Arctic MISSION

Arctic

WILLIAM F. ALTHOFF

MISSION

90 North by Airship and Submarine

NAVAL INSTITUTE PRESS
Annapolis, Maryland

This book has been brought to publication with the generous assistance of
Marguerite *and* Gerry Lenfest.

Naval Institute Press
291 Wood Road
Annapolis, Maryland 21402

Library of Congress Cataloging–in–Publication Data
Althoff, William F.
Arctic mission : 90 north by airship and submarine / William F. Althoff.
p. cm.
Includes bibliographical references and index.
ISBN 978-1-61251-010-1 (hardcover : alk. paper)
1. United States. Navy—Aviation—History. 2. Airships—United States. 3. Arctic regions—Aerial exploration. 4. Underwater exploration—Arctic regions. 5. Arctic regions—Description and travel. 6. Nautilus (Submarine : SSN-571) I. Title. II. Title: Arctic mission, by airship & submarine to the far north.
VG93.A867 2011
910.911'3—dc23

2011024314

⊗ This paper meets the requirements of ANSI/NISO z39.48-1992 (Permanence of Paper).
Printed in the United States of America.

19 18 17 16 15 14 13 12 11 9 8 7 6 5 4 3 2 1
First printing

Frontispiece: Painting by Ken Marschall © 1994 / Courtesy of KenMarschall.com

To Pen,

whose idea this was.

It took me north.

Contents

Preface

FROM THE AIR, the camp is a jot of shapes and shadows, dissolved in white.

On the ice, the horizon line is a low, brooding wrinkle—hummocked sea ice. The U.S. Air Force has designated this berg "Target 3." Bravo rides its ice—a "drifting station" for research in the Arctic Ocean. This field season, Bravo is supporting the International Geophysical Year of 1958. Logistical support is by military airlift, so air force personnel are on board to sustain and protect the researchers.

Beneath their boots, Target 3 is 120 feet thick and 9 miles across—an immense tabular iceberg. Unlike sea ice, T-3 has calved from a freshwater shelf in the Canadian High Arctic. Invulnerable to ice pressure and breakup, "ice islands" offer semipermanent platforms for occupation. Adrift with the polar pack, T-3 has inscribed an erratic orbit off northern Alaska–Canada and, this season, is tracking westward off the Canadian polar margin, about 60 miles out. Approximate coordinates: 79° N, 121° W—760 miles from the geographic pole.

It is August. The freeze-dry cold has eased, and a gray calm prevails. A feeble sun shuns the horizon as the "days" of circumpolar summer fold together.

Air temperature: 34° Fahrenheit.

Off island, open water and puddling blush the pack. Snow and slush have vanished—and the island-slab itself is ablating. Dampness is pervasive. Errands now are expeditions: heavy slogs across ponds and meltwater channels. In camp, soot (from the diesel hut) and general traffic have darkened the surface, accelerating ice loss. Ironically, any structure is protection from the sun; as the ablating white melts and drops away, Bravo elevates atop pedestals of ice. To gain access to trailers or mess hall, wooden steps have been improvised

Most vexing, the runway has melted out, shutting down Bravo's life-support system resupply option: paradrops. But for weeks, supply flights from Thule (Greenland) have been promised then repeatedly postponed.

On island, fresh supplies are exhausted. As private caches of cigarettes, beer, and candy vanish, a growing sense of quiet desperation pervades life on ice. Smokers especially are hard hit.

"When things got desperate," one Bravo resident will recall, "we searched for old butts in the ice, dried them out, and smoked those."[1]

As it happens, an aircraft *is* en route. It is not heavier-than-air machine, not even an airplane, but an airship of the U.S. Navy. Word spreads. Though dismissive, most personnel are disposed to follow the flight as it approaches. A blimp offers absolute novelty—a welcome break to routine. More to the point, the navy may be delivering mail and fresh supplies.

In circumpolar wastes, aircraft are lifelines. Landings are charged moments at any outpost. Mail and cigarettes, fresh fruit and vegetables, beer, new faces, gossip—each is a balm for stale routine and protracted isolation.

The "morning" of 9 August has cloud and fog enshrouding IGY Bravo—the gray realities of boreal summer. Through occasional breaks, a pale blue is visible. Following breakfast, personnel scatter, most to work sites. About midmorning, the throb of engines invades the silence. Navigating precisely, the airship has found Bravo's radio beacon and is "riding" its signal in. A series of ambling passes commences, the aircraft orbiting over and near the main camp area.

Communications are therapy at any outpost. As the airship loiters about two hundred feet off, an exchange continues via radio.

Visibility—the range of horizontal vision—is nil. Straight down, though, a narrow cone of view is granted the airmen. On the ice, some are unaware of the ship. Few will see it. "Suddenly the clouds parted slightly," one researcher recalled, "and we saw this long, ghostly, silvery airship for a few seconds. It was much longer and more slender than we expected—as well as more beautiful."[2]

Until rendezvous, Bravo was but a mark on a navy chart. Professional satisfaction pervades the control car of U.S. Navy airship Bureau Number (BUNO) 126719: nearly a thousand miles above the Arctic Circle, its naval aviators are circling their audacious objective.

In the North Atlantic, a low, dark form is steaming southeast, toward Iceland. On board, the mood is celebratory. That June, the world's first nuclear-powered vessel had set a course from U.S. Submarine Base, Pearl Harbor, for abyssal Arctic waters. Top secret orders: Operation Sunshine, a submerged transit from Pacific to Atlantic via the North Pole. Bering Strait astern, shoal water and deep-draft ice (pressure ridges) had barred passage—the navy had rushed the season. Sunshine is rescheduled—Phase II. Northing again blocked, *Nautilus* (SSN 571), surface-running the shore lead off northern Alaska, logged (on 1 August) the Barrow Sea Valley—the boat's boulevard to deep water. Descending the continental slope, speed and depth increasing, *Nautilus* gained the basin's nether regions—sea bottom all but uncharted. On 3 August, the boat pierced 90° N then steamed for the Greenland–Spitsbergen Passage. *Nautilus* surfaced at 79° N, just beyond the sea-ice disk enfolding the geographic pole.

The transit has no precedent—an epic feat. Washington savors a tonic dose of good news; the cruise (an admiral exults) is "America's answer to the *Sputnik*." At the White House, President Dwight D. Eisenhower announces the polar crossing to a rapt television and newsreel audience. As well, *Nautilus*' skipper is awarded the Legion of Merit and his command the Presidential Unit Citation—a first for a navy ship in peacetime.[3]

Nautilus concludes Sunshine with a rave-up British welcome. Back home, a media bonanza is under way.

Three days following takeoff from base Resolute, on the Northwest Passage, navy airship *719* returns from Arctic Canada—concluding an unclassified mission. Local media attend the touchdown, at a naval air station near Boston. That same hour, on 12 August, *Nautilus* secures at a Royal Navy yard.

The feasibility of far-northern operations stands verified—for *both* navy crews. In his report, the officer in charge of the air expedition will recommend airships for observation, photography, and special instruments. Deployed between May and mid-August, when fixed-wing craft are denied the rotting ice, lighter-than-air offers unique capabilities in support Arctic research.

In contrast to the nuclear-powered attack and ballistic-missile submarines (SSNs and SSBNs), no airship has since crossed the Arctic Circle. The hours logged by *719* and its research-and-development command stand unique in naval aviation.

This work recounts that long-ago expedition for the Office of Naval Research and, as well, pioneer under-ice penetrations by the U.S. Navy.

Acknowledgments

THIS RESEARCH AND WRITING has incurred numerous obligations, most especially to Brigadier General Keith R. Greenaway, RCAF (Ret.). Contacted in 1988, Keith instantly agreed to an interview; in the ensuing years, he assisted by in-depth correspondence and telephone—and meeting. Keith also reviewed portions of the draft manuscript. Captain Harold B. Van Gorder, USN (Ret.), also hosted the author. Answering countless questions, he loaned documents, diary notations, and images, then critiqued selected chapters. No less gracious, Lieutenant Commander Aage J. Schou, USN (Ret.), met with the author, provided materials, and later reviewed the written results. Lieutenant Harold D. Koza, USN (Ret.), also reviewed draft chapters, providing comment and correction.

Commodore O. C. S. Robertson, RCN (Ret.), invited me to his Ontario home. A gifted raconteur, he offered remarks as to the penetration of Arctic Canada via airship that proved delightful as well as informative.

Squadron Leader William P. Becker, RCAF (Ret.), described duties at Resolute Bay and, in particular, the 1958 visit by a U.S. Navy airship to "the base." Tom A. Levine shared an appraisal of his former skipper, Commodore "Robbie" Robertson.

AD1 Elmer B. Lord, USN (Ret.), and ATC Frederick L. Parker, USN (Ret.), lent personal scrapbooks and answered queries. Lieutenant Commander Cecil Manship, USN (Ret.), clarified several points regarding advance operations. Commander Max V. Ricketts, USN (Ret.), helped explain Project Lincoln and the NADU command as an element of ONR.

Mr. Robert Kopitzke, Curator, History of Aviation Collection, unearthed the log book for BUNO 126719. Commander Charles A. "Charlie" Mills, USN (Ret.), provided documents and recounted his icing tests flown for NADU. Mr. Louis Mancini described the production intricacies attending the ZPG-2 airship.

Mrs. Jeanne Harris loaned materials concerning her late husband, Dr. Guy S. Harris of the Underwater Sound Laboratory. Mr. Walter L. Clearwaters, Senior Scientific Consultant, Naval Underwater Systems Center, took time to reminiscence about Dr. Harris. Ms. Kathleen P.

O'Beirne provided useful data pertaining to the Arctic programs of USL. Mr. Walter H. Bailey answered questions pertaining to the airship as platform in Arctic Canada.

Dr. Maynard M. Miller, who conceived the Polar Project, passed along a number of reports and offered background and context. Special correspondent Hugh A. Mulligan, of the Associated Press, consented to be interviewed and dug out his dispatches from a long-ago assignment.

Dr. Norman G. Gray was most helpful, making available portions of his personal journal and answering follow-up questions. Thanks to Mr. David F. Barnes and Dr. Max Britton for their remarks. Dr. Louis De Goes provided materials pertaining to Cold War polar programs. Mr. William I. Wells provided materials concerning Lincoln Laboratory.

Special mention is due Barry Jan Countryman. Through him, the author was able to know Canadian opinion: official, editorial, and public.

Captain William R. Anderson, USN (Ret.), granted an informative interview, then consented to review selected chapters in draft. Captain Shepherd M. Jenks, USN (Ret.), and the late Captain Frank C. Adams, USN (Ret.), prepared (recorded) responses to questions. Vice Admiral Kenneth M. Carr, USN (Ret.), submitted written replies. Thanks to these naval officers, heretofore unpublished material is included. The late Dr. Waldo K. Lyon of the Arctic Submarine Laboratory, San Diego, granted a interview and, further, copied pertinent pages of his personal journal—a priceless record of the evolution of under-ice sailing. Dr. Lyon's trusted colleague, Richard J. Boyle, also provided documents.

Captain Edward L. "Ned" Beach, USN (Ret.), described the genesis of *Nautilus* (SSN 571) and offered insights into the force behind the boat's creation, Admiral Hyman G. Rickover, USN. Vice Admiral James Calvert, USN (Ret.), commented on the Arctic cruises of *Skate* (SSN 578) under his command. Captain Robert D. McWethy, USN (Ret.), recreated the era when *Nautilus* and the Arctic were compelling visions. Admiral Arleigh A. Burke, USN (Ret.), kindly answered a query.

Lamont-Doherty's Dr. Marcus G. Langseth sent materials relating to SCICEX-93, an Arctic cruise he accompanied.

The Department of the Navy assisted. Ms. Anna C. Urband, Office of Information, was a valuable aid, uncovering a wealth of materials and helping to connect the author with retired personnel. The Office of Naval Research sent data regarding its programs in the Arctic. At the Naval Historical Center, Roy A. Grossnick and Bernard Cavalcante located important documents. Ms. Marie A. Ivaskewitz, Public Affairs Office, NAS South Weymouth, found materials pertaining to that naval air station.

Through Mr. Leonard C. Bruno, the Library of Congress researched *New York Times* reports on the flight, after which the New York Public Library provided copies. The Thunder Bay Public Library (Ontario) sent photocopies regarding a singular visit by U.S. Navy airship.

Regarding T-3 and life on ice, Dr. Gerry H. Cabaniss, Dr. Arthur E. Collin, Mr. Don Plouff, and Dr. Charles C. Plummer extended themselves on my behalf. Dr. Collin also made time for an interview. Dr. David D. Smith, another researcher from that IGY summer, assisted with publications and advice. Andy Heiberg, Polar Science Center, Seattle, supplied information on the final days of Ice Island T-3. Archivist Janis Jorgensen and librarian Mary Kearns-Kaplan provided research assistance to the author.

The Department of the Air Force was helpful. The U.S. Air Force Historical Research Center, Maxwell Air Force Base, responded to several inquiries for information. The Headquarters Alaskan Air Command, Elemendorf Air Force Base, provided a history of the Alaskan Air Command.

The Arctic Institute of North America clarified a number of points. Courtesy of Sergey Priamikov, the Arctic and Antarctic Research Institute in St. Petersburg (former Leningrad) granted access to its singular staff and archives.

I am inexpressibly grateful to the Canadian government. Among the agencies assisting were the Geological Survey of Canada, Indian and Northern Affairs, the National Archives of Canada, the National Aviation Museum, and the Canadian War Museum. Invariably, inquiries to all these were professionally handled. Mr. P. W. Cole of the Ice Centre, Atmospheric Environment Service, Environment Canada, outlined sea-ice conditions in the Northwest Passage. In 1989, courtesy of Thomas B. Kilpatrick, Chief, Ice Reconnaissance Division, I accompanied Canadian Ice Patrol missions over the very landscapes seen from airship *719* decades earlier. For those days, Bernard "Bernie" Wyer proved to be an excellent guide. The following spring, thanks largely to George D. Hobson, former Director, Polar Continental Shelf Project, Energy, Mines and Resources Canada, I logged a few days on an ice island off the Canadian polar margin, in the Arctic Ocean.

Thanks to Richard "Rick" Russell, this (much-revised) work is again in print.

Penny—as ever—was supportive, patient, understanding.

Without such splendid support and cooperation, this manuscript would scarcely have been realized.

A Note on Times, and List of Acronyms and Abbreviations

THIS BOOK, as the participants in the events it recounts did, uses military-style twenty-four-hour time. The hour 0000 is midnight, 0600 is 6 a.m., and 1200 is noon. Thereafter subtract twelve from the first two digits to derive familiar twelve-hour time: 1500 is 3 p.m., 1515 is 3:15 p.m., 1800 is 6 p.m., 2230 is 10:30 p.m., etc.

AC	aircraft commander
ADC	chief aviation machinist's mate
AD1	aviation machinist's mate 1st class
AD2	aviation machinist's mate 2nd class
AEC	chief aviation electrician's mate; Atomic Energy Commission
AEW	airborne early warning
AE1	aviation electrician's mate 1st class
AE2	aviation electrician's mate 2nd class
AE3	aviation electrician's mate 3rd class
AFB	Air Force Base
AMC	chief aviation structural mechanic
AM1	aviation structural mechanic 1st class
AP	Associated Press
ARL	Arctic Research Laboratory
ASW	antisubmarine warfare
ATC	chief aviation electronics technician
AT1	aviation electronics technician 1st class
AT2	aviation electronics technician 2nd class
BHP	brake horsepower
BUNO	bureau number
CDST	Central Daylight Savings Time
CF	Canadian Forces

CinCLantFlt	Commander in Chief, Atlantic Fleet
CNO	chief of naval operations
CO	commanding officer
ComSubLant	Commander, Submarine Force, Atlantic
ComSubPac	Commander, Submarine Force, Pacific
ComSubRon	Commander, Submarine Squadron
CST	Central Standard Time
ECM	electronic countermeasures
EDST	Eastern Daylight Savings Time
ETA	estimated time of arrival
ETD	estimated time of departure
FBM	fleet ballistic missile
GHO	ground handling officer
GST	Greenland Standard Time
HTA	heavier-than-air
ICS	intercommunications system
IGY	International Geophysical Year
INS	inertial navigation system
JATO	jet-assisted takeoff
LTA	lighter-than-air
MAD	magnetic anomaly detection
MK	Mark
MP	member of Parliament
NADU	Naval Air Development Unit
NAS	Naval Air Station
NEL	Navy Electronics Laboratory
nm	nautical mile
O&R	Overhaul and Repair Department
ONR	Office of Naval Research
R&D	research and development
RCAF	Royal Canadian Air Force
RCN	Royal Canadian Navy
rpm	revolutions per minute
SSBN	nuclear-powered ballistic missile submarine, or boomer
SSN	nuclear-powered attack submarine, or fast attack
USL	Underwater Sound Laboratory
USN	U.S. Navy

Arctic MISSION

You don't know how splendid it is up there. That's where I want to die.
—Roald Amundsen

1 The North American Arctic

On the map of North America, look above the familiar outline—*north* of the United States. For Americans, the word "Canada" has a vague, reassuring association. Most Americans are oblivious of the huge, contiguous country that is their neighbor and trading partner to the north.

As a nation, Canada emerged from a tangle of rivalries. By 1760, England had wrested control of New France and assumed political mastery in North America. A century later, in 1867, a fragile confederation of four provinces was fashioned from the British Empire's continental holdings. In 1870, the Dominion of Canada obtained transfer of the Hudson Bay territories and, in 1880, the Arctic Islands. Canada had become the second-largest country in the world.

Britain's holdings in North America had ended, save for Newfoundland.

Throughout the 1800s, the northernmost fringe of this realm was poorly defined. An explorer's map from 1814 labels the offshore circumpolar blank as the "Icy Sea." The first European to reach the Arctic Ocean overland—an officer of the Hudson's Bay Company—had done so less than fifty years before. For Europeans, the Arctic was an alien blank. Unimaginably harsh and without apparent value, the continent's boreal reaches were consigned to explorers and trappers, whalers, adventurers, and entrepreneurs, plus a sprinkling of resolute settlers. As yet, boundaries and matters of sovereignty concerned few officials.

The U.S.-Canadian bond is a special partnership. Strains and discord occur, to be sure. Economically, the United States dominates the continent and exerts a seductive cultural influence—a force resented north of the border. Canadians cherish their cultural distinctions from their dominating neighbor to the south.[1]

On national issues of mutual interest, Canadian collaboration is expected. With respect to continental security, the strategic concerns of Washington are overriding. Canadians crave a national identity separate from the United States; in consequence, there resides at least a particle of anti-Americanism in the Canadian soul. "The Americans are our best friends, whether we like it or not," is a sentiment emblematic of the relationship.

[Opposite] Unlike Antarctica, the central Arctic is maritime—morphologically, an oceanic basin. Here sea/ice/atmosphere interactions play a major role in deep-ocean circulation, and in regulating global climate. Superpower rivalry anointed the North as strategic space, an exposed flank. Note the wide continental shelf off Eurasia.

The two nations enjoy an undefended geographic frontier: no fortifications and few barriers disfigure the forty-ninth parallel of north latitude, sea to sea. Absent also are the incidents that chafe ministries of foreign affairs elsewhere. Towns, even buildings, straddle the line. The 5,500-mile border is nearly unique in the quarrelsome history of modern international diplomacy.

Canada dominates North America, including its huge Arctic geography. Like every continent "platform," this colossus is a grand mosaic of geophysical processes and biological evolution.

The earth's continental crust is broken into more or less rigid plates that float atop the slush-like upper mantle. Over *geologic* time, forces in the deep mantle bearing upon their edges raft and stress the plates. (Sea ice is an analogue: floating pans under constant stress.) Continent-sized, the plates are pulled apart as, elsewhere, they converge and buckle. Slow yet insistent, geologic forces destroy, reprocess, and renew these errant platforms. As landscapes are recycled, life is marked by movement and adaptation—passengers for the ride.

During glacial periods, immense ice sheets overlay the Northern Hemisphere. In a recurring pattern, they enlarged and coalesced, then collapsed. The retreats sent bursts of meltwater and icebergs' ice along drainage systems into the northern North Atlantic—disrupting global patterns of ocean and atmospheric circulation. When the last deglaciation began about 20,000 years ago, ice masses were close to their greatest area and volume. Nearly all of what is now Canada and the territory as far south as the Ohio and Missouri River Valleys were interred. In the east, Manhattan Island lay entombed.

The continent shouldered ice two miles thick, depressing bedrock and obliterating landscapes. Ottawa and Washington share the mixed forests of the east, the tallgrass prairie of mid-continent, the spine of the Rockies, and a craggy Pacific seaboard.

The North America we know today is but the most recent expression of an infinitely complex, unimaginably powerful evolution.

To Americans, it is "their" continent—a conceit that denies geography. Canada extends east–west across six time zones and to the rim of the Arctic Ocean. Given the sheer scale of his country, Prime Minister W. L. Mackenzie King (1874–1950) remarked, "If some countries have too much history, we have too much geography."

Canada "north of sixty" is a sprawl of 1.5 million square miles—40 percent of the nation.[2] So vast is the Canadian Arctic that maps tend to omit its far-northern reaches. The Canadian Archipelago, an area of .5 million square miles, is seldom shown in full. Here the continental platform is broken into a labyrinth of bays, inlets, channels, and straits, including the famed Northwest Passage.

These islands were little known and poorly mapped well into the prior century. Except for a brief thaw, snow and sea ice camouflage the line between land and water. As recently as 1944, the explorer Vilhjalmur Stefansson could still remark, "Besides being inaccurate, most Arctic maps carry only the names of explorers, patrons of exploration or friends of the map makers." In places large sections of coastlines were only approximately outlined, and details of inland features were practically nonexistent. Accordingly, the dead reckoning of sailors and airmen could prove lethal. "Until the Arctic is accurately mapped, all elevations indicated on maps must be considered as only approximate. When low stratus cloud is encountered it is far better to fly above the weather than to descend and attempt to navigate by map reading."[3]

Canada has three bordering seas—only two of which are "used." Fringed by continental massifs, the Arctic Ocean is the dominating feature. Canada has nearly six thousand miles of coastline, second only to Russia. The north geographic pole lies within ever-shifting pack ice.

Sea ice derives its importance from its influence on ocean and atmospheric circulation; these in turn define hemispheric climate. Although perennial in the central basin, the ice canopy is ever changing. Subject to the pull of tide, wind, and current, it is horrendous to cross on foot and daunting to icebreakers. From the air, patterns are crazy-quilt. As floes shift and rotate, open water appears. Under pressure, floes deform and thicken or, floating loose, disperse like ships. And with freeze-up, first-year ice binds floes into a near-continuous canopy.

Off Alaska/Canada, the polar pack circulates in a huge clockwise spiral called the Beaufort Gyre. As elsewhere, local physiographic conditions dictate the formation and the fate of local sea ice. Geologically, the Arctic Islands are part of the continental platform, with water depths correspondingly shallow. This High Arctic is the largest island group in the world. Except for a bold, mountainous strip in the east, the surface is a flat to rolling tableland. As well, here are marine plains and unbroken tundra, swampy shores and sheer escarpments, alpine peaks and clinging glaciers. In eastern Arctic Canada, immense ice sheets arch into vacant interiors.

The islands of the Queen Elizabeth group fringe the deepwater basin and are gripped by perennial ice. The large eastern islands are harshly sculpted and indented; here yawning fiords host calving glaciers born of icebound peaks and ice caps.

When adjustment from continental ice is complete, crustal rebound will alter the map of Canada. For example, Hudson Bay is shallowing; with time, this inland sea will drain almost to its entrance.

Relics of the Pleistocene linger—Greenland and the pack ice its largest remnants. Vestigial white grips the eastern Arctic. Ellesmere Island lies interred: five ice sheets grip hundreds of square miles and, at their highest, rise to 6,200 feet above the sea. Dissected peaks—the highest in eastern North America—pierce the white. Fed by ice sheets, glaciers drain the interiors, rumpling into lower valleys drowned by sea-level rise. Within its fiords, icebergs parade beneath sheer walls—the signatures of glaciation. This is Earth reduced to stark landforms, a majestic, timeless realm—a window into the last ice age.

Exceeding 11,000 feet in places, the Greenland ice sheet inters 700,000 square miles. Exposed at the coasts, bedrock throughout the interior has been pressed below sea level. The island is an immense, ice-filled bowl rimmed by alpine peaks and fiords and broad glaciers.[4] The spectacle that is Greenland has awed even seasoned airmen: "There, then, was the enormous mass of Greenland, and I could not look away from it. It held me as it took on coloration and I finally distinguished the warts as the peaks of great mountains. And all about them, choking their gigantic necks, lay the awesome ice cap. This all-embracing coverlet formed its own horizon and stretched north and eastward beyond my comprehension. I had never in all my flying days seen anything to compare with this fantastic exhibition."[5]

This is a realm of protracted dark and enduring cold—a haunting place. Northland spaces hang heavy with silence—a soundlessness vaulting clear to Asia. On walking reconnaissance, one can fail to note a single living presence. Creatures patrol; indeed, the North is robust with life. Yet evidence of occupation—insect or avian, plant and animal—may be unapparent. But for the dome of sky and water, this might be a lunar landscape.

Brief summers of nightless days persist from about early May to mid-August. A protracted winter arrives in September; in short order, a half-light prevails, then total darkness. It is the persistence of cold that defines the region.[6] On the average, there are only forty to sixty frost-free days north of the tree line.

A desert, the Arctic suffers scant precipitation—an annual average of less than five inches over most of the Queen Elizabeth Islands, about equal to that of the Sahara.[7] As one moves north from the sixtieth parallel, the climate, terrain, and vegetation change. Coniferous forest gives way to open woodland, then to tundra, before, finally, desert.

Transportation in all that space is an obstacle. A 1936 map is devoid of roads anywhere in the Northwest Territories—an area the size of Western Europe. A handful of unpaved roads marked the Yukon Territory. Ten years later, only two serviced the territories, both roads located in the Mackenzie area for the oil field at Norman Wells. A handful of "winter tractor trails"

Sea ice is the dominant factor in polar operations by sea. Deformed by wind and current, thin ice is compressed between converging floes, forming hummocks and pressure ridges. The submerged keels of pressure ice may hang to a depth of 100 feet or more. (Author)

rounded out the ground-based transport system. At the end of the Second World War, no road of consequence had been constructed in the whole of the eastern Arctic.

At any outpost, the matter of supply is crucial. Historically, waterways were the all-weather highways. Today, rail transport is confined to the familiar strip along the U.S.-Canadian border. (Most Canadians reside within a hundred miles of the forty-ninth parallel—squeezed, as it were, by subpolar vastness to the north and American pizzazz to the south.) A single rail line snakes to Churchill, in Manitoba, an outpost of the fur trade on Hudson Bay. The North's first major road, the Yukon's Alcan Highway, was built for the Second World War. No definite roads policy for the northern territories, indeed, emerged until the 1950s. Many sites remain without road transportation or are sustained only on a seasonal basis. Systems of year-round ground links through permafrost emptiness are difficult to engineer then maintain—a challenge inherent to all northern construction.[8]

In the Arctic, aircraft provide ideal transport. Movements of people as well as light, valuable, or urgent freight are conveyed almost exclusively by aircraft. Heavy or bulky freight—fuel particularly—is reserved for seaborne arrival, exploiting the breakup. Today, the sole means of regular and reliable access to most camps, settlements, weather stations, bases and resource-development projects is by air.

In Canada, as elsewhere, the Great War helped nourish aeronautics. The first commercial bush flight occurred in 1919. Two years later, aerial photography for mapping began. In Canada,

Alaska, and Russia, the twenties were a period of "quiet development" for high-latitude aviation. Small companies delivered passengers, equipment, supplies. Mail was flown, geographic and geological reconnaissance conducted.

Still, few airports were built; floatplanes shouldered bush operations. The adventures of Canada's bush fliers in this immensity have passed into legend. A zone of largely uncontrolled airspace, in it flying is comparatively freewheeling. As one result, the level of judgment demanded of pilots is high.

The region poses headaches for government—its scale and the absence of road-rail infrastructure among them. About sixty towns, villages, bases, and outposts are scattered throughout the territories in what amounts to a vast, loosely linked network. The upper tier of the archipelago is devoid of permanent settlements. Only weather outposts dot the map. The scarcity of forage and food inhibits occupation even by subsistence hunters.[9] Two settlements are present in the Queen Elizabeth group, one of which is Resolute, on the Northwest Passage. Both postdate the Second World War. The major thrust of southern-based enterprise into the northland, indeed, dates from the 1940s.

Man reached North America 30,000 years ago, possibly much earlier. Gradually, determinedly, down the millennia hunter-gatherers moved east, across the difficult, boundless blank of what is now the Alaskan and Canadian north, adjusting to coastal conditions and developing a subsistence culture based on marine hunting. Achieving permanent residence, the Inuit ("Eskimo" is a southern label) have inhabited the High Arctic for at least 5,000 years—the earth's most adept survivors. Essentially pacific, these peoples attained a remarkable accommodation to their fragile environment, adapting in efficient, complex ways—establishing a culture and economy that, until the modern era, have remained based on hunting, fishing, trapping, gathering.

For generations beyond memory, communities thrived along the Northwest Passage before the first Europeans appeared, in search of a route to the Far East. John Cabot met the Inuit in 1498; Martin Frobisher landed on Baffin Island in 1576; Henry Hudson came in 1610. The explorers had limited contact with native peoples, and, by 1650 this phase of the search for a northwestern passage stood abandoned.

The Hudson's Bay Company was founded in 1670. A commercial marvel, "the Bay" flourished—a continent-spanning empire. Based in London, it exerted an abiding influence on the exploration of colonial North America, pursuing its mandate, as one author writes, "across a vast sweep of North America, establishing a corporate presence imprinted deeply in Canada's history and character." By establishing posts throughout the North, the company's traders helped map the contours of the upper continent. At its peak, the network reached from the Arctic Ocean to Hawaii.[10]

Contact with European whalers and traders, explorers and profiteers introduced the Inuit to other-culture goods, attitudes, and religions. Basics like metal tools and utensils, cloth, and firearms proved irresistible. In the early 1800s the British began a new phase of expeditions. William Parry, John Ross, and Sir John Franklin, among others, commanded these penetrations. The hunting culture of the Inuit gave way. European missionaries pursued their pernicious business. Under pressure to shed many of their traditions and beliefs, the Inuit saw their way of life largely succumb.

Few of the new colonists appreciated what native Americans had accomplished in an unforgiving environment. Writing of contact with the mounting number of white men, a sympathetic Canadian geologist observed in 1906, "As a people, they [the native populations] are very hospitable and kind; but like other savages would probably soon tire of continuous efforts to support helpless whites cast upon them, especially when the guests assume a superiority over their hosts."[11]

Chauvinism has embittered the native–white relationship. When Admiral John Franklin explored the Northwest Passage in the 1840s, he was celebrated as its discoverer. Yet the Inuit had built communities along its shores before the seventeenth century. Motivated by profit from whale, fur or fish, the Europeans imported a technology to exploit a demanding realm; they could not, however, subdue it. The native populations, in contrast, had achieved a perfect (if brutish) harmony with their physical world. Predictably, decimation accompanied the colonizers. And racism toward the inhabitants led to indignities, injustices, and atrocities. The anger burns still. "Explorers you call great men were helpless. They were like lost children, and it was our people who took care of them," a native leader observed bitterly.[12]

Canada and the United States are Arctic sovereignties, two of eight nations that share the northern rimworld. Viewed from above, Russia is not so very distant from the West; Asia indeed is closer to Canada than is any European nation. At the Bering Strait, forty-five miles of shallow shelf interpose between the United States and the Russian Far East.

The North is distant, inhospitable, alien. Most Canadians reside in a congenial strip within a hundred miles of the States. Canadians, one journalist harrumphed of his countrymen, are "somehow schizophrenic about the Arctic. At one level, the North is part of us, part of our self-definition and occasionally the object of our passion. Most often, though, we simply forget about it, remain doggedly unaware of what is happening there, and are disinclined even to visit."[13] Another has lamented, "We do not think circumpolar. Only in recent years, through technology, are we finally lifting the fog on the northern perimeter of the country." Historically, the focus has been east/west—Canada's patriotic direction. With barely 33 millions distributed over an area equal to the United States, it is a horrendous task to fashion an infrastructure, especially so when much of its land cannot be cultivated and easily settled.[14]

In 1896, gold deposits were discovered in the Yukon. An influx of hopefuls ensued: by summer 1898 the boomtown of Dawson City had soared to 30,000—the largest settlement in Canada's northland. The Yukon district of the Northwest Territories became a separate entity. This is generally regarded as the first major period of mining activity in northern Canada. Mineral development has since become an economic cornerstone and remains the territories' largest private-sector employer. Gold production has persisted; other minerals—silver, copper, lead, coal, uranium, diamonds—also occur. The intensity of exploitation has varied, depending in part on world prices. As for the Klondike Rush, that boom, like others before it, was short-lived. A northern economic staple, the fur trade experienced a gradual decline.

Northern development slowed.

A renewed push accompanied the Second World War. Knowledge relative to the Arctic and its resources immediately assumed utmost urgency. Advances in construction and other technologies were stimulated, experience acquired, near-revolutions realized. Weather stations were established, airfields constructed, roads graded, communications transformed.

In 1942, thousands of U.S. troops and civilians began construction of a defense route to Alaska. The impetus: the need to protect the northern Allied flank. Japan had gained a foothold in the western Aleutians, an intolerable threat to the home continent. The Canada–Alaska ("Alcan") Highway provided a land connection and helped link the chain of airfields on the northwest staging route ferrying aircraft through Alaska to the Soviets. As well, wartime requirements were responsible for the first pipeline in northern Canada. In 1942, construction began on a pipeline from the field at Norman Wells, in the Mackenzie Valley, southwest to a refinery in Whitehorse.[15]

The need urgent to protect North Atlantic convoys, Washington acquired the right to establish coastal bases in Greenland.[16] Construction began on a staging route to embattled Europe. As in Greenland, a chain of airfields was installed: sites at Churchill and Coral Harbour, at Goose Bay in Newfoundland and Kuujjuaq (Fort Chimo) in Quebec, and at Frobisher Bay on Baffin Island. These became stepping-stones on a great-circle route across the North Atlantic.

Ironically, a presence in the Canadian north was established not by Axis powers (as had been feared) but by the United States, projecting its power in a global war.[17]

The combatants had shunted thousands of men northward. The logistics attending these incursions were thrown into place on fearsome timetables. Knowledge of Arctic conditions exploded. As air operations multiplied (for example), so too the body of experience, data, and expertise. The circumpolar north—a peripheral realm hitherto on the outskirts of military notice—had become strategic space.

Cold War Arctic

The Soviet challenge shifted center stage. In the nuclear age, the shortest arc between the superpowers lay across maritime boreal wastes. Concern for this transpolar threat translated into a sustained U.S. presence in the North.

Sovereignty is a vexed issue in Canada—the western country with the greatest frontage on the Arctic. Every generation or so a sovereignty panic sets in. Nationalists decry the U.S. presence, insisting Canada take control in the North or risk losing it. "Full sovereignty is vital to Canada's security. It is vital to the Inuit people. And it is vital to Canada's national identity."[18] Still, Ottawa can hardly begrudge access: strategic transpolar threats to the United States are inseparable from those to Canada. The U.S. armed forces, along with Canadian agencies, installed outposts, stations, and air bases. And so the circumpolar north factored in geopolitical rivalry for more than four decades.[19]

The threads of military and scientific enterprise intertwined. Arctic, Canadian, and U.S. weather are closely associated. Wartime land, air, and sea campaigns had exploited data available from Allied and Axis observers. Now such were indispensable.[20] Within months of VJ Day, the United States proposed construction of a network of weather stations. Fearful of unilateral action by Washington yet appreciative of it, and mindful of its own requirements, in 1947 Ottawa announced an agreement to establish permanent *joint* weather stations in the Arctic islands. Its main stations: at Thule, in western Greenland (a joint Danish-U.S. operation), and at Resolute Bay, on Cornwallis Island.

Accurate analyses and forecasts were crucial not only to military commanders but, as well, to the international ambitions of the airlines. Global war had transformed aviation, compressing years of innovation into each year of conflict. "War-time experience made long-range flying a routine matter and brought the inter-continental airlines into overnight existence," an airman observed. "Flights that would have made headlines as late as 1939 now go almost unnoticed."[21]

In summer 1946, a U.S. Navy task force carried out a reconnaissance in Baffin Bay and within the archipelago. The convoy bulled its way north to build a weather station and lay out a strip at Thule.[22] In spring 1947, the first Canadian High Arctic station was established at Eureka, on Ellesmere. That same summer, four hundred tons of cargo was offloaded at Resolute Bay. A telecommunications and weather station was erected, an airstrip surveyed. Resolute was intended as an advance base, reachable by ship, from which smaller stations would be established by air. The next year, supplies were airlifted to the outlying sites. Mould Bay and Isachsen are icebound and unreachable by sea; the stations there were built and resupplied entirely by air. Responsibility for establishing the stations rested with the U.S. Weather Bureau and the Canadian Meteorological Service. Resupply was handled by the U.S. Navy; the U.S. Air Force airlifted the cached supplies to outlying stations and provided long-range ice reconnaissance ahead of the probing ships.

In 1948 supplies were landed at Alert, on northern Ellesmere Island. The station went operational in 1950—the planet's northernmost permanent habitation.

Canada had accepted a nettling reality: membership in the Western alliance and its proximity to the United States foreclosed straying far from that superpower's policies toward the Soviet Union. Washington has sustained an abiding northern presence—a factor Canadians have come to resent. By contracting out its own defense, Ottawa has abrogated a sovereign responsibility. "Certainly co-operation with the U.S. is desirable," an editorial grumped, "but we must not, in effect, abandon our own territory." "The United States has been pouring men and materials into our North," another complained. "Military installations have risen on the ice covered islands. American planes patrol the ice fields, American construction crews have built radar stations with equipment ferried in by American ships."[23]

In 1958, and not for the last time, resentment peaked. The minister of northern affairs confessed to "shame and chagrin" upon learning that even cabinet ministers required clearance from Washington to visit U.S. radar installations on Canadian territory. "The American mania for military security has long been a source of amazement—and at times, acute inconvenience—to the friends and allies of the United States [a Toronto newspaper fumed]. So long as it is applied to Americans on American soil, it is clearly that country's own business. But when it is applied to Canadians on Canadian soil then . . . it is time Ottawa set Washington straight."[24]

A fully satisfactory solution has yet to emerge. The issue continues to simmer and, intermittently, to boil over.

In 1952 a group of U.S. scientists recommended a Distant Early Warning (DEW) Line of radar stations across the full sweep of North America—to prevent a nuclear Pearl Harbor. The largest assault on the Arctic ever attempted, the line forever altered the North. The speed and range of manned bombers and the nascent threat from intercontinental ballistic missiles (ICBMs) had rendered the problem of defending the United States one of utmost priority. The shortest, most probable route of approach: over Canada. These were the Eisenhower years, the era of

"bomber gap" and superpower posturing. In this overheated atmosphere, upgraded air defenses were deemed urgent. These would have to be in place, moreover, before new Soviet bombers and missiles became operational later that decade.[25]

The early-warning network covered all continental approaches—an electronic fence. "To provide the first line of warning on the northern border of the United States," *Air Force* magazine intoned, would be "manifestly absurd when precious hours could be gained by having a warning line far to the north."

Construction began in 1955. Relays of aircraft lifted in tons of supplies; logistic support by ship delivered thousands more. That June, a convoy set sail from Halifax, Nova Scotia. Steaming northward, vessels peeled away to unload onto beaches. Pioneering the way was the icebreaker HMCS *Labrador.* Commissioned in 1954, she was the biggest (6,400 tons loaded), most complex vessel yet built in Canada. Designed as a scientific and hydrographic survey ship, *Labrador* was part laboratory, part warship. Under Captain O. C. S. Robertson, RCN, ship would log the first combined operation of scientists and sailors in the Canadian Arctic, the first deep-draft vessel to transit the Northwest Passage, and the second to circumnavigate North America.[26]

Robertson's was an affable leader personality—on the bridge, his remarks often were hilarious. At his first mustering of the ship's company, he stared at the ranks before offering a vintage appreciation: "You've all had a good look at me. You may be disappointed but you'll have to get used to the sight. We're going to be together for some time."[27] This splendid officer will reappear later in our narrative. (See chapter 3.)

Labrador had preceded the eastern convoy, setting up temporary navigation stations, surveying a route, and charting the way. That July, a convoy of fifty-seven ships departed Seattle. The western convoy steamed for the Beaufort Sea and the Northwest Passage, to supply the western and central sectors of the DEW Line.

On 31 July 1957, the line was declared operational: a semicircle of radar stations arcing from Alaska across Canada to Baffin Island, thereby connecting the U.S. Air Force's Alaskan and Northeast Air Commands. The system provided warning, tracking, and interception capability against enemy aircraft far into the Canadian north, as well as advisory service to friendly aircraft.

The project had verified that humans supported by technology could work effectively and live comfortably in the far north. The DEW Line brought with it an enduring "outside" influence. Military and scientific operations irretrievably affected the Inuit and other ethnic groups. Installations in their ancestral lands came fully equipped with southern-style accommodations, and the latest communication and transportation paraphernalia. Along with modern conveniences, employment opportunities were delivered direct to local populations. Attracted, many Inuit moved close. Contact with nonnatives increased, reinforcing Inuit reliance on outside goods and services.

This coincided with a federal policy of centralizing social services to native Canadians. The distribution of health, education, and social-assistance benefits to far-flung families was thought to be impractical. Services were therefore established at existing trading posts. Drawn in, native populations relocated into permanent settlements; in time, groups scattered across the region congregated into about forty permanent communities, thereby ceding control over most of their day-to-day affairs.[28]

[Opposite] In 1946 the U.S. Weather Bureau and the Canadian Meteorological Service installed the first of the Joint Arctic Weather Stations (JAWS) on Cornwallis Island, in the center of the Arctic islands. A network of stations followed. Here USS *Wyandot* (AKA-92) steams the Northwest Passage as part of the sealift for JAWS. Unloading at Resolute Bay began on 30 August. (National Archives and Records Administration)

Northern Sovereignty

"North" exerts an enduring allure. Incursions have led to territorial claims, allegations, and counterclaims. Explorers passing through what is now the Canadian Arctic made random claims as recently as the First World War. In 1925, Canada proclaimed its sovereignty over everything between 61° E (between Canada and Greenland) and 141° W (the Yukon border with Alaska). Geographically, this represents a wedge arching to the North Pole. Despite sustained U.S. objection, this claim endures on maps published in Canada. (Washington also opposes the "internal" status claimed for the Northwest Passage, viewing the waterway as international.)

Implicit to the exercise of sovereign rights is occupation and control of territory. The Inuit hunted and trapped the islands but established no permanent settlements. In 1953 and again in 1955, Inuit families were relocated onto Cornwallis and Ellesmere Islands—transplanted to exert Canada's sovereignty.[29]

The U.S. military, for its part, incited an insatiable demand for information. Aviators and mariners, surveyors and cartographers, geologists and geophysicists, marine biologists, botanists,

[Opposite] Airmen provided brilliant logistic support and services throughout the Soviet Arctic. The Antonov An-2 (here the floatplane version) still provides air-link service over the tundra and taiga of Siberia and far eastern regions—a vastness of few roads or rail lines. (Boris Vdovienko, courtesy R. E. G. Davies)

glaciologists, oceanographers, meteorologists, and hydrologists streamed north in ceaseless parade. In order to improve infrastructure, engineers, contractors and entrepreneurs attended these visitations. Ottawa was obliged to respond to requests for information—and often that information was not available.[30]

The launch of *Sputnik I* in October 1957 intensified the pressure. National resolve rejuvenated, Ottawa pushed a vigorous presence in its own northlands. Mapping and other programs were accelerated, a "Roads to Resources" program initiated (later abandoned), commercial development encouraged. One enduring initiative: the Polar Continental Shelf Project, an agency that provides logistics support in the Canadian High Arctic. Each year, "Polar Shelf" still coordinates field parties working to seaward and ashore in all fields of science.

In 1958 the United Nations convened the first Conference on the Law of the Sea. One outcome: all nations were granted dominion over their respective continental shelves. Rights to mineral and other resources, moreover, were conferred to as far out as two hundred miles. Canada thus found itself claiming jurisdictional responsibilities for a polar margin about which very little was known—save for what the Americans and the Soviets disclosed. "We didn't even know where the continental slope *was* in the Arctic," George Hobson, a geophysicist and former director of Polar Shelf, remembered. "Yes," he agrees, "we were pushed to express our sovereignty." Scientific investigation was the cheapest yet most effective means of deploying the flag. "What better way," Hobson continues, "to express sovereignty in the Canadian Arctic than to have a thousand scientists walking around there peacefully every summer."[31]

"This Arctic, this Canadian Arctic, is our business—ours to defend," Captain Robertson avowed. Contracting out Canada's defense weakened the case for sovereignty. Washington's northward push "caused us to pull up our socks," a fellow officer remarked. Incited to control its own scientific destiny, Ottawa mandated programs of basic research—for Canada. "It is the oldest goal of post–Second World War Canadian sovereignty protection that, to the extent possible, defense activities undertaken in Canada not be left entirely to US forces, especially in the north."[32]

The specter of the Soviet Union—the most probable enemy—incited an orgy of humiliation and introspection. Many were convinced that Soviet science was ahead of the West. For the Arctic, this view was justified. In Leningrad, the Arctic Institute had amassed decades of observation. Soviet icebreakers were marvels of modern technology, their deployment pioneering. Along northern Eurasia, a network of polar stations, reporting vessels, and air reconnaissance supported Northern Sea Route shipping. The level of coverage granted the Soviets a near-synoptic map of the route (Northeast Passage) fully to the Bering Strait. As well, the institute's aggressive, air-supported oceanographic, meteorological, and hydrographical programs *on the ice* had Western officials nervous.

The Arctic Ocean is an enclosed theater, access to which is controlled by a few narrow passages. Ottawa was pressed to survey approaches between the archipelago—potential submarine routes. A U.S. Office of Naval Research report was blunt: the concept of the Arctic as a barrier to an aggressor had ceased to be tenable. Renewed programs of research were "essential" if Washington was to advance its northern frontier to the Soviet Arctic littoral. Military personnel and civilian specialists streamed north. The dominant presence in the non-Soviet Arctic, the United

States worked to dominate those programs it did not already control. Grumblings arose: were Canadian rights of sovereignty again being prejudiced?

The prospect of the North as an American-dominated militarized zone was granted a very noisy examination. With nettling Yankee bravado, magazine and press articles were referring to developments within Canada as in "our" Arctic. By 1958 Canadian public fears stood acute. Did the United States covet Canadian geography? Was Washington really after the Canadian Arctic? Politicians worried openly.

The Soviets, for their part, had returned to the ice, deploying "jumping" air expeditions (air-supported parties) to record oceanographic stations on the Arctic Ocean. (No camps were set.) Landings were logged throughout the polar basin—representing apparent mastery of theater airspace. Riding the ice, moreover, two semi-permanent Severnyy Polyus, or "North Pole," drifting

[Top] Arctic ice is a natural if hazardous runway. At-sea landings call for seasoned eyes, to "read" the surface. Unlike turbines, piston engines take a beating in the cold. (National Archives and Records Administration)

[Bottom] Deployed via ski-equipped Lisunov Li-2, a field team measures pack-ice thickness. Old ice is preferred for Severnyy Polyus ("North Pole") drifting stations, with refrozen leads nearby to serve as runways. The technique of air-supported ice camps was pioneered by the Soviet Union. (Boris Vdovienko, courtesy R. E. G. Davies)

stations were operational. Unprecedented in scale, Soviet programs to understand the Arctic were meticulously planned, superbly equipped. In Ottawa, a Defence Research Board paper painted a dark picture: "Unfortunately . . . it can be said without dispute that the ice covered sea beyond the north coast of Canada is now scientifically, and possibly from a military viewpoint, entirely dominated by the Soviet Union. . . . While there may be some dispute over the value of the polar basin from a strategic point of view there can be little doubt that the presence of [polar stations] manned by the USSR in this period of tension should invite profound concern in their activities."[33]

What, then, was to be done about the Soviets *and* the Americans? That August, Prime Minister John Diefenbaker, speaking on northern policy, asserted his intention to ensure "that everything that could possibly be done should be done to assure that our sovereignty to the North Pole be asserted, and continually asserted, by Canada." Speaking before the House of Commons, Lester Pearson (future prime minister) remarked that it had become "more important than ever before that there be no doubt left in the mind of anybody that it is the Canadian Arctic."[34]

Amid this atmosphere of anxious cooperation and competition, two U.S. Navy craft received singular operational orders.

What is now proven was once only imagined.

—William Blake

Platforms 2

Lighter-than-Air Flight

In the book of manned flight, lighter-than-air is the opening chapter. LTA has contributed much to the venture, including the aerospace sciences. Yet balloons and dirigibles seem mere footnotes to heavier-than-air (HTA) aeronautics.

An enduring element, buoyant flight commenced a century before the Wright Brothers' machine skipped free at Kitty Hawk. Balloons came *first.*

The first passengers eased aloft in the eighteenth century. The brothers Montgolfier, sons of a French papermaker, were thoughtful men of persistent curiosity. Their consideration of an aerostatic machine began in 1782, from observations of the "levity" of smoke from chimney fire. To exploit its lifting power, they constructed a bag of taffeta open at the bottom. (Hydrogen, the lightest element, had been discovered in 1776. As yet, though, its application to flight stood unexploited.) Applying burning paper to the aperture, the bag promptly swelled out to full size then sailed to the ceiling—the first balloon.

The brothers persisted—out-of-doors and in private. Enclosing hot air within containers of their own devising, they dispatched ever-larger balloons until, on 5 June 1783, a demonstration was held. Their aerostat—about 110 feet in circumference—ascended to 6,000 feet and flew a horizontal distance of 7,668 feet. (The inaugural aerial voyage of the first hydrogen balloon would occur on a rainy afternoon late in August.)

The work of the Montgolfiers reverberated throughout Europe. The first manned ascent took place that October, in Paris. With Jean-Francois de Rozier as passenger, the balloon rose to eighty-four feet on its tether. After four and a half minutes, de Rozier descended: his flight, he reported, had been exhilarating. Further captive ascents followed. An untethered flight was inevitable, of course: on 21 November 1783, from outside the capital, a large machine of Montgolfier design was released from its moorings with two on board. A gathering watched transfixed as the world's first successful *aircraft* (for such it was) ascended "into the world of the birds" for a flight of five miles in twenty-five minutes. Its aeronauts were the first humans to travel the atmosphere.

A veritable parade was soon aloft: the year 1784, indeed, was extraordinarily rich in experiment. Early in 1785, the English Channel was crossed by air.

In America the first ascension took place in 1793, achieved by the celebrated French aeronaut Jean Pierre Blanchard. Departing Philadelphia, his hydrogen sphere crossed the Delaware River into New Jersey. Blanchard augmented his flight by attempting scientific observations. Among the witnesses: George Washington, John Adams, and James Monroe.

Ballooning would dominate aeronautics for a century. (In our time, balloons have an established niche in aerospace engineering and in science.) Over eight hundred English ascents alone were recorded. The American Civil War would provide the first large-scale military application. As yet, buoyant flight offered the sole means for aerial transport. Sole rival: the glider.

The balloon's natural descendant is the airship, or dirigible. The first attempt to propel a balloon occurred in 1784. Genuine progress awaited reliable engines, however. As fast as a new source of propulsion seemed to reach practicability, designers seized upon it, hoping its ratio of horsepower to weight might prove satisfactory. In time, workable power-driven balloons were under design. In 1872 an airship propelled by an internal combustion engine rattled aloft.

What of the airplane? For them as with airships, controlled flight against the wind had awaited the advent of light, reliable aero engines—after which the whole of aeronautics was transformed. As a new century opened, squadrons of imaginative aircraft—aeroplanes *and* dirigibles —dotted the skies.

Count Ferdinand von Zeppelin nourished a distinct technology. The hull of a rigid-type airship consisted of girders running longitudinally and transversely, braced by wires. The gas space for buoyancy was subdivided into compartments. Progress was such that an aerial-transport company was founded; by the outbreak of the world war, the fledgling—and fortunate—carrier had lofted more than ten thousand passengers without injury. Germany stood preeminent in the airship arts. In terms of lift, range, and endurance, the rigid types boasted performance unmatched by any HTA machine. The war, moreover, saw the first serious use of lighter-than-air craft as combat weapons; indeed, the wartime application of zeppelins (long-range bombers, naval scouts) accelerated development in England, France, Italy, and in the United States.

In the commercial realm, Germany dominated dirigible transport: "The modern rigid airship [1927] is an evolutionary development from the historic airship *Zeppelin I,* built by Count Zeppelin in 1900. During the course of the quarter century of progress since . . . , the Zeppelin Company has always been in the foreground, although other constructors in Germany, Great Britain, and the United States have contributed not a little to the evolution of the type."[1]

Due largely to international barnstorming of *Graf Zeppelin,* Germany nurtured the airship to the brink of commercial reality. In the era of jet airliners, it is little appreciated that the rigid airship was first to demonstrate the feasibility of transoceanic, intercontinental, nonstop air transport.[2]

In the United States, the U.S. Navy maintained an active interest in the rigid airship until the Second World War. A Zeppelin Company product, the German *LZ-126* was delivered in 1924 to the naval air station at Lakehurst, New Jersey.[3] Christened USS *Los Angeles*, *"L.A."* proved indispensable for training and for developmental projects, so as to advance the art. USS *Akron* (1931–33) and USS *Macon* (1933–35) were commissioned strategic scouts for the fleet.

To enhance search capability, both carried airplanes that could be launched and retrieved in flight via trapeze. In the military environment of the interwar years, the LTA "carrier" offered an unmatched instrument of very-long-range reconnaissance over ocean areas.

For a variety of reasons—technological, military, and political—the large airship failed to prove its value for naval warfare. *Akron* foundered in 1933—with a loss of seventy-three, the worst aviation tragedy to that date. *Macon* was lost in 1935. And in 1937, *Hindenburg* took fire at Lakehurst—a defining calamity. The next war imminent, the crying need was for airplanes, not rigid airships—a military and commercial platform with a public record of failure. Late in 1939, *Los Angeles* was dismantled; the following spring, convinced that *Graf Zeppelin* and *Hindenburg*'s sister ship were militarily useless, Berlin ordered their destruction.

In June 1936, American Airlines had launched Chicago-to-New York service. American and the DC-3 went on to make aviation history, of course. That same year, *Hindenburg* inaugurated regular transatlantic service.[4] In the air-transport environment of the thirties, transoceanic travel was an incomparable experience. *Graf Zeppelin* and *Hindenburg* offered a fast crossing *on schedule*. The flying public liked their comforts, quietness, and dependability. For 1936, the service *Hindenburg* offered was fast: about fifty-two hours on the eastbound leg, about sixty-five hours westbound. But in 1937, the last paying passenger was conveyed.

Pan American introduced the first transatlantic air mail and passenger service by airplane in 1939; outbreak of the European war forced abandonment of the routes.

The Second World War foreclosed a big-ship revival: aeronautics had advanced too far and too fast for the commercial or naval rigid to catch up. Thanks to generations of airliners, the airplane has matched the operating cost and range of large airships. (The maximum range of 747s, 777s, and Airbus A340s is halfway round the world.) And the advantage of speed has suffocated "the inflated competition."[5] "In . . . five generations, the commercial airliner has grown from a 14-seat, 100 mph, 100-mile range, noisy, temperamental, and unreliable Ford, to a 360-seat (530 seats in Japan), 600-mph (550 on the cruise), 6,000-mile range, quiet, comfortable, and reliable Boeing or Airbus."[6]

No rigid airship has flown in three generations. As a transportation system, the transoceanic airship never recovered from a few moments in 1937.[7] Today, little is recalled of the airship's achievements and unique military promise—which we'll look at momentarily.

Throughout the interwar period, the nonrigid type was consigned largely to duty as trainers. The shape of helium-filled hulls is maintained by internal pressure of the lifting gas. Compensation for contraction and expansion (due to temperature and altitude changes) is regulated by air-filled "ballonets" inside the envelope, or "bag," using automatic and manual valves to maintain pressure within predetermined limits. "The smaller sizes of pressure airships as developed in the United States [1927] have been primarily for military and naval purposes, such as scouting, transportation, ship convoys, harbour defense, anti-submarine offensive operations, and as a preliminary stage of training for the crews of rigid type airships."[8]

The U.S. Navy was not the sole operator of blimps. Unable to procure a rigid type, the U.S. Army Air Corps inaugurated a competing program—abandoned in 1937. Goodyear, for its part, deployed an aerial fleet for public relations and for training aircrews for the never-authorized commercial ships. In recent years, barnstorming from Connecticut to California, blimps have ferried thousands of passengers—customers and celebrities, VIPs, the media, and a curious public.[9]

Marketers are image-mad; the craving for breaking news, visuals, and ratings is unquenchable. So network sports and news broadcasters deploy skycams. Often, they're orbiting blimps. Today, a number of firms build, own, and operate airships in the United States, Europe, and elsewhere.

Lighter-than-air was an operational element of U.S. naval aviation for nearly five decades. What were its *military* applications? Airships offer a unique performance package: phenomenal endurance, large lift, economy of operation. Unlike fixed-wing craft, which require continuous use of engines, an airship *floats* in its medium. (The atmosphere is a fluid.) This makes them comparatively fuel efficient: most of the *static* lift is provided by the contained gas. Engines propel the craft forward; when they do, *dynamic* lift is gained from the "bag," which acts as a crude airfoil. Most planes fly high and fast. Airships are slow-speed, low-flying craft. Speed, though, is adjustable in a way impossible for fixed-wing (if not rotary-wing) aircraft—from a maximum down to zero (hovering). Here, then, were instruments of relatively high speed and extraordinary endurance that, in the environment of the interwar years, could not be matched by any other means.

In both the eastern and western Atlantic, Great War U-boats operated offensively against merchant shipping. A ring of coastal stations was erected; flying boats and small coastal blimps pressed a campaign of antisubmarine warfare (ASW) and convoy escort, helping to blunt the undersea threat.

Following the Armistice, the nonrigid was marginalized. In the teeth of tragedy and criticism, a program of experimentation and development for the rigid type would persist to another world war. Meanwhile, carrier aviation and flying boats were the major constituents of U.S. naval aviation.

Dismantling of the last rigids in 1939 shifted emphasis to blimps. When Berlin's U-boats applied near-crippling pressure in the western Atlantic—the locus for shipbuilding and imports to Britain—coastal bases were rushed into commission. By 1944 the U.S. Navy Department was deploying the largest LTA fleet ever, augmenting antisubmarine airplanes and surface forces with newfangled sensors—radar, Loran, sonobuoys, magnetic anomaly detection (MAD) gear. On VE day, its airships were operational in North, Central, and South America—and in southern Europe and northwest Africa.

Tied to surface oxygen and batteries, the diesel submarine was not a true submersible. The mere presence of aircraft—HTA and LTA—had obliged the enemy to submerge. No panacea had defeated the U-boat; rather, the *combined, integrated weight* of responses had rescued the tonnage war. LTA had benefited greatly, but so had heavier-than-air aeronautics. Further, the blimp's combat record seemed problematic. In 1939–40, the navy's LTA forces were outmoded and marginal—it was a time of frantic growth in naval air forces. Readiness proved slow: in trained personnel, material support, advanced sensors, effective weapons. One outcome: no U-boats were confirmed sunk by blimps, unassisted.[10]

This apparent failure—no *offensive* successes—deprived LTA of political leverage; in the postwar period, the officers and bureaus whose influence would dominate policy and procurement saw little reason to sustain the program. Competing against long-accepted hardware, U.S. Navy lighter-than-air would fall (in 1961) to competing programs and weapon systems.

In the meantime, peace brought demobilization—and a return to stepchild status for LTA. Still, lighter-than-air retained a few high-level proponents. Admiral Chester W. Nimitz, USN, was one. Promoted to chief of naval operations, he acknowledged in testimony on the 1948 appropriations bill the blimp's "vital defensive role" against the submarine. The deputy chief of naval operations for air, Vice Admiral Arthur W. Radford, in his own testimony worried as to the consequences of further austerities, remarking that the LTA organization "has been reduced to an absolute minimum, and that further reductions will completely destroy the morale of personnel currently associated with this valuable part of our program."

New Platform

The years 1948–53 proved to be a time of healthy expansion in U.S. Navy lighter-than-air. As part of the "Aviation Navy" package for 1948, a new platform was authorized. A total of nearly $4 million was earmarked for an LTA development program, $1.5 million of which was allocated for the prototype.[11] The production version would become the primary LTA postwar platform of the naval service.

The Second World War had transformed the at-sea battleground. Newfangled sensors, communications and navigation gear, information processors, and weaponry had become indispensable. For antisubmarine aircraft, the desirability of increased range and lift was clear. Equipment represents weight. For aircraft, each pound is critical. Nonetheless, an array of sophisticated avionics would have to be mounted if the new ship were to have any military relevance. The wartime K-type airship could lift 28,000 pounds, granting a *useful* lift of about 8,700 pounds for fuel, crew, ordnance, supplies. Any new ship would have to exceed this. Hence, large size was an inescapable design objective. The navy wanted an ASW airship capable of blue-water patrol—a true "seagoing" platform.

Goodyear Aircraft, the prime contractor, submitted a package of proposals. However, the design competition yielded a surprise entry: Douglas Aircraft. The interloper (one assumes) was outclassed: Goodyear had been active in aeronautics since 1911, having designed, built, and flown over two hundred airships. Douglas, for its part, had built none.[12]

Neither firm was a stranger to the politics of procurement. Indisputably, Goodyear excelled in airship design. For its part, the Navy Department seemed comfortable with its special relationship. Yet Douglas was selected: the West Coast firm would fabricate the control car, Goodyear the fins and envelope—and, as well, be responsible for the final erection.

Months of haggling ensued. In the end, Douglas elected to sell to Goodyear for actual production. Douglas' foray into the field had realized a number of innovations, notably in the control car. The contracts were signed in May 1948.

Design specifications called for an airship 324 feet in length. Envelope capacity: 875,000 cubic feet of helium. When flown, the prototype N-1 would be the world's largest nonrigid airship.

Among its innovations was equipment for in-flight replenishment—a means of obtaining ballast via a seawater pickup system. Why? As fuel is burned an airship becomes progressively lighter. Helium can be valved, but this is operationally undesirable—and expensive. Reballasting would offset the weight of fuel burned, thus extending loiter capability hence on-scene hours with cooperating surface units.

Protracted flying imposes physical and psychological demands. Habitability for aircrews is vital.[13] A two-deck car was Douglas' design solution—a first for the nonrigid type. Under way, crews would berth and mess "topside"—a short physical remove from the lower deck, with its operating and ASW equipment. A fully equipped galley was incorporated: electric refrigerator, freezer, coffeemaker and range, and serving counter, plus storage spaces. A roaster and pressure cooker, even a sink and freshwater storage, were installed. The wardroom held two tables, seating eight. Two bunks were installed forward, above the flight deck, six immediately aft. Two washrooms were fitted, equipped with deliberate amenities, such as a drink-cup dispenser, a receptacle for electric shavers.

These were quantum improvements. Early nonrigids had been open-cockpit affairs, scarcely adequate for moving—theirs were cramped, noise-filled patrols. Later models were far more habitable. The ZPG series introduced a singular in-flight environment.

Power plant: two air-cooled Wright radial engines. Their location was the most novel feature of the model—both engines were mounted *inside* the car instead of outboard. As a result, the engines were accessible for in-flight maintenance and repair. Two reversible-pitch propellers (a boon to ground handling) were mounted on outriggers; small-diameter nacelles accommodated the prop hubs and gearboxes—a feature enhancing streamlining. The aircraft, moreover, was designed for one-engine operation, an option offering exceptional fuel economy. During normal operation, each engine would deliver power via a long drive shaft to its prop. When wanted, an interconnecting clutch and transmission system engaged a shaft between the port and starboard inboard gearboxes, an arrangement making it possible to drive both props with either engine.[14]

Another feature was its X-type empennage. Four "ruddervators" (combining the function of rudders and elevators) were moved to forty-five-degree positions about the stern, to facilitate heavy takeoffs. Retractable, tricycle-type landing gear was yet another innovation.

A mock-up of the prototype (designated N-1, later ZPN-1, then ZPG-1) was ready in 1949. Noting its innovative features and design advances, *Aviation Week* called the prototype "an interesting example of how far lighter-than-air nonrigid design has progressed from balloon days."[15] As is the case with prototypes, work was punctuated by a variety of design and engineering difficulties. The power-transmission system, heretofore untried, proved especially troublesome. The fin design, ballonets, the new neoprene-coated rayon envelope, and the control system generated challenges for engineers. Problem components were ground tested, the results evaluated, deficiencies corrected, improvements worked in. Preliminary design to final rollout, testing, fabrication, and assembly consumed three years.

The inaugural flight was logged on 18 June 1951. A series of in-flight and ground tests ensued. As the trials program advanced, it became clear that various refinements were in order; Goodyear, indeed, would wrestle teething problems for another twelve months before N-1 was ferried to the navy at Lakehurst.

On 16 June 1952, course was set for east-central New Jersey. Concluding an uneventful flight, the new ship circled in fog before rolling out into the hands of a ground crew—VIPs and

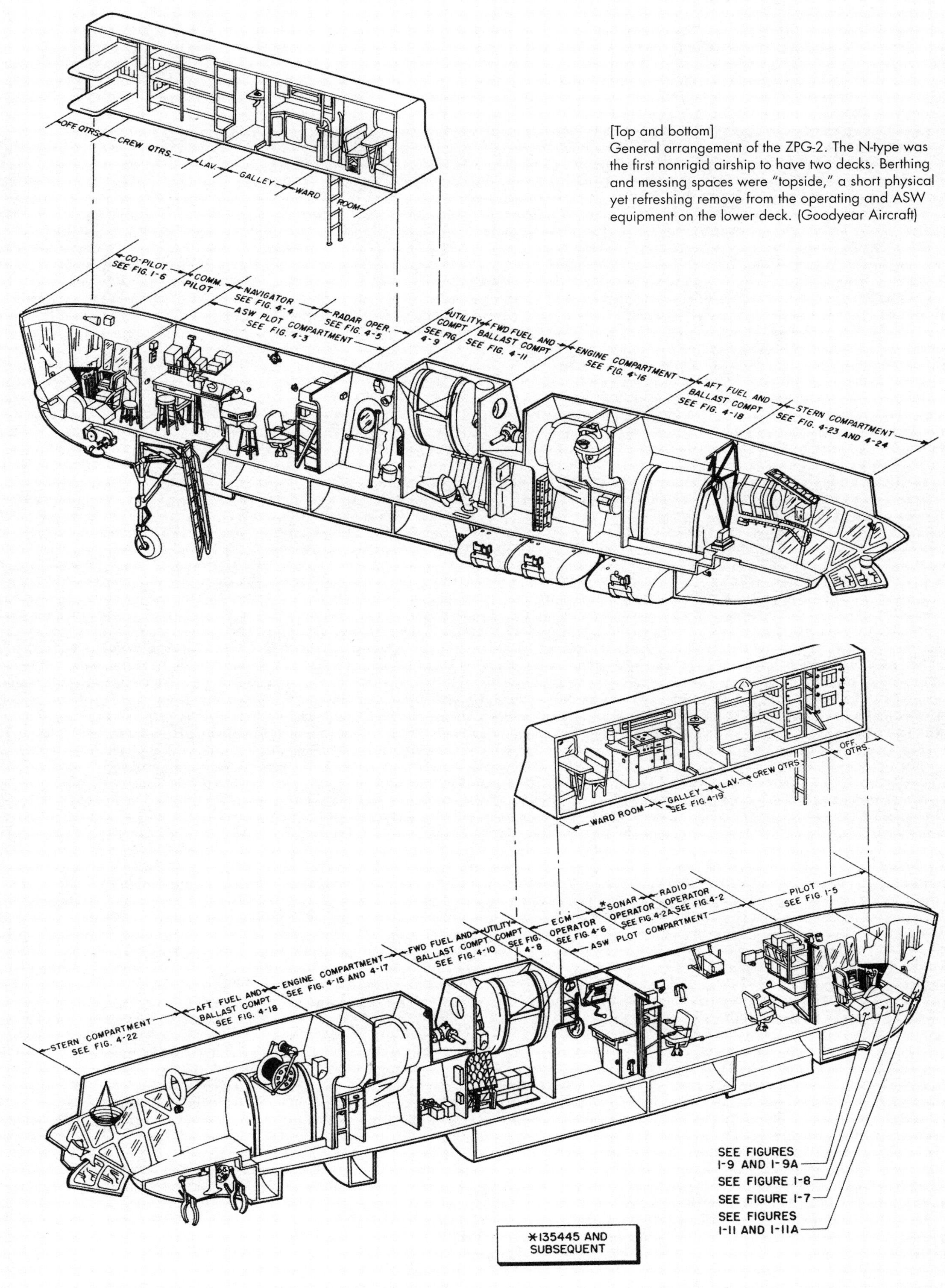

[Top and bottom]
General arrangement of the ZPG-2. The N-type was the first nonrigid airship to have two decks. Berthing and messing spaces were "topside," a short physical yet refreshing remove from the operating and ASW equipment on the lower deck. (Goodyear Aircraft)

media representatives duly assembled. Secured to a mobile mast, N-1 was shunted under a roof; there it dominated the hangar's berthing space, the ship's envelope curving well above the older ships secured nearby.

N-1 had advanced the state of the airship arts. The ZPG series had much greater range/endurance and habitability than any preceding airships. Mission loaded, they were good for thirty-six-hour flights as a matter of routine (longer, if not mission configured). ZPGs could also cope with severe weather better than could smaller airships, simply by virtue of their larger size. They were more stable—not unlike the difference of the performance of a destroyer compared to that of a cruiser in a full gale.[16]

Delivery marked a gratifying moment for all who had worked to realize a prototype. It remained to be seen how the surface fleet would exploit this novel platform.

The First Arctic Submarine

The notion that a submarine might convey men to the North Pole had been suggested, surprisingly, in 1648. The visionary: Bishop John Wilkins, founder and first secretary of the Royal Society of London. Jules Verne, the French novelist and prophet of technology, popularized the notion of the polar submarine. His tale of the fantastic—and prophetic—submarine boat *Nautilus* was published in 1869. Still, Verne's dream would not be fully realized until the advent of nuclear power.

During the winter of 1903–4, *Protector* navigated under ice off Newport, Rhode Island, and surfaced by breaking through a floe eight inches thick. The experimental boat was built by the American naval architect-engineer Simon Lake—a pioneer submarine designer. In Russia, where transportation was (and remains) a key to development, the submarine *Kefal* operated in ice-covered waters off Vladivostok and in the Gulf of Finland.

In 1928 the first expedition by submarine into the Arctic Ocean was announced. Australian-born explorer Hubert Wilkins was a hard-edged, globe-trotting adventurer. Wilkins had accompanied the irrepressible Vilhjalmur Stefansson into the Canadian Arctic, then Ernest Shackleton on an expedition to Antarctica. In 1928 Wilkins and Carl Ben Eielson made the first airplane flight across the Arctic. The pair landed off northern Alaska to record a sounding (16,000 feet) from the ice canopy.

The first flight over Antarctica followed, piloted by Eielson. In 1929 Wilkins was a passenger on board *Graf Zeppelin* during its world circumnavigation—a feat that altered air-transport thinking. And in 1936 he booked passage on board *Hindenburg* on its maiden flight to the United States.

Partnering with Lake and Sloan Danenhower, a former submarine officer, Wilkins had resolved to cross the Arctic Ocean, conducting scientific work throughout the passage.[17] The notion had been seeded in 1913, during talks with Stefansson, who, it appears, grasped the submarine's polar potential. A submersible, the pair reasoned, would unlock a new field of inquiry.[18]

The northern ocean, many held, is capped by an unbroken canopy. In winter, the ice is a more or less consolidated sheet. Still, zones of compression and tension realize pressure ridges and cracks. By his own observation, Wilkins knew that open water (leads) broaden in spring then persist until freeze-up. These were basic to Wilkins' strategy: they would allow a short-legged diesel boat to "puddle jump" across.[19]

Wilkins put up his own funds then embarked on a lecture tour. Major support was secured from Lincoln Ellsworth, a wealthy American obsessive about polar exploration. Friends helped; institutions endorsed the venture. And to popularize his notion, a book on the prospective voyage *(Under the North Pole)* was published.

A vintage U.S. submarine *(O-12)* was leased, modified, and renamed *Nautilus*. Wilkins was no scientist; nor did he have experience with submersibles. He was relying on experts, some of whom may have held reservations. And though his theory of under-ice navigation was sound, Wilkins' platform and its Lake-installed equipment would fail him.

On 4 June 1931 *Nautilus* departed Provincetown, Massachusetts, for London. Following breakdown in mid-Atlantic, delays, and misadventure, the boat reached its first ice on 19 August (80° 20′ N)—months behind schedule. Then a maddening discovery: in a lead, attempting to

[Opposite] ZPG-2 (1953–62). Note the tricycle landing gear, radome beneath the car, and small-diameter nacelles. Both engines were mounted internally, enabling in-flight access. Either engine could drive both propellers. (AMCS Daniel Brady)

dive, the boat simply did not respond: the diving rudders had carried away. Wilkins radioed, "Now we were in a submarine that had come 5000 miles to a point within 600 miles of the Pole, and was no longer submersible!"[20] The expedition was reduced to a scientific probe, albeit a fruitful one—the first submarine penetration of the Arctic Ocean.

North and west of Spitsbergen the sea is open in summer; there the pack-ice edge curves poleward. Wilkins' plan: to submerge in that sector and, with slight positive buoyancy, slide *Nautilus* along the underside of the ice canopy. (The boat's conning tower had been removed, leaving a topside that was smooth, curved, clean swept.) *Nautilus* would inscribe a profile of the ice, using sledlike runners installed on the main deck.

Two test dives were logged. Trimmed down by the bow, the boat bulled into an obstructing floe then fought to slide beneath. *Nautilus* stalled, propellers thrashing. Positive buoyancy was too great. Further, the ice-drill mounted topside had jammed above deck. As Sir Hubert described the predicament: "The vessel [on 31 August] went half its length under the ice and there stuck. The noise of the ice scraping along the top of the vessel was terrifying. It sounded as though the whole superstructure was being demolished. An inside inspection proved that it was undamaged."[21] All hands were relieved to regain the surface.

These were the first attempts to dive beneath polar ice. By design, the ceiling had to be sensed visually ("quartz peep holes") or by contact; no sonar assisted. Through sheer force of character, Wilkins took *Nautilus* farther north than any vessel before—82°. Another measure of the man is the expedition's scientific accomplishment: the first core sample taken in the Arctic (depth 5,220 feet), bathymetry by echo sounder, gravity measurements, temperature and salinity profiles, plankton samples, and other data. As well, both visual and photographic observations of the under-ice profile were recorded. "We looked out from the portholes [on 4 September] to see the steel-like fangs of ice moving stealthily past us. . . . We had at last made some progress beneath the ice. We could not, of course, without the diving rudders, dive beneath it. I would have liked to continue further, scraping beneath the scattered ice, but to continue to do so was considered by some on board to be too risky and too dangerous, so we pulled up beside a heavy flow, blew tanks and let the men ashore for exercise."[22]

Valuable research data had been compiled. Results of the Wilkins-Ellsworth Trans-Arctic Submarine Expedition would, in a later era, assist the navy and a new breed of *Nautilus*.

Convinced that his boat could do no more, Wilkins logged the last scientific observations on 6 September. Hull battered and leaking, *Nautilus* retreated to Spitsbergen. "There were, undeniably, certain circuslike aspects to the expedition, but these were resorted to only in order to raise money for a privately financed expedition of a sort usually attempted only with total or substantial government financing. Overall, it was eloquent testimony to stalwart determination of a remarkable man."[23]

Why had Wilkins—who had flown over the pack and walked its surface—assumed that he could skate its underside without meeting deformed (pressure) ice? Had *Nautilus* been able to run under ice, the expedition might well have ended tragically.

Wilkins' dream would be vindicated, of course—long after two rhetorical follow-on cruises. In 1937 Wilkins was reported to be making preparations for a submersible trip under the ice, to

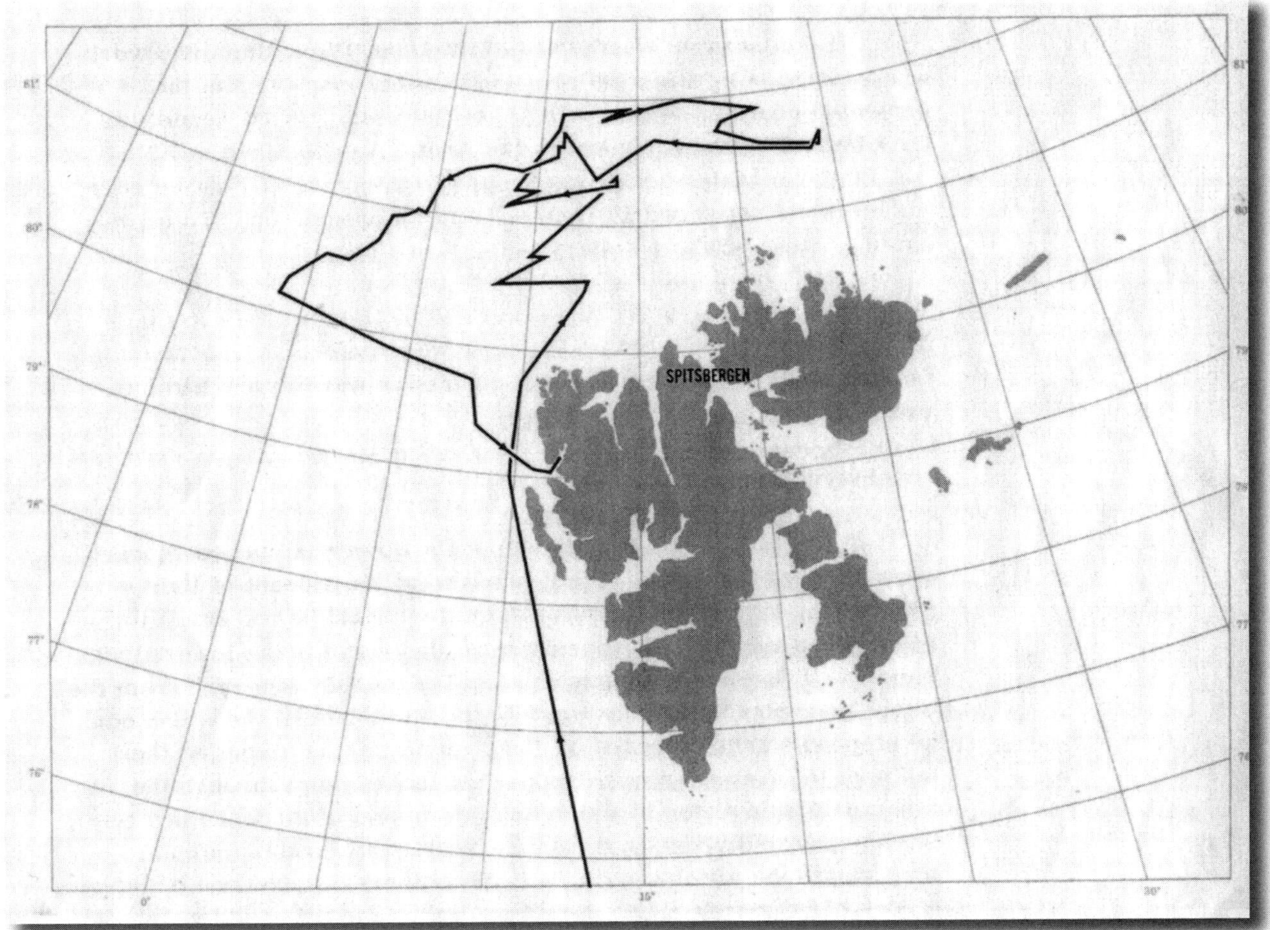

Track of Sir Hubert Wilkins' *Nautilus* (former O-12) in Spitsbergen waters, August–September 1931. The boat had pressed farther north than any other vessel on its own power—the world's first Arctic submarine. (U.S. Navy Electronics Laboratory)

establish and maintain a scientific base. Also, nurtured by the euphoria attending their own transpolar flights, Soviet authorities hinted of a submarine expedition to the Pole, to aid a proposed Arctic air route.

Rhetoric notwithstanding, these notions came to nothing.[24]

SSN

The concept of propelling ships with newfound energy had, in fact, predated the Second World War. Within months of Japan's surrender, scientists and engineers were discussing its practicability. Among senior submarine officers, a consensus was coalescing: development of a true submarine appeared probable within a decade, provided nuclear power was made available for propulsion. Voices of opposition in the Navy Department (rather few) were to vanish, swept away by a surge of endorsement and support.

A nuclear ship-propulsion system (first studied in 1939) gestated quickly. Not long after the war, Commander Edward L. Beach, USN, a decorated submariner, began hearing that The Bomb could be made into an engine, maybe. "I remember at that time thinking to myself, by George, there's the way to go. The nuclear engine would give a submarine tremendous capability, because, you see, the submariners right away relate to air—you have to have air to run the [diesel] engines. That requires that you come up all the time; you can't run the engines submerged. . . . But if you could run a *nuclear* engine—not need air—it could go indefinitely."[25]

In 1947 Beach was the submarine officer assigned to the Atomic Energy Division of the Navy Department, at that time oriented entirely to atomic bombs. That October he and Captain Elton W. Grenfell, in the office of assistant CNO for operations, prepared a secret memorandum for signature by Rear Admiral C. W. Styer, USN. It called for the navy to initiate action "to prompt development, design, and construction of a nuclear powered submarine." That December Admiral Chester W. Nimitz, CNO, endorsed the concept to Secretary of the Navy John L. Sullivan. In 1948 the General Board (the senior panel then responsible for such matters of policy) went on record endorsing the nuclear boat.

Construction of one nuclear-powered attack submarine (SSN, in naval parlance, nicknamed "fast attack") was recommended to Congress in April 1950. A joint resolution approved 1 July 1951 made funds available for SSN 571 and, as well, for other vessels in the 1952 shipbuilding program.[26] In August the contract was awarded to the Electric Boat Company, Groton, Connecticut (soon the Electric Boat Division of General Dynamics Corporation). Basic designs were prepared by the Bureau of Ships, with design of an atomic propulsion plant falling to the Argonne National Laboratory of the Atomic Energy Commission (AEC), together with the Westinghouse Electric Corporation.

Research, design, and production work for the world's first nuclear-powered vehicle advanced with startling alacrity. The "Bunsen cells" of Jules Verne's imaginary vessel became, in the new *Nautilus,* a fission reactor. Conventional submarines were submersible *surface* ships. But nuclear propulsion offered freedom from surface oxygen, and so prolonged submerged operation—true undersea ships. One application of this potential (so far, it was only that): exploiting the open sea that lies beneath the ice canopy. Few yet foresaw this. Still, within a brief, fruitful span, *Nautilus* (special equipment installed) would confirm the notion of under-ice sailing.

Meantime, the effort to realize a nuclear platform was driven with obsessive force. A submariner as well as engineer, Captain Hyman G. Rickover, USN, headed the nuclear-propulsion program, holding concurrent positions in the Bureau of Ships (charged with developing a nuclear boat) and at the AEC. En route to becoming the navy's most controversial officer, iconoclast Rickover became its most powerful.

The design of a propulsion plant—extracting power from an explosive, heat-producing, radioactive substance to drive a propeller—was the product of an all-out program. "As he built and manned the *Nautilus,* [Rickover] was creating a new submarine navy." He helped design its systems, making crucial engineering and also operational-related decisions. The man was a taskmaster, and his pace was furious. No corners were cut, no technological shortcuts approved. He insisted on safety and reliability and performance. Rickover, characteristically cajoling and badgering, oversaw virtually every element of the program. "He drove everyone with a relentless fury to produce it," Beach said. "*Nautilus* was built in a *phenomenally* fast time."[27] "We really had support" for the project, the boat's prospective commanding officer, Commander Eugene P. Wilkinson, USN, would recall. Snared by Beach into the nuclear program, Wilkinson (not an

Academy man) had become the navy's expert on nuclear power as a line officer—and second to Rickover as a constructor. Nominated by Rickover to command the first SSN, and despite a faction endorsing Beach for the command, Wilkinson was assigned.

The entire project (in Wilkinson's words) was "hard-driving, take-a-chance, get-it-done." Anything needed was procured—immediately.[28]

On 14 June 1952, with 12,000 dignitaries and well-wishers attending, President Harry S. Truman presided over the keel-laying ceremonies at Electric Boat. "This ship will be something new in the world," Truman remarked. "She will be atomic-powered"—the force that heats the sun. "Think what this means," Truman exulted.[29]

On 21 January 1954, the keel of SSN 571 met the sea. Admiral Robert B. Carney, now CNO, remarked that the fleet was "hungry to put *Nautilus* to work." Altogether, the 2,800-ton vessel had consumed $55 million: forty million for the hull, fifteen million for design and construction of its nuclear reactor. Builder's trials well along, *Nautilus* became a commissioned ship in the U.S. Navy on 30 September 1954. At Groton, Admiral Jerauld Wright, USN, commander in chief, Atlantic Fleet, addressed the implications: "The entire free world watches as a new instrument of power comes into being. The placing of the USS *Nautilus* into commission means the beginning of a new era whose horizons are beyond the scope of our accurate vision. The atom has been harnessed and now, here today, it goes to work."[30]

Months of construction and dockside testing concluded on 17 January 1955, when Wilkinson ordered the lines cast off and signaled to the Submarine Force commander, "Underway on nuclear power."

Sea trials confirmed an astounding capability. For a time, *Nautilus*—rated at 15,000 horsepower and about twenty-one knots submerged—was the world's fastest combat submarine.[31] Her steam turbines granted a performance that, one publication noted, "virtually wiped out progress in anti-submarine warfare techniques."[32] More or less unassailable in antisubmarine exercises, "he [the boat's skipper] was, with that ship, all over the navy with it. They couldn't lay a finger on it." Improved sonar was stimulated to help counter this new weapon system. The potential of undersea ships had now been realized, with *Nautilus*—the first true submersible.[33]

In May 1956 *Nautilus* was accepted "for unrestricted service." Still, the boat had not been designed for polar operations: its sail and superstructure, for instance, were constructed of aluminium—unsuitable for upward impact. Nonetheless, the Arctic Ocean—heretofore closed to conventional maritime passage—now, plausibly, might be accessible. Still, the submarine would become Arctic-capable only through a testing procession of operations using SSN 571 and her successors, building upon the first trials in Arctic operations by diesel-battery boats.

Field Trials (Submarines in Ice), 1946–57

Among Wilkins' admirers was a physicist from the U.S. Navy Electronics Laboratory (NEL). Since the Second World War, Dr. Waldo K. Lyon, encouraged by Otto Neumann Sverdrup (1855–1930), a Norwegian advocate of submersibles in the Arctic, had maintained an abiding interest in submarines and their scientific potential. The urging of this soft-spoken civilian would deliver polar submarining to a practicable, operational reality.

[Top] One of two shafts for the first nuclear-powered submarine, Electric Boat Division of General Dynamics, Groton, Connecticut, 1953. Note that the screws will extend out—which will be a concern of Adm. Hyman Rickover when, in 1956, USS *Nautilus* is ordered into Arctic waters. (U.S. Naval Institute Photo Archive)

[Opposite] USS *Nautilus* (SSN 571) is commissioned into the U.S. Navy, 30 September 1954. (U.S. Naval Institute Photo Archive)

"Literature and comment," Dr. Lyon records, "treated the expedition with disdain and the submarine concept as fantasy." Yet Wilkins' original *Nautilus* had brought out a great deal of information. (At the time, expedition results were ignored; later, though, its data proved "most valuable.") Sir Hubert had demonstrated, moreover, the taking of oceanographic and other observations from a submerged platform, thereby pointing the way to future penetrations.[34]

During 1939–45, German U-boats had applied near-crippling pressure on Allied merchant shipping. Operating against Arctic convoys, for example, a few boats went under ice—exploiting acoustic conditions that complicated detection. In September 1944, *U-957* operated against a convoy and covering forces in the Kara Sea, on the Northern Sea Route. During the hunt and chase, collisions with drift ice bent both periscopes, leaving the boat blind and trimmed down by the stern. Its captain probed the pack's underside with the bow—"feeling" for open water. He was able to surface and make port, the outer doors of his boat's bow tubes buckled.[35]

No submarine was yet properly equipped to sail under ice. A polar submersible awaited nuclear propulsion. Meantime, the wartime U.S. Navy—occupied throughout the global ocean—held scant interest.

> After conference in the Navy Department [1944], including conference with representatives of the Office of the Commander in Chief, it has been determined that the use of a submarine designed to go under the Arctic ice would have no Naval use. . . . It does not appear that any desirable objective could be attained by a submarine operating under ice that could not be accomplished by other means. . . . The general question

of underwater Arctic exploration has been discussed with Rear Admiral Richard E. Byrd and with Sir Hubert Wilkins. It was agreed that if such an expedition is contemplated after the war, minor changes on a standard submarine would meet the requirements.[36]

In July 1946, USS *Atule* (SS 403), a diesel-electric boat, navigated under pack ice between Greenland and Ellesmere Island but suffered collisions with ice keels—deformed or pressure ice. Its sonar installation included an upward-beamed, high-frequency, high-resolution set. In January 1947, USS *Sennet* (SS 408) struggled in the Ross Sea of Antarctica. In his report, *Sennet*'s commanding officer noted, "Handling a submarine in an ice pack was an entirely new and different experience for everyone on board." This operation would benefit shiphandling near the opposite pole, including navigation by sonar in the vicinity of icebergs.[37]

The navy initiated an eight-year study. As senior scientist, NEL's Dr. Lyon accompanied each of the service's experimental patrols, bringing a wealth of experience, information, and continuity with him, together with special equipment. Utterly dedicated to under-ice submarine operations, "Dr. Waldo Lyon was the premier expert on Arctic ice and submarine operations for many years. He used submarines as his vehicle for exploring the ice, ice passages, and ice lakes. He was the driving force behind the Navy's many voyages to the Arctic from 1947 on. He rode on most of the trips. He was instrumental in obtaining the *Nautilus* to extend the range of his studies."[38]

In August 1947, USS *Boarfish* (SS 327) passed through the Bering Strait into the shallow, flat-bottomed Chukchi Sea—and held there. "When we first went up there with the diesel boats in 1947, we didn't dare go east of Point Barrow—we stayed in the Chukchi Sea—'cause there wasn't any chart. Didn't know *what* you were going to get into. So we did all the work in [the] '47–'49 period with the diesel boats in the Bering Sea and Chukchi Sea, which we had charts [for]."[39]

Special equipment was a prerequisite. Through Dr. Lyon, *Boarfish* was equipped with three sonars: forward-looking scanning sonar plus upward- and downward-pulsed sounding systems, to measure distance to the canopy above and clearance to the seabed. Northwest of Point Barrow, the boat sailed between floes, maneuvering to avoid deep-draft ice—the first excursion under polar pack. Diving in clear water for an initial run, "We travelled a distance of twelve miles under the ice and learned the art of interpreting the scanning sonar pictures of the ice canopy. We learned to pilot the submarine around and past heavy ice masses which appeared on the sonar screen to threaten our passage. . . . Having successfully completed the first dive, the mystery of underice submarining vanished, and an objective to develop an Arctic submarine and underice operating technique was established."[40]

Ten hours (three dives) were logged—a distance of about thirty miles using scanning-sonar guidance—a major part of the solution. As well, *Boarfish* compiled the first sonar records of ice profiles (under-ice topography). The 1931 *Nautilus* had represented the first *attempt* to dive under ice. These were the first extended *dives* under ice. The practicability of under-ice navigation stood demonstrated. Still, hostage to batteries and to oxygen, exploratory work was necessarily slow, tentative.

[Opposite] *Nautilus* is backed clear for its first sea trial, 17 January 1955. On the bridge are Adm. Rickover (center) and Cdr. Eugene P. Wilkinson (right), commanding officer. As yet, the Arctic Ocean is not a naval theater on or beneath the pack-ice canopy. The exploratory phase of the true Arctic submarine soon opened—courtesy of nuclear propulsion. (U.S. Naval Institute Photo Archive)

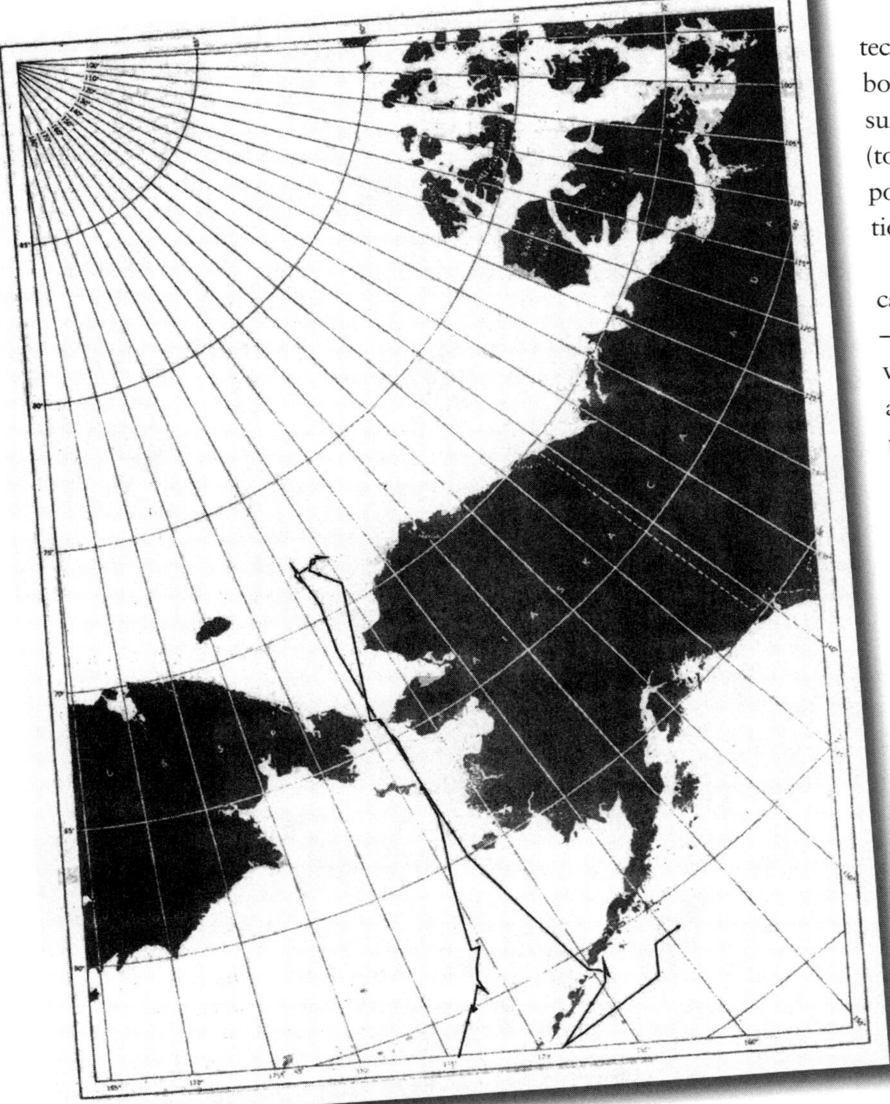

Emphasis shifted to operating technique for fleet-type diesel-electric boats and to navigation: locating and surfacing in open water between floes (to recharge batteries and determine position), adapting sonar and navigation systems.

Development of an Arctic-capable submarine advanced nearer—boats able to operate anywhere within the deepwater basin and its approaches.[41] The northern half of the Bering Sea and the Chukchi Sea are shallow—and flat-bottomed for great distances. Trials persisted in this known area of the Chukchi. (The Arctic Basin was unsurveyed; few soundings were yet recorded.)[42] In September 1948, USS *Carp* (SS 338) located open-water polynynas and conducted vertical dives and ascents between floes. Experimental scanners were tested: installed on *Carp*'s upper deck was an inverted fathometer developed by Dr. Lyon and colleagues. *Carp* penetrated more than fifty miles into scattered ice, to the limit of consolidated pack (72° 10′ N). "Unquestionably," diving control was practical in ice areas.

During both the *Boarfish* and *Carp* patrols, oceanographic data were collected under the direction of Dr. Lyon. In his view, an under-ice submarine was "far closer than had been envisioned." Extended navigation was feasible, given the prerequisite equipment: efficient fathometers and scanning sonars. The Arctic—plausibly—was a navigable operational area for science, for surveillance, and for combat. According to the *Naval Arctic Operations Handbook* (1949), however, "development of the trans-arctic submarine remains in the realm of fantasy."

In 1952, using new Hydrographic Office charts for the shelf east of Point Barrow, USS *Redfish* (SS 395) logged an exploratory cruise with *Burton Island* (AGB 1), an icebreaker modified for surveys and trials. Primary objectives: under-ice navigation, conditions of combat, and sonar transmission beneath sea ice, along with oceanographic and geophysical observations. The cruise completed experiments with conventional fleet-type submarines. "The diving and ascent procedures in ice lakes are completely solved," Dr. Lyon reported.

[Opposite] Track chart, USS *Boarfish* (SS 327), August 1947. (U.S. Navy Electronics Laboratory)

> The necessary sonar system is provided by a scanning sonar (QLA), a topside echo sounder system and any simple searchlight (pinging) sonar. The searchlight sonar is needed to assist scanning sonar in the detection of icebergs and separation of sea ice targets. . . . Considerable caution is necessary because the topside sonars and periscope shears are very susceptible to damage by sea ice.

As well, warfare in sea ice stood tested. Simulated runs by *Redfish* on the icebreaker indicated that, properly equipped, a submarine under ice possessed "nearly overwhelming combat advantages of maneuverability, choice of opportunity to attack, detection range, and ordnance. The sea ice provides a very effective protective cover for the submarine. . . . Another submarine appears to be the only conceivable weapon for attacking a submarine in sea ice areas."[43]

The cruise had logged deep-basin acoustic work with T-3—an ice island occupied since March by the air force. (See chapter 6.) Why joint work with an ice-rafted "drifting station"? The attenuation of radio waves in seawater is even more severe than that of light waves. Despite the problems (e.g., increase in attenuation with increase in frequency, background noise at low frequencies), underwater sound is the best tool for submarine detection. Underwater TNT explosions—sound sources—set off at T-3 (then at 88° N, 96° W) were received by listening equipment on board *Redfish* nine hundred miles away, in the Beaufort—direct, long-range measurements. A 1949 expedition had examined propagation of acoustic energy in the Bering and Chukchi Seas—prefatory to high-priority research on the sound-velocity structure of the Arctic Ocean by the Navy Underwater Sound Laboratory (USL).

As yet, underwater navigation and communications were the "big problems." (For transpolar aviation too, the problem was navigation—specifically, nearness to the magnetic pole. See chapter 3.) Converts to the polar submarine were yet few; it would take the advent of nuclear propulsion to change that. The theory of under-ice sailing may appear elementary. In operational practice, skilled seamanship is vital, as are thoroughly dependable equipment and machinery. Further, as *Nautilus* would discover, a superstructure built to withstand upward impact is basic.

In January 1955, meanwhile, *Nautilus'* signal lamp on the bridge blinked out its historic signal.

Dr. Lyon and Commander Robert D. McWethy, USN, a submariner, had together embraced the concept of polar submarining. The two had met by chance in 1951, on board *Burton Island.* Having requested icebreaker duty, McWethy was serving as executive officer, Lyon as chief scientist. (McWethy's first clue that the Arctic might be a place for submarines had come in 1948, when he had flown over the Pole with the air force. He'd been "amazed" by the open water.) "That [1951] is when we started exchanging notes. . . . We started plotting there," off Alaska. "At that time, neither Dr. Lyon or I was thinking in terms of nuclear power."[44]

Nautilus—the ideal instrument—changed that. In October 1956 Dr. Lyon recorded in his journal: "Discussion with Cdr. McWethy Op 311 [in OpNav, the CNO staff] re arctic submarine, nothing new. [H]e hopes to get OP[erational] requirement out soon, but is still waiting for comment from ComSubLant [Commander, Submarine Force, Atlantic] re use of nuclear subs under ice. Still possibility that *Nautilus* will be assigned to dive under ice north of Spitzbergen, summer 1957, stated distance order of 500 nm [nautical miles]. I agreed to take part and provide necessary topside sonar gear."[45]

The two lobbied anyone who would listen, among them *Nautilus'* first commanding officer, Wilkinson, and his relief, Commander William R. Anderson, USN. Hesitant initially, Rear Admiral Rickover offered support.[46] Still, arousing high-level commitment proved decidedly uphill, fraught with inertia and outright resistance. When a student at the Naval War College, in Newport, Rhode Island, for example, McWethy had written a paper on under-ice operations. Sent to the Submarine Warfare Branch in OpNav, the paper received a cool reception. One concern was the boat itself: *Nautilus* had not been designed for ice-covered seas. Some deemed it foolhardy to risk the navy's first nuclear platform on an escapade into an uncharted ocean. "Everyone seemed interested," McWethy would recall of his advocacy, "but that was as far as it got." One admiral baldly predicted: "That trip you are talking about will never happen. You might as well relax."

When Captain "Ned" Beach learned of the proposal (winter 1957–58), it held top secret classification. "I was told," Beach recalled, "this is not to be talked about." Even at that date, the visionaries of sailing the Arctic by submarine were—still—straining to assure continuation of under-ice excursions "in order to give necessary impetus to Navy Department policy, for there is always the school that will immediately use any item to discourage any further effort to solve the Arctic basin operation problem."[47]

Development work persevered, notably underwater navigation (determining position) and communications. Environmental data attendant to under-ice piloting—oceanographic/bathymetric survey work, underwater acoustics—were yet fragmentary.

As Lyon and McWethy proselytized, a boost for the polar submarine reached Admiral Arleigh A. Burke, CNO, in the form of a letter. It was dated March 1957; its sender: Senator Henry M. "Scoop" Jackson (D-Wash.), chairman of a subcommittee on military applications of atomic energy. The senator had flown over the basin (with the air force) and been impressed with the extent of open water. Why couldn't the navy exploit this? A hearing on the Hill was scheduled, so McWethy and Dr. Lyon hurried up a plan. Among its main points: modifying a submarine for experimental under-ice fieldwork.

"Let's really look into this," the admiral had told his staff. The Navy Department, Senator Jackson was advised, was working on it.

Flight Trials—into Production

As flight trials for N-1 advanced, the need for improvements became evident. These would be incorporated into the follow-on production models, designated ZP2N-1 (or ZPG-2). Among the changes: improved radar and a larger envelope to accommodate heavier electronics and armament loads (including towed sonar). In Akron, these and other, minor alterations realized countless conferences and design changes.

At Lakehurst, this team effort had Goodyear field representatives working closely with navy engineers and flight personnel to assess the prototype, note deficiencies, and define areas for improvement. Recommended changes were resolved by the engineers and quality-control personnel with a call, a meeting, or a bit of slide-rule work.

As finally configured, ZPG-2 had a length of 343 feet, a height of 97 feet, and a volume of 1,011,000 cubic feet. ZPG-2 was the largest nonrigid airship yet flown.[48] Cruising speed was forty-five knots, with fifty-five-hour endurance at forty knots. The endurance capability of this singular aircraft, indeed, would be verified in two record-breaking demonstrations later that decade.

Meantime, the "factory" was the Goodyear Airdock at Akron Municipal Airport. In the heady days of the twenties, Goodyear had invested in a hangar of its own so as to avoid interfering with operations at Lakehurst—and, it was hoped, lay the foundation for a new industry. *Akron* and *Macon* had been built here; later, the world's first (and only) mass-production line for blimps had sped antisubmarine blimps to the navy.

The design went into production. The navy had elected to order only a few units; ultimately, follow-on orders pushed the procurement to a dozen aircraft. As well, concerns over an aerial Pearl Harbor sponsored a version incorporating electronic features designed for airborne early warning (AEW) missions, the ZPG-2W.

As materials and components arrived at the Goodyear complex, fabrication of the first subassemblies commenced. Materials, equipment, parts (propellers, instruments, engines, motors) streamed in from subcontractors. Fabricated at the firm's Litchfield Park (Arizona) plant, envelopes and accessories were rail-shipped to Akron.

Inside the hangar, erection work proceeded. Each control car (eighty-three feet long, eleven feet wide *sans* outriggers) was hand assembled. As work progressed, inspectors checked each phase, from construction of parts to final assembly and flight testing. Specialists in engines, rubberized fabrics, and general aircraft construction hunted for discrepancies, which then were reworked by quality-control personnel and, if necessary, Goodyear Engineering. In overall charge of quality control for the navy: Mr. Louis D. Mancini. "My boys," he recalls, "checked it out as they were building those ships."[49]

In pioneer days, control cars had been straightforward affairs: rugged, fabric-covered tubular steel. Later, wartime cars were welded-steel tubing over which was riveted aluminum-alloy sheeting. The N-ship's car, in contrast, consisted of "sandwich" material: two thicknesses of thin-sheet aluminum between which was set a thicker layer of balsa wood or aluminum honeycomb.

Fabrication and assembly proved painstaking, many parts having to be hand-formed—no mass-production efficiencies. Production time for each ship: twelve to eighteen months.

Nearing completion, a control car soon was mated to an envelope—seven thousand square yards of fabric weighing 14,000 pounds. Unpacked, each envelope was stretched across the deck, after which it was partially inflated with air. Inside—an eerie, floodlit space—workmen checked seams (using black light) for leaks and inspected the fabric for imperfections. The control surfaces and accessory equipment (e.g., air and helium valves, suspension cables) were attached.

When in all respects ready for inflation, a net was draped to tether the assembly as it filled with helium. Inflation line attached, valve handles were turned. Limp fabric began to stir and rear itself. Stiffening, the entire mass assumed its full shape as, gradually, the chamber lifted clear of the deck. Restrained by the net (itself ballasted with bags of sand and shot) the envelope hung fully aloft.

A car was shunted beneath. The load imposed by the car must be transferred to the envelope and distributed by a system of cables. (It is not practical to suspend a car from the bottom of a ship: distension of the envelope would result.) On ZPG-2, two suspensions were employed: an internal system attached to the inside top of the bag and an external one attached around the car's upper edge. As the remaining accessories were attached and connected, the first production N-ship neared completion. It was 1953—more than twenty-four months after fabrication of the initial components.

Military aircraft are assigned identifying numbers. In the navy, this unique designation is termed a "bureau number"—a relic of the Bureau of Aeronautics. BUNO (pronounced "byoo-no") assigned to the first production N-ship: 126716. It flew on 1 April 1953, lifting off on its first trial. Following a flight program, then a delay to correct a transmission problem, the ship was air-ferried to Lakehurst for full navy trials. In Ohio the next two aircraft—BUNOs 126717 and 126718—were undergoing flight trials by the contractor.

The ZPG-2 series (1953–62) provided superb detection and tracking capabilities—a formidable weapons system. Gross lift (approximately 64,500 pounds) allowed a full range of electronic capability. In it the largest search systems adaptable to aircraft were combined: the best ASW radar, Loran, sonobuoys, MAD, and other sensors, plus (then unique to airships) variable-depth towed sonar. Generous spaces provided ample room for plotting and control facilities. Moreover, its stable, vibration-free environment and slow speed were congenial to the delicate electronic gear essential to its military mission. And the car's size and low noise levels provided a hospitable, relatively comfortable in-flight environment for aircrews, which was important particularly on long searches.

The next in the series—BUNO 126719—would serve U.S. naval aviation more than five years, logging 1,356.8 hours. Further, *719* would make history as the only nonrigid airship to cross the Arctic Circle *and* as the only military airship of any nation to do so. Its penetration of the Canadian Archipelago and Arctic Ocean stands unique in aeronautics.

Construction began in summer 1952. On 13 January 1954, a first flight was logged—duration, 7.4 hours. Purpose: check out and test ship's systems. A second trial was held two days later.

On 24 January, the ship was accepted by the navy, its future operator. In the ZPG-2 series, only *719* would return—briefly—to its Ohio birthplace.

Two days later, *719* rolled out to a ground crew at Naval Air Station, South Weymouth, Massachusetts. Assigned to a research-and-development command, this ship would support various classified projects. Time on airframe so far: 26.1 hours.

Few expeditions proceed according to plan; nor would the two unique missions now in planning.

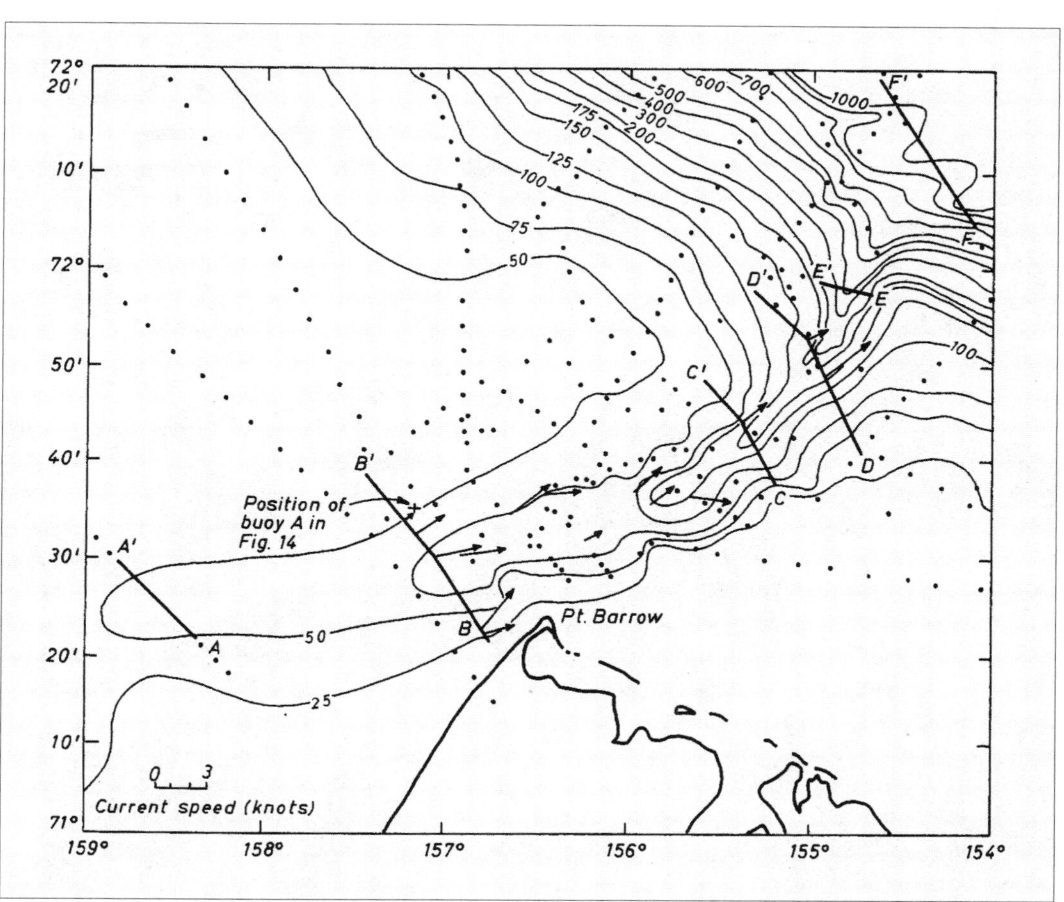

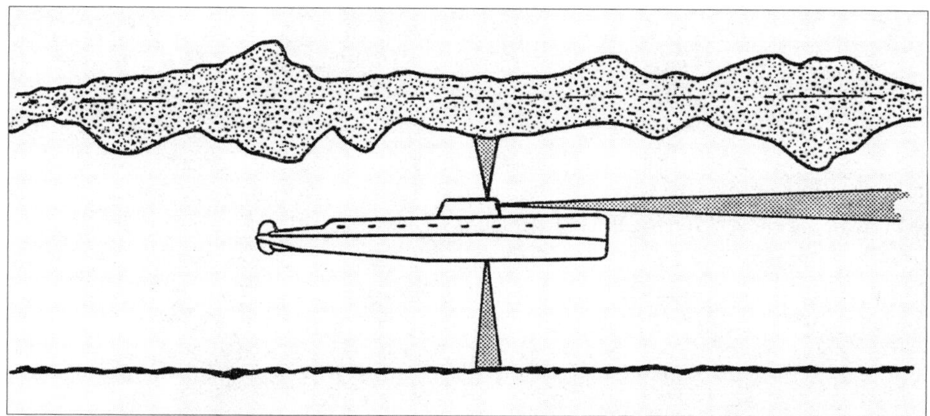

[Top] Bathymetry and current flow, Barrow Sea Valley–in 1958, *Nautilus'* boulevard to deep water and 90 North. Chart used on board. (U.S. Navy Electronics Laboratory, 1953)

[Bottom] Diagrammatic sketch of under-ice sonar system, USS *Nautilus*. (Lyon, 1963)

The success of a polar expedition principally depends upon the preparations which were made before the expedition started out.

—Fridtjof Nansen

3 Preparations

Backdrop

The Battle of the Atlantic—in its first months—meant staggering German success. Great Britain's naval forces were stretched past reasonable limits. "I can assure you, Mr. President," Winston Churchill advised, "we are absolutely extended." Following a declaration of war, a U-boat campaign was orchestrated against all U.S. shipping.

For the harried defenders, this was a frenetic, fearful time of furious reactions against a resolute, elusive undersea enemy. Off the eastern seaboard, the masts and stacks of torpedoed hulks multiplied alarmingly. And along the beaches, grisly proof of the struggle began to come ashore.

Offshore, the need of destroyers and antisubmarine aircraft of all types was urgent. Accordingly, the U.S. Navy's few blimps represented a welcome—if paltry—addition to the defenders' assets.

Against this backdrop, the lighter-than-air fraternity pressed forward with a modest expansion: more aircraft and facilities shoreside to sustain them. When Oahu was raided, however, only Lakehurst was operational. But two air stations *had* been authorized: one near Boston (First Naval District), the other at Weeksville, North Carolina. The former, about 1,250 acres at South Weymouth, southeast of Boston, is a military installation still. In 1941 the place was a soggy expanse of marsh.

Filling commenced, then actual construction. Steel arches were soon climbing skyward—ribs for a great hangar enclosing eight acres of floor. Auxiliary facilities to support a LTA squadron were erected as well: shop, office and classroom spaces, a landing mat, fuel and helium storage, and a power plant, as well as subsistence and housing for both station and squadron personnel.

But the U-boat threat sponsored a new program of construction before the first was concluded. A timber hangar (by 1942 steel was being rationed) for a *second* squadron rose across the mat, plus corresponding increases in fuel storage, helium, housing.

At a cost of $6 million, Naval Air Station (NAS) South Weymouth was the largest wartime project on the Massachusetts south shore. In mid-1942, with local, state, and national

[Opposite] NAS South Weymouth, Massachusetts. Note the WV-2s on the apron—"Willie Victors" in navy parlance. Commissioned in March 1942, the naval air station is located southeast of Boston. (Hank J. Applegate)

representatives attending, the station was commissioned into the naval service. Wartime operations would consist primarily of antisubmarine patrols and convoy escort.

The Second World War transformed the services. At sea, vessels with names like *Enterprise, Wasp,* and *Yorktown* proved the decisive element in a string of campaigns across the island-dotted Pacific. Deemed useful if unproven as the forties opened, the aircraft carrier rose to stardom and remains instrumental to naval strategy and naval politics—only the nuclear submarine has challenged the carrier's status as a major instrument of power projection. Navy lighter-than-air, in contrast, was destined for termination.

For the Battle of the Atlantic, however, LTA enjoyed unprecedented fiscal attention: about $228 million altogether. Most of the appropriations went in those years to air stations and to related support. While generous, relative to the overall defense expenditure this was a trifle. The high-level salute attending the war would not survive the Cold War decades. Though proponents could not know, the high-water mark of U.S. Navy lighter-than-air lay astern.

LTA and Cold War

With general demobilization, NAS South Weymouth descended into protracted somnolence. Its ASW squadron disestablished, the air station was placed on a "reduced complement" status and turned over to the Naval Air Reserve Training Command. In June 1949 the base was deactivated.

The 1950s proved resurgent—one outcome of the Korean conflict. South Weymouth was rehabilitated and, in December 1953, recommissioned as a naval air station. Renewed operations reflected revived defense spending and a general expansion throughout U.S. naval aviation. The number of LTA squadrons doubled, and an AEW squadron commissioned. Research and development (R&D) units were established as well.

In mid-1957 LTA had forty-four airships operational, of which four squadrons (twenty-two aircraft) were part of the Atlantic Fleet, their primary mission: ASW. Early Warning Squadron ZW-1 had four ships operational. Another nine were assigned to R&D, a further nine to training.

The deputy chief of naval operations for air, a senior officer responsible for planning and a principal advisor to the CNO, testified before Congress in favor of LTA. *Aviation Week* also was upbeat: "The Navy appears to be convinced that the modern advantages of the blimp for anti-submarine warfare and radar picket duty far outweigh its vulnerability. The blimp will be an essential part of the Navy's airpower for some time to come."[1] And the popular literature seemed approving.

U.S. Navy lighter-than-air was thriving. Or so it seemed. In fact, appearances to the contrary, the program's political base was (as it had always been) tenuous. And opposition festered within heavier-than-air aviation. The blimp, in truth, had yet to be integrated into the "mix" of weaponry or into the overall command structure. Nor was it destined to be. Naval aviation was preoccupied with the carrier and with high-performance jets. Guided missiles were replacing guns. The capability to deliver nuclear weapons preoccupied military thinkers. Speed, firepower, versatility, mobility: these were the catchwords of the day.[2] And a new age loomed: man in space. In this high-tech Mach-2 atmosphere, most high-level officers could not imagine a significant role for the lumbering airship.

For a "new Navy," weapon systems were reassessed. Some would be adapted to the time, as others—deemed obsolete—were consigned to be discarded. High-level commands reached the decision to phase out LTA.

The first cutback was announced in June 1957. Within weeks, the number of operational antisubmarine units stood halved. Two squadrons—twelve aircraft—were abruptly withdrawn. Official explanation: none. Flight crews and support personnel were transferred, the aircraft ferried to Lakehurst for war-reserve storage.

Rumors swept the Navy Department: LTA was phasing out. Amid the shambles, though, force-reduction orders had yet to reach NAS South Weymouth.

At South Weymouth, where it had been established in 1953 by the Office of Naval Research (ONR), was the Naval Air Development Unit (NADU)—a tenant R&D command. Primary mission: support of Project Lincoln—a program of the Lincoln Laboratory, itself an adjunct of the Massachusetts Institute of Technology. NADU assisted development of airborne detection and tracking systems. In the "Power for Peace" environment of the 1950s, most projects related to the threat of surprise aerial attack. Jointly funded by the U.S. Air Force and Navy (through ONR), the lab served multifarious needs of the Department of Defense.[3]

Project Lincoln was a source of theoretical studies and prototype equipment.[4] NADU, for its part, provided test platforms—an odd assortment of aircraft. A half dozen jets, including fighters (to serve as radar targets) were assigned. Also in inventory: a P2V patrol bomber and a R4D transport (test beds for armament and electronics). Three WV-2Es ("Willie Victors" in service slang—otherwise Constellations, or "Connies"—of that era), three airships, and a Beechcraft rounded out the flight line. NADU, in short, was a flying laboratory.

In 1958 Captain Harold B. Van Gorder, USN, was its commanding officer. Commissioned an ensign in the reserves in 1936, "Van" had qualified as a naval aviator a few months following the raid on Pearl Harbor. Following service in England and as operations officer for a Georgia-based LTA squadron, he served as CO of a squadron at Lakehurst. Command of a training unit had followed, thence orders to NADU. A hard-driven, no-nonsense taskmaster, Van Gorder was both LTA and fixed-wing qualified.

When queried decades later, the captain was characteristically straightforward: "We were busy." His executive officer, Commander Max V. Ricketts, concurred: "It was," he remembered, "an interesting and challenging assignment for we who were involved."

Projects were unusual. One team was dispatched to Brazil to help collect, near Ascension Island, a down-range tracking station of the Atlantic ballistic-missile range, meteorological data pertaining to long-range communications.[5] Closer to home, radar clutter tests were being flown. And in cooperation with Lockheed, Lincoln Lab, and the North American Air Defense Command (NORAD), Van Gorder had given the press its first glimpse of the navy's newest early-warning platform. The WV-2E was about to receive six months of preliminary evaluation prior to duty as a radar picket.[6] Fearful of attack, the navy and air force had established a twenty-four-hour watch against Soviet intruders.

Another: a three-year, all-weather evaluation of the ZPG-2. Ice can be lethal to flight. Accordingly, conditions conducive to icing are to be avoided. For this NADU project, the intent was to go looking for ice, exploiting BUNO 126561, equipped with special recording instruments as well as television monitors mounted topside, on the bow, and on the upper fins.

"The real problem was *finding* ice," Commander Charles Mills, USN, later remembered. "We would go hunting for it—punching weather—in a 'Connie' and P2V till we could find ice at an altitude that we could handle. And then the job was to get the airplane down, get into the airship and get up and punch it."[7]

On a December 1955 mission, ice was noted by *561* during a climb. An airspace reservation was promptly granted between three and four thousand feet. As the ship ambled, the accretion thickened—the yaw meter, outriggers, drift meter, radome, air scoops, and antennae hosting buildups. Window ice began to form. Within twenty-five minutes a vibration commenced. "Getting into ice was difficult enough," Mills recalled. "Once you're *in* it, and you are icing up, the windshield's icing, the props are icing, it began shaking the ship a lot." The reaction became pro-

Capt. Harold B. Van Gorder, USN, commanding officer, Naval Air Development Unit at South Weymouth. Established by the Office of Naval Research, NADU provided support for Project Lincoln, a program of the Lincoln Laboratories of the Massachusetts Institute of Technology. (AD1 Elmer B. Lord)

nounced, then excessive: the propellers were icing unevenly; soon, prop ice was banging against the car. Instruments became unreadable. The vibration "built steadily in amplitude," a test report records. "The car vibrated at a high frequency estimated to be about five cycles per second. The instrument panel began shimmying to the limits of its shock mounts, moving about an inch to the left and right of centerline."

Full propeller anti-icing dampened the vibration, but buildups worsened; still, the pilots persisted. In protest to a hideous burden, shaking became "very pronounced throughout the ship" with prop ice hammering the car continually. (Nearing the Alaskan coast in 1926, *Norge* had experienced a like bombardment. See page 118.) Frost blanked the forward windows.

The decision was taken to bring as much ice as possible to the mat, for photographs. Within two hours of liftoff, shedding sheets of white, *561* landed—the veneer across the pilots' position sliding clear just before touchdown.

Two years before, in 1953, the first production ZPG-2 had reached the operator. As trial data had accumulated, it had become evident that performance might possibly exceed that guaranteed by the contractor. The idea of an endurance flight had been born. In May 1954, following exhaustive testing, conferences, and slide-rule work, BUNO 126716 set a course to seaward.

The airship loitered off the eastern seaboard, pressed south to Bermuda then ambled toward Puerto Rico. Island-hopping northwest, *716* touched down at NAS Key West, having established a world's record for self-sustained, unrefueled flight: two hundred hours (8.3 *days*) in the air.[8] The potential for extended missions was becoming evident.

As part of an all-weather evaluation of airships, a joint barrier test was held during the winter of 1956–57, using five ships (including two from Lakehurst). One ship held station to

[Opposite] In January 1957, the NADU and Lakehurst commands flew a joint all-weather barrier exercise for ONR. Here ZPG-2 BUNO 141561 readies for takeoff during Operation Whole Gale. Note the ground-handling "mule"—"the best thing since reverse-pitch propellers—even better." (Capt. Harold B. Van Gorder)

seaward for ten consecutive days. Conditions that New England January proved miserable: icing, fog, snow, sleet, rain, and winds to sixty knots. One N-ship loitered above angry ocean more than fifty-six hours. This test appeared to confirm the practicability of overwater operations in virtually all weather conditions.

Concluding the evaluation, ZPG-2 141561 was assigned a singular trial. On 15 March 1957, eleven days following a South Weymouth liftoff, a tired but elated flight crew touched down at Key West. *561* had flown nonstop across the Atlantic, overflying Portugal, then Africa before ambling back across. Among the well-wishers: Admiral William F. Halsey Jr., USN, who, on behalf of President Dwight Eisenhower, presented the Distinguished Flying Cross to Commander Jack R. Hunt, USN, command pilot.

The test had logged 264.2 unrefueled hours—eleven days aloft.[9] Capability for sustained surveillance and "station keeping" stood confirmed.

The navy had procured a superb platform. *Jane's All the World's Aircraft,* for one, was impressed: "The ZPG-2," it noted, "has the latest developments adaptable to aircraft for locating and attacking submarines." And in its own report, NADU underscored the model's "great potential," declaring, "The results of this flight combined with those of the all-weather tests indicate that the unique qualities of the airship and its systems potential have not been fully explored."[10]

To what extent, though, would the naval service "explore" the capabilities of the platform for *any* naval mission?

The Polar Project

In 1957 a geoscientist posed a question: Could airships help support science in the Arctic? Dr. Maynard M. Miller is today a seasoned polar hand. Specialties: high-latitude glaciology, remote sensing, climate. A research associate at Columbia's Lamont Geological Observatory in the latter fifties, Miller also held a senior scientist position in the Geology Department at the university's New York campus. As it happened, he was also a lieutenant commander in the Naval Reserve.

Miller knew the exasperations attending Arctic research. Given the environment and extreme isolation, its logistical burdens were stupendous. Field camps were dispersed over a roadless hinterland. Runways were few, the weather capricious. Offshore, on the polar pack, sea ice cracks and floes disperse. With spring breakup, the pack is a nightmare of slush, leads, and meltwater ponds—meaning closed airstrips. (Half a runway is no runway.) But airships, Miller reasoned, could hover. If they proved deployable in circumpolar airspace, sensitive equipment incompatible with airdrop might become deliverable throughout the melt season.

Dr. Miller foresaw further applications. A low-flying, long-endurance platform is ideal for surveillance. Already, variations in sea-ice extent had begun to intrigue researchers, foreshadowing climate change. (Today, sea ice is a critical parameter for climate computer modelers.) The Arctic is an indicator: secular (that is, long-term) changes in snow and ice extent might, just might, yield insights. "Even then," Miller observed, "it was obvious that with respect to naval operations in arctic waters the behavior of arctic sea ice and Alaskan glaciers as indicators of global climate change were practical subjects in which the navy had long-term interest."[11]

Airplanes had yet to match an airship's endurance. Further, air force missions to the Pole were narrow in terms of scientific return. Ubiquitous today, helicopters were still short-ranged and limited in capacity. And satellites (for surveillance) were still few and unsophisticated.

In Miller's opinion, proof of concept lay to hand.

The success of the Navy's prolonged ZPG flight to Africa [he said] provided a timely springboard for us formally to propose a similar mission to the Arctic Basin. The rationale was that we could demonstrate the feasibility of applying LTA techniques to a broader region and with the possibility of more continuous surveillance of ice-covered waters of the Arctic Ocean and bordering shorelines. . . . In such a situation, a slow-moving, low-flying airship, which could remain aloft for three or four days, could provide unique advantages for close surveillance, as well as be an ideal platform for scientific instruments.[12]

Dr. Maynard M. Miller. A specialist in high-latitude geoscience, Miller conceived the Polar Project for ONR—an expedition by airship into the Arctic Ocean. Objective: to assess the platform's suitability for support of northern science. (Ira Spring)

Could blimps deploy effectively at extreme latitudes? Might winds foreclose deployment of a slow-speed platform? As it happens, smooth air conditions characterize late winter and spring. And between June and September, as Miller observed, the Arctic Ocean is "the quietest in the world." Light winds predominate.

The lieutenant commander queried the Office of Naval Research. Established in 1946 "to plan, foster and encourage scientific research" as it relates to naval power, ONR manages funds for basic research. During the Cold War, propelled by superpower suspicions and the notion of a strategic Arctic, the region was a Defense Department priority.

At ONR, Miller conferred with Dr. Louis Quam (head of the Earth Science Division) and his staff, including ecologist Dr. Max Britton. The concept offered potential. The navy was eager to maintain a robust northern presence. And why cede dominance to a major competitor, the U.S. Air Force?

That fall, Miller made it his business to visit both South Weymouth and Lakehurst. Among his conferees: Vice Admiral Charles E. Rosendahl, an irrepressible spokesman for lighter-than-air, and Commander Jack R. Hunt, officer in charge of the March 1957 record transatlantic flight. During fall and winter of 1957–58, specific research applications were assessed, to gain advice and to stimulate interest.

Given Rosendahl's "unqualified endorsement," NADU embraced Miller's notion. Among its proponents: Captain Van Gorder, NADU's CO, who was convinced of the airship's efficacy. "The staff at NAS South Weymouth," Miller recalls, "accepted the assignment with enthusiasm, vigor, and professional readiness." An expedition to the Arctic was, as Van would recall, "a big project which I was delighted to take on." Why? "I wanted to do it for the sake of doing it—be able to prove that airships could fly in the Arctic."[13] These were the final wilderness years of U.S. Navy lighter-than-air. Struggling for relevance, staggered by cutbacks, and (justifiably) fearful of further reductions, the program was hungry for new applications. A role in polar research might, again just might, forestall termination.[14]

Dirigibles in the far North were hardly a novelty. Explorers such as Roald Amundsen and Lincoln Ellsworth had considered airships the *preferred* platform. In May 1926 the semirigid *Norge* had reached 90° N mere days behind Richard E. Byrd and Floyd Bennett in their airplane. Was *Norge* actually first to gain the Pole? Credible evidence undermines Byrd's claim of primacy. The capabilities inherent to airships seemed ideal for exploring the Arctic—a trackless realm empty of emergency airstrips.

Still, and for a variety of reasons, airplanes became the platform of choice. Northern logistics remain daunting and expensive. Airlift capability is indispensable. In the fifties the U.S. Air Force was already the dominant military presence in the Canadian Arctic, in Alaska, and in Greenland.[15]

In addition to military and contractor personnel, untold quantities of supplies and aircraft and about a hundred scientists were scattered throughout the continent's upper tier. The air force was providing most of the support, deploying and resupplying field parties, then retrieving them. The International Geophysical Year (IGY) intensified the quest for data and observations.[16] The *Sputnik* shock accelerated the northward flow.

And so it happened that, in May 1958, a proposal was submitted to the chief of naval research. Title: "The Use of Non-rigid Airships in Support of Geophysical Research and Related Studies in the Region of the North Pole Sea." Prospectus: "[The project report of results] may be of special interest and significance to the Navy. It is stressed that it would not detail operational aspects of LTA activity, since it is expected that these would be well covered by the experienced air crews involved. The report will instead highlight the research advantages and disadvantages to be gained in field work in the Polar regions through the use and support of such airships."[17]

Peer review for scientific merit and relevance to naval needs yielded approval, after which funding was allocated to support the oceanographic and surveillance goals of the proposed study.

On 18 June a letter reached NADU headquarters at NAS South Weymouth: the Polar Project had been assigned for prosecution. As a logistical-support arm of ONR, NADU was the logical command to execute an exercise unique in naval aviation: to conduct airship flight operations in support of research in the area of the Arctic Ocean and to determine the feasibility of such operations. Proposed date for execution: immediately.

A plans and project officer had been assigned: Lieutenant Commander Maynard M. Miller, USNR, returned temporarily to active duty.

The orders were exotic. No naval aviator had flown anywhere near the Arctic in a blimp. And no airship of any type, from any nation, had penetrated far-northern airspace since 1931. Reference information, let alone a body of experience, was nonexistent. Still, an operational plan had to be formulated—and quickly. The boreal summer would end in September, less than three months off.

Word spread. NADU was going to check out the all-weather characteristics of the LTA platform in a remote, demanding climate. The flight, one newspaper jested, would provide its crew with one of the "coolest" summer trips.

What of the platform? Concluding a search, a ZPG-2 in overhaul at Lakehurst was assigned. Mission-specific modifications were essential, of course. These would be installed at South Weymouth: after all, adapting special equipment to aircraft was a NADU forte.

BUNO 126719 had left the contractor in 1954. Inaugural mission: R&D work for the Bureau of Aeronautics. Overhauled in mid-1956, *719* had operated with Airship Squadron 3 (ZP-3), an antisubmarine warfare unit. By winter 1958, ship's logbook had recorded nearly a thousand hours. That February, at NAS Guantanamo Bay, a heavy landing had damaged the control car and props. Once the squadron's maintenance officer had supervised provisional repairs, the bird had been flown north to Lakehurst, where it had been remanded to the Overhaul and Repair Department (O&R). A full renovation was effected. It was during this work that NADU found her.

Squadron aircraft typically are unavailable for research work. But the heavy landing had deleted *719* from operations. For NADU, this ship would do in other respects as well. The airframe was comparatively new. And thanks to overhaul, *719* was airworthy. Further, the aircraft carried extra fuel: four 300-gallon tanks mounted on the envelope above the car. (Envelope mounting avoided overloading the car, important in light of limits imposed by the car's cable support system.) In consequence, slow-cruise range could be augmented by about 1,200 miles.

On 27 June a brief checkout flight was logged. Finding all systems satisfactory, O&R signed over the aircraft. A ferry crew put Lakehurst astern on 4 July, destination NAS South Weymouth. Temporary airship commander: Lieutenant Harold D. Koza, USN, a thirty-six-year-old hailing from Wyoming. Easygoing and likeable, this officer was to spend almost two hundred hours at these controls over the next five weeks.

NADU, meantime, was awash in preparations. Van Gorder—a sometimes brusque, unsentimental personality—brought his energy to the project. Much needed doing. A crew needed to be chosen, flight routes assessed, weather information compiled, then analyzed. Liaison work with Canada also was initiated, to obtain clearance over Canadian territory and use of airfields. NADU spaces buzzed with conferences, calls, briefings, and the clatter of telexes and telephones.

Near Maintenance Department spaces, personnel lavished attention upon the platform. All nonessential gear was unshipped to save weight. Crucially, alterations were made to the compass systems, necessary if *719* was to navigate near the magnetic pole. As well, a gaudy international orange was applied to the bow, so as to enhance recognition over northern terrain.

An air of excitement pervaded the command, a reaction naturally attending a venture of this kind.

The success of any operation ultimately depends upon the effectiveness of the personnel involved. "The human factor," Roald Amundsen had observed, "is three quarters of any expedition." Fourteen men were selected, each handpicked. Lieutenant Commander Henry D. M. Collins, USN, would command the aircraft. A skilled pilot, Collins had enlisted during the war. A qualified HTA pilot, he also held naval aviator (airship) designation. In 1958 his flight log recorded hundreds of hours—HTA and LTA. Collins was highly regarded as an officer and leader, not least by his commanding officer, Van Gorder. Their professional relationship, the captain later noted, was "absolutely perfect."

Earlier, Collins had been responsible for the ground-handling crew flown ahead to help support the record endurance flight. Quiet, proficient, and capable, Collins was to prove wholly qualified for the expedition now taking shape.

ZPG-2 BUNO 126719, May 1958. A platform for R&D initially, *719* was assigned to Airship Squadron 3 (ZP-3) in mid-1956. Damaged on landing at Guantanamo Bay, the ship was remanded to Lakehurst's Overhaul and Repair Department where, in June 1958, NADU found her. (AMCS Daniel E. Brady)

Since each leg might demand thirty to forty flight hours, reliefs for each position were essential. Collins would be assisted by three pilots: Lieutenant Koza, Lieutenant Commander Aage J. Schou, and by George Kalnin. Schou, thirty-four, was a likeable, easy-to-smile professional flier from Minnesota. Like his CO, he was qualified in both airships and fixed-wing aircraft. Kalnin, an enlisted pilot, was thirty-five and a Massachusetts native.

The temporary-duty orders cut that July for the mission's officers were without precedent in LTA. "On or about 26 July 1958, proceed to (1) Churchill, Manitoba, Canada; (2) Resolute Bay, N.W.T., Canada; and (3) such other places as may be deemed necessary in connection with the Polar Project." Before that summer was out, these bland words would translate into an experience utterly unique in U.S. naval aviation.

The enlisted crew included a pair of mechanics to handle flight engineering: Elmer B. Lord and Floyd W. Johnson. Both were aviation machinist's mates—"first mech" and "second mech," respectively. Given the importance of electronic systems, three specialists were selected: William

H. Eels and Francis M. Hughes, aviation electronics technicians, and Rudolph J. Cabral, an aviation electrician. Frederick L. Parker, a chief aviation electronics technician, would act as crew chief. Two seasoned riggers, James P. Quinn and Wendell H. Dunlevy (both aviation metalsmiths) rounded out the aircrew. Mission responsibility: ship's airframe.

This team was outstanding. "Van Gorder, Collins, Koza, and the entire crew were exceptional people," NADU executive officer Ricketts later told me. "In 1958, when you were selected for duty in NADU you had to be exceptional, and these gentlemen satisfied that criteria."[18]

The North was an alien realm to these airmen; they had little previous knowledge of it. Van Gorder required exceptional talent in all departments. And his navigators were crucial. "Practically nowhere else is the navigator so completely on his own and nowhere else can he and his crew find themselves more isolated from help should he make a mistake. No one, therefore, should navigate in arctic regions without, first, a thorough understanding of the importance of the two basic components of navigation, Dead Reckoning and Astro; secondly, a full knowledge of the particular problems and procedures involved; and finally, the most careful flight planning."[19]

NADU would be operating where the magnetic compass is unreliable. Reason: the weak horizontal component of the earth's magnetic field at high latitudes. This realizes a decreasing force on a compass needle until, at the magnetic pole, the force goes to zero. Except for ice reconnaissance and research flights out of Alaska, the U.S. Navy had logged precious little flight time near the magnetic pole.[20]

The intricacies of air navigation generally are difficult to fathom: the magic by which aircraft are conducted to distant dots, alighting within moments of the times predicted. Decades ago, a navigator's calculations were unaided by an inertial navigation system (INS). Visual contact with the ground, the sun, or stars is desirable, certainly. But such are dispensable to these airborne merlins: their magic works as well in darkness or cloud. Before INS, position and direction were charted with deceptive ease, the navigator recomputing the most advantageous direction almost constantly as he corrected his heading over the rotating surface below. It was—and remains—a ceaseless foiling of natural forces, the collectivity of which insists that he straggle about the sky.

In the North, alternate airfields were yet few. So too were navigation aids. Detailed en route and area forecasts were often lacking, as was the reliability of existing maps. The business of navigation would impose constant demands on these navy aircrewmen. Lacking high-latitude experience itself, where was NADU to find the expertise to assist them?

Canadians had been overflying the upper tier of North America for decades, gathering experience unmatched outside the Soviet Union, perhaps the world. "The initiation of transpolar flights indicates the future importance of the Canadian north to commercial as well as military aviation. The RCAF [Royal Canadian Air Force] has already established a lead in research and development and have [*sic*] a greater proportion of crews qualified for polar flying than any other western air force."[21] That long-ago spring, Wing Commander Keith R. Greenaway was serving in the Royal Canadian Air Force Headquarters in Ottawa. His logbook recorded years of northern flying, with emphasis on long-range navigational and other problems—including assistance to the U.S. Air Force (USAF). In 1946 he had helped navigate the first U.S. military aircraft to gain the North Pole. Next year, he had photographed (from a B-29) an unusual rippled pattern later identified as T-3—the earliest known image of that ice island. (See chapter 6.) In 1954 Greenaway was posted on a two-year exchange with the Strategic Air Command, his joint USAF/RCAF unit introducing the technique of steering by gyro at high latitudes in B-47 and B-52 intercontinental bombers.[22] The High Latitude Twilight Computer (which he codeveloped) was adopted by the RCAF (among others) for use in planning flights. By mid-1958 the wing commander's flight log held six thousand hours, most logged over Arctic Canada.

In sum, this energetic, agreeably outgoing officer was, at forty-two one of the world's leading authorities on Arctic air navigation.

On 15 June, Greenaway's desk telephone rang. Caller: Group Captain E. M. "Marty" Mitchell, director of air staff services, RCAF Headquarters. A delegation from the U.S. Navy would be arriving: it seemed the Americans wanted to fly an airship into Arctic Canada. Since he knew the area, would he sit in?

Next day, a contingent led by Captain Van Gorder conferred with Canadian counterparts. The NADU mission was outlined, along with logistic requirements: basing, quarters, ground handling. Primary topic, though: the proposed route.

The problem of maintaining an airship away from its base—even briefly—is a formidable one. An airship needs a mooring mast, ground crews, and helium storage. NADU intended to operate from a temporary mast installed at Resolute Bay, an RCAF base on the Northwest Passage and the most northerly airfield capable of supporting a blimp and accompanying WV-2. If Ottawa approved, the ship would cross the Gulf of St. Lawrence, then follow the Atlantic margins of Newfoundland and Labrador, using expeditionary masts installed at Argentia and at Frobisher Bay, on Baffin Island. Departing Frobisher, course would be set for Resolute.

Naval airships were sea creatures; to the Americans, the proposed route seemed logical. But, Greenaway asked, had they considered an *inland* route? Interior Canada offered several advantages. Not least, it was shorter. As well, NADU could avoid the coastline's unpredictable weather, including fog, strong winds, and rugged terrain—hardly ideal conditions for a slow, low-altitude machine. The topography between Boston and northern Ontario, in contrast, was low—once the mountains of New York were astern. Exploiting the Hudson and Mohawk River Valleys to the international border, Greenaway continued, *719* could push into northern Ontario and base halfway up Hudson Bay, at Churchill. From there, the aircrew could press due north, following an overwater track for a thousand miles, clear to Cornwallis Island and its base.

The meeting ended. The wing commander returned to his duties; the matter passed from his attention.

Back at NADU headquarters, Van Gorder and his team studied their charts and climatological summaries. After a bit of map rustling, the merits of Greenaway's arguments stood clear. The inland track, Van Gorder recalled, "made a lot of sense." It *was* shorter, and, further, it presented no daunting physiographic obstacles; land-surface elevations, for one, were less than two thousand feet throughout.

These airmen were accustomed to operating low and offshore, where conditions are relatively congenial to temperature-sensitive helium. But flying overland in high daylight temperatures would not, NADU reasoned, introduce trouble. This particular aspect of the expedition was to prove an embarrassing miscalculation, however.

A few days following the conference in Ottawa, a message arrived from the Navy Department. The suggestion had been taken: a portable mast at Churchill was now proposed. Still, certain logistical arrangements remained to be settled. The project would require fuel, quarters, and messing for two flight crews; further, the all-important masts themselves had to be shunted north, then erected—and, with them had to go (via WV-2) the ground crew that would accompany the expedition. Moreover, clearance for operations in Canadian territory had yet to be secured.

For any mission so thoroughly removed from routine, let alone in another country, advance operations are crucial. Lieutenant Commander Cecil Manship was made responsible for advance-base preparations. Manship had enlisted in 1940; by 1958 his flight log recorded more than 5,300 LTA hours. For this project, Manship confronted a number of headaches, prominent among them helium and ground-support personnel. Regarding helium, small stockpiles were found (quite by chance) to be potentially available along the proposed route. At Churchill, there was helium under U.S. Army custody and, at Resolute, under that of the U.S. Weather Bureau. But it sat on foreign soil at both. Its release to the navy was to involve a promenade through several bureaucracies.

"For the Resolute operation," Manship remembered, "I was in charge of the blimp ground crew (ground handling) and material." The to-be-available facilities required inspection. "The first trip to Resolute [and Churchill] was primarily for checking the possibility of operating a blimp" from Arctic Canada. "The second trip was for taking material up and erection of mooring masts. The third trip was with the blimp."[23]

Early in July, an official message reached Resolute. Could the base, Ottawa inquired, support a blimp overnight? Squadron Leader William P. Becker, RCAF, was commanding the detachment there. Aristocratic in bearing (he had been personal pilot to the Duke of Edinburgh during part of his 1954 Canadian tour), Becker gave an affirmative reply. "The answer," he recalls, "was based on our responsibility to work closely with the United States military and, perhaps more likely, our strong desire to host this unknown visitor which, no doubt, would put a smile on the face of every human being at Resolute." Living and working conditions at 75° N were yet primitive, base personnel attending to their duties in extreme isolation. Moreover, the workload was demanding, often with extra duties ("We all thrived on work[;] . . . it made the time go faster"). Regulations were necessarily tight, recreational opportunities minimal. In short, *any* respite from routine would be welcomed.[24]

[Opposite] Coastal Baffin Island east of Frobisher—a proposed mast site for the airship. A shorter interior route via Fort Churchill on Hudson Bay was chosen, so as to avoid the unpredictable weather and bold coast of Newfoundland waters, the Labrador Sea, and north—hardly ideal for a slow, low-altitude aircraft. (Author)

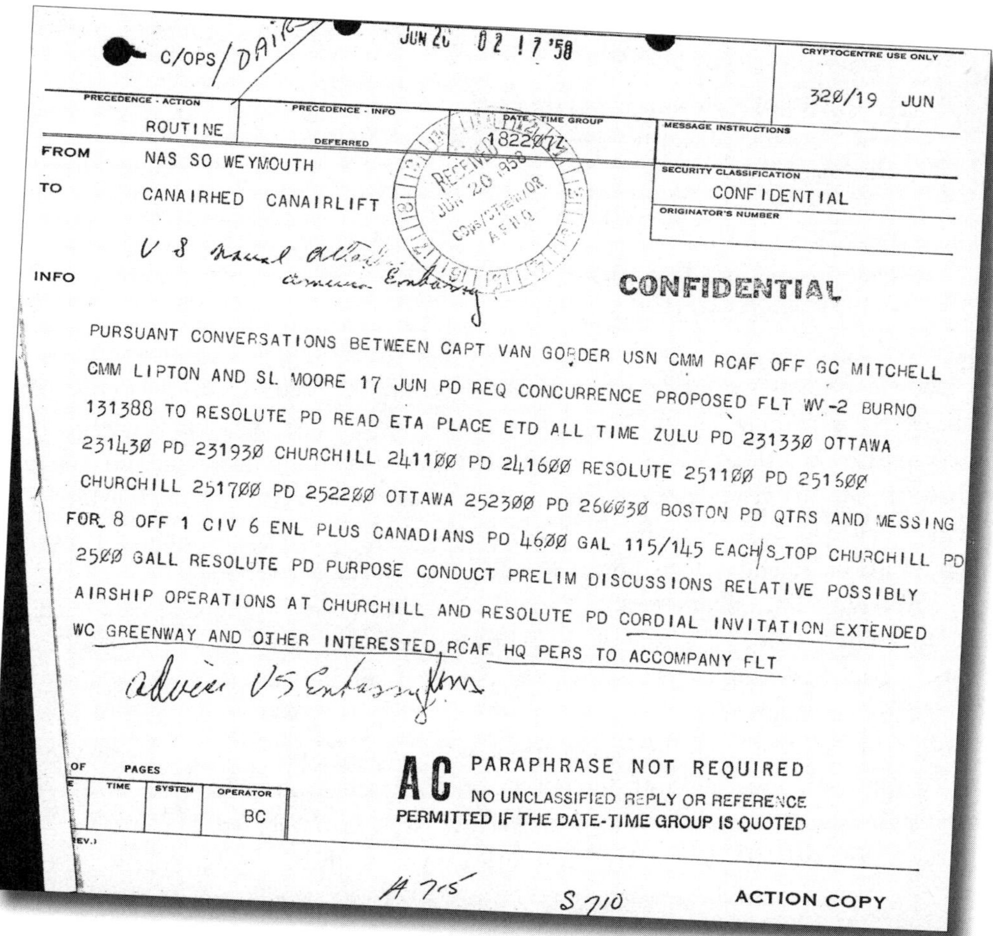
C/OPS / DAir

JUN 20 02 17 '58

CRYPTOCENTRE USE ONLY

320/19 JUN

PRECEDENCE - ACTION: ROUTINE

PRECEDENCE - INFO

DEFERRED

DATE - TIME GROUP: 182207Z

MESSAGE INSTRUCTIONS

FROM: NAS SO WEYMOUTH

TO: CANAIRHED CANAIRLIFT

SECURITY CLASSIFICATION: CONFIDENTIAL

ORIGINATOR'S NUMBER

INFO: U S Naval Attaché, American Embassy

RECEIVED JUN 20 1958 C/OPS/D AIR OR AFHQ

CONFIDENTIAL

PURSUANT CONVERSATIONS BETWEEN CAPT VAN GORDER USN CMM RCAF OFF GC MITCHELL CMM LIPTON AND SL MOORE 17 JUN PD REQ CONCURRENCE PROPOSED FLT WV-2 BURNO 131388 TO RESOLUTE PD READ ETA PLACE ETD ALL TIME ZULU PD 231330 OTTAWA 231430 PD 231930 CHURCHILL 241100 PD 241600 RESOLUTE 251100 PD 251600 CHURCHILL 251700 PD 252200 OTTAWA 252300 PD 260030 BOSTON PD QTRS AND MESSING FOR 8 OFF 1 CIV 6 ENL PLUS CANADIANS PD 4600 GAL 115/145 EACH/S_TOP CHURCHILL PD 2500 GALL RESOLUTE PD PURPOSE CONDUCT PRELIM DISCUSSIONS RELATIVE POSSIBLY AIRSHIP OPERATIONS AT CHURCHILL AND RESOLUTE PD CORDIAL INVITATION EXTENDED WC GREENWAY AND OTHER INTERESTED RCAF HQ PERS TO ACCOMPANY FLT

advise US Embassy

AC PARAPHRASE NOT REQUIRED

NO UNCLASSIFIED REPLY OR REFERENCE PERMITTED IF THE DATE-TIME GROUP IS QUOTED

OF PAGES | TIME | SYSTEM | OPERATOR: BC

A 715 S 710

ACTION COPY

[Left] NADU message to Headquarters, Canadian Air Forces. Subject: logistics for operations into Arctic Canada. An airplane can be landed and serviced almost anywhere; an airship needs a mooring mast, generous manpower—for ground crews—and helium storage. (National Archives of Canada)

At about this time, a telex reached Ottawa from the Canadian embassy in Washington, D.C.: Could Greenaway be made available? A man of persistent curiosity, his national service had been shaped by the unconventional. Greenaway's abiding interest in R&D and its working environment pervaded a distinguished career. The Polar Project of the Americans tendered a unique opportunity. "Fascinated" by the prospect (and despite impending leave), he agreed.

Polar navigation demanded well-qualified men. When the crew list was posted, *two* navigators were named: Lieutenant (junior grade) James Malloy, USN, and the wing commander.[25] A quiet man, Malloy was the junior officer with respect to navigation. Though well regarded ("possibly our best non-aviator navigator," one pilot told me), Malloy was relatively inexperienced. He adapted quickly to the peculiar full-time demands of the expedition.

Basic survival equipment—tents, sleeping bags, extra parkas, emergency rations (such as dehydrated foods)—was requisitioned, a clothing list posted. Each crew member, it announced, was to have in his possession the following:

One summer flight suit
One two-piece winter liner
One parka hood
One suit long underwear
Two pair heavy socks
One pair heavy shoes ("boondockers")
One pair arctics (galoshes)
One pair sunglasses
One sheath knife
One wool shirt
One pair summer flying gloves
One pair winter flying gloves

"Individuals may use their own discretion," the navy advised, "in their selection of other optional items of clothing." A small bag was recommended. "This bag should contain one winter dress uniform and shoes, extra sox, and handkerchiefs and so on. It should also contain two towels, soap, shaving gear, extra underwear, sox and any other necessary small items. A small bag may be taken aboard the airship if desired." This kit was to contain a minimum of clothing, enough for use on a flight of forty hours' duration. Personal cameras: allowable.

At midmonth, Captain Paul B. Ryan, U.S. naval attaché in Ottawa, was briefed. Ryan would be responsible for all liaison work relative to clearance for operations within Canadian territory. A back-and-forth of telegrams, correspondence, phone calls, and meetings ensued, to flesh out plans and approvals.

In a 19 June message to the headquarters of the Canadian Air Forces, South Weymouth requested approval for a flight to Churchill, thence to Resolute. The fuel needs for the visiting plane plus subsistence for the air crews during layover were now outlined.[26]

Less than a week later, a NADU contingent arrived in northern Canada. Purpose: to conduct general reconnaissance and familiarization and to gather on-scene information unavailable in flight-planning publications. Following a stopover in Ottawa, the WV-2 filed for Fort Churchill. En route, the plane was diverted: Churchill was fogged in. At the Coral Harbour alternate ("a drear stretch of flat brown-grey tundra"), the Willie Victor refueled. The NADU aircraft had the 6,500-foot gravel strip at Resolute beneath in the early hours of 24 June.[27]

The base detachment was unacquainted with airships. A briefing was held to outline the upcoming exercise ("We [found out] all the facts about the blimp," Becker remembers.) Requirements included quarters and messing, fuel, ground handling, and—not least—an unobstructed site for the expeditionary mast. NADU inspected the facility. Located in the middle of Canada's Arctic islands, this outpost lies about 2,500 miles northwest of Boston and 1,000 miles from the Pole.

Business concluded, the Americans set course for Churchill. In Manitoba they found a relatively modern facility—by Arctic standards. Built by the United States as part of the "Crimson" air route to Western Europe, Fort Churchill was duty station for units of the RCAF, the Canadian Defence Research Board's northern laboratory, and a training center for the Canadian Army. The U.S. Army's First Test Center also was sited there.

Facilities for support of aircraft and flight personnel were deemed adequate. Resolute also was found to be ample—barely. ("Comparing Resolute to Churchill in 1958," Becker later observed, "was like comparing Rattlesnake Gulch to Hollywood.") Still, NADU could stage through Fort Churchill, a thousand miles to the south, and exploit it again on the return run. At Resolute, a mast site would have to be graded and a taxiway prepared. No one could yet know, but carving a mooring site and taxiway from Cornwallis Island tundra was to harrow the operation.

NADU WV-2 on Resolute gravel, Northwest Territories, 24 June 1958. The Americans have come to assess Canadian facilities for handling an airship and to brief base personnel. In August this NADU bird—BUNO 131388—would accompany *719* into Arctic Canada. Note the tundra terrain and lingering snow. Sited at 74° 43′ N, 94° 59′ W, Resolute is 2,500 miles from Boston. (ATC Frederick L. Parker)

[Opposite, top] U.S Army drill rig boring holes for mast-support cables at Fort Churchill, Manitoba, July 1958. This subarctic outpost (60° N) would receive the airship on its northbound run, and return. At Resolute Bay (nearly 75° N) shaped explosives were used to penetrate rock-hard permafrost. (ATC Frederick L. Parker)

[Opposite, bottom] A mooring mast is shunted into position at Resolute. Sited on the Northwest Passage, the airstrip here is midpoint between Churchill and the geographic pole. This expeditionary mast along with equipment and supplies for the expedition—slated for August—had arrived via WV-2. (AD1 Elmer B. Lord)

[Left] Lt. Cdr. Cecil Manship, USN, and his advance crew at the Resolute mast site, 13 July. (Cdr. A. J. Schou)

The NADU bird returned to base on 25 June. Captain Ryan drafted an "entirely unofficial" note to Group Captain Mitchell. Tentative flight itinerary: South Weymouth to Fort Churchill, then to Resolute. From there a round-robin, nonstop via Alert, on Ellesmere Island, would be conducted before departure for Churchill and, finally, the return to Massachusetts. Estimated elapsed time: twelve days. "The services which would be required," Ryan advised, "are quarters and messing for fifteen persons, POL [petroleum, oil, lubricants], and a working party of thirty men to assist the advance party in ground-handling of the airship." The aircraft's radio call (voice), he noted, would be "Navy 26719," or "N6719," on continuous wave. Both government and personal cameras would be on board the unarmed aircraft. "I am instructed," Ryan continued, "to state that the U.S. Navy would be honored if two Canadian Military or Governmental representatives could be nominated to make the trip in the airship as representatives of Canada."[28]

On 2 July, the expedition was authorized by Admiral Arleigh A. Burke, CNO—full sanction. Approval from the Canadian government would conclude the organizational hurdles.

On the third, the U.S. embassy drafted its official request. "The primary objective," the embassy wrote Air Marshall Hugh Campbell, chief of the Air Staff, is

> to undertake airship (blimp) flight operations in support of research in the area of the Arctic Ocean. The U.S. Naval Air Development Unit based at South Weymouth, Massachusetts, has been designated by the Chief of Naval Operations to conduct a feasibility study and an exploratory flight to determine the feasibility of the airship

as a suitable research vehicle in the region of the Arctic. The blimp will investigate weather affecting airship operations near the Arctic Ocean, among other factors. Using advance bases, its potential (distance and duration) for research and exploration flights in the region will be assessed. The air-drop and pickup of both personnel and equipment also will be explored.

Whether an airship could operate under Arctic conditions, and the logistical requirements for such operations, would receive a practical field test. Ryan's letter to Air Marshall Campbell continued, "I have now received instructions from the Chief of Naval Operations to seek agreement and approval of the Chief of Air Staff for clearance for this exploratory flight, or flights, of U.S.N. aircraft and airship." A WV-2 would transport one mooring mast to Resolute, another to Churchill. The proposed flight route and its duration, the blimp's call sign, and the services needed en route were again outlined. The blimp

EMBASSY OF THE UNITED STATES OF AMERICA
OFFICE OF THE NAVAL ATTACHE
OTTAWA

IN REPLY REFER TO
EN3/EF13/wsw
A4-3
~~Serial: G-0291-58~~
3 July 1958

CONFIDENTIAL

CONFIDENTIAL

Air Marshall Hugh Campbell, C.B.E., C.D., RCAF
Chief of Air Staff
Department of National Defence
Ottawa, Ontario

Dear Air Marshall Campbell,

I have the honor to refer to a U.S. Navy Project with a Class A priority. The primary objective of the project is to undertake airship (blimp) flight operations in support of research in the area of the Arctic Ocean. The U.S. Naval Air Development Unit based at South Weymouth, Massachusetts, has been designated by the Chief of Naval Operations to conduct a feasibility study and an exploratory flight to determine the feasibility of the airship as a suitable research vehicle in the region of the Arctic.

As you may know, Captain VanGorder, Commanding Officer of the Naval Air Development Unit, has been in communication with Group Captain E.M. Mitchell, RCAF, Director of Air Services at RCAF Headquarters. As a result of meetings between representatives of the USN and the RCAF, it is understood that the RCAF Commands at Churchill and Resolute would be prepared to collaborate with the Naval Air Development Unit in support of a feasibility, or exploratory, flight during the summer of 1958.

Matters to be investigated would be:

a) Weather conditions affecting airship operations in the area of the Arctic Ocean.

b) Utilizing advanced bases, determine distance and duration of research and exploration flights that can be conducted.

c) Air drop and pickup of personnel and equipment.

d) Logistic requirements.

e) Ground handling.

[Left] Page 1 (of three), U.S. Naval Attaché confidential letter to the Department of National Defence, Canada: official notification to Ottawa concerning the upcoming exercise. (National Archives of Canada)

[Opposite] Letter to U.S. Naval Attaché, Ottawa, granting approval for the Polar Project, 8 July 1958. (National Archives of Canada) would depart South Weymouth, it was hoped, about 27 July, based on advice of RCAF officers at Resolute, "who state that weather conditions would be most favorable at that time. . . . A detailed itinerary will be provided later when details are firm."

Ryan concluded: "As you know the airship has certain capabilities such as long distance, personnel and equipment accommodations, hovering, low altitude and slow speed, which make it particularly suitable for Polar work. The fact that this project has an *A Priority,* suggests that we are in immediate need of basic data in climatology and oceanography, polar ice cap information and sea ice. Consequently, if this project is successful our two countries would derive many mutual benefits therefrom."[29]

The air marshall, replying, was "pleased to approve the subject operation." RCAF facilities would be made available, with one exception: because quarters at Resolute were limited, the navy would be obliged to provide its own. As for the invitations, both were accepted: Mr. G. M. Carty, Department of Northern Affairs, and Wing Commander Greenaway would accompany the U.S. aircraft.[30] For whatever reason, Carty was later dropped, replaced by Commodore Robertson, naval attaché in Washington.

U.S. officials fretted over publicity. As much as possible, the navy wished to avoid "too big" an advance buildup. The Navy Department had resolved to avoid a "Vanguard-type" debacle should the expedition be aborted or, worse, suffer failure or casualty.

CONFIDENTIAL

S530-105-1(CAS)

Ontario

JUL 8 1958

Naval Attache,
Embassy of the United States of America,
100 Wellington Street,
Ottawa, Ontario.

Attention: Captain Paul B. Ryan

Special Flights - US Aircraft over Canada
USN Airship Operations

1 Reference is made to your EN3/EF13/WSW A4-3 Serial: G-0291-58 dated 3 July, 1958.

2 I am pleased to approve the subject operation as outlined in your letter. All RCAF facilities required to support the operation are available, with the exception of accommodation at Resolute Bay. Captain Van Gorder was advised of the lack of accommodation during his visit to Resolute Bay 24 June.

3 I am also pleased to accept the invitation for Canadian personnel to participate in the operation. Mr. G.M. Carty of the Department of Northern Affairs and Wing Commander K.R. Greenaway of RCAF headquarters have been selected as the two Canadian representatives.

"Original Signed By"

(Hugh Campbell)
Air Marshal
Chief of the Air Staff

F/L WAWright/MMc
2-5392

Copies to
CAS
VCAS
COPS
DAIRS
orig
circ
file

Internal Canadian Forces message concerning planning for the Polar Project. (National Archives of Canada)

CONFIDENTIAL
S530-105-1

RECEIVED
1958
DEPUTY MINISTER
NATIONAL DEFENCE

JUL 15 1958

Under-Secretary of State for External Affairs,
Room 267 East Block,
Department of External Affairs,
Ottawa, Ontario.

Dear Mr. Leger:

Please be advised that permission has been granted, on a service to service basis, for the US Navy to carry out airship operations from Resolute Bay N.W.T. during the month of August this year.

The purpose of the Operation is to determine the feasibility of using airships as research vehicles for polar regions. The operation will consist of a 36 hour flight by an airship from Resolute Bay along the north coast of Ellesmere Island and return. The airship will stage through Churchill enroute to Resolute Bay and on the return flight to the U.S.A. Twelve hour crew rests are planned at Churchill and Resolute Bay northbound and southbound. The estimated time of departure from Naval Air Station, South Weymouth, Mass is 27th July. The total elapsed time for the operation is approximately twelve days.

Temporary collapsible mooring masts have been erected at Churchill and Resolute Bay. All RCAF facilities required to support the operation have been made available with the exception of accommodation at Resolute Bay. The USN will provide accommodation at that location.

An invitation for two Canadian representatives to accompany the airship has been accepted. Mr. G.M. Carty of the Dept of Northern Affairs and W/C K.R. Greenaway of RCAF Headquarters have been selected to participate.

Yours sincerely,

Original Signed by
JAMES A. SHARPE
Assistant Deputy Minister

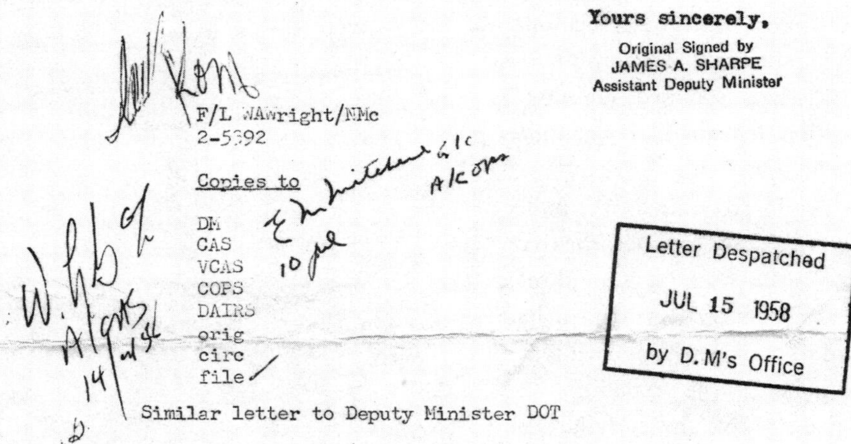

F/L WAwright/NMc
2-5992

Copies to

DM
CAS
VCAS
COPS
DAIRS
orig
circ
file

Letter Despatched
JUL 15 1958
by D.M's Office

Similar letter to Deputy Minister DOT

Project Vanguard was the recently discredited program to lift IGY satellites into orbit. (Out of seven operational Vanguard satellites, only two had gained orbit.) The launch vehicle had been developed under the direction of the Naval Research Laboratory.[31] The Soviet Union had been first: *Sputnik*s *I* and *II* had opened the Space Age. Soviet technology had been underrated. In the United States, an orgy of introspection and accusation had ensued. Amid the hue and cry, pressure had been applied to the Vanguard team to loft a small earth-circling satellite—and quickly. The navy had been chosen to conduct the launch, even though the army was technologically more advanced in rocketry. On 6 December 1957, the nation had suffered humiliation when the vehicle lifted off the pad, then exploded.[32]

Both the White House and Navy Department had shouldered acute embarrassment. Now, a bit of public-relations insurance was purchased for the Polar Project. "At the same time," ONR noted brightly, "it is felt that the trip and its hoped-for results will be of sufficient general interest to warrant an effort to secure good public information treatment."[33]

Nautilus, 1957: First Trial

At Submarine Base Pearl Harbor, another crew was making ready. A submarine modified for under-ice "ops" had been ordered into far northern waters. Its operational orders (unlike *719*'s) held ultrahigh security: few senior commanders knew the actual objective. USS *Nautilus* (SSN 571) was to penetrate the Arctic Ocean fully to 90° N latitude then transect the basin, to complete mankind's first voyage from Pacific to Atlantic by way of the North Pole.

Planning had advanced at the Pentagon, in New London and San Diego, and even at the White House. Now skipper of the world's first atomic submarine: Commander William R. Anderson, USN. Lieutenant Commander Paul J. Early, USN, the boat's chief engineer, was to recall a major premise at the operation: absolute maximum secrecy. Security was not to be broken. (See appendix 5.) "The Captain initially told only the Executive Officer, Frank Adams; me; and 'Shep' Jenks, the navigator. We were forbidden to tell anyone else, but we were required to make all preparations and modifications." One security headache: charts for waters from basin to basin across the Pole.[34] "The four of us," Anderson would write, "then tackled what is undoubtedly the toughest job I have experienced in my naval service: preparing *Nautilus* for a transpolar cruise in utter secrecy." Later, Early continues, "the other officers were told."[35] In the know, initially: eleven names, including CNO, Rickover, ComSubLant, and the president. "You could talk only to those people *by name,*" Lyon recalled. "And some of them weren't too useful—such as Eisenhower."

The advocacy of McWethy, Lyon, Anderson, and like-minded figures was about to pay off. Operation Sunshine was top secret: the president himself would announce its success.

When Senator Jackson had posed his question, the matter had passed to McWethy at Op 311, the submarine desk in CNO's staff. Following two years in command of a New London–based boat, McWethy had been assigned to the Pentagon. It was early March 1957. "I was the only submariner in OpNav with ice experience, and my interest was well known. So when Senator Jackson posed the question . . . his letter came to my desk for action. I suggested we could do that; and ADM [Admiral] Burke in his green pencil indicated we should work up a program."

McWethy phoned San Diego. And Dr. Lyon immediately flew east. Having conferred with Dr. Louis Quam at ONR, Lyon and McWethy worked to formulate a five-year effort to develop an under-ice capability for nuclear submarines, *Nautilus* being in the picture. Among Lyon's main points was major field investigations of the Arctic Ocean and its approaches: bathymetric survey, oceanography, ice conditions, sound transmission, reverberation studies. As well, methods of access to the surface needed investigating—and a boat itself modified for "experimental field work," to make it Arctic-capable. As for the military mission: field study of target detection and recognition, weapon requirements, and approach doctrine. Here is McWethy, bringing a plan to fruition:

> This [plan] covered ops in various seasons and localities. I worked to smooth out the plan; and, eventually, it was sent out to the Atlantic and Pacific Fleet commanders for their comment. Pacific came back saying they didn't have a nuclear submarine and would defer to the Atlantic. CinCLantFlt [Commander in Chief, Atlantic Fleet] sent it to ComSubLant to prepare a reply. By that time I was assigned to Submarine Squadron 10 in New London, and I had the pleasure of preparing ComSubLant's reply which, of course, was favorable.[36]

Submarine Squadron 10 was assigned. (*Nautilus* had become a unit of ComSubLant in April 1958. Rickover had hesitated as to sending *Nautilus* under ice; for its part, ComSubLant (influenced by McWethy) had ordered an experimental excursion under the polar pack. Tacking the excursion onto a NATO exercise in the North Atlantic, that summer the command arranged for *Nautilus* and *Trigger* (a diesel-electric boat) to steam north. His upward-beamed fathometers installed, Dr. Lyon accompanied *Nautilus*—now modified for Arctic operations.

Casting off at 0800 EDT, 19 August, at New London, SSN 571 logged test dives before settling the next day into cruising at 20.5 knots, three hundred feet. Two days out, the boat's echo sounder trace showed a maximum wave height of twelve feet in the sea overhead, wave roll felt a hundred feet below the surface. *Nautilus* sped its crew across the Atlantic in steady (and stealthy) comfort. "Makes one realize," Lyon felt, the "great change capable by SSN type submarine, i.e., have been cruising at 15–18 knots, 300 feet deep without fighting high seas and consequent strain on personnel or working of ship's hull, means that any moment vessel & men are in top shape for combat and can immediately concentrate on task, terrific advantage when think of surface vessel fighting seas overhead."[37]

Passing eastward of Iceland, Anderson pressed toward the slot between Greenland and Spitsbergen—a deepwater approach to the basin. On 29 August, at four hundred feet and flank speed, *Nautilus* crossed the Arctic Circle at 66° 33' N, 9° W. The taking of water samples in the engine room commenced, along with hourly tabulations of temperature and salinity. *Trigger* entered the rendezvous area late—having detoured around a Russian fishing group to avoid detection. The pair closed range, *Nautilus* taking station abeam the diesel boat. Anderson surfaced his command on 1 September, concluding eleven and a half days continuously underwater from New London—more than 3,900 miles. ("Need more be said in contrast to conventional boat," Lyon jotted.) *Trigger* holding station at approximately 80° N, beyond the ice margin, Anderson made preparations to dive at about 2100 on 1 September to run under the pack. Two topside echo sounders began recording ice coverage as *Nautilus* continued north under sea ice at a running depth from three to five hundred feet.[38] "We steamed northward," the commander would write in his public account, "plunging deeper into the unknown."

The boat was relying utterly on its machinery and equipment. Advancing in, scanning sonar topside, echo sounders, and a topside BQN (sonar) unit monitored the canopy. As yet, no vessel had gained 90° N. Nor yet would *Nautilus*. On 2 September, a small block of ice damaged the sail and periscopes while the boat was surfacing in a polynya. A reversal in course ordered, the boat turned slowly, carefully—by reference its known turning radius. Holding rudder, "we hoped we were going south," Lyon remembers. "But *what* south?" At 87° *every* direction is south. Back in open water, repairs were made. At 2000 on 4 September, the boat having steamed to within 180 miles of the Pole (87° N, 8′ W by dead reckoning), the decision again was taken to retire: the power supply to both gyrocompasses had failed (a fuse had blown). Ability to steer a known course stood problematic. Anderson dared not rely on dead reckoning. "After we recovered," Early records, "the Captain decided to turn south since we could not demonstrate that we could find the North Pole accurately, even though our dead reckoning, in retrospect, showed us to be within five miles of our fix when we surfaced."

To regain a reference direction, the auxiliary compass had been aligned on a true meridian as defined by the auxiliary *magnetic* compass, possibly introducing a large, unknown error. *Nautilus* being unable to surface, "no other means," Lyon notes, "was available to reset direction." As they ran to the south then southeast for open water, they studied "all possible clues from the ocean" to determine if, in fact, the boat was on course for Spitsbergen, not Greenland. Water temperatures, the overhead cover, and bottom contours (bathymetry) were compared to that recorded during the Sverdrup and Wilkins expeditions, and from Russian sources. These, along with dead reckoning, argued that *Nautilus* in fact was riding the outflowing Greenland current. After more than seventy-four hours under ice, the boat began breaking clear; around 1000 hours, on the 6th, *Nautilus* cleared the pack altogether.

Backup systems, plainly, were essential for navigation, for direction. Experience gained from the 1957 cruises would "really pay off" the following year.

Disappointment aside, *Nautilus* had logged a new northing.[39] As well, useful data had been collected: the distribution of floe types, thicknesses, open water (leads) inside the pack—continuous, "uniquely extensive" records of under-ice profiles. A decade after *Boarfish, Nautilus* had demonstrated *unlimited* movement. The polar submarine, dismissed five years earlier as fantastic, was now demonstrated fact. The Arctic Ocean had become an operational area for submarine forces.

Following participation in two exercises, *Nautilus* returned to New London on 28 October. An extended availability at Electric Boat commenced; it would persist into February: improvements, modifications, and routine overhaul items were completed. As well, all the NEL sonar gear and other special equipment on board for the 1957 Arctic cruise were removed. Reinstallation came unexpectedly soon—in March 1958. Late in February, ordered to Washington, Anderson learned of Operation Sunshine: the proposal to cross the Arctic Basin in June.

That March, meantime, the navy secretary commended *Nautilus'* officers and men for its "significant naval accomplishment" in the Arctic Ocean in the period August–September 1957: "The report of your cruise indicates that the USS *Nautilus* made three submerged sorties under the Polar Ice Cap, including one 962.5 mile submerged run under ice of over 74 hours duration in which an approach was made within 180 nautical miles of the North Pole. This superb display of seamanship by *Nautilus* crew has added a new significance to the mobility of forces at sea." This had been accomplished despite the known hazards of polar operations and the unknown perils of long transits under solid ice with the possible entrapment thereunder. "The results of this operation have provided invaluable scientific data and operational information. In accumulating this data, the officers and men demonstrated a skilful application of professional knowledge and devotion to duty which are in keeping with the highest traditions of the Naval Service."

Notable among the obstacles remaining were under-ice navigation and communications. *Nautilus* had had difficulty determining position. Bottom charts had yet to be surveyed; as well, data as to water masses and currents remained incomplete. Precise bathymetry would offer a direct, reliable method for rough positioning. For Dr. Lyon, then, the major field chore for the Arctic operational theater was bathymetric survey.

Nautilus (in Lyon's words) had "opened the entire Arctic Ocean to a new era of high-speed operations." Still, diving procedures devised for diesel boats in ice needed modification for high-speed operations. As well, hull changes were required to permit surfacing in all ice conditions. And bathymetric survey of the Arctic Ocean and its approaches were deemed "essential."[40]

Nautilus, 1958: Transect Arctic Ocean (June Attempt)

A planned joint SSN operation was next: *Skate* (SSN 578) and *Nautilus* steaming north in company, for mutual support. As it happened, Commander, Submarine Squadron [ComSubRon] 10 continued Arctic work with *Skate,* the third nuclear submarine—but was cut from further plans involving *Nautilus.* Operating alone, *Skate* would log the first surfacing at the North Pole. *Nautilus,* for its part, was to garner the lion's share of media glare and public fanfare.

In his report, Anderson had recommended a further phase. In this, he discovered, he enjoyed rock-solid support, the best. President Eisenhower had plans for *Nautilus.* By February a special mission had been put up for study: a transit of the Arctic from ocean to ocean: a submerged northwest passage. If possible, the White House wanted passage from west to east, so as to arrive at the World's Fair in Brussels in June. Plans were initiated, to be known as Operation Sunshine. Two nuclear boats were assigned: *Skate* would penetrate from the Atlantic, press to the Pole, then retire. On 17 February the cross-basin operation was authorized. Conferences at the Pentagon focused on modifications to *Nautilus*—to make her more Arctic-capable—and on conditions anticipated not only for the Bering Sea but also, particularly, the shallow Chukchi Sea, and on the latest soundings.

Nautilus, meanwhile, was ordered to the Pacific Fleet under strict security—with an attending cover story floated by the navy. Late in May, Anderson received operational orders for the final phase of Sunshine.

Nuclear propulsion, as we have seen, had transformed the submarine into a true undersea (hence under-ice) vessel. In this period, however, natural obstacles to polar sailing remained. The key was under-ice topography—deformed, deep-draft ice. It was not enough, Dr. Lyon knew, to predict coverage and ice movement. Ice *draft* was crucial: the maximum keel depths of pressure ridges as well as their drift and probable concentration in the shallow approaches to deep water. The Chukchi Sea presents the most difficult part, the governing factor, of any Arctic Ocean transit, because of its shallow depth for great distances, lack of identifiable bottom features, and confused current patterns. The difficulty rapidly decreases with retreat of the ice northward during the summer. Hence, the transit attempt was to be from Pacific to Atlantic Ocean.[41] Sunshine, that is, would be a west-to-east transit, because ice conditions on the approach might end the penetration.

On 4 June, aerial reconnaissance was flown via Cessna 180, Anderson and Lyon as passenger-observers. From the air, ice cover appeared "completely congruent with experience and observation of previous years," Dr. Lyon recorded. "Particular effort was made to note any heavy pressure ridging in floes. The small slow plane permitted easy observation of surface detail. *No heavy pressure ridges were observed.*"[42]

On 9 June, SSN 571 set sail from Seattle en route to England via the North Pole.[43] Her approach to the basin: Unimak Pass through the Aleutians, thence the Bering Sea into the Chukchi. This "door" requires passage over flat bottom contours with water depths less than 180 feet for a thousand miles. Ship's complement: thirteen officers and ninety-three enlisted personnel. Assisting with special equipment were four civilians, two from NEL. Senior scientist: Dr. Waldo Lyon.[44]

Nautilus' wardroom during first phase of Operation Sunshine (June 1958)—a top secret Pacific-to-Atlantic transect of the Arctic Ocean via the North Pole. (U.S. Naval Institute Photo Archive)

Upon departure, the watches were stabilized on a one-in-three basis. Special sonar watches were assigned, each under the supervision of a leading sonarman. Three officers manned the watch. And the skipper or his "exec" was awake at all times. "By the time the shallow Bering Sea was entered," Anderson records, "each section was a well trained and operating team."

Around 2200, 14 June, rounding the Northwest Cape of St. Lawrence Island, *Nautilus* began meeting ice. As she pressed in, coverage increased. This ceiling soon became worrisome: old, blocky pressure ice thickened to about thirty feet: unexpected, unanchored ice. The SubRon command had had neither experience nor observations to offer on spring breakup in that sector. This mass was landfast in character, from coastal Siberia, Alaska, or Canada. (Air reconnaissance had detected virtually no ice of land origin in open sea.) Twenty-five miles under the pack, and with twenty-fathom water ahead, approach was blocked.

Anderson retreated, retried: exploiting the shallower but more ice-free route east of the island. There the Bering Sea opens earlier—a gift of warm-water inflow through the strait.

Course changed to 180°, Anderson headed for a point about fifty miles south of St. Lawrence Island, then pressed back in. The Chukchi Sea was logged at 0530, 17 June, the Arctic Circle at 1108. Breakup here begins in late June or early July and proceeds from south to north, open water following the current. A transit was made as far as Point Hope, dodging occasional patches and blocks (and walruses) before diving to run under the pack—ice ahead in all directions. Northwest of Cape Lisburne, the submarine having run thirty miles under scattered floes, detectors showing good correlation on ice ahead *and* overhead,

> the ship suddenly and unexpectedly underran a very thick [47 feet] mass of ice, probably of considerable age, and of coastal origin. The water depth was 160 feet. *Nautilus* was cruising at 120 feet. After passing under a ridge of 63 feet draft, depth was increased to 140 feet, speed was changed to 4 knots, and extricating maneuvers [reversal of course] commenced. In this process the ship underran a ridge of about 80 feet draft which cleared the top of the sail by 5 to 10 feet. This body of ice was observed to be over 1600 yards in the dimension across our track and at least 500 yards along track. Since even shallower water lay ahead (23 fathoms charted) and having observed that drifting ice of coastal origin and uncommonly large size was present in the Chukchi, the operation was reluctantly abandoned in favor of a later attempt under more ideal conditions.[45]

On sonar, the first deep mass had not shown up before *Nautilus* passed beneath. The SQS-4 sonar had been in "maintain close contact" mode. This had proven best for detecting ice, pressure ridges, leads. This time, however, SQS-4 had granted no advance warning of very deep ice. Switch was made to search mode; this made the beam horizontal—and the keels showed up clearly.[46]

Nautilus had rushed the season—a result of failure to appreciate spring breakup of shorefast ice in the Bering–Chukchi approaches. (As noted, aerial reconnaissance had seen virtually no ice of coastal origin early in June. Probably, the unusually warm winter just past had caused heavy ice of land origin to break free.) The boat cleared this ice at 2315, proceeding south. By 0800, next day, *Nautilus* was running the Bering Strait at periscope depth in a flat calm, speed nine knots. Ice covered the strait's western side "completely." The return trip also proved eventful. Influenced by southwest winds, ice from the Siberian coast—including many large pieces of fair draft—had drifted across *Nautilus'* northbound track. Most were evaded by running closer to the Alaskan side, making small changes of track to the east to pass clear. "However, during the transit of a 40 mile shallow water reach it was necessary to make an under-ice penetration in as little as 105 feet of water. By this time we had become expert in interpreting the ice picture on the various sonars and were able to weave in between and around the ice floes to the end that no thick ice was allowed to pass overhead. This is undoubtedly the most classic example to date of under-ice maneuvering and afforded superb training for conning officers and sonar operators."[47]

A dispatch to CNO had recommended return to Pearl (approved), to await opening of the Point Barrow passage to deep water. Early June ice had excluded that route, dictating the now-aborted track across the Chukchi in water of twenty-three fathoms, minimum—roughly the 169° W meridian.

Self-critiquing to his journal, Dr. Lyon revisited the decision for a *June* transit. During February's deliberations, he'd held that the Chukchi could be crossed. Probable maximum thickness: fifty feet—pressure ice formed *at sea*. Ridges of landfast origin would normally still be anchored. Though this conclusion had been based on years of (submarine and icebreaker) observation, a nagging uncertainty had persisted, that greater thickness might be met—"now an obvious reality." He had urged the shore-lead route to the Barrow Sea Valley (see page 39), so as to have maximum sea room and a precise fix for departure across, to the Greenland Sea. This would have necessitated transit at periscope depth and, in June, icebreaker support—thus complicating security, "a primary factor governing the operation."

Lack of knowledge had foreclosed further northing. Among the senior scientist's conclusions:

> The difficulties experienced during the Bering–Chukchi transit illustrate the sterile character of these shallow seas for submarine operations. Neutralization of the area can be readily accomplished because of the lack of sea room, from both constricting shoreline and shallow depth, and susceptibility to mining and all detection devices. Patrol of the Arctic Ocean should be developed from the Atlantic Ocean entrance and Canadian Archipelago.
>
> The second phase, the transit of the Arctic Ocean is expected to be made easily. The transit across the Chukchi Sea will be made during the summer period for which we have maximum information and operating experience. The transit into the Barrow Sea Valley will duplicate 1952 *Redfish* transit.[48]

Nautilus ended Sunshine's first phase at 1000, 28 June, amid a noisy aloha: ships, helicopters, flowers, bands. Dr. Lyon saw none of it. "I missed it all secure in [a] cabin awaiting security clearance to avoid visitors that might recognize me." *Nautilus* on standby, a three-week leave and upkeep commenced—during which photographs, charts, logs, and all material relating to or indicative of the prior operation were retained on board, under top secret security classification and control.

In his report to CNO, Anderson expressed confidence: "The training and experience received on this cruise will be a major contribution to the success and the speed of a subsequent transpolar transit by *Nautilus*. The Commanding Officer is proud to report that there is no one in *Nautilus* who is any less a volunteer for such an operation than before the disheartening experiences of this attempt."

He recommended Sunshine be rescheduled, with a target-date departure of 30 July from Pearl—with a four-day standby commencing 8 July, if ice conditions permitted an earlier castoff. His information indicated "a high probability" of clear water to the hundred-fathom curve in the Chukchi or western Beaufort by August—perhaps before, depending on wind history during the standby. Accordingly, air reconnaissance of the pack boundary and ice configuration between longitudes 150° W and 169° W was recommended, "starting immediately."

Meantime, a cover story was floated. Until departure, Anderson would fret that his true objective would, somehow, leak out.[49]

An instrument of geopolitics, SSN 571 was sailing under the direct order of the commander in chief. Sputniks were chirping—a priceless Soviet propaganda coup and, for Washington, a humiliation. Stunned by the furor (compounded by U.S. failure on the Vanguard launchpad) the White House craved a technological success. Gaining the North Pole would reaffirm America's prowess and affirm, along with *Explorer I* (heaved aloft in January 1958), what the United States could do—respite from the unrelieved bad news since October. In short, a further *public* fiasco was intolerable. The world would know of *Nautilus'* true objective only if the boat succeeded.

In contrast to this high-level indigestion, the concurrent airship expedition was unclassified—a mere research project. Washington elected to impose few restrictions. Security concerning *Nautilus* foreclosed any joint operation; the two naval crews were unaware of each other. Had they known, the submariners would have changed—nothing. Admiral Early explains: "Coordination would not have been a good idea," he said. "There would be no opportunity or means for communications. The two trips were completely independent. There was not even the opportunity for rescue of one by the other. Hinging completion of one operation on the other would have introduced complexities that could easily have reduced the chance of success."

Timing was one. Thwarted in June, *Nautilus* tarried in Hawaii before again steaming in. And deep water (as we shall see) would again eat the calendar. Early again: "What," he asks, "would the blimp have done in the meantime?"[50]

Ten days prior to departure, on 17 July, a notice to the press was released. Media coverage of the airship, the Pentagon announced, would be by a pool. No more than three representatives could be carried. One berth could be guaranteed for nonessential guests. Further, there was the possibility that the media might not make the round-robin to Ellesmere at all. That decision would rest with the expedition leader, based on conditions at Resolute at the time of takeoff.

Accordingly, a ranking had been instituted: if one pool representative accompanied, ONR preferred that it be a wire-service writer. Assuming cooperative atmospherics (the Arctic is notorious for poor radio communications), wire copy would be transmitted directly from the aircraft. Anyone left behind at Resolute would be obliged to find copy there. If two guests accompanied the flight, a photographer could accompany the press writer. Lowest-priority passenger: network announcers.

As it happened, only one correspondent would accompany the expedition. Hugh A. Mulligan, a feature writer for the New York bureau of the Associated Press, was "certainly pleased" to bag the assignment. Feature writers handle the human-interest side of a story, focusing on background, analysis, color. Though not a heavy political story, an expedition by airship *was* unusual. Already, Mulligan was developing a reputation for offbeat coverage, often involving what was to become a career trademark: bizarre transportation.

Why just AP, no one else? Formed in 1848, the Associated Press was by now the world's biggest news agency. It was and is a cooperative, owned jointly by newspapers and radio and television outlets in more than a hundred countries. A premier wire service, today it has its own satellites. Members receive their copy from the service, tailoring it to their needs and local interests.

Telecommunications aside, news gathering is (as it has always been) an arena of cut-throat competition. If the *New York Times* had been selected, the *Boston Globe* might well have protested. Similarly, if CBS had been chosen, NBC could have whined. Picking the AP meant that in effect *everyone* was riding along.[51]

Mulligan's dispatches were to make fascinating reading for papers "on the wire" electing to use his copy and for listeners of radio stations using them as "rip and reads."

[Opposite] *Nautilus* edges into berth at the U.S. Submarine Base, Pearl Harbor, 28 June 1958. Blocked by shoal water and deep-draft ice, the boat has retreated to Hawaii, to await favorable pack-ice conditions. *Nautilus* lay pierside to 22 July, a cover story masking its true objective. (U.S. Naval Institute Photo Archive)

The Pentagon news release outlined the upcoming expedition.[52] Destination had changed: instead of Alert, on Ellesmere, the navy would rendezvous with Drift Station Bravo, the air force IGY base riding Ice Island T-3. Adrift in the Canadian sector, the errant slab's encampment was manned by scientists and military personnel. "A Navy blimp will leave from the Naval Air Station, South Weymouth, Massachusetts about July 26, 1958, for a trip which will take her farther north than any U.S. Navy blimp has ever flown."

> This scientific flight will have the primary mission of testing the feasibility of using blimps for future Arctic research. Sponsored by the Office of Naval Research, the airship will travel via Churchill, Manitoba, Canada, and Resolute on Cornwallis Island, Northwest Territories. From there, it will fly to ice island "T-3," the U.S. floating weather station in the Arctic Ocean. Ice Island "T-3" is 45 square miles in area and is floating in the Arctic Ocean. Manned by IGY personnel who are conducting weather, oceanography and other research, the station is now located near 80 degrees north latitude, north of Borden Island of the Queen Elizabeth group. The expedition is under the command of Captain H. B. Van Gorder, USN, Commanding Officer of the Naval Air Development Unit at South Weymouth.
>
> Several scientists will be along on this trip, conducting tests as practicable. However, the testing of the blimp operations themselves remains the primary mission of the flight. The entire flight is not expected to last more than 12 days.
>
> It is hoped that future flights will enable scientists to conduct tests and experiments in the fields of geology, glaciology, meteorology and oceanography. There is an additional possibility that the flight may give an indication of the feasibility of future military operations in the far north in the fields of AEW, ASW, search and rescue, and resupply.
>
> Two Canadian military representatives, Commodore O. C. S. Robertson, RCN, and Wing Commander K. Greenaway, RCAF, will be observers on the trip. Commander Greenaway devised the grid system of navigation now widely used for operations in the Arctic.[53]

A scattering of press reports ensued, most editors electing to give the probe only matter-of-fact coverage on inside pages. Television expressed little if any interest, radio somewhat more. At South Weymouth, time slots were set aside by WBZ Boston for briefings as the mission unfolded. Still, Commander Ricketts remembers, media interest was "minimal."

With full control of the story, the AP decided to include the flight in "the budget"—its list of the day's top ten stories that advises editors as to what's worthy of front-page treatment. "Offbeat news is always prized," Mulligan explains, "and the blimp trip qualified although never as the lead story." On 18 July, the *New York Times* published its first article (on page 11), under the headline "Navy Blimp to Fly to Arctic Isle," datelined Washington, 17 July (AP): "The Navy announced today that a blimp would fly to the Arctic Ocean this month on a combined scientific and military exploratory mission. The blimp will leave the Naval Air Station at South Weymouth, Mass., about July 26. The flight will take about twelve days and carry the lighter-than-air craft within 100 miles of the North Pole. The Arctic goal will be the floating ice island now manned by a group of scientists studying northern waters, ice and weather conditions in connection with the International Geophysical Year."

Primary purpose: to determine the feasibility of using blimps for Arctic-related research. The secondary mission (according to the navy) would be to assess if blimps could be used successfully for antisubmarine warfare in the far North. Deeming it second-order news, the *Times* would print eleven pieces concerning the expedition—each short, and all on the inside pages. The flight led the local Boston news, in contrast. And in the airmen's hometowns, the mission provided good copy for the small-town sheets.

Fifty-one hundred miles from New England, on Oahu, a low, black form eased from berth S-11, Submarine Base Pearl. It was 1958 hours, on 22 July 1958. It was 2000, dusk. As the boat shoved slow ahead, lights on navigation aids danced indolently on a quiet harbor.

As she cleared the entrance channel, the glow of Honolulu eased astern. The maneuvering watch was secured, regular steaming watch set.

The Hawaiian island chain is a stupendous volcanic outpouring, the tallest mountains on earth. The islands rise abruptly off the enclosing sea floor, standing 30,000 feet off the bottom, the highest peaks breaking the surface. To seaward, there is no fringing offshore shelf: the seabed falls away to abyssal ocean.

The final phase of Sunshine was under way. Commander William R. Anderson (Academy class of 1943), thirty-seven, from Tennessee, manned the bridge with his officer of the deck and lookouts. Quiet, dedicated, handsome, imperturbable—Central Casting need search no further for a hero. Imaginative and bold, Anderson had long dreamed to steam fully to the Pole. Risk attends every unknown. In a submarine, risk is proportional to the reliability of the

As senior navigator, Wing Commander Keith R. Greenaway would navigate a U.S. Navy airship into the Arctic Ocean and back. (*The Star Weekly* [Toronto], 21 May 1955)

23 July 1958

FF12/NADU/P16-3/00-1/WH:cag

From: Commanding Officer, Naval Air Development Unit, NAS, South Weymouth 90, Massachusetts
To: LCDR H. D. M. COLLINS, USN, 395833/1310 SOW-17
LCDR Aage J. SCHOU, USN, 391070/1310 SOW-18
LT Harold D. KOZA, USN, 460090/1312 SOW-19
LTJG James F. MALLOY, USNR, 608780/1355 SOW-20

Subj: Temporary additional duty orders

Ref: (a) BUPERS ltr Pers-B114-rek dtd 29 Nov 1957

1. Proceed to the places indicated below for temporary additional duty; this is in addition to your present duties, and upon the completion thereof you will return to your station and resume your regular duties. This temporary duty will be approximately twelve (12) days.

On or about 26 July 1958 proceed to (1) Churchill, Manitoba, Canada; (2) Resolute Bay, N.W.T., Canada; and (3) such other places as may be deemed necessary in connection with the Polar Project.

2. Travel by government air is authorized where available. Class TWO priority is hereby certified.

3. Upon completion of travel you will submit to the NADEVU Administration Office the original and all copies of these orders, all endorsements and a signed travel statement of itinerary and cost of claims. In the event these orders are not utilized, return them immediately to the NADEVU Administration Office.

4. ALLOTTEE. Commanding Officer, Naval Air Development Unit, NAS, South Weymouth, Massachusetts. Cost of this travel is chargeable to appropriation and subhead 17X1319.98 [illegible], object class 022, expenditure account 46014, chargeable activity 101, allotment number 101 524. The estimated cost is $156.00 per diem.

5. Issuance of these orders is authorized by reference (a).

6. You have been granted access to Classified Material up to and including:

LCDR COLLINS - SECRET (BI, 22 Mar 1956)
LCDR SCHOU - SECRET (NAC, 20 Apr 1953)
LT KOZA - SECRET (NAC, 17 Mar 1954)
LTJG MALLOY - SECRET (NAC, 23 Jan 1956)

H. B. VAN GORDER

ORIGINAL

DISB. OFF., USNAS SO. WEYMOUTH, MASS. JUL 25, 1958
PAID TA/ADV PER DIEM $ [illegible] which has been
charged on pay record NPR/ # [illegible] /CWO T. PAJAK, USN /s/

ship and its captain. Anderson had relieved Wilkinson in June 1957. (While still on duty in the Naval Reactors Branch, Anderson had met with Dr. Lyon and McWethy to discuss the feasibility of a try on the Pole.) In the ensuing months, Anderson had won the crew's unqualified respect—"a pleasure to work for," one officer told me.

The ship's executive officer, Lieutenant Commander Frank M. Adams, USN, was Academy class of 1947. (A classmate, Lieutenant James Earl "Jimmy" Carter, would in time also be selected for the Silent Service, en route to a larger responsibility.) Lanky and soft-spoken, Adams, a Mississippian, was seasoned in diesel boats, including USS *Tang* (SS 563), in which he had served with Anderson. *Nautilus*, though, was the lieutenant commander's first nuclear assignment.

Speed increased, America's largest submarine (319 feet) surged forward on surface run. Below, the team of engineers under Lieutenant Commander Paul Early monitored the vitals of this superb machine. The propulsion plant and auxiliary equipment were performing perfectly, all within tolerances.

The echo sounder pinged a dipping line: the seabed's plunge. A wide turn was made to starboard, to round Oahu through Kauai Channel. As the boat steamed northeast, seamen painted out the identifying numbers on the sail.

Ample water beneath, the conning officer was told he could clear the bridge. The rasping "Aaa-*oooo*-guh, Aaa-*oooo*-guh" of the diving klaxon reverberated throughout the hull, followed by the hiss of escaping air. As ballast tanks filled, and with increasing negative buoyancy, the boat assumed a gentle down-by-the-bow angle. *Nautilus* began to settle. At 2321 she nosed under, only a dying swirl left to betray her presence. The boat was slowed for a good trim, after which full speed was ordered: 22.5 knots. His command rigged for deep submergence, Anderson took her to test depth to check for leaks, then rose to three hundred feet, cruising depth. The boat came to course 343° true.

[Opposite] Temporary additional duty orders to Lt. Cdr. Aage Schou, USN—one of five pilots assigned to the ONR-sponsored evaluation. (Schou Papers)

This was no ordinary operation; "Bill" Anderson was a man preoccupied. His mission, he told me, was one "that had to succeed." Failure, he added, was "not a part of my contingency planning." Ship's crew—each man handpicked—was no less determined. Concerning Operation Sunshine, Engineman William Furholm was to remark, "There was not a soul on board who visualized failure."

In that part of consciousness reserved for anxieties, however, the crew *was* accompanied by genuine doubt and tension. Shallow ice-prone sea interposed, all knew, between them and the deepwater Polar Basin.

As he stood out, Anderson had in mind his recent too-early, straight-across approach. Shallow water and deep-draft ice had scuttled transit of the central Chukchi—and had nearly trapped the boat. Sonar had traced sinister profiles: hanging keels of deformed ice. As if to pinch the boat in a hideous vise, sea room had narrowed alarmingly. One ridge had hung halfway to the bottom, with *Nautilus'* fathometer showing 162 feet of water. Had the boat become wedged, one submariner's terror would have acquired a tragic reality.

The image did little to relieve inner tension. "I felt," Anderson confided, "there was a wee better than a fifty-fifty chance of getting through the tricky part of the trip. But by no means did I feel we had a 100 per cent chance. In leaving Pearl, I was a fella relying very heavily on the Almighty."

Still, the commander held excellent assets. Among his resources: the world's best ship and crew. "I had everything going for me that any skipper could ever want."[54] His officers and men were expert in interpreting the ice picture on the various sonars, thereby able to weave between and around thickened, deformed ice.

Anderson had further assets as well. The Pacific approach to the Arctic Ocean would be made in summer, a season for which the navy held chart (and at least incomplete ice) information—courtesy of the Hydrographic Office and other sources.[55] The probability of clear water to the hundred-fathom curve during August stood high. Further, ice reports now were encouraging: air reconnaissance had the rim of the polar pack retreating farther each day.

Next landfall: the Alaska Peninsula. Swept by winds and fog, the Aleutian chain—a volcanic mountain belt—is the longest archipelago of small islands on earth. Immediately north is the Bering Sea, with its slot to the Chukchi, thence deep water—and the geographic pole.

No one has a sorrier lot than the weather-man. He is ignored when he is right, and execrated when he is wrong.
—Isaac Asimov

False Starts 4

Concluding an overnight run from Ottawa, the train conveying Wing Commander Keith R. Greenaway, RCAF, clattered through Boston's drowsy suburbs. South Weymouth is a short drive; by late morning, the Canadian officer reached the naval air station. It is 24 July 1958. An oppressive summer heat had enveloped the northeastern United States.

Formalities done, the Canadian officer was waved on board. Greenaway is a few days early. Departure for Arctic Canada, he knows, is set for the 27th—three days hence. As yet, the airman has no clear indication of his exact role in the upcoming operation by NADU command.

He met with Captain Van Gorder; introductions to his prospective shipmates followed. This day was spent with a NADU crew and support personnel, going over operational plans. Greenaway had no direct experience with airships, so his early arrival was welcome—and something of a surprise. "This lead time was even more appreciated," he would recall, "when advised by Captain Van Gorder on arrival that they were counting heavily on me to assist with the navigation."

Climbing on board, the wing commander checked out BUNO 126719 and its systems. An introductory flight followed, next day. Modifications, he realized, were in order. "I had two interests," he said of preflight planning. "Not only to see that we had the right equipment aboard, but also I wanted some experience . . . so I'd have some feel for the airship. And they were very good to give me that. From my point of view, the cooperation couldn't have been better down there."

At one of his recommendations, a maintenance crew installed a switch in the gyromagnetic compass: by cutting out magnetic "slaving," the directional gyroscope could operate "free," that is, independent of the magnetic field. This would be critical beyond Fort Churchill, in northern Manitoba, where magnetic headings become unreliable. "Once we got to Churchill," Lieutenant Commander Schou later told me, "we had to literally forget our magnetic compasses."

Further, an N-1 gyro system was installed as backup. (The merit of this change would become plain over Hudson Bay.) At that time, the N-1 was among the best gyro-based compass systems available. But it required an external reference to maintain a heading. And since much of this upcoming operation would be flown in continuous light, the astro compass (which uses the

[Opposite] NAS South Weymouth, July 1958. Here BUNO 126719 is being modified for operations near the north magnetic pole—notably its compass systems. The pattern applied to ship's bow is to enhance recognition in Arctic airspace. (ATC Frederick L. Parker)

sun as the arbiter of direction) was the answer. "During the summer months with the long hours of daylight, the sun plays an important part in navigation and must always be taken into consideration when planning flights into the Arctic. When above the horizon, it is the only celestial body available for navigation, with the exception of the moon at certain times."[1]

At Greenaway's direction, four astro compass mounts were installed along the control car: two forward and two aft. The search radar—a primary navigation aid—was "very modern," as good as that on any plane. Ship's radar and drift meter required no alteration.

719 had flown a twelve-hour maintenance and test flight on the 17th, Lieutenant Koza in the left seat. As first pilot and maintenance officer, Koza was responsible for mission preparations. On 25 July, fully loaded, *719* was again aloft—to familiarize the Canadian officer and the entire aircrew with a maximum-heavy ship.

As NADU readied for departure, philatelists reacted—sending in envelopes for special-flight cachet. Altogether, about three hundred pieces of mail would be put on board. One bag held round-trip items: having attended the flight South Weymouth to South Weymouth, its contents returned to collectors.

As preparations concluded in Massachusetts, *Explorer IV* was flung into orbit—its payload a contribution to the International Geophysical Year.

Boston-area press now headlined the expedition. "Weymouth—Arctic Flight Set for Start Tomorrow Night," one newspaper reported; "Flight from Weymouth to Blaze Trail for Blimp Operations in Arctic Area," another declared. The expedition promised the first penetration of the Arctic by an American airship—and the first ever via blimp. Few editors beyond the immediate Boston area would grant the flight more than passing attention, however.

A day or two prior to liftoff, the media were briefed, Van Gorder officiating. Emphasizing that the flight was no "stunt" or attempt to set records, the thirty-seven-year-old NADU commander explained that portable masts, support equipment, and personnel had been sent ahead. "This is," he outlined, "a routine airship flight to investigate the feasibility of using the airship for arctic research." The blimp would gather data for both military and scientific purposes. As for its destination, the ice-island base floated six hundred miles from the North Pole and a thousand miles inside the Arctic Circle. Most of the scientific work, he continued, would be conducted en route to T-3. Upon rendezvous, mail and scientific equipment would be dropped to the encampment. Would he land? That was uncertain but unlikely. The mission, the captain added, was "not directly connected" with the International Geophysical Year, although its results would have a role in IGY research.

When questioned, Wing Commander Greenaway—an affable, handsome man looking quite at home in a flight suit—noted that navigation posed special problems. As of the north *magnetic* pole (within the archipelago a hundred miles from Resolute) a conventional magnetic compass was unreliable. "We have to steer by a free gyro compass monitored by celestial observation." And, since all meridians merge at the geographic pole, ship's navigators would be obliged to rely on a special grid system in order to track position across the charts.

The international aspect of the expedition, the fact of Ottawa's "full co-operation," was spurring interest. Navigational duties would be shared by Greenaway and Lieutenant Malloy. The wing commander, reporters learned, had devised the grid system then in wide use in polar

air navigation. "This grid [one paper explained] operates in areas where the magnetic compass is either extremely erratic or weak. In fact, the north magnetic pole is actually south of the expedition destination."

In an editorial, the *Boston Traveler* sounded a nostalgic note: "In this age of rocketry, satellites and lost nosecones—with *Explorer IV* the latest conqueror of gravity—the blimp's expedition seems sort of simple and comforting. . . . We wish the blimp Godspeed and for its crew the wisdom to determine what is 'feasible' for such craft."[2]

Into Canada—Briefly

Sunday, 27 July 1958, dawned cool and damp over Boston. Fog was likely. The day passed in final loading of the aircraft, in farewells, and in monitoring the all-important weather, particularly air temperatures. By early evening, the thermometer had sagged into the upper seventies. In preparation for takeoff, *719* had been towed onto the mat through the west doors of the station's steel hangar. Onlookers saw that the emerging bow had acquired an eye-shocking orange.

[Right] Food, supplies, and personal effects are shunted on board *719*. The bulge beneath the 83-foot-long car houses ship's radar. Note the size of the aircraft. (AD1 Elmer B. Lord)

[Opposite] Early evening, 27 July 1958: a mobile mast tows *719* onto the apron at South Weymouth. Takeoff will await lower air temperatures. (ATC Frederick L. Parker)

No flight crew was yet on board. Liftoff would await more agreeable temperatures. The twilight deepened. The thermometer—heedless of human ambition—eased a reluctant decline. Scattered fog was reported. In hangar spaces, last-minute matters were concluded. A sense of quiet excitement was pervasive: the mission was about to embark for an extreme, alien realm—airspace unique in U.S. lighter-than-air aeronautics.

The airmen made ready. For the officers, uniform of the day was lightweight flying suits, for most of the enlisted complement more informal dungarees. Suited up and ready, they walked to their ship, swinging to its mooring on the mat. At about 2100, the blimp's aircrew began to board.

Via ship's ladder, the men filed up through the nose-wheel well. Inside, Collins and Koza moved to the flight deck, the others to their takeoff positions aft. Forward, Collins eased into the portside seat. A diminutive man, he slid his seat forward, adjusted height, strapped on its belt. To his right, first pilot Koza settled in. Donning headsets, both pilots connected into the ICS (intercommunications system). In the after compartments, the crew commenced their own preflight checks. The spaces along the eighty-three-foot-long car began to hum—the elaborate, quiet intensity of professional flying.

Van Gorder would not accompany the first leg. Still, he fretted through the preflight. "I felt," he later explained, "the project did not need me aboard until we got to Churchill. Departing South Weymouth would be just a long flight which could be handled by the flight crew." NADU would stay in contact—"fortunately or unfortunately, I'm not sure which," he added, chuckling. The captain would board in Canada.

The flight deck of the ZPG-2, by aviation standards, was spacious. In multiengine military planes, cockpits tend to be tiny compartments fitted with stingy windows. Here, the pilot and copilot occupied a veritable solarium. Ahead and around, five-foot Plexiglas panels extended from the deck to the overhead. Farther back, along each side, windowlike panels reached aft to the first bulkhead. Visibility from each position: superb. On the starboard side, behind the copilot, a small "jump seat" was built in. Here the aircraft commander sat out of the way yet able to confer

Flight crew and their ship, 27 July. Front row, l. to r.: Francis M. Hughes, electronics mate (AT1); Frederick L. Parker, chief aviation electronics technician (ATC) and crew chief; William H. Eels, aviation electronics technician (AT1); Rudolph J. Cabral, aviation electrician (AEM3); Elmer B. Lord, aviation machinist's mate ("first mech"); James P. Quinn, aviation structural mechanic ("first rigger"). Second row: Lt. Cdr. Henry D. Collins, command pilot; Lt. Cdr. Aage J. Schou, pilot; Wing Commander Keith R. Greenaway, RCAF, senior navigator; Lt. Harold A. Koza, pilot; Lt. (jg) James F. Malloy, navigator; George Kalnin, pilot (AC1); Floyd W. Johnson, aviation machinist's mate ("second mech"); William H. Dunlevy, aviation structural mechanic ("second rigger"). Capt. Van Gorder and Commodore O. C. S. Robertson, RCN, met the aircraft at Lakehead Airport, Ontario. The accompanying scientists along with Hugh Mulligan, of the Associated Press, met the ship at Resolute. (ATC Frederick L. Parker)

easily with his pilots as he monitored mission progress. Between the forward seats but slightly aft, a moveable stool was used by crewmen coming forward to confer. Normally exploited by the flight engineer when he was not aft on his rounds, it was used by most visitors forward.

Airship handling is exacting. Trim, angles of attack, power settings: these and a myriad of related factors are instinctively integrated by all who press aloft in powered craft. Unlike the airplane, however, an airship is exquisitely sensitive to its medium. A blimp is a balloon plus engines. Airships are analogous to submarines; the fundamentals of operation are similar, as both are submerged—afloat—in a fluid. Pilots must be intimate with the complex physical laws that govern static condition and aerodynamic control. Atmospheric temperature, for example, is of scant consequence to a speeding plane but crucial for the plodding airship, because it defines lift. "Normal airship handling," Schou emphasizes, "is a constant battle with Charles' and Boyle's Laws"—equations describing the fundamental properties of gases.

Still, flight controls of the ZPG-2 resembled those of an airplane. There was a control column and wheel, duplicated at both seats; each was manipulated by a yoke that incorporated both the elevator (altitude) and rudder controls. (Historically, two pilots had been required—the senior man on the elevators, copilot on the rudders. One-man control, introduced with the N-ship, simplified handling.) An array of standard flight instruments were presented, along with several peculiar to airships.[3]

The panels were granted a knowing scan, after which Collins and Koza commenced their checks of gauges, indicators, switches, levers, lights. As well, the panels at their sides and the console between them were checked. All systems normal, preflight routines continued.

Aft, the crew ran their checks. The navigator, for example, ensured that his equipment and supplies were on hand and that the armament switches were set to "off," and he set his clocks. All power switches were set to "off," and all circuit breakers on his panel were closed.

Crew complement was fourteen, allotted to eight stations. A command pilot, first pilot, and copilot flew the aircraft;[4] a navigator, ASW plot officer, radio operator, radar operator, and ECM (electronic countermeasures) operator occupied stations in the large ASW compartment behind the flight deck. This was no fleet operation; the ASW station this evening was unoccupied.

In the glare of floodlights, a ground crew took up position. On hand were family members plus a handful of photographers and media representatives, including an Associated Press photographer from the Boston bureau. The media glanced at their watches, checked equipment, killed time. A nighttime takeoff was an inconvenience; now, thanks to fog, departure stood delayed ninety minutes.

On the apron, the ground handling officer (GHO) had taken up station ahead and slightly to starboard; here he could maintain visual contact with the pilots. Preflight preparations concluded, the two Wright engines barked to life. The sudden throb reverberated in the heavy air—a deep, throaty rhythm characteristic of the model.

At about 2200 EDT, the mooring mast began to move.

Collins kept his eye on the GHO, who was walking alongside. Until the ship was released, primary responsibility for its safety rested with the GHO. This man's duties were comparable to those of any marine pilot. Near port, ship's masters typically defer to the pilot's ship handling—and to his knowledge of the vagaries of the waters they are transiting. In LTA, Collins was similarly dependent. The GHO orchestrated the awkward ground-handling ballet: the men grouped on the lines, atop the mast, and on the two ground-handling "mules"—self-propelled winches assisting ground operations.

Pulled by the bow, *719* was shunted to the point of takeoff. As the assembly of men and equipment advanced, Collins and the GHO exchanged hand signals over idling propellers.

After ten or so minutes the tractor and mast was in position—into the wind at the southwest end of the northeast–southwest runway. Departure would be to the northeast. On board, final checks concluded. All was ready. The station tower (in contact throughout) granted clearance.

The GHO assured himself that the runway was clear and that the nose wheel was down and locked. He signaled his satisfaction. Collins, also ready, gave *his* signal. The airship was cast off. Alongside, the "mules" retained their grip, holding *719* into the wind, engines just turning over. At 2232, Collins gave the sign. The GHO signaled "Release," the lines were let go. The throttles advanced. Inertia had the big ship hesitating before, slowly, it edged forward.

The Polar Project was under way.

Departure had been chosen to exploit lower evening temperatures; cooler air would allow more helium to be pushed on board. Every cubic foot was needed. The aircraft was ten thousand pounds "heavy" (well over maximum gross), mandating a long, rolling takeoff.

Collins let most of the runway slide by. "We intended to use most of it," Schou told me. "We did." The pilots were exploiting the dynamic lift inherent to ship's envelope: a crude airfoil, it augmented the static lift.

As *719* drove down the runway like a plane, Collins held a slight "down elevator": this kept the bow from rising abruptly and allowed buildup of airspeed while holding his ship on the wheels. "We *had* to get some airspeed and dynamic lift," Schou explains, "to get airborne." The pilots concentrated on trim and speed. The runway end was closing. Max load at last carried dynamically, Collins eased his wheel—and the deck dropped away.

Fourteen are on board this humid evening: five officers and nine enlisted men. Destination: Fort Churchill, in the subarctic of Manitoba, an old Hudson's Bay Company settlement. Estimated flying time for 1,100 miles: about thirty-six hours.

> South Weymouth, Mass., July 27 (AP)—A Navy blimp eased its way into an overcast sky tonight on the first leg of an anticipated 2-day flight that is expected to take it farther north than ever penetrated by a nonrigid airship. The giant blimp is scheduled to carry its research to within 100 miles of the North Pole. It took off at 9:32 p.m. (EST).
>
> The no. 1 job of the flight is to explore the possibilities of using such craft for Arctic research.
>
> The blimp plans to fly to ice island "T-3," this country's floating weather station in the Arctic Ocean.
>
> Its trip will take it by way of Churchill, Manitoba, and Resolute on Cornwallis Island, Northwest Territory.[5]

Climbing away, *719* assumed a westerly heading. The aircraft was struggling. The pilots leveled off at three hundred feet—well below their assigned altitude. Cruising speed: thirty-five to forty knots. The airship plodded out of the traffic-control area, the night glare of metropolitan Boston fading astern.

Flight plan: west to the Hudson Valley in New York State, then along the river path to Albany, thence the Mohawk Valley to Lake Ontario. Interposing, however, is the higher terrain of central and western Massachusetts.

Minutes out, visual contact with the ground was lost. The airmen were meeting widespread, low-hanging fog. And the air temperature was higher than expected. The forecast had misled them.

The first crisis (already) was at hand. Its cause: the temperature.

As the ship climbed to its assigned altitude, elevated air temperatures enveloped it. This had not been forecast. Typically, atmospheric temperature *declines,* and at a more or less predictable rate—about five degrees per thousand feet. The pilots had flown into an inversion—a thin layer of air warmer than that near the ground. The fog was largely a nuisance. In light of the airship's very heavy condition, however, the inversion was cruelly inopportune. When every pound of lift was needed, the ship was *losing* buoyancy.

Schou on the iron laws of aerostatics: "Immediately after take-off we discovered we were involved in a temperature inversion and therefore the helium—the safety valves—on the envelope were automatically "popping" [as they are designed to do]. In other words, [he continued], we were losing helium as a result of the increased temperature as well as the decrease in [atmospheric] pressure as we climbed. That's why we leveled off at 300 feet—we couldn't make it to a thousand—we were just losing too much lift."[6]

Lighter-than-air flight blends conventional airplane handling with a nuanced understanding of ballooning. The conditions besetting the pilots illustrate.

The aircraft was *very* heavy: indeed, static weight exceeded the recommended maximum. (A waiver had been granted.) In the hours before takeoff, Koza had twice taken advantage of lowering temperatures to push aboard additional lift. The one-million-cubic-foot envelope was near to full inflation. But the rise in temperature was expanding the helium. Where was it to go? Normally, ship's ballonets were used to compensate. They were air-filled fabric chambers along the underside of the "bag," used for trim (in effect, the trim tabs) and to control envelope pressure. By deflating them, the pilot freed internal volume. But in this instance, for all practical purposes the ballonets were already deflated.[7] When internal pressure rose, and with no spare volume to occupy, the automatics opened, sending helium—and its precious lift—"overboard."

Maintaining envelope pressure was (and remains) a basic operational requirement. An airship's pressure-control system maintains a prescribed differential between helium and atmosphere—while skillful pilots minimize loss of lift. Normally, the center ballonet of a ZPG-2 was set to a predetermined pressure—thereby relieving pilots of managing internal pressure. But with the center unit largely deflated, the ability to meet certain in-flight situations was absent. And with the fore and aft ballonets "flat," the aircraft could not be trimmed.

The pilots' headaches did not end there. The ballonet system is fundamental to pressure control. Since atmospheric pressure changes during flight (in response to changes in temperature and altitude), the ballonets compensate: internal air is valved when the helium expands, pumped in when it contracts.[8] A nonrigid *must* maintain its shape—for aerodynamic reasons and to ensure proper distribution of the loads imposed by the control car. The envelope, literally, is a structural element of the aircraft.

Further tangles: a blimp is said to be "heavy" when gross *weight* exceeds gross *lift*. A heavy ship requires extra power. To maintain altitude, Collins was flying up by the bow, to gain dynamic lift, thereby easing static heaviness. As the blimp pressed westward, the weather did not improve. "We were losing lift and getting heavier and heavier," Schou remembered, "to the point where the engines, with max continuous power, could just barely hold it." One penalty: fuel consumption. The rate would not ease until the temperature dropped or sufficient fuel had been burned off to help lighten ship.

Soon after departure, South Weymouth radioed that visibility had deteriorated below minimum. The ship was committed.

Calculations were made, a decision taken. If conditions did not improve during the next twelve or so hours, the fuel reserve margin of safety would drop below an acceptable minimum, ruling out Churchill.

Course was altered south, to the coast. Open water would deliver lower temperatures and less fog. The aircraft could then loiter just east of Long Island Sound under New York radar control until morning, then, if necessary, follow the water west to New York and the Hudson River.

An hour or so out, *719* reached the greater Providence area, then pressed south-southwest along Rhode Island's Narragansett Bay, passing west of Newport. The coast was crossed near Point Judith. Block Island Sound was shrouded in fog when, at about midnight, Collins turned his command toward Long Island Sound.

The pilots conferred with South Weymouth as to their options—and quietly cursed the temperature as the automatics still "popped" helium overboard.

NADU had planned to reach Canadian airspace in about eight hours, Churchill in thirty-six. Now it might not even escape the Northeast. About two hours out, Schou contacted New York approach radar control, requesting permission to proceed west, to the harbor, thence north—up the Hudson. Air traffic control was not about to oblige. Some of its radars were down: commercial traffic was stacked over the metropolitan area. With three major airports and smaller fields to satisfy, the navy was told to wait. Koza advised New York Approach of the navy's on-board radar, that *719* on its own could loiter clear of inbound/outbound traffic. "We were still refused passage." The lieutenant commander acknowledged.

A "hold" commenced over eastern Long Island Sound. Assuming a wide circle, the blimp would orbit lazily, as if forgotten, for the next five hours.

On the flight deck, the pilots were dim silhouettes against the glow of panel lights. Quiet comments and radio chatter blended with the snore of the engines reverberating along the car. Forward, it was a steady, almost humming vibration; in the engine compartment, the two radial engines hammered inside their cowlings hardly six feet apart. An occasional figure (usually the flight engineer on his hourly rounds) shuttled in with some business or to chat, or climbed topside. At the navigator's station, Greenaway and Malloy monitored their progress via radar, providing position reports when requested by traffic control.

Lieutenant Koza was a qualified airborne radar controller. That night, he expended a bit of off-duty time observing the night traffic in their general area. He "secured the radar around 0430 hours and helped make breakfast," he would recall.

Shortly after 0530, the eastern quadrant began to pale. On board, a tired disappointment was evident. But Collins and Koza (Schou's relief) were outwardly relaxed—a natural, easy manner these professionals were to display throughout the mission. Topic of the hour: alternate airfields. Churchill had been ruled out. In light of the temperature and static heaviness, the pilots could not hope to press up the Hudson at a thousand feet. Permission to traverse the city had not been granted, anyway.

This was maddening: north of Poughkeepsie, sixty miles upriver, visibility was good. But fog, cloud, and high temperatures blanketed New York City and vicinity. Fog had played havoc with other aircraft as well: helicopters on a ferry flight from the Sikorsky plant in Bridgeport, Connecticut, had been forced down.

At daylight, the decision was taken: divert to Lakehurst, about fifty miles from New York. Air station conditions were reported acceptable. There *719* would refuel and get minor maintenance, including repair of an inoperative compass. As well, Lakehurst offered a low-altitude approach to the Hudson. At about 0930, *719* arrived over the naval air station in steady drizzle.

Contrary to the rushed arrival of planes, an airship returns to earth almost reluctantly. A Boeing 707 lands at about 125 knots and requires a six-thousand-foot runway.[9] In navy LTA, standard practice was to land about two to four hundred pounds heavy, touching down and rolling out with just enough power for control. This morning, despite dumping fuel, *719* would log a very heavy landing.

Lakehurst's steel hangar dominates the local pine and scrub oak—it is the tallest structure for miles. The "barn" in sight, checks concluded, the aircrew assumed landing stations. The pilots' checklist (more than two dozen items) included computation of static heaviness. This was accomplished via "weigh-off"—that is, a turn into the wind, after which power was eased off. The airspeed at which the decelerating ship settled or rose defined static condition, hence optimum landing speed.

On approach and on signal, Koza pulled a handle, extending and locking the tricycle landing gear. Slowing to fifteen knots, the pilots made a gradual descent. In light of ship's static condition, theirs would be a fast landing.

Leveling off just above the mat, Collins retarded his throttles slightly—and *719* stalled down. Aloft for twelve and a half hours, a linear distance of 242 statute miles had been flown. Average ground speed: forty miles per hour. At 0950 EST, throttles in reverse, handling lines well in hand, on the mat but not yet moored, Collins and Koza continued to "fly" the ship, holding bow into a light breeze so as to assist the ground handlers.

On final approach, an absurd figure was noted amid the ground crew, wearing red. A "North Pole" sign in hand, Santa Claus was pointing north.

> Lakehurst, N.J., July 28 (AP)—The "flying sausage" Navy exploration blimp, was tucked away in a hangar today [she was, in fact, not docked], waiting for a break in the weather to start a trip to the North Pole.
>
> The navy said the blimp may not get into the air again until tomorrow morning.
>
> The 343-foot aircraft took off at South Weymouth, Mass., last night in what it hoped would be a flight to Churchill, Canada. But bad weather forced it to detour to the naval air station here.
>
> Destination of the ZPG-2 type blimp is the ice island known as T-3, a floating weather station in the Arctic Ocean. A crew of 14 and scientists of the International Geophysical Year are making the trip to do arctic research.
>
> If the expedition is a success, the blimp will be the first Navy airship to fly over the North Pole.

Ship secured to it, the mast was towed to a mooring-out circle. There *719* would swing to its mooring like a ship at anchor. A pressure watch climbed on board (to relieve the flight crew), and the latter disembarked.

The Polar Project at NAS Lakehurst, 28 July—a two-day layover. Note the sandbag ballast on the control car and open hatch, amidships. At this moment *Nautilus* is approaching the Bering Strait, the Pacific Ocean approach to the Arctic Basin. (U.S. Navy)

Refueling and replenishment commenced. The troublesome compass was unshipped for repair ashore, Greenaway assisting. The aircrew messed, then rested. Still, the weather charts and forecast had to be monitored: a drop in temperature would dictate departure.

This watch on the weather lengthened to almost forty-eight hours. Assisted by station personnel, the duty crew busied itself about the ship. Ashore, meanwhile, paperwork and various duties awaited. Naval messages as well as personal communications passed between Lakehurst and the Boston area. And both Washington and the CNO were advised.

As the layover extended, the station's officers club hummed with the chatter of professional airmen. A new subject was dissected around the bar: navy airships and the Arctic.

A good story had dropped in. Lieutenant Commander Schou, for one, was interviewed by the *Minneapolis Star*. (After all, a Minnesotan was copiloting the first navy airship ordered to the Arctic.) "The blimp offers a very stable platform," the thirty-four-year-old told the folks back home. "We're trying to prove that it is an ideal ship for operations which would contribute to exploration in the Arctic." He outlined the itinerary: Lakehurst to Fort Churchill thence to Resolute, 1,100 miles farther north. There the blimp would sortie for T-3. "We will not land on the island but will drop things of a scientific nature to personnel of the International Geophysical Year who are stationed there," the officer explained. The newspaper offered a crash course on the capabilities of naval airships and offered a review of its creature comforts: two decks for messing and sleeping, a five-hundred-pound "deep freeze" (in fact, a refrigerator-freezer), storage space for four hundred pounds of food, an electric range, "and a pilot's compartment like the crew cabin of a commercial airliner."[10]

Except for the miscreant compass, Greenaway had no navigating to do. He used the time to study ship's manuals and to look around.

Dominating the field is Hangar No. 1. Completed in 1921, for a time it was the largest single room in the world. *Shenandoah,* the navy's first commissioned rigid, had been erected inside. From the same field where *719* now vaned lazily, each of the navy's rigid airships had operated. And commercial airships had called, *Graf Zeppelin* first. Its transatlantic crossing in 1928 had been among that year's biggest stories. Ten of the twenty passengers who had disembarked had paid for their crossing—the first-ever transatlantic airfares.

And 1936 had reestablished Lakehurst as an international airport. *Hindenburg* had inaugurated regular transatlantic mail, freight, and passengers. The zeppelin had arrived then departed for Frankfurt ten times between May and October. When travel by plane was still a noisy adventure, *Graf Zeppelin* and *Hindenburg* were pioneering the transoceanic air service.

Those airships now were anachronisms. Still, the big ships flew on in the memories of former crewmen, many of whom were naval station employees.

High temperatures and humidity blanketed the East Coast. And the forecast held scant promise. On the 29th, daytime temperatures refused to dip below the mid-eighties. A tolerable forecast for 30 July sponsored a ray of optimism: if the temperatures eased as predicted and the gradient held, Churchill would be possible.

The crew awakened early: takeoff had been set for 0100. Minor engine trouble brought delay. At 0620, 30 July, the horizon crimson with promise, *719* took departure.

> Lakehurst, N.J., July 30 (AP)—a Navy blimp took off from here today on a historic, lighter-than-air flight to the North Pole.
>
> The 343-foot blimp rose into the morning sky at 6:20 a.m. about as gracefully as a blimp can rise and pointed its prow northward.
>
> It will follow the Hudson River and is scheduled to land in Churchill, Canada, late tomorrow night. . . .
>
> So far, however, the huge craft has been dogged by lighter-than-air gremlins.
>
> Foul weather delayed its departure from South Weymouth, Mass., until Sunday night. The following day, rough weather and a temperature inversion—warm air at a high altitude—forced the blimp to set down at the air station here.

An operational unit of the U.S. Navy, the aircraft kept the department informed of its location and progress. As *719* pulled away, a situation report ("sitrep," in naval parlance) was transmitted to the appropriate commands and agencies.[11]

Naval messages are more cryptic than, say, copy from the wire services. The transmission: "Airship Arctic flt X Sitrep two X Navy airship BUNO 126719 Dept Lakehurst 301020Z for Fort Churchill Canada X ETA 40 plus 00 hrs." This line is a masterpiece of compressed information. Its shorthand fleshed out, this told the Atlantic Fleet and other commands on the distribution list, "This is the second situation report for the Arctic airship flight. The U.S. Navy's airship

Under way for Arctic Canada. (Cdr. A. J. Schou)

Bureau Number 126719 departed the Naval Air Station, Lakehurst, New Jersey, on 30 July, 1020 Greenwich mean time ["Zulu" time], for Fort Churchill, Canada. The aircraft's estimated time of arrival after takeoff is forty hours."

Position reports would be transmitted about every six hours throughout the mission.

Malloy's course was nearly due north. The temperature hovered in the sixties. Visibility: excellent. To the east, the glinting surface of the Atlantic arched away to a flaming horizon.

Lakehurst eased astern. The blimp cruised over the coastal plain of east-central New Jersey—a low, sandy terrain extending fully to the curve of Sandy Hook and the magnificent harbor that is New York.

Back at South Weymouth, a telephone briefing by Commander Max Ricketts, NADU executive officer, had reached the papers. Sea ice, he explained, melts during the brief polar summer, making conventional landings difficult. A blimp, however, can hover or drop vertically onto its wheels; no runway is required. A helicopter also can do this, he admitted, but a blimp can hang aloft for fifty hours—something no helicopter can do. The advantages, the officer advised, "are obvious." "Washington," he continued, "wondered what would be the problems of logistics involved in maintaining a blimp in the Arctic. They wanted to know the feasibility of using blimps for Arctic research. Besides, they could be a valuable asset to the DEW [early warning] line." The advantage, Ricketts concluded, might come from not "having to keep all your eggs in one basket."[12]

Lakehurst less than an hour astern, the coast was crossed near Sandy Hook—a barrier island at the approach to the port of New York. The airship pierced the Narrows, the sea door to the Upper Bay.

The harbor spread wide across the windows. Liberty Island, then Ellis Island, came abeam, slid aft. The spires of Manhattan were abeam at 0700, the Hudson below. Geologically, this superb port is a "drowned" estuary swallowed by the sea-level rise attending the last deglaciation.

The blimp droned upriver. Portside, the Palisades walled in the river's west bank. The parapet appears much as it did when Henry Hudson sailed these waters.[13] Ahead, the catenary of the George Washington Bridge eased from the haze.

Altitude: barely eight hundred feet off the water. Collins was staying low, to conserve helium. (The gas expands with increasing altitude.) On occasion, the cliffs framing the river seemed higher than the ship. The Tappan Zee Bridge was crossed. Here the Hudson River is wide, its valley magnificent. The pilots, Greenaway remembers, "just lifted it over the bridges."

Not long after, West Point lay to port. Visibility: good. By 0840, the blimp had reached Poughkeepsie; about ninety minutes later the crew had Albany below. Here the pilots abandoned the Hudson to follow the Mohawk River and its valley. At about 1020, *719* advised South Weymouth of its position: twenty miles west of Schenectady. The expedition hung above Utica a bit more than an hour later. From Utica a heading was taken almost due north. Next landfall: Watertown, near the shore of Lake Ontario.

Now air temperatures again were confounding. The mercury had climbed, obliging the pilots to valve helium, so as to stay within pressure limits of the ballonets. Lieutenant Koza had checked valving time, that is, the corresponding volume (and lift) lost overboard. The results proved worrisome, as did the fuel log. Despite burn-off, the aircraft was *still at takeoff gross weight*. Throttles set to max power (to maintain altitude) abused the engines; moreover, the demand gulped fuel at an unacceptable rate.

At about 1300, over the St. Lawrence near the town of Kingston, *719* penetrated Canadian (Ontario) airspace.

Here the St. Lawrence is wide, crowded with islands. Crossing very low, the ship droned in over the Kingston waterfront. Collins intended to steam north, to the Ottawa Valley, then upriver fully to the Hudson Bay lowland of northwest Ontario and eastern Manitoba.

Time in Canada proved brief. The press had the ship fighting "rugged head winds," when in fact it was in a high-pressure cell with practically *no* wind. The problem was—as it had been—elevated air temperatures. A safe reserve of fuel was vanishing. A request for weather info brought nothing to ease the strain: high temperatures were expected to persist.

The visitor crept across town. "The blimp," according to the *Kingston Whig-Standard*, "was given a relatively close inspection by Kingston citizens as it flew over the city at almost rooftop level about 2:15 p.m."

The navy struggled inland about twenty miles, by which time, to conserve helium, the airship was on the treetops. On the flight deck, the manometer levels ("You're checking your manometers all the time") indicated excessive ballonet pressure. Short on inland experience in such temperatures, the crew had not been anticipated the heat's impact. "We were flying the ship off the performance charts," Greenaway would recall. All calculations had showed that Churchill was a feasible objective in *normal* air. "In retrospect," Van Gorder conceded, "I should have realized the possibility of higher temperatures and the inability to have enough lift to carry enough fuel to make the trip all the way to Churchill. I should have elected to refuel, probably at Akron [in Ohio]." When Greenaway was queried in later years, he was philosophical: "This was," he said, "a developmental exercise, so you expect things to happen."

Collins was reassessing. As command pilot, he was responsible for the safety of ship and crew. He conferred with his crew and with the captain back at South Weymouth. Should they persist or instead abort to an alternate? And if so, which one? Collins re-reviewed the operational situation: he was losing helium, fuel usage had climbed beyond acceptable limits, and the rate was not about to drop. Churchill was hours from their position—and well away from any other field having facilities to receive an airship.

Inclined to press on, Collins knew the mission was riding on his judgment as on-scene commander; the decision was his. His face—young, almost boyish—betrayed little of the pressure which, now, was his alone. Outwardly relaxed, the lieutenant commander assessed his information, weighed his options.

He elected to turn west, to seek out more agreeable over-water temperatures. South Weymouth was advised. "Higher and higher power settings," Greenaway wrote, "had to be used as the lift capability was reduced. This raised fuel consumption beyond acceptable limits and made it impossible to reach Churchill."[14] To press on posed an unacceptable risk: the safety margin was too narrow. Continuing, Collins remarked, "just wasn't worth the chance."

An airplane can land for servicing almost anywhere; a blimp, in contrast, needs a mooring mast, along with a generous supply of manpower (for ground handling) and helium. Which alternates had facilities? Suitable airfields were few and scattered. "The one at South Weymouth and the other at Brunswick, Maine," Greenaway remarked, "meant backtracking and going over mountains in the case of Brunswick; whereas Akron was relatively close by, surrounded by low ground and the route to Churchill was excellent."[15]

Decision: divert to Akron airport—to Goodyear. From northeast Ohio the expedition could follow water into Canada. Van Gorder was advised, Akron contacted. Collins received clearance to proceed.

Van Gorder summarized a frustrating day: "On 30 July," the NADU CO would report, "departure was taken for Churchill, but again high temperatures, turbulence, and terrain clearance altitudes resulted in unacceptable helium losses. The flight diverted to Akron, Ohio."[16]

This morning, another NADU aircraft had filed for Churchill. Accompanying the captain, an advance party boarded a Willie Victor: Lieutenant Commander Manship (in charge of ground crew), an aerologist, and two pilots, plus six ground handlers and maintenance personnel. Four guests accompanied: Commodore "Robbie" Robertson, RCN, up from the Canadian embassy in Washington; Paul B. Swenson, a geographer from the Arctic Institute of North America; Walter H. Bailey, also a geographer; and Mulligan, from the AP.

Aircraft commander: Lieutenant Commander James Goodman, USN. Unlike the public travails of *719,* an uneventful flight (seven and a half hours) had NADU in Churchill. Officers and passengers were assigned quarters in the officers' mess, enlisted personnel the sergeants' mess. One prospective expedition passenger was already there. Norman G. Gray, Dominion Hydrographer, had logged five days awaiting the navy.[17] And his wait would lengthen: Churchill would not see *719* for four days more.

Collins, meanwhile, had turned southwest, to follow the axis of Lake Ontario. At its far shore, he crossed into New York State, in the vicinity of Niagara Falls, then took course over Lake Erie.

The ship hung off Cleveland at nightfall. Airmen have an aversion to severe air. Now thunderstorms threatened—a line of thunderheads along the south shore. The towering cumulonimbus appeared no less menacing on radar: Greenaway and Malloy were at the screen, measuring the height of the roiling wall of cloud.

Severe conditions did not abate until early morning, so the night was spent offshore, north of Cleveland, well away from the cells. The next morning, at 0810, 31 July, a beleaguered aircrew rolled to a mooring mast at Akron Municipal Airport. Time aloft: nearly thirty hours.

> Akron Ohio, July 31 (AP)—An Arctic-bound blimp, its fuel supply diminished battling rugged head winds, today was forced to delay a polar-expedition for the second time.
>
> The ZPG-2 set down at Akron Municipal Airport to wait for a break in the weather.
>
> "We are going to get off as soon as possible," said Lieutenant Comdr. Don Collins, skipper of the ZPG-2.
>
> "The weather looks unfavorable this evening, but there's a possibility we can leave tomorrow morning," he added.
>
> Thundershowers were predicted for tonight and tomorrow.

A further wait on the weather began—an embarrassment for the Navy Department. For its part, the flight crew would wait out the heat for another two days when air temperatures refused to ease. "The two failures to reach Churchill," Greenaway observed, "clearly indicated that another attempt would have to wait until surface temperatures along the route dropped from the mid-80s to the low 70s."

And so the first of the month brought postponement:

> Akron, Ohio, Aug. 1 (AP)—The Navy again called off a planned Arctic flight by one of its blimps tonight because of adverse winds and temperatures. The ZPG-2 already is six days behind schedule on its ultimate destination to an ice island known as T-3, an Arctic weather station.
>
> Rough weather and fog forced the craft to turn back in the first attempt for the northern trip from South Weymouth, Mass., last Sunday. The blimp landed here yesterday after strong winds spoiled a second attempt from Lakehurst, N.J.
>
> A Navy spokesman said it is "a 50–50 chance" as to whether the ZPG-2 would take off tomorrow. He said the best bet for departing would be Sunday night.
>
> At Churchill, Man., the ship's first scheduled stop, a team of international geophysical year scientists will board the craft. The 1200-mile trip to Churchill will take about 40 hours from here, the commander of the blimp said.

Air temperatures had intensified in-flight static conditions, realizing the two aborts. In Akron, a reexamination was ordered. Collins would lighten ship. One pilot and three technicians—Dunlevy, England, Kalnin—would be "valved," leaving two pilots and six men to crew the next leg. Every possible pound was jettisoned commensurate with safety and aircrew fatigue. The

matter of fatigue pertains to the need for continuous watches. Aircrews were divided into port and starboard watches of approximately four hours each; Koza and Schou, for instance, took opposite watches. To further ease heaviness, about a thousand pounds were offloaded, including much of the expedition's survival gear.

Phase II, Operation Sunshine

As airship *719* tarried, well south of Arctic airspace, *Nautilus* was probing the polar pack, on the very lip of the deepwater basin.[18] Dr. Lyon had made *Nautilus*' circumpolar cruises possible. Once again, the physicist was on board—his thirteenth polar expedition. As Early told me, "the cruise would not have taken place without his presence and equipment."

The shelf linking northeast Asia with Alaska is broad and flat. Depths in the Chukchi hold shallow (averaging 120 feet) for great distances, and the bottom is devoid of features. Further, current patterns are confused. In short, a submerged passage here was the most critical part of any transpolar attempt. Accordingly, this phase of Operation Sunshine would again track from Pacific to Atlantic, given that ice here would likely govern success.

As in June, the problem was to find at least three hundred feet of sea room: water enough to bypass deep-draft pressure ice.

Late on the evening of Saturday, 26 July, Anderson had land in sight: the Pacific side of the Aleutian group—useful now for radar fixes. (At that moment, *719* was loading stores at South Weymouth.) Below lay the Aleutian trench, a colossal trough more than two thousand miles long, with depths exceeding 25,000 feet. Here continental plates converge, the edge of the Pacific plate plunging beneath that bearing the Americas. Crustal heat from these forces has constructed the Aleutian volcanic arc—the crests of volcanoes. Here also, the Bering Sea meets the warm air masses and currents of the North Pacific. Result: cyclonic storms, ferocious winds, rain, fog, mist, and snow.[19] Pushing on, the boat slipped through the narrow passage between Herbert and Yunaska Islands into Arctic waters.

Undetected, Anderson had maintained a high-speed run at three hundred feet, slowing only to approach the surface to snorkel-ventilate and to receive radio traffic, including ice summaries. (Today's boats suffer this restriction still: an inability to transmit submerged unless antennae are near-surface.) *Nautilus* had steamed 2,900 miles in slightly more than six days. Average speed: just below twenty knots—a record run.

The island arc threaded, *Nautilus* entered the Bering Sea at 2159. West of the Pribilofs, course was changed to stay in deep water as long as possible. At 1540, 27 July, *Nautilus* crossed the two-hundred-fathom curve. Soundings shallowing, speed was changed to eighteen knots (from twenty-two), depth to 150 feet (from 300). To port, the rim of northern Siberia arced west toward Europe, half a world away; to starboard, the dark line of the northern Alaskan coast slanted east, to the international line with Canada.

The Bering and Chukchi Seas overlie a vast plateau—continental shelf. Soundings now were continuous (instead of at fifteen-minute intervals). "We've crossed the 100-fathom mark," Lieutenant William G. Lalor, USN, main propulsion officer, wrote in a personal log, "and the deepwater honeymoon is over."

Radar landfall on St. Lawrence Island was logged at 1032, 28 July—the first ascent to periscope depth since castoff. "Now necessary to be very careful during snorkel, radio, radar and periscope runs," Lyon wrote, "to be sure to avoid contact by land radar stations, ship or air patrol."[20] At 1330, "Came to periscope depth. Took a visual cut on St. Lawrence Island. Siberia in sight. Visibility unlimited. Sea flat calm. Came to 340° T because we were 5 miles inside our track. Making 8 knots."

At 0140, 29 July, SSN 571 came to course 357°, entering Bering Strait. The Pacific "door" to deep water, it separates the Eurasian and American continents and connects the Bering and Chukchi Seas. At 0625, the keel crossed the Arctic Circle at longitude 168° W 42′ W. (At this moment, *719* swung to a mast at Lakehurst.) Occasional ascents to periscope depth continued, to fix position and for radio reception. Fixes also checked the newfangled inertial navigator—the first ever installed in a combatant ship.

Sonar contact on possible ice was recorded at 2230. Anderson came to periscope depth—and held. The first ice was sighted at 2324, range about five miles: small pieces becoming numerous as visibility deteriorated. As the smaller pieces were difficult to pick up, Anderson surfaced. Lyon readied his recorders and checked the topside echo-sounder system for the run under ice. Confidence level on board: high. As the physicist fiddled, a contest was held for a flag to commemorate the Pole and impending transect.[21]

[Opposite] Akron, Ohio, 30 July. Elevated temperatures again have delayed penetration of Canadian airspace. Attached to ship's envelope (l. to r.) are an ECM direction finder, ECM receiver antenna and tuners, and a magnetic anomaly detector (MAD). Early on 3 August, the airship will cast off for Canada—North Pole Day on board *Nautilus*. (Capt. Harold B. Van Gorder)

Ship's complement: 116 officers and enlisted men, plus civilian technicians, all encased in comforts never before accorded so far north. *Nautilus* was designed to berth a full crew; the shared, or "hot," bunks familiar to every submariner stood banished.[22] As in all submarine services, privacy within these steel tubes is impracticable. Only the CO had a privileged space; all others shared quarters.

For ship's crew, *Nautilus* was hotel-class. Needing stowage for only emergency diesel and batteries, its designers had devoted unusual attention to "habitability." This pioneer SSN represented "an extraordinary advance" over diesel boats and their space-robbing fuel tanks. "The comforts necessary to good morale and healthful living were not overlooked when this fighting ship was designed. In addition to the equipment necessary to fight the ship, *Nautilus* was also equipped with a spacious dining, comfortable living spaces for all hands, and convenient wash rooms."[23]

Nautilus was about twice the submerged displacement of most conventional boats. Her nuclear reactor, moreover, bought generous habitability. A huge air-conditioning system—for handling heat generated by the power plant and, secondarily, for crew comfort—maintained an inside temperature between 68° and 72°. Oxygen was obtained through electrolysis of seawater, using electricity produced by reactor-core heat. An air-monitoring system provided a continuous check on interior atmosphere, to ensure a proper mixture of vital gases. A scrubber removed carbon dioxide; oxygen bled in as necessary.

The wardroom space (on the upper deck just forward of the sail) was nearly four times that of conventional boats. Cream-colored linoleum covered the deck, and imitation wood-grained paneling helped create an agreeable impression. Framed photos of pinups hung in the mess and other spaces. Heretofore, hull interiors had been cramped and bare, hollow worlds circumscribed by all-business plating and machinery draped in tapestries of pipe and cable snaking overhead, alongside, and underfoot.[24]

Nautilus delivered yet another quantum improvement: the reactor banished the dank, pervasive smell endemic to all diesel boats. As exec Frank Adams confided, diesel "penetrated your clothes, and your life."

Underway drill: watch standing, sleeping, working, eating. During the off watch, the crew enjoyed unheard-of diversions, such as a Seeborg Selectomatic jukebox—five plays for a nickel. (It seemed to play almost continuously.) Coke and ice-cream machines were installed. Also available: a library, films, and games—chess, cribbage, acey-deucy.

Good chow was on board, enough for seventy-five days. Menus and food preparation: excellent. For Phase II, as it happened, lettuce and tomatoes quickly vanished, due to the limited supply available at Pearl. Still, milk and fresh meat would be served throughout the polar transit.

On the run from Hawaii, there was "absolutely no motion"; the boat was as steady and level, Anderson would write, as a living room. Operating submerged was more comfortable than surfaced. "Four hundred feet down at 20 knots," recalled Steward 1st Class Walter J. Harvey, "you feel as though you're tied up in harbor. No oil, no smell, no rock and roll—just like a club car on a good train."[25] One significant deprivation: an almost total lack of news from the world outside.

[Top] Cdr. Anderson (seated, center) in the wardroom. From left: Lt. John W. Harvey, reactor control officer; Lt. Cdr. Frank M. Adams, executive officer (hidden); Lt. Kenneth M. Carr, electrical officer; Lt. William G. Lalor, navigator; Capt. Jack L. Kinsey, a medical observer; Dr. Waldo K. Lyon, senior scientist and father of the polar submarine; and Lt. William S. Cole Jr., electronics and supply officer. (U.S. Navy)

[Bottom] Lt. Shepherd M. Jenks, USN, briefs fellow officers while under way. For ice reconnaissance, navigator Jenks had been flown secretly over the proposed second-phase track, then back to Pearl, to rejoin the boat. (U.S. Naval Institute Photo Archive)

[Opposite, top] Chukchi Sea, 30 July–1 August. As *Nautilus* probes for deep water clear of pressure ice, *719* waits out high air temperatures in Ohio. (U.S. Navy)

[Opposite, bottom] Cdr. William R. Anderson, USN, commanding officer, USS *Nautilus* (r.) during the surface run to Point Barrow. Exploiting the shore lead off North Alaska, working south and east, *Nautilus* would reach the Barrow Sea Valley on 1 August—boulevard to abyssal depths. (U.S. Navy)

Nautilus logged the west corner of St. Lawrence Island on 28 July. At 1100, the hull was snorkel ventilated, a fix recorded. The boat steamed on at twelve knots in twenty-five-fathom water along meridian 169° W, noting occasional brash (ice fragments). At 0139, 30 July, Anderson surfaced, to make better time and to avoid damage to the scope. Lyon exploited this surface run to effect repairs to the hydrophones. The bow was again cutting the Chukchi. "Where before was jammed with deep-draft ice," Anderson was to write, "now it was clear. As we ripped along over the forty miles of shoal water that had caused us so many anxious moments on the previous trip, someone summed up the feelings of all of us: 'a piece of cake.'"[26]

Reconnaissance flights by the Alaskan Sea Frontier command and the ice summaries relayed to *Nautilus* seemed to be paying off.[27]

Along 168° W, the ice boundary had receded to about 73°—approximately the fifty-fathom curve. In the shore lead to Point Barrow, total coverage concentration did not exceed four-tenths. "The second phase of Operation Sunshine in July," Lyon recounted, "we were using charts that we had made in 1954 that were very critical because we had to find the Barrow Sea Valley right north of Barrow to get the closest deep water, to get under the ice."[28] If the valley were reached, *Nautilus* could transit longitude 168° into abyssal depths before meeting difficult ice.

Probing in flat calm and fog, the barrier was approached. Depths proved shallow; heavy ice to the west, Anderson jogged east then nudged north again. "We continued nuzzling at the edge of the ice pack," he observed, "pinging for deep water. We ran into one dead end after another."

A cautious routine would hold. Anderson had hoped to locate a northward passage—depth thirty-five or so fathoms—in the Chukchi. But progress stopped at 72°. The boat turned east, to 165° longitude, then turned again north. "We were hoping by cautious, step-by-step probing," the retired captain told me, "we could get through, build up speed and be on our way." By the midwatch (0000–0400) of 31 July, the boat was working east and north (Lyon recorded) "on all or any longitude before being stopped by ice." Excerpts from Anderson's narrative:

> 0345U [i.e., in the "Uniform" time zone, or Pacific Standard time, eight hours earlier than Greenwich] After running 14 miles and finding ice from 270° to 120° T visible decided to ease north to check for possible deep water. Now in 30 fathoms, deepest water since the Bering Strait. . . .
>
> 0356U Changed speed to 4 knots. No passage here! From Northeast through North and Southeast the sea is filled with brash and block ice, and what definitely looks like the pack is directly beyond. . . .
>
> 0401U Changed course to 150° T, changed speed to 12 knots. Proceeding toward Pt. Barrow, attempting to skirt the southern projection of the ice pack. Set an ECM watch, especially for aircraft frequencies. . . .

The way blocked and with "high-level eyes" hoping for a high-speed transit the decision had been taken to make for Point Barrow. The shelf off North Alaska is narrow, with deep water close inshore.[29]

Reconnaissance and commercial air traffic transit that sector. To avoid detection, Anderson had ordered a close topside watch; at 1230, to better his odds, the boat was dived to periscope

[Opposite] Point Barrow, Alaska: latitude 71° 21′ N, longitude 156° 46′ W—home to the Naval Arctic Research Laboratory. Surveyed in 1951 by icebreaker, the Barrow Sea Valley lies nearshore—bathymetrically a notch in the continental shelf. Note the sea ice; in bad years, heavy ice is close to shore all season. (U.S. Naval Institute Photo Archive)

depth. Clear of ice, surface-running thirty to forty miles off the beach, the submarine pressed southeast on various courses and speeds along the edge of the pack (port side) in intermittent fog, avoiding occasional ice.

Objective: Point Barrow—71° 20′ N, 156° 46′ W. There a scar cleaves the continental shelf. The Barrow Sea Valley had been found in 1951, then charted by *Burton Island* during joint Canadian-U.S. expeditions. If it can be reached, no deep-draft ice can thwart further northing.

From October until July, the Beaufort hosts a near-continuous cover. In those years ships seldom were able to reach Point Barrow prior to 1 August. Each thaw season, however, the pack recedes: a zone of shear develops between shorefast ice and polar pack. The charts tantalized: limitless sea room a mere twenty or so miles off the port beam.

Dr. Lyon and his assistant monitored equipment, waiting out the delay. The physicist had shaped the polar submarine program; now, atomic power was propelling a platform for extending the range of his work. Dedicated to the concept that the Arctic Ocean was potentially navigable, Lyon had fathered *Nautilus*' sonar systems, making under-ice piloting practicable.

The near-shore zone of seasonal ice offered a shallow, indirect path to deep water. Meantime, the fathometer plotted shoal water. "For two days," Lyon wrote, "we searched for a northward passage through the ice pack to reach deep water. Dodging ice floes on the surface, the *Nautilus* worked her way south and east." On 31 July, the probability of passage neared, "0800U Position 71° 57′ N/164° 02′ W. Maneuvering on various courses at various speeds attempting to go southeast toward the Barrow Sea Valley along the edge of the pack by dodging between small and medium floes, brash and block. Courses vary between 151° T and 300° T, with most courses 180° T–200° T."

The day's last hours were expended skirting the pack, proceeding thirty to forty miles off the beach and clear of ice, alternately slowing and speeding as visibility changed—clear (surface) passage to Point Barrow. At 0135, 1 August, *Nautilus* made radar landfall on Point Franklin, bearing 155° T, fifteen miles. Here the valley originates, deepening to the northeast. A precise fix was taken—final navigation check before diving. Early on 1 August, fifty fathoms beneath the keel, ventilation commenced in anticipation of a dive. "When you are ready, clear the bridge and submerge," Anderson ordered. At 0437, "Submerged on course 045°T. LT Kassel dived the boat to 200 feet. At diving time the sky was clear overhead, sun rising and moon full. Wind 12–15 knots, sea state 1, from the direction of Pt. Barrow. And as Alaska faded slowly into the moonset, *Nautilus* set course for deep water, North Pole, and Atlantic Ocean."

Rigged for deep submergence, the boat steamed down-valley, descending the steep continental slope toward the basin's nether regions. Bottom deepening, *Nautilus* pushed toward longitude 155° W, to begin the transit. Position verified by echo-sounding the depth to the seafloor (the valley was charted), speed and depth were gradually increased.

At 0852, helmsman David Greenhill came left to north at longitude 155° 04′ W. Dead ahead, 1,094 miles distant, across sea bottom all but uncharted, lay the north geographic pole. Cruising conditions were set: northward at six hundred feet and eighteen knots. "Soon," Anderson writes, "we were well under the true polar pack." *Nautilus* had reached her true medium.

Why a running depth of six hundred feet? The chart was essentially that used by Fridtjof Nansen, in the 1890s. Soundings had been added taken from T-3 and from Soviet drifting sta-

tions, plus *Nautilus'* own soundings north of Spitsbergen. Accordingly, position (Lyon writes) "could not be determined by bathymetry or any other observation under ice; it had to be reckoned from one's last known position in Barrow Sea Valley."[30] What of T-3, at that moment drifting south off the Arctic islands? "The position of T-3 was known to us in both 1957 and 1958," Admiral Early reminded. "It was well off any intended track. Rather than consider it for rendezvous, we considered it an object to avoid because of its deep draft."[31] Cruising depth was set sufficiently deep to clear all pressure ridges—and the rare ice island.

"Our major problem now," Lieutenant Lalor remarked, "navigation."

Toward Churchill

As *719* waited out the heat, arrangements for a refueling were completed by the support group awaiting her in Ontario. Captain Van Gorder, in overall command, was not about to suffer further delay—not for want of fuel, anyway.

In 1958 Lakehead Airport served the twin communities of Port Arthur and Fort William, on the Canadian shore of Lake Superior, roughly halfway between Akron and Churchill. (Today, the two cities are consolidated as Thunder Bay.) Although small, the field's location and facilities sufficed. And a U.S. Air Force detachment was available to serve as an improvised ground crew.

At last, the air temperature dropped, and a favorable gradient was forecast. Late on 2 August, an (abbreviated) navy crew prepared for flight. A welcome departure from Akron airport was taken in the very early hours of the 3rd.

> Akron, Ohio, Aug. 3 (Sunday) (AP)—a Navy blimp sailed early today on a third attempt to get close to the North Pole.

It started last Sunday from South Weymouth, Mass., hit bad weather and came back. The second attempt began at Lakehurst, N.J., but more rough winds turned it back here on Thursday.

The departure from Goodyear Airdock was at 1:33 a.m. (EDT). The weather here was clear, but a slight overcast at about 8,000 feet shut off the starlight.

Main purpose of the trip is to study whether a non-rigid aircraft may be used in Arctic research. The craft is type ZPG-2, with a capacity of about one million cubic feet of helium. . . .

The first destination, taking about 36 hours, will be Churchill, Man., where the ship will pick up a team of scientists on a project of the international geophysical year.

The ultimate destination, about 100 miles from the North Pole, will be ice island T-3, which is a floating weather station in the Arctic Ocean.

Over Lake Erie, a heading was taken direct for Sault Ste. Marie, about four hundred miles to the northwest. Halfway across, *719* penetrated Canadian airspace. When the far shore slid beneath, the rolling Ontario countryside filled the flight-deck windows.

Daylight found the navy cruising above Lake Huron. Jointly, Lakes Michigan and Huron form an immense liquid arch drapefolded onto Michigan. Here the international boundary cuts Huron's long axis: maintaining a northwest course, the airship tracked cross-border, peeking out, then back into Canadian airspace.

To the Pole

In another world, *Nautilus* was approaching the Pole. The boat was running fast and deep, holding to a steady course—due north—along the 155° W meridian. Speed: twenty knots—one degree of latitude every three hours. "We just went down deep—and ran," one of the enlisted men, Alfred Charette Jr., later remarked.

At 1630, 2 August, the boat was at the 74° curve. At 76° 22´ N, soundings jumped abruptly from 2,100 fathoms to 1,500, then decreased slowly, steadying at 510 fathoms. A subaqueous wall lay athwart her track. Here the bottom was all but uncharted; in the attack center, eyes on the fathometer, Anderson called for reductions in speed: fifteen knots, then ten. "You can't ever be sure," navigator Jenks remarked, "when a rise like that will level off." For a time soundings varied sharply from 450 to 725 fathoms. However, within fifteen minutes, the shoaling bottom was put astern: soundings gradually increased throughout the watch, smoothing out again. *Nautilus* had found a nine-thousand-foot highland, wholly uncharted and unknown. Or was it? "Appears to be extension of Chukchi plateau," Lyon recorded, "to east of area we had assumed. This requires study of fathograms and Russian data before stating positively."[32]

Ice profiling continued. Its trace spoke of mutability: zones of pressure ice as well as large areas of flat floes averaging five to eight feet. Coverage: from about seven-tenths to full (ten-tenths). Overhead, the ice was nearly continuous and very rough. Dr. Lyon held station at his sonar gear, "watching the recording pens trace the contour of the underside of the ice." Around noon, 2 August, the boat crossed 80°—six hundred miles to the Pole. At 2000, 452 miles remained. Maintaining twenty knots, the vessel advanced at six hundred feet—except where the bottom shallowed and to dump garbage or blow sanitary tanks.

At 1000 on 3 August, the boat crossed 87° 00′—180 miles to 90°. *Nautilus* had penetrated farther north than any previous ship in history.

Cruising depths must allow for an adequate margin of safety—for this cruise, deep enough to clear deformed ice *and* the rare ice island. Drift Station Bravo was known to be to the southeast, off any intended track. As for Alpha, *Nautilus* would close to about a hundred nautical miles of the floe camp. No contact was attempted. "No means of direct communication was planned nor set up," Admiral Early told me. "Submarine communications in those days," he explains, "was [*sic*] difficult at high latitudes because of low power, antenna height, and atmospherics on short-range frequencies." Running depth had been dictated in part by T-3. Anderson explains: "While our projected route would not take us near the reported position of T-3, a navigational failure could change this. Thus, I used the draft of T-3 (about 130 feet as I recall) as a maximum for ice to be encountered and thus a depth to stay below whenever possible."[33]

This was history's farthest push beneath ice. Mile by extraordinary mile, the upward-looking sonar plotted a continuous profile of the canopy overhead. And the echo sounder pinged a continuous record of bathymetry—the first contour map of the Polar Basin.

Submarine duty is fraught with risks: loss of propulsion or depth control, collision, flooding, sinking, grounding, a foul atmosphere. Under-ice operations introduced a further hazard. That May, running north from Panama en route to the Bering Sea, fire had broken out in the engine room, obliging Anderson to surface.[34] Nonetheless, *Nautilus* hands were at ease with protracted submergences. Mood on board: professional—with a tinge of apprehension.

"There was," Admiral Early cautioned, "a feeling that we were pushing into the unknown, and that it was possible to get lost."[35] Among the concerns: to locate open water for surfacing. Conning officer Carr was "busy plotting polynyas, that is, holes in the ice which we might need

Dr. Lyon (l.) and Cdr. Anderson check ice profiles at the boat's upward-scanning fathometer. (U.S. Navy)

in case of an emergency." "We plotted every hole in the ice we passed," a sonarman recalled, "so that we could go back to it if necessary."[36] Yet, as Carr summarized, "staying submerged for long periods was old hat to the *Nautilus*." Adams agrees. "There was no significant concern," he recalled. "We had people who had been under the edge of the ice before." According to Electrician 1st Class James Sordelet, "As far as the men were concerned, we could have been in the China Sea or the Mediterranean. Physically it was no different from other times." "It was pretty routine," Steward Thomas Emanuel added.

These were "nucs": volunteer professionals artfully culled and burnished—the entire crew selected and trained by Rickover. His exacting standards met, excellence prevailed.

A closed-circuit, upward-beamed television system (completed at Pearl) granted views of the pack's underside in the attack center. Courtesy of "Polar TV Network, Channel 571," an uncanny seascape scrolled past. It was, a crewman reported, as if they were flying beneath an implausible cover of cloud.

The inertial navigation system and the automatic control equipment were holding the hull exactly on course. Still, for the officers responsible for navigation, tension was building: "North Pole Day" would test their skill. Two hours out, Jenks mediated a "quarrel" among the Mark 19 gyro and the inertial navigation system. (One of two civilian engineers attended the on-board INS equipment constantly.) Jenks found for the INS. Later, Anderson would concede (to *Life*): "I was skeptical about the inertial gear at first but I must say I am amazed at its accuracy." Built by North American Autonetic for the Navaho missile (a cruise missile, recently canceled), the N6A autonavigator was providing an independent check on steering and position.

Throughout 3 August, *Nautilus* pressed poleward at twenty knots, depth six hundred feet, her instruments recording continuous ice profiles as Dr. Lyon analyzed water samples (for salinity). As noted in the log, "0400U Coverage generally 10/10ths with numerous 60 foot deep ice. Water [that is, open water on the surface] scarce."

The boat closed on the place. Just prior to the Pole, the Lomonosov Ridge was passed over; bottom readings, Lyon recorded to himself, appeared to agree with the USSR chart on board (from Ottawa). *Nautilus* had pushed more than a thousand miles out, into the central Arctic. And her crew had been under the canopy more than sixty hours.

The off watch had gathered in the crew's mess; in the wardroom, two or three officers lingered. Others, though, had thronged into the attack center; there Anderson waited. Frank Adams advised: "Two miles to go, Captain." Minutes later, Lieutenant Jenks reported: "The Pole lies one thousand yards dead ahead."

They were about to drill 90° north latitude. Tenths of a mile remaining, Anderson stepped to the intercom to count down. Chief Engineer Early, off watch in the wardroom, was surprised to hear the CO's voice: "It was very unusual for him to use the announcing system and I thought, when he began, that it would disturb those off watch who were sleeping." Then, all data plots and computations agreed. The hour: 1915 local time (2315 Eastern Daylight Savings Time). Anderson later recreated the scene:

> The juke box was shut off, and at that moment a hush literally fell over the ship. The only sound to be heard was the steady staccato of pinging from our sonars steadily watching the bottom, the ice, and the dark waters ahead. I glanced again at the distance

[Top] The inertial navigation system is checked—the first ever for a combatant ship. Maintaining a continuous electronic plot of position, the INS is attended "as though it were a sick child." Should it fail, *Nautilus* was equipped with magnetic and electronic compasses. 90° N was logged at 1115 (EDT), 3 August 1958. (U.S. Navy)

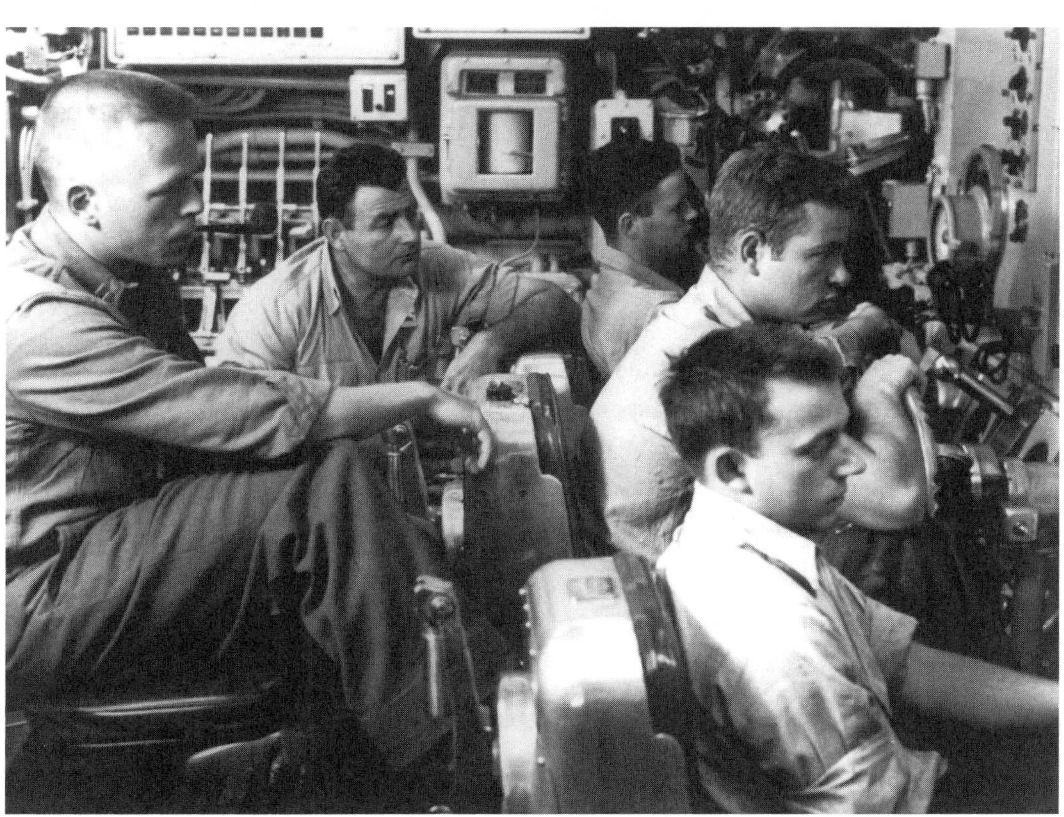

[Bottom] Watchkeepers monitoring course, depth, and speed as *Nautilus* steams beneath the polar pack at a running depth of six hundred feet, maintaining twenty knots. Holding to a steady course along the 155° west meridian, *Nautilus* is approaching the north geographic pole. (U.S. Navy)

indicator, and gave a brief countdown to the crew. "Stand by. 10 . . . 8 . . . 6 . . . 4 . . . 3 . . . 2 . . . 1. *Mark!* August 3, 1958. Time, 2315 [11:15 p.m. EDST]. For the United States and the United States Navy, the North Pole." I could hear cheers in the Crew's Mess.[37]

As well, the skipper signed a letter prepared for President Eisenhower thanking the commander in chief for his "personal interest, approval, and support." Santa Claus joined celebrations as the machine persisted in its remarkable business, its course changing from 000° T to 180° T; "Continued on across the Pole," Lyon dryly noted to his journal, "maintaining straight course, taking water samples, etc., continuous profile." "When the Captain finished the announcement [Admiral Early continues], I went in to the Attack Center and congratulated him and Dr. Lyon. I then looked at the track chart on which our inertial and DR [dead-reckoning] positions were being kept and spoke to the Exec, Frank Adams, and Shep Jenks, the Navigator. . . . We were at 400 feet at 20 knots, headed 000 or due North one instant and 180 [degrees] or South the next."[38]

Upset and uncertain, the compasses would not settle themselves until about 88°. "As we watched in awe [Lalor was to write], our gyrocompasses swung, finally to point back to where we had been. Tom Curtis [a civilian technician babysitting the INS] was manipulating his slide rule beside the inertial navigator. I asked how close we had come to the exact Pole. . . . 'We pierced it, Bill.'"[39]

This day's final entry, at 2000: "Continued on course 180° on longitude 26° E with MK [Mark] 19 compass slewed around and settling, steering by MK23 in direction gyro. Headings comparing closely with N6A (INS). Ice coverage remaining 9/10ths—10/10ths coverage floes and some brash and block."

More men had gathered at the north geographic pole than at any time in the history of exploration.[40]

To Hudson Bay

Sault Ste. Marie lies at the southeast corner of Lake Superior. Here the blimp changed course, to the north-northwest. This track would take it direct to Lakehead, Ontario, on the opposite shore of earth's second-largest lake. As before, *719* kept well offshore, seeking constant and lower temperatures. The hours added. The weather: excellent.

This leg (so far) was proving a welcome respite. On board, the residue of seven unrewarding days had softened.

The aerial expedition had at length edged north. Off to starboard, beyond a vacant, craggy shore, the Canadian Shield filled the curve of a green horizon. A nearly flat but rugged expanse, this district is the crustal core of North America.[41] Ancient bedrock extends for hundreds of desolate miles, to the lowland muskeg fronting Hudson Bay. This is the taiga of Canada—part of the coniferous belt girdling the subarctic. Inaccessible save by water, its only sign of habitation are the threads of rail and road, few of which cut far northward.

The shield is edge of the inhabited world; there, the presence and unrestrained impact of man is largely imperceptible.

Fifteen hours out, *719* lay abeam of Lakehead. For the first time since liftoff from South Weymouth, the expedition was proceeding as planned. Collins nonetheless elected to exploit congenial conditions. He would refuel.

The aircraft settled onto the northwest runway; it had been closed for the arrival. To assist with operations on the ground, a NADU Willie Victor had flown in from Churchill—three hours flying away. As well, an estimated three thousand residents had streamed to the field. The Sunday crush gaped at the craft, the first of its kind here, as if an apparition had come among them. The American visitor (as the *Daily Times-Journal* phrased it) was "longer than a football field and higher than most Fort William buildings."

The refueling (in Greenaway's estimate) was carried out in less time than that required to untangle the traffic caused by their arrival.

A fuel truck with a hose (extra long for clearance) was positioned astern. Free to vane on its undercarriage, the blimp was held in position (in light winds) by about two dozen men—among them U.S. Air Force recruits—assisted by ship's idling engines. As *719* pivoted, the truck maneuvered to remain astern, the hose's length allowing the airship to swing with minimum reaction from the truck. One thousand gallons of gasoline were pumped on board, plus extra oil.

NAVSHIPS 1111 (REV. 11-54)

SHIP'S POSITION

U. S. S. NAUTILUS

TO: COMMANDING OFFICER

AT (Time of day): 1915U
DATE: 3 August 1958
LATITUDE: 90° 00.0'N
LONGITUDE: Indefinite
DETERMINED AT: —
BY (Indicate by check in box): [X] N6A [X] D. R. [X] MK19 [ ] RADAR [ ] VISUAL
SET: —
DRIFT: —
DISTANCE MADE GOOD SINCE (time) (miles): Honolulu 4844
DISTANCE TO: North Pole
MILES: Zero
ETA: —
TRUE HDG.: 180°
ERROR: MK19 GYRO 3 E MK23 GYRO 0°
VARIATION: 170 °E
MAGNETIC COMPASS HEADING (Check one): [ ] STD [ ] STEERING [X] REMOTE IND [ ] OTHER M 244 G 359°
DEVIATION: 126E
1104 TABLE DEVIATION: 3° W
DG: (Indicate by check in box) [ ] ON [X] OFF
REMARKS:
N6A DR: σ = 0, ν = 0
N6A: n_x = 0, n_y = 0, n_z = 1

RESPECTFULLY SUBMITTED (Navigator): LT Shepherd M. Jenks, USN

CC:

Commodore Robertson, the Canadian naval attaché, marveled at his hosts. "Well, to me it was impossible. To them, it was just[,] . . . they were experts."[42]

Thanks to advance work by the support group, a successful refueling was accomplished in forty minutes.

Takeoff nearing, Captain Van Gorder elected to board. Heard to remark something similar to "Damn it, I'm getting on this thing," he climbed ship's ladder. Enjoying himself, Commodore Robertson followed. As well, ADC Herman England (here via the Willie Victor) along with Dunlevy, Kalnin, and Schou (flown up from Akron) reboarded. For the run to Churchill, Lord and Quinn were "valved" temporarily.

Granting it page-one treatment, a Fort William paper described the departure: "Acting like an enormous weather vane, the craft wanted to swing so as to face the wind. Sixteen men on either side anchored a long rope and held the machine steady until the wind was blowing directly down the runway. With a signal from a crewman standing in front of the nose, ropes were dropped, engines roared and the craft began a lazy movement down the tarmac. When sufficient speed was attained the nose rose and the monster lumbered into the sky amid cheers from the sweating ground crew."[43]

Persistence would grant its reward. In about seventeen hours, a U.S. Navy airship would find mooring at Fort Churchill, on the subarctic shore of Hudson Bay.

In nature there are neither rewards nor punishments—there are consequences.

—Robert Green Ingersoll

Northward 5

Unlike the Lakehurst-to-Akron contest, conditions in east-central Canada proved ideal: superb visibility, high ceilings, winds from abeam to following. And the heat wave had ceased—air temperature was in the upper sixties. Lakehead eased astern. Hugging Thunder Bay, U.S. Navy airship 126719 droned northeast. Near the town of Nipigon, a highway traced east to escort the bedrock rim of Lake Superior. This would be the last road of consequence the aircrew would see for eight days.

Course was taken due north. Near Armstrong Station, the trans-Canada railroad was crossed.

A low, soggy terrain was presented: the all but roadless taiga of northern Ontario. Vacant and forlorn, the Canadian Shield rolled away to each horizon: a blanket of trees, swamp, and bog pocked by lakes and ponds. Relics of continental glaciation, a webwork of shimmering threads struggle to drain this scoured waste to Hudson Bay. At about 60° N, evidence of tall green life would vanish altogether. Meanwhile, no inhabited scars broke the swampy sameness until Chesterfield Inlet, near the northwest corner of Mr. Hudson's inland sea.

Deep in Ontario, the airship throbbed past Trout Lake, then the Severn River. Altitude: about five hundred feet. The sky retained a splendid, almost crystalline aspect, with winds light. In terms of weather, the mission was having an exceptional day. Ground speed: about forty-five knots.

In-flight routines were a familiar cycle of shared duties: four or so hours on watch, a meal, snatched private time, perhaps a turn in the bunks, coffee, relieve the watch—a well-worn ritual as old as the naval service.

By 0500, the shore of Hudson Bay was near. At 57° 14′ N, 92° 40′ W—a point over the subarctic blank of eastern Manitoba—a position report was transmitted. Estimated arrival Churchill: 0712 Central Daylight Savings Time (CDST), 4 August.

York Factory was close aboard around 0530. Here the shore curves west and south, forming a dent of water. The town site, on a long peninsula, slid into view.

In the salad days of the Hudson's Bay Company, this had been headquarters. A flood tide of trade goods—and the furs garnered in exchange—had passed through this place. The economic life of York Factory is inseparable from the history of "the Bay" in North America. And it tracks the development of Canada itself.

The annual supply ship from England would arrive in late summer with guns, brandy, axes, knives, wire, cookware; countless transactions moved these and other commodities into the interior. In exchange, pelts of beaver, fox, mink, ermine, and lynx were transported bayward by canoe. The shuttle from London thrived for more than a century, persisted for yet another.

When *719* arrived, only scattered ruins were evident. A depot, cemetery, and assorted relics and remnants were left to commemorate two centuries of merchandising. Nature was reclaiming the site. But decay is constrained by cold; even if untouched by preservationists, evidence of occupation will persist in such climates.

Next the Nelson River. Course: north-northwest, direct for Churchill. At 0725 (local time), 4 August, the navy realized its belated Churchill arrival—five days behind schedule. Flight hours since Akron: thirty-two.

As if to chide its tardiness, no ground crew had yet assembled. The field's layout was unfamiliar to the support group from the WV-2. And local volunteers were new to airships. So the ship circled as preparations on the ground were sorted out. "It was," Greenaway remarked, "just a case of getting organized and coordinating activities in a strange environment with a volunteer crew unfamiliar with the routine."

The wait was unlamented. The harbor itself was enjoyed from aloft, as was, across the river, the remains of Fort Prince of Wales. Offshore, the cold-blue surface was broken by sporting white whales. In scattered groups, two hundred or so beluga animated the Churchill River. The off watch was at the windows. Beluga calves gamboled among the adults, which are snow white. Throughout the car, excited murmurs mingled with the click of cameras. A low pass was flown, about fifty feet off from them. Sensing the intruder and alarmed, the whales swam for open water. The blimp, Greenaway mused, was superb for observation.

Easing in, the navy touched down, rolled out, slowed. Temperature: 60° F. The entire base had turned out, along with gawking sightseers at the perimeter fence—and clouds of insolent mosquitoes.

Churchill is the oldest settlement in the Canadian north. In the 1950s, the port was a scattered collection of shacks and frame houses. And Fort Churchill, about a mile from town, was a sprawling complex. During its busiest season, the government post supported as many as eight hundred personnel. Lieutenant Commander Schou was surprised by the facilities. Captain Van Gorder thought it "a considerable base." Mulligan too hadn't expected such a large installation so far north—on the order of Thule Air Base or Gander.

The facility had been a staging base for wartime aircraft on the stepping-stone air route to Western Europe. By 1958 the place had begun hosting a mix of activities—mostly research and cold-weather testing of equipment and clothing. And now, staff from the U.S. Army's First Test Center would assist the ground-handling operation.

The mast had been installed on a taxi strip between the north–south runways. Greenaway recalls, it "was rather awkward to reach." Fifty or so U.S. soldiers had received a crash course

719 on approach to Fort Churchill, on Hudson Bay. High surface winds and a predicted headwind on the track to Resolute will delay departure here for two days. (ATC Frederick L. Parker)

in ground handling. As the ship rolled to them, men rushed to grab its dangling lines, under the command of Lieutenant Commander Manship and *his* men. Mooring here involved "walking" *719* across taxiway gravel to the mast—a distance of about 1,300 feet. Emplaced over irregular ground, the taxiway's surface dropped off several feet on each side. The imperative to keep the ship's undercarriage on its narrow path would complicate all ground handling here.

Ground operations much farther north, at Resolute, would prove less satisfactory still. "It's one thing to drive a mobile mast close up to the nose of the airship and ease the ship up to within the mast cone—and secure it. It's another thing to maneuver by hand and walk the airship ahead. You could do it a lot easier with a [much smaller] K-ship. This [ZPG-2] is a big monster, as you know. It took a lot of manpower, but everybody really bust[ed] their gut."[1] A difficult mooring was completed by 0900.

A half-day layover was planned, long enough to refuel and top up with helium. Sitrep sixteen was terse: "ARR [arrived] Churchill 041425Z PD ETD [estimated time of departure] 050200Z for Resolute Bay."

Once down, Van Gorder and Greenaway elected not to wait out the mooring; ship in hand, both clambered off in search of a brief on the weather.

Crew chief Fred Parker scribbled a note to his wife. "Long tiring trip . . . ," he wrote. "Had some delays en route due to weather [an understatement], but looks good from here on out. Lift was our big problem. . . . Quite cool here in Churchill. Just got in this morning, leaving again this afternoon for the north."[2]

[Opposite] The road from Fort Churchill and adjoining muskeg. "It was not a shore-leave town," according to Hugh Mulligan, feature writer for the Associated Press. Castoff from the mooring mast: 7 August, in fog. (Hugh A. Mulligan)

The U.S. Navy would not be taking off. An intensifying "low" centered over northern Saskatchewan was moving southeast toward James Bay, a polar "high" advancing south behind it. The combination was breeding "tight isobars" (a steep pressure gradient) for the Churchill area, as well as strong headwinds along most of the planned route northward.

Dawn blew in with gusty winds sweeping the field—east-southeast from twenty-five to thirty-five knots and higher. Unmooring: problematic. "Plans for departure washed out due to weather," Norman Gray recorded to his journal. A patient man, the Canadian hydrographer had now invested ten days in waiting.

Throughout the 5th, *719* held to the mast. And there it would swing for two days more, as winds refused to abate. The wing commander framed the matter: "We just waited out the weather, which is common in the North."

This first experiment was necessarily cautious. Thanks to mobile masts and hard-fought experience, airships could be handled safely in moderately strong winds. But airmen are prudent; conditions signaling hazard are avoided if an operation can be postponed or rerouted. Churchill was no South Weymouth—and Van Gorder was taking no chances. Along with rough ground, a drop-off paralleled the taxiway. If he elected to cast off and *719* got away from a green ground crew, the expedition might well end in the Manitoba muskeg.

A watch on conditions was punctuated by frequent visits to the weather office. At Van Gorder's urging, the airmen tried to snatch some rest. As well, there was opportunity to sample the mess, read, do laundry, and relax at the local "club" meeting their Canadian and American hosts. Challenges of "Do you play darts?" broke out. A dusty road led to the town for local excursions. Though uninspiring in terms of scenery or distractions ("It was not a shore-leave town," Mulligan chuckled), Churchill does offer a singular history.

A pause here is useful.

The first Europeans to occupy the mouth of the Churchill River had come in the 1600s. Durable tenant: the Hudson's Bay Company. Today, the Bay store, the RCMP post, and the old Fort Prince of Wales (built against French incursion) recall the era of empire.

Churchill's contemporary history dates from the Hudson Bay Railway, which reached here in 1929. (A popular wilderness adventure for tourists, the line is still one of the most northerly in Canada.) A town was surveyed, harbor cleared, grain elevators installed. The latter explain Ottawa's investment: prairie wheat would be stored here for transshipment to Western Europe through Hudson Strait.[3]

The seaport scheme has disappointed. Hudson Bay is ice covered in winter. Ice forms in November and breaks up late in June, rendering the bay accessible to unstrengthened ships only from late July to the mid-October—barely three months open to navigation. (Port conditions may sometimes slash this further.) Courtesy of the Labrador Current, moreover, ice obstructs entrée to the bay January through June. And icebergs are found in the approaches throughout the year.

Mindful of the hazards, the insurance industry imposes horrendous charges on Churchill-bound shipping. Currently, a giant terminal elevator stores the precious grain, which arrives each autumn over the narrow-gauge line and is stored until breakup, when seagoing ships can reach the harbor.

The airship's guest-passengers assembled.

Hopeful of converts, the Navy Department had invited experts to assess the project. Gray has been mentioned. Paul B. Swenson, a sea-ice specialist, had flown up from New England. That summer, Swenson was under contract to ONR, investigating the application of aerial photography to ice forecasts. The scientific party also included Walter H. Bailey, a geographer, and ONR's Captain Frank A. Nusom, USN. Leader of the group: Dr. Guy S. Harris, a specialist in sonar technology and head of research for the Navy's Underwater Sound Laboratory and the U.S. Hydrographic Office.[4] (Colleague and fellow collaborator: Dr. Waldo Lyon.) AP feature writer Hugh Mulligan completed the roster.

Exploiting the furlough, the passengers-to-be chatted, inquired as to takeoff, explored the town, shopped.

Harris, fifty-eight, was an animated personality. Not one to loiter about, he was known to tell associates, "Nobody has more fun than I do." For his part, curious for something to write about, Mulligan learned that local Cree and Chipewyan hunt whale. The AP's official photographer declined to accompany a hunt. Harris, however, was pleased to go. The quarry: beluga.

The whales enter Hudson Strait in spring en route to James Bay, a thumb-shaped basin to the south. There the young are born. After about a month, the return migration begins. Following the western shore, the creatures feed in the shallows of debouching rivers on fish, squid, and crustaceans. One place they frequent: the mouth of the Churchill River.

There beluga were hunted with rifles and harpoons from small boats or canoes equipped with outboard motors. Mulligan and Harris join a party. "We got two whale and got a story and Guy took all the pictures for Associated Press," Mulligan said. The carcasses were sold locally for butchering—the blubber rendered, then refined into oil valued for its vitamin content and its inability to spoil. Chopped and ground, the meat was sold to mink and fox farmers.

A complimentary chunk was sent to the mess. To round out his experience, Harris tried a steak. "The meat has no fat though it must be fried," he reported. "In color, it is almost black; in taste, well, it tastes like whale!" "It was one of those situations," Gray reported, "that the more one chewed it, the bigger it became."

Blustery conditions persisted throughout 6 August, with gusts as high as fifty knots sweeping the runways. (The airship's wheels had been locked in athwartship position, allowing *719* to vane with the wind.) To ease strain on the mast, the engines were used, obliging pilots to be on board. A "pressure watch" also was on station, monitoring envelope pressure and checking systems. Static condition can change abruptly: moored out, a constant watch was needed to counteract the effects of temperature, barometric pressure, and wind.

As a precaution, a rip-cord tie-off had been rigged. Should a breakaway from the mast occur, the envelope would rip. An emergency deflation would end the mission, certainly, but would save the ship and forestall further damage.

Blimps are pampered machines; in this, they resemble surface vessels. Naval airships had no haven while in operational status. A fixed-wing pilot shuts down, walks away. Airships require twenty-four-hour attention. Before flight crews would disembark, a pressure watch would go on board—and stay until relieved by the next watch or a crew with flight orders. Even in the hangar, a watch was still needed.

A lengthening layover bred unease. Collins and Van Gorder fretted: their operational "window" was narrowing. All available data pointed to the desirability of concluding the project before mid-August, when conditions affecting air operations deteriorate. Falling temperatures and failing daylight would be uncongenial to an airship.

On 7 August, conditions eased. Though visibility held poor (fog is common in summer), the forecast had improved. All hands were eager to be away—the expedition was eight days behind schedule. A flight plan was filed for Resolute, via Roes Welcome Sound. The mast erected there stood about midway between Churchill and the Pole—and nearly 1,250 miles north of Churchill. Estimated flying time: about twenty-four hours. The nose wheel tilted clear shortly before 1000.

One nonessential person was on board. "Robbie" Robertson's assignment was to offer an appreciation of the platform. A vivid, voluble personality, the commodore had a wholehearted interest in all things nautical; he would thoroughly enjoy the NADU exercise.[5] Commander Burt Hickman, NADU operations officer, also was on board for this leg to Resolute. As for the scientists and Mulligan, departure from Churchill was taken nearly four hours behind the loping blimp, on board the WV-2.

The ship emerged into the clear at five hundred feet. Greenaway had set course north-northeast, a flight track about thirty miles from shore. Visibility held poor until the vicinity of Marble Island; near the hamlet of Rankin Inlet the fog and low stratus dissipated.

As if in welcome, brilliant sunlight flooded the car. Spirits had sagged, deflated by yet another delay. The crystal sky and fine visibility softened the mood. In the jump seat behind Schou (copilot, this morning), Van Gorder granted himself a measure of relief: "After many delays and some frustrations," he scribbled,

> today our Arctic trip really begins. We took off this morning from Churchill at 0947 in fog which soon dissipated. We are now (1600) flying over Hudson's Bay in perfect weather. Our first point of interest will be Chesterfield Inlet where there is an Eskimo village. This flight to Resolute will be approximately 25 hrs. I'm now completely relaxed," he recorded with rare emotion, "for the first time—the airship withstood more than 50 mph of wind at Churchill without trouble. I'm fully confident that the remainder of the trip will be eminently successful.[6]

The operation would now enjoy near-ideal conditions. "It was," Greenaway recalled, "the type of weather you would order up for your first experimental flight."

Water filled the view forward and to starboard. Here Hudson Bay is more than four hundred miles wide. Placid and drained of menace, its waters defined the full arc of the eastern horizon.

Offshore, a faint line bespoke lingering pack. East of its margin, roughly half the surface was littered by a confusion of first-year ice—a melange of slush, brash, blocks, and floes adrift with the wind. West of the line, the blue gray of open water danced in the sun.

Excepting the wing commander and commodore, this aircrew had no experience in the subarctic. Greenaway had logged thousands of Arctic hours; Robertson, for his part, had skippered *Labrador* through every type of ice. "We were operating in an environment which was foreign to them," Greenaway recalled. "I was familiar with the environment, but the airship was foreign to me." Among the aircrew, Schou alone had logged northern hours: ice-patrol missions out of Iceland.

Roused by the view, the aircrew posed questions. Greenaway was encyclopedic on all matters Arctic, Robertson a beguiling guide and raconteur—these were master classes.[7] Few are prepared (one suspects) for their first polar encounter. Yet not so very far from the cosmopolitan ease of New York, barrens brood. Van Gorder was correct: one forgets just how immense Canada is. Flying low and slow over its reaches, he remarked, was an experience "none of us will ever forget."

To port, a sweep of country presented itself. The Canadian Shield offers scant visual enticement. It is a quagmire pierced and pocked and scattered with outcroppings of continental bedrock. Very nearly flat topographically and empty of landmarks, this treeless plain occupied the visual field to the west, arcing a half-circle of vacant horizon to the edge of sky.

A zone of transition between boreal forest and open tundra had been crossed. Tall-growing vegetation had all but vanished. A greenish veneer—ground-hugging tundra plants—seemed painted on. Lost in featurelessness, the tree line lies fifty to sixty miles north of Churchill.

"Tree line" is a misnomer. It is a *zone*, in which trees diminish in size as, gradually, they disappear altogether—the boreal coniferous forests giving way to open woodland in which trees are stunted, finally to a dense cover of tundra in which scrub birch and willow, berry, lichens,

and other species dominate. The line snakes erratically across Newfoundland, Quebec, and the Northwest Territories to the Arctic Ocean, hostage to latitude and to surface topography, altitude, and nearness to the sea. The tree line marks the average southward extension of polar air masses during the growing season and, thus, the absolute limit for trees.[8]

Minutes out of Churchill the primary compass system failed. The N-1 gyro system (installed for this eventuality) was put to work. It proved indispensable.

The sixtieth parallel was logged. Soon Chesterfield Inlet lay abeam. Steeped in history, this had been a strategic harbor for exploration, trade, and commerce. Inuit here retain a fairly traditional lifestyle; in 1958 the village was home to perhaps a hundred souls—an outpost of humanity. One can only imagine the effect as the aircraft droned past.

Abruptly, several polar bears were sighted. Someone sang out—and all hands claimed windows. "Polar bear on the starboard beam," Mulligan would recall, caused a stir. "[One bear] charged the blimp's shadow as it moved across and one tried to jump at the unknown prey 800 feet above him."[9]

Bear are common along this shore, where upon breakup the animals exploit ice floes to hunt seals. When the ice vanishes, they come ashore to await the freeze-up. Females den for the winter, emerging with their cubs in March or April. After a few days, the family makes for the nearest floes. Six to seven thousand of these magnificent carnivores are estimated to inhabit the Canadian Arctic.[10]

Off Chesterfield Inlet, the display was unforgettable. Plunging off their pan, the bears swam furiously in one direction then another. Greenaway watched one dive in dragging a partially eaten seal. The bears, Lieutenant Koza said, were "very impressive." Robertson also was impressed—by the platform. "You were cruising at, what, forty miles per hour and flying very seldom over 500 feet. So as an observation platform it was marvelous." His countryman agrees: "You were low," Greenaway told me, "you were down there and you could see things." Crew chief Parker stared at the bloodied floe from which the seal carcass had been pulled—an unforgettable image.

[Opposite] The subarctic tundra of northern Manitoba, as seen from *719*. (Hugh A. Mulligan)

Ahead lay Roes Welcome Sound. Off Cape Fullerton, lineations appeared as narrow lakes. The pattern is caused by zones of weakness in bedrock accentuated by weathering. The northern landscape—coastline, topography, and drainage, as well as its tenacious vegetation and animal life—is a vestige of continental ice and enduring cold.

Roes Welcome Sound is a migration route for beluga. In the nineteenth century, it was a center for whaling. Ship's shadow crossed it early that evening. The coast to starboard (Southampton Island) is a waterlogged lowland of lakes and wide tidal flats; in winter, its shoreline is difficult for airmen to distinguish.[11]

Whale, seal, and walrus are hunted from the hamlet of Repulse Bay, a tucked-away dot fronting the sound. It came abeam in less than an hour—a settlement of about 350 individuals. "Flying at 175 meters above ground level, we were not noticed until practically overhead. Suddenly the entire community emerged from their tents and houses, stopping all activities to see this strange monster so close at hand. . . . Our airship, 106 meters long, 33 meters in diameter, looked like a giant whale to the Inuit. They had never seen anything like it before. The children in particular were very excited, running about in all directions, some appeared to be waving at us."[12]

Repulse Bay lies astride latitude 66° 33′ N.[13] "Crossed Arctic Circle at 2132—saw polar bear," the captain wrote to his diary. A position report about due, a sitrep was drafted to inform NADU command and official Washington. A single sentence sped south: "Airship Arctic flight X Sitrep 25 X Crossed Arctic Circle 8638W at 080317Z X Witnessed by one polar bear." Lighter-than-air had broken a new horizon.[14]

At Resolute, the Willie Victor was monitoring its NADU companion. Shown the transmission, Mulligan prepared a dispatch; it flashed to Navy Radio in Washington, thence to CNO. As well, the national press services were informed.

> Navy blimp crossed Arctic Circle at 9:17 (CST) tonight in the Repulse Bay section of Melville Peninsula PD Blimp now has proceeded further north than any non rigid airship in history STOP Capt HB Van Gorder in charge of the scientific expedition radioed that his airship crossed the circle witnessed by one polar bear STOP Next stop on the 4600 mile flight to the polar region is Resolute Bay here on Cornwallis Island.

The sixth lighter-than-air craft to penetrate boreal airspace and the only military airship ever to cross the Arctic Circle, ZPG-2 BUNO 126719 was making aeronautical history.

Arctic Air Exploration

The first attempt at polar exploration *by air* occurred in 1897. Platform: a balloon. Salomon August Andrée, a Swede, had a passion for aeronautics. "Ruthlessly curious," he was the first to dare the Arctic Circle.

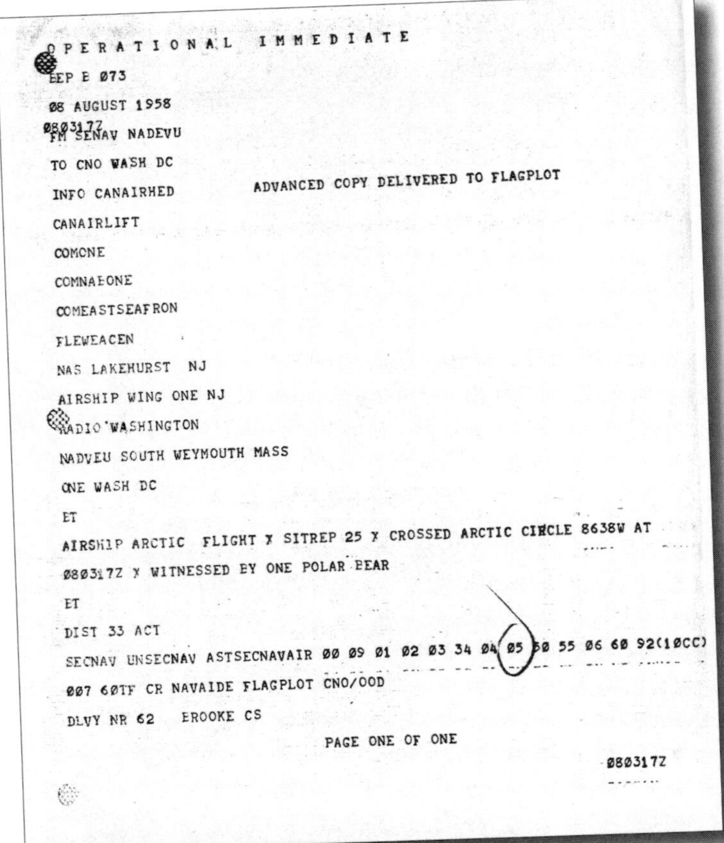

OPERATIONAL IMMEDIATE
EEP E Ø73
Ø8 AUGUST 1958
Ø8Ø317Z
FM SENAV NADEVU
TO CNO WASH DC
INFO CANAIRHED ADVANCED COPY DELIVERED TO FLAGPLOT
CANAIRLIFT
COMONE
COMNAEONE
COMEASTSEAFRON
FLEWEACEN
NAS LAKEHURST NJ
AIRSHIP WING ONE NJ
RADIO WASHINGTON
NADVEU SOUTH WEYMOUTH MASS
ONE WASH DC
ET
AIRSHIP ARCTIC FLIGHT X SITREP 25 X CROSSED ARCTIC CIRCLE 8638W AT
Ø8Ø317Z X WITNESSED BY ONE POLAR BEAR
ET
DIST 33 ACT
SECNAV UNSECNAV ASTSECNAVAIR ØØ Ø9 Ø1 Ø2 Ø3 34 Ø4 Ø5 5Ø 55 Ø6 6Ø 92(1ØCC)
ØØ7 6ØTF CR NAVAIDE FLAGPLOT CNO/OOD
DLVY NR 62 EROOKE CS
PAGE ONE OF ONE
Ø8Ø317Z

On 11 July, Andrée with two associates ascended from northwest Spitsbergen in *Eagle,* a hydrogen-filled, specially engineered free balloon. Objective: the geographic pole. Men and machine drifted northeast from view. Three messages later were recovered; however, the balloonists were not seen again—their fate unknown for thirty-three years.[15]

Walter Wellman, an American journalist-explorer of means, was next. His "aerial craft" was the French-built *America*—a nonrigid airship. From Spitsbergen, the Wellman *Chicago-Record Herald* Polar Expedition realized two attempts on the Pole. The first, in 1907, lifted off from the same spot as Andrée. The width of the fiord was the length of the flight. Undeterred, in 1909 it made a second try with a rebuilt *America.* It began propitiously. "The weather was fine [Wellman later wrote,] a light breeze was blowing from the south. At the wheel I steered her several times around the strait which lay in front of our camp to learn if everything was in good order. All going well I headed her north." He was obliged to abort after two hours and forty or so miles. *America* was towed back by steamer and salvaged. "The task [of gaining the Pole by air] was not an easy one," he conceded. "I never thought it was."[16]

In 1910, at the instigation of Count Ferdinand von Zeppelin, an official commission inspected Spitsbergen, to study its feasibility for exploration by rigid airship. Favorable findings notwithstanding, no expedition resulted. (But see page 120.)

The Italian-built *Norge,* a semirigid type, would log 90° N during a continent-to-continent transit—Spitzbergen to Alaska. Officially, it is relegated to *second* place, behind Richard E. Byrd and Floyd Bennett in a Fokker monoplane.[17] The modern disputing of Byrd's claim of primacy implies *Norge* indeed was first. At 1:25 a.m. (GMT), 12 May 1926, concluding an untroubled, sixteen-hour penetration, First Navigating Officer Hjalmar Riser-Larsen announced: "Now we are there." "Under us lay the polar basin, [Riser-Larsen wrote] bathed in sunshine. We slackened speed, and went down to 200 meters altitude. One by one the flags were dropped there, whilst we stooped with uncovered heads."[18]

It had been a triumph of planning, but the Amundsen-Ellsworth-Nobile transpolar expedition nourished tragedy and disgrace. Roald Amundsen had organized the expedition, Lincoln Ellsworth its principal backer. *Norge,* however, had been designed and built at the Italian State Airship Factory, under the direction of Colonel Umberto Nobile, an officer in the Italian Military

[Opposite] 2132 hours (EDT), 7 August 1958. Sitrep 25, a singular moment in naval aviation. Airship BUNO 126719 was the sixth lighter-than-air craft to penetrate Arctic airspace and, to date, the only military airship to cross the Arctic Circle. (Naval History and Heritage Command)

[Left] 14 April 1926: *Norge* departs Oslo, Norway, for North America via Spitsbergen and the Pole—the first air crossing of the Arctic. The Italian-built semirigid will land at Teller, Alaska, on 13 May—four days after Richard E. Byrd's now-disputed claim to 90° N. The Aero Club of Norway was the expedition's official sponsor. (Author)

Air Service. Hired on, Nobile had commanded the airship. Explorers are proud men. Disagreements and resentments were ignited. One outcome: bitter and disparate accounts of the *Norge*'s expedition across the top of the world.

Nobile had resolved to return, this time with an expedition unquestionably his own, in a new airship, *Italia*. On 23 May 1928, the expedition departed Kings Bay, Spitsbergen. *Italia* reached the Pole next day with little difficulty. On the return, dropping temperatures, fog, and adverse winds hindered navigation—an obstacle no less than the extreme cold. Moreover, the ship became increasingly, unaccountably heavy—due, probably, to ice buildup and pieces thrown into the bag by the props (see page 45). Descent uncontrollable, the control cabin impacted, spilling ten crewmen onto the pack. Adrift before the wind, the derelict took six to oblivion.

The search-and-rescue effort was high theater—an international tragicomedy. Coming out of retirement, Amundsen vanished while assisting the search. The mounting fiasco introduced questions regarding Nobile's judgment and conduct: following his rescue, the general was disgraced by the fascist government.[19]

In Russia various official schemes for lighter-than-air transport were investigated. The Soviet Union, some argued, needed airships to help connect its nearly roadless immensity. "In no other country," *Flight* magazine noted (in 1932), "not even in America, is the construction of lighter-than-air craft undertaken with such enthusiasm and complete official support as in Russia." The national program (assisted by Nobile) concentrated on the smaller types—semirigids and blimps.

Some mail and passengers were carried. In 1937, *V-6* crashed during a training flight. Thirteen were killed, three injured. And in May, *Hindenburg* burned at Lakehurst. Official fever for airships cooled.

Graf Zeppelin was last to penetrate the North. In July 1931 Dr. Hugo Eckener commanded a scientific and geographic flight off the coasts of European Russia. No try was made on the Pole (reason: insurance); instead, the expedition devoted itself to science. Passenger comforts stripped, spaces were appropriated for instruments—magnetometers, mapping cameras, survival gear. The roster was an international *Who's Who* of experts, led by the energetic director of the USSR's Institute of Arctic Studies, Professor R. L. Samoilovich. Not one to inhabit an office, Samoilovich had led the Soviet rescue of *Italia* survivors, saving seven.[20] Three comrades included Professor P. A. Molchanov, aerologist and inventor of the first radiosonde. Accompanying: Lincoln Ellsworth and Lieutenant Commander E. H. ("Iceberg") Smith, U.S. Coast Guard.[21] All on board were granted a spectacular tour.

Three radiosondes were dropped—a polar first—and measurements of air pollution over the Soviet Arctic recorded.[22] Such was the scientific harvest, Eckener joked, that Samoilovich might faint from the burden.[23]

Northernmost penetration: 81° 50′ N, off Prince Rudolf Island—less than five hundred nautical miles from the geographic pole.

On to Resolute

North of Chesterfield Inlet, the coast changed in aspect; by Repulse Bay, a rugged terrain offered welcome contrast to the muskeg enclosing Churchill. Rae Isthmus was crossed in clear twilight. It connects the mainland with Melville Peninsula, now filling the windows to starboard. From October to June, natives hunt its interior for caribou, polar bear, and wildfowl.

Crossing the head of Committee Bay, *719* again had water below. Ahead lay the Gulf of Boothia. It lies between Baffin Island and the Boothia Peninsula—the northmost tip (71° 58′ N) of North America. Waters here may be icebound even in summer: late in summer, deteriorating pack ice from Prince Regent Inlet tends to collect there, where it rots and, in good years, melts entirely.

Visibility deteriorated. This leg would be flown at about eight hundred feet, keeping between fog and intermittent stratus, changing course to keep well off shore. When the fog level climbed, visibility dropped to zero. Moisture began collecting; at its altitude, fortunately, tem-

Graf Zeppelin. In July 1931, an international roster of scientists on board—including Sir Hubert Wilkins—the "Graf" explored the polar wastes off European Russia. Northernmost penetration: latitude 81° 50′ N. (*Luftschiffbau-Zeppelin*)

perature precluded ice on the ship. "As with airplanes," the explorer Vilhjalmur Stefansson observed, "dirigibles have found in the Arctic that they can usually control the formation of ice by rising and dropping to levels of different temperatures." Recalling his test-flying for NADU, Commander Charles Mills concurred. "You could usually maneuver out of icing by either going up or down."[24]

No sun sight was possible. The N-1 did yeoman's service, holding *719* to a steady heading. "When it was overcast and the sun not available, as on part of the Churchill-to-Resolute leg, I used a combination of track-made-good and drift angle to compute the heading flown, and then compared it with the gyro reading. This technique was o.k. when we could get radar fixes off the islands. [Greenaway adds,] It was fortunate that the primary direction system failed when in good weather over Hudson Bay and not while flying between layers in Prince Regent Inlet."[25]

A bleak shoreline paraded astern. Visual contact obscured, radar bearings on prominent landmarks were used to maintain track. Though no permanently settled Inuit occupy the region, this coast is an important hunting area for ringed and bearded seals, narwhals, and beluga.[26]

[Opposite] Lancaster Sound—eastern entrance to the Northwest Passage—shimmers under an August sun. Today the sound is a suggested marine conservation area, but, in 2010, was slated for geophysical exploration for oil and natural gas. (Author)

At about 0600, the blimp's huge shadow was gliding across Bellot Strait (72° N). Its waters separate Boothia Peninsula from Somerset Island—a sedimentary flatland about the size of Vermont.

Creswell Bay came abeam. The living resources here are remarkably productive: narwhal, seal, caribou, ducks, geese, ptarmigan. The bay is also an important beluga calving area. And in the freshwater streams and lakes, Arctic char abound. The species is an important food to Inuit and, more recently, a quest for sport fishermen.

To port, the ruler-straight shore of Somerset Island climbed in elevation; soon, a thousand-foot escarpment and ribbon of beach were parading astern. To both port and to starboard, however, the shore passed unseen, save for the "eyes" of the radar.

The final two hundred miles would be dominated by stratified cloud decks plus low-hanging fog. Radar navigation—taking bearings on the shore, as check points to maintain track—was exploited throughout this leg.

Gateway to the Northwest Passage on this track: Prince Regent Inlet. Cornwallis Island and its airfield at Resolute lie astride the waterway, about thirty miles north of Somerset Island.

The final minutes dropped away; heading: almost due north. The blimp approached close to the northeast tip of Somerset Island, a smooth, bold coast of striking cliffs.

Breaks in fog and cloud yielded snatches of visibility. Vegetal life was unapparent. Island plants become increasingly scarce as one proceeds north. At 74°, no hint of green splashes the tans and chocolate black browns: here the airship had reached the High Arctic. The few plants able to defy the protracted cold, scant moisture, and months of near-total darkness are scattered and few, thus unapparent from the air.

Abruptly, Prince Regent Inlet lay astern: Lancaster Sound is the eastern arm of the fabled east–west highway through the archipelago.

A turn to port brought a new heading, so as to pass between Somerset and Prince Leopold Islands—the latter an islet off Somerset's northeast tip. It is a prominent check-point for airmen: flat topped and surrounded by magnificent banded cliffs standing sheer a thousand feet above the water. On approach to Resolute, the spectacle of its bold cliffs and the extraordinary setting are unforgettable.

This desolation had scant impact on the expedition leader: Van Gorder was a man preoccupied. "I was concentrating," he recalled years later, "with Collins about the problem of getting the ship on the runway"—a narrow gravel strip.

New heading: north-northwest, direct to the airfield. Below, the open water gave no hint of ice, having cleared this sector less than a week before. In the diffused, filtered light, Barrow Strait offered a dull mercury-gray hue.

Arrival was spiced with concern: the ceiling was low, and dropping. Fortunately visibility held to at least ten miles: to starboard, the flat-topped cliffs of Devon Island brooded on the passage; to port, the smooth coast of Somerset Island extended westward into haze. Ahead, to the northwest, an indistinct line appeared; on approach, it darkened and enlarged: Cornwallis Island.

Waiting at base "Res," Squadron Leader Becker recalled "a wonderful day in every way. The supply ships arrived in the harbor and the resupply operation of Resolute Bay was about

to start. The weather was borderline excellent and the winds were reasonable. Available station personnel, both military and civilian, were looking south for the first glimpse of the strangest aircraft ever to arrive at Resolute. The control tower was operational and anxiously awaiting for radio contact."[27]

Radio Resolute contacted, the clipped banter of tactical communication ensued.

> Resolute Bay, this is USN Airship *719*. How do you read?
>
> Roger *719,* this is Resolute Bay reading you 5 by 5. What is your position?
>
> Resolute Bay, Navy *719*. We are 40 miles south—request local weather conditions and permission to land.
>
> Roger *719*. You are cleared for a straight-in approach—anticipate a crosswind of about 40 degrees, wind 25 knots. What is your ETA [estimated time of arrival]?
>
> Resolute *719:* Our ETA is one hour from now.[28]

Fog might blank their flight path, so today's was an instrument approach for the pilots—no particular danger. Still, an unfamiliar field in deteriorating conditions is an unwelcome prospect for any airman.

Through thick cloud, Cornwallis Island began to frame the forward windows—a smooth plain cut by flat-topped bluffs at water's edge. Resolute Bay itself is a gray indentation rimmed by a cinnamon-color shore. Inland, spatters of bright orange on a canvas of yellow brown peeked into view: the Canadian base.

Airship in sight: an enlarging pinpoint to the south. In 1958 Resolute boasted a single gravel strip. When graded (in 1947), it was not aligned into the prevailing wind. The remains of six or seven wrecks blot the nearby tundra—proof of the hazards of operating here. A Lancaster bomber is one: impressed into ice-patrol duty, one day the "Lanc" did not make the airstrip. The wing commander knew this place: for "years and years, we flew in and out of there with a strong crosswind."

On approach, the landing itself tempered the satisfaction of arrival: a crosswind landing. Fortunately, despite a ton or so of moisture picked up since Committee Bay, *719* was light and free of ice. Base temperature: 41° F.

The airship slowed, then initiated a descent. Exploiting the local beacon and directional gyro, it aligned with runway. The beach line was on the scope, radar providing distance from runway's end. On final radar approach, *719* broke through a ragged underdeck at about three hundred feet. Despite a fluctuating ceiling, forward visibility now was good: dead ahead lay 6,500 feet of gravel quite free of fog.

Collins and Koza compensated for an insistent crosswind. A wide, sloping beach was crossed. Storage tanks scooted past to starboard (the all-important fuel depot), then the Inuit settlement. Abruptly, runway gravel lay beneath.

The navy touched down at 0830 local (CDST) time, 8 August. Considering conditions, Greenaway deemed it an excellent landing. The crosswind, he would recall, combined with an unfamiliar approach beneath a low ceiling and a narrow runway "added up to a not very relaxed landing, although quite safe." For the captain, the landing was "somewhat hazardous." "Considering all factors," Becker recalls, "it was an excellent landing indeed."

Undercarriage skidding, the airship rolled out against a crosswind. Props set in reverse pitch, *719* slowed amid dust and skittering gravel.

On hand to meet the airship were the support group from NADU, the expedition's scientists and Mulligan, a few journalists, Squadron Leader Becker and his RCAF detachment—and just about every white man and Inuit on the island. "The arrival," in Becker's phrase, "was nothing less than spectacular."

Resolute is a fascination. A staging point for anyone pushing elsewhere into the islands, the outpost is indispensable—a jump-off point for anthropologists, geologists, wildlife biologists, and assorted researchers, as well as airmen and contractor personnel, nearly all of whom slosh in (and out) with the field season. The author well remembers the base. The dining hall was host to a diverse lot: grizzled laborers (there to regrade the runways) chatted with specialists in satellite communications. Crowding nearby tables were university scientists, airmen, government personnel.

Decades before, Commander Schou had met a similar scene. He was struck by the "diversity of humanity" in the mess: scientists, engineers, PhDs, laborers, crisply uniformed Canadian "Mounties." Today, the Polar Continental Shelf Project provides logistic support for scientists who come then scatter throughout the region. A few miles away, the Canadian military conducts survival training.

Morning of 8 August 1958: the base at Resolute (lower left) and enclosing tundra from the airship's flight deck. In the bay, the annual resupply ship swings to its anchor. (Cdr. A. J. Schou)

"The base," as everyone calls Resolute, is now a civilian airfield. In 1958 it was military—manned by an RCAF detachment. Among the ground handlers for that long-ago arrival were six or seven officers from Canada's Tactical Ice Reconnaissance Unit. Eager to impress, they had donned their number-one uniforms. "The aircrew went out to the ramp just before the landing," Tom Kilpatrick, chief of the ice unit, recalled. Deprived of sleep from weeks of round-the-clock exertions, and despite the excitement, Kilpatrick had taken "a rain check on this affair because of extreme fatigue." Now mooring lines were tossed to his men. "We probably had," Schou observed, "people from blue collar workers to Ph.D.s on those long lines helping." For their trouble, the Canadian officers were promptly dragged through mud when the blimp answered a gust. "I was in bed but awake when the aircrew returned," Kilpatrick continued, "and it was just about the funniest sight you ever heard or saw. Of course, there were no dry-cleaning facilities at Resolute."[29]

"With the wind, the soft gravel and no proper ground handling equipment," the base commander told me, "taxiing from the runway to the mooring mast was, to say the least, difficult and time consuming but the airship crew made it. The United States Navy had arrived in Resolute Bay!"[30]

There is nothing like arrival at one's destination to prove a point.

> Resolute Bay, Cornwallis Island, Aug. 8 (AP)—The arrival of a Navy blimp today gave this remote Arctic island, about 500 miles north of the Arctic Circle, a double reason for celebrating.

[Opposites, top, and bottom] Arrival at Resolute, in the Canadian Arctic islands. (Hugh A. Mulligan)

[Bottom] Ship secured, Capt. Van Gorder and command pilot Collins confer with Squadron Leader William P. Becker, RCAF—officer-in-charge of the Cornwallis Island detachment. Note ship's ladder. (Hugh A. Mulligan)

Last night the Canadian icebreaker *C. D. Howe* was the first ship of the year to appear in the harbor. The blimp, first ever seen in these parts, stole some of the ship's thunder by poking its nose through the low-hanging clouds this morning.

Practically the whole island's population turned out for the double visitation. Completely uninhabited until 15 years ago, the island now has about 150 Canadian airmen; about 35 American and Canadian civilian technicians and scientists; 68 Eskimos and 1 Canadian Mountie.

The blimp's orange and silver painted body blended nicely with the local decor. All of the one-story corrugated huts on the airfield and at the weather station are done up in bright orange for easy identification in the snow, of which there is none at the moment.

Contrary to popular opinion, there is little snow above the Arctic Circle during the summer months of almost continuous sunshine. The blimp, coasting along on a 10-mile an hour tail wind, covered more than a 1,000 miles in 22 hours.

It now goes to T-3, a floating ice island manned by scientists of the International Geophysical Year, to accomplish its primary mission of demonstrating supply and observation possibilities. The station at T-3 is less than 500 miles from the North Pole.

Beyond the Pole

On approach to 90° N, *Nautilus* had recorded generally ten-tenths coverage ("water scarce") with numerous sixty-foot ice keels. Now the Pole stood logged: "1915U Passed under geographic North Pole." Now, on course 180° T, beneath near-continuous ice, *Nautilus* steamed unimpeded into the next phase of Anderson's operational orders: the first under-ice transit Pacific to Atlantic.[31] "Without changing course," he was to write, "we were heading due south." In his journal, Lyon jotted, "Continued on across pole maintaining straight course, taking water samples, etc, continuous ice profile."

Nautilus in fact recorded a near-continuous acoustic under-ice profile. Beyond the Pole, in the Eurasian side of the basin, the ceiling's underside became progressively more severe. An inverted topography of floes, refrozen leads, and deep-draft keels gave way to

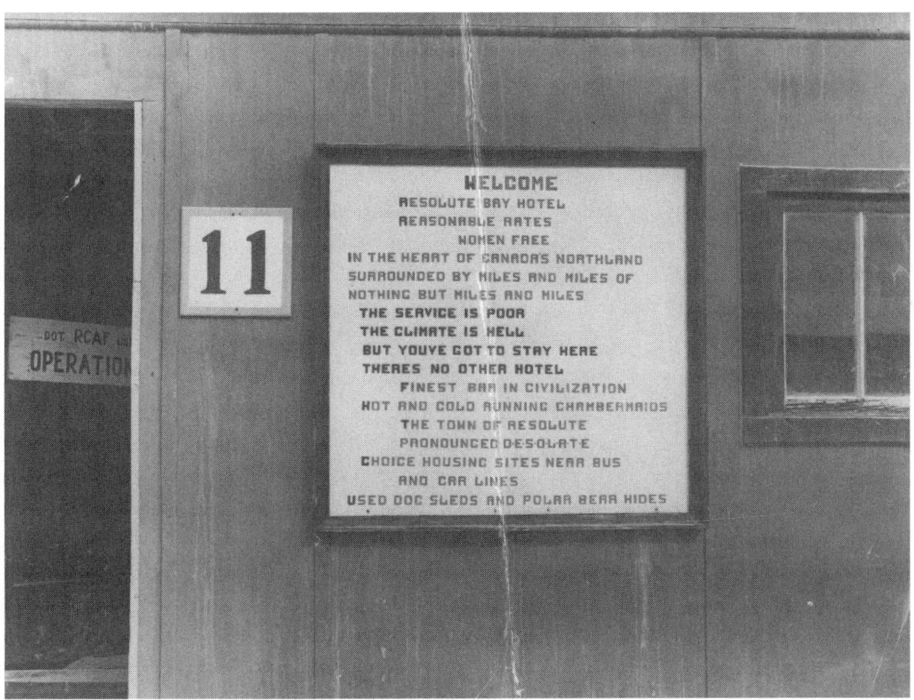

Entrance to "Ops." In 1958 the base and airfield facilities at both Resolute and Fort Churchill were administered by the Air Transport Command, Royal Canadian Air Force. (Capt. Harold B. Van Gorder)

a rougher profile. A heretofore unobserved sector, this most rugged topography was recorded. The deepest-draft ice keels were underrun—more than a hundred graphing off the recording charts.[32] Sea ice, the submariners knew, is a shifting, broken sheet riven by cracks, leads, and ridged ice. First-year ice is about a foot thick or less, multiyear pack ice perhaps ten feet. Pressure ice—broken, crushed, refrozen—is thickened to tens of feet and can reach a hundred or more. Prevalent on the Atlantic side of the basin, no large leads were now detected.

Unable to surface, though safe from the deepest ice, the boat could make no transmissions until surfacing.

Nautilus steamed south. The gyrocompasses did not slew around until the boat reached below 87° N. In the meantime, every half hour, as the helmsman was relieved he reported, "Steering 180 True, 000 by gyro, Sir!"

Chief engineer Early had returned to his stateroom, where he filled in the date and time on commemorative letters. "Since it was late, I undressed, took a hot shower, and turned in," Early recalled. "Later, I learned that I had taken a shower within ten miles of the North Pole, the only one to do so!"

The most difficult phase lay astern. And not so much as a light bulb had failed. "The material performance of the ship, and particularly the nuclear plant," Anderson would report, "can only be described as remarkable." Mood prevailing? "It was a feeling of accomplishment. [But] we still had a hell of a long way to go, so we didn't get carried away with it. . . . We had at least found with very primitive navigation for those days the North Pole. We were pioneering navigation equipment, we were pioneering under-the-ice equipment. It had been successful, and we looked forward to completin' the mission—and announcin' it to the world."[33]

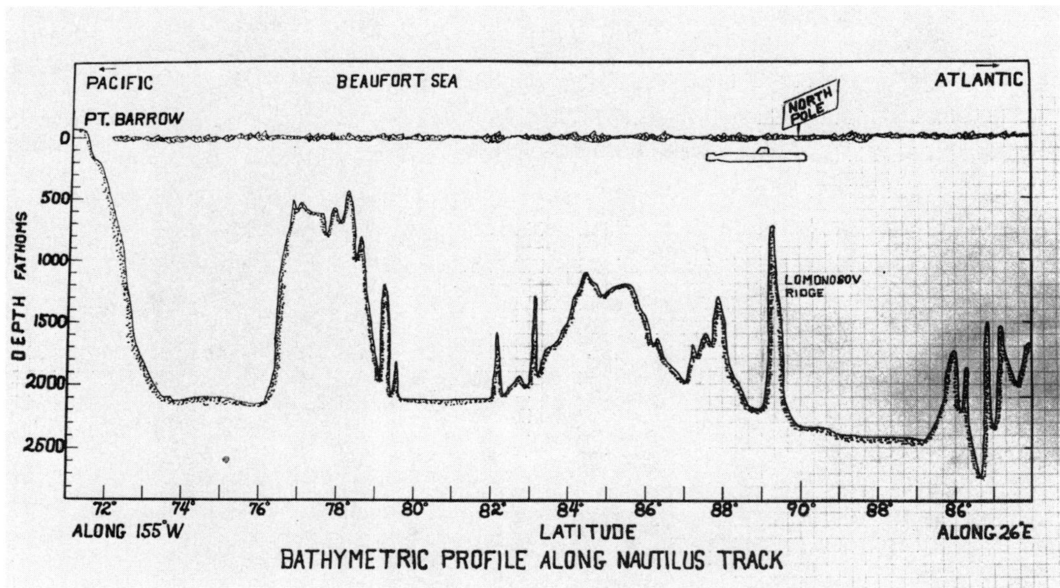

Acoustic depth profile for Operation Sunshine, 1–4 August 1958. The transit also recorded ice thickness from below the canopy. Detected by Soviet *polyarniks* (polar researchers) in 1948, the existence of the Lomonosov Ridge was confirmed the following year. A continuous feature, it divides the Polar Basin into two deep basins. (U.S. Navy)

On the run out, 4 August, Anderson held his command to twenty knots, steering various true courses "to make good 198° grid heading for 81° N/00°." The compasses, for their part, had appeared to settle. Via periscope, the ice appeared as black or dark gray masses, a light gray for leads. As 5 August opened, "At 22 knots, 600 feet, course 170° T. Soundings are varying from 700 to 1200 fathoms indicating we are on the Nansen Ridge west of Spitsbergen. All positions—N6A, Navigator's EP, and DR are within 25 miles. Ice is getting thinner with more water openings indicating we are near the pack edge. Injection [Dr. Lyons' hourly water samples] is up to 38°–39° indicating we are in the Gulf Stream off-shoot west of Spitsbergen."

The surface was watched for signs of large polynyas or the pack-ice edge. Nearing the Greenland–Spitsbergen Passage, Anderson relied in part on observations the boat had collected earlier. On hand was a chart with soundings taken in 1957 by *Nautilus* north of Spitsbergen. As he approached, it was "comforting," Early acknowledged, "to pass from a blank chart to an area that showed the soundings we ourselves took the year before."[34]

Sonars and television showing negative for ice, *Nautilus* was trimmed for a vertical ascent; all stopped, Anderson hovered up to periscope depth. The log recorded 1,830 miles since Point Barrow, ninety-six hours since submergence. At 09:54 EDST, clear overhead, Anderson surfaced in the Atlantic Ocean, completing the first Pacific–Atlantic transpolar crossing. *Nautilus* floated northeast of Greenland, coordinates 79° 19′ N, 4° 12′ E. "Surfaced easily," Lyon wrote, "thus ending the transit from Pt. Barrow."

Swells and wave size spoke open sea. For the first time since Hawaii, Anderson broke radio silence, to broadcast "*Nautilus* ninety north," followed by, "Ninety-six hours, Point Barrow to the Greenland Sea."

Navigator "Shep" Jenks climbed topside. In passage, he had been relieved and "terribly excited" when all the navigational systems had agreed, especially at the Pole. Still, a doubt nagged.

> I ran up on the bridge with my sextant and back to the old methods—and started taking sun lines. . . . When we surfaced we were in a sort of hazy fog. But you could see the sun and certainly bring it down to the horizon and get good sun lines. I don't know exactly how accurate they were but after four days submerged from our last "fix" on land at Point Barrow it was pretty exciting to get our sun lines and find that position by conventional sextant methods and position by estimated position—which was based on a lot of things, from dead reckoning, inertial navigation—that once again positions tracked. As I remember the figure was somewhere about a mile and a half between the sun lines position and the estimated position that we were keeping at the time.[35]

For the thirty-year-old, it was exhilarating. Anderson's remark: "Fan-damn-tastic," a *Nautilus* expression.

Though it was a story of the highest moment, the Navy Department withheld any public statement: President Eisenhower would announce success personally.

Nautilus submerged; at four hundred feet and twenty-three knots, Anderson continued his run toward rendezvous off Iceland, surfacing only to copy radio traffic.

Reverberations

In American eyes, *Nautilus* had never been in Canadian waters, and thus the need to inform Ottawa had not arisen. Still, Canada was the ally most directly affected. North of the border, the transit (announced on 8 August) reignited concern for sovereignty. Further penetrations were certain to use approaches claimed by Ottawa. (Indeed, submarine interaction between the superpowers would intensify the strategic value of Canadian Arctic waters—the archipelago particularly.) True, the Canadian media echoed the universal plaudits. "There is a dash of Jules Verne romance in the voyage of the American submarine *Nautilus* under the polar ice cap," one sheet trumpeted. "It is a triumph for American science, imagination and courage and should go far to restore the self-confidence of the people of the United States and its friends abroad so badly shaken by recent Russian achievements."[36]

Still, the portents were plain enough. At a stroke, the transpolar crossing had underscored the basin's strategic importance—open now to military exploitation. On the floor of the House of Commons, one MP remarked that the strategic and commercial potential of "this magnificent achievement" on Canadian national life "must be very much in our minds." A colleague went to the heart of the matter: "No longer can Canadians think that because we have ninety per cent of our country to the north unexplored and undeveloped, because we have a great cold ocean to the north, this is our defence line. We are now fully aware of the fact that the water underneath that ice is available for the movement of underwater craft and this affects the whole future of this country and, I believe, much of the world."[37]

Eisenhower chose to underscore the commercial applications. In its wake, according to the president, *Nautilus* had opened a new seaway connecting two major oceans. In his own remarks Anderson also emphasized the commercial angle.[38] Most officials and defense analysts—skating over the harsher implications—avoided calling attention to the strategic significance of the transpolar cruise.[39]

[Opposite] Canadian reaction to the transpolar crossing was admiring—but also concerned. (*The Telegram* [Toronto], 12 August 1958)

On 10 August, Admiral Rickover (under no constraint save his own) commented for the press. Due to his no-nonsense evangelism, ego, and indispensable contributions, *Nautilus* "belonged" to Rickover.[40] Outspoken and a point-blank personality, the admiral was the navy's most notorious active-duty officer.[41] Not coincidently, his congressional connections were terrific. The transit, he told reporters, could be duplicated by *Skate* and *Seawolf.*

As Rickover spoke, *Skate* was at sea. Commander James Calvert had "waited by Spitsbergen" until word from *Nautilus*. Prior to Sunshine, both were to have operated together, though not under the ice. In the Denmark Strait, *Skate* passed *Nautilus* to port at about noon on 7 August. Four days later, *Skate* reached the ice margin. "We were equipped to break through the ice," Admiral Calvert would tell me. *Nautilus* was not. "That was all planned by the White House," he noted. The intent of a two-boat operation: to underscore U.S. technological prowess and realize a public-relations bonanza. After all, Calvert reminded, "Wherever we [nuclear boats] went, there was a tremendous amount of coverage."[42] White House press secretary James Hagerty had intended to exploit that reaction. And the Navy Department was not about to object.

Nautilus' success, Rickover added, "shows that we now have a ship that can hide under the ice. Now any nation knows that if they attack us they will inevitably be destroyed." Incited, Radio Moscow responded, claiming that the United States employed every scientific discovery for "war preparation." *Nautilus'* contribution to science and exploration was acknowledged. Yet, "on the very same day when President Eisenhower lauded the courage of the crew of the *Nautilus* there was a separate voice which exposed the designs of the U.S. military leaders."

Canadian media devoted column inches to the exchange.[43] According to one vexed editorial, Rickover's talking up the missile-carrying submarine as a deterrent implied nuclear warheads "infest[ing] our hitherto innocent polar seas." The issue was no idle anxiety: nine of the navy's first thirty-three nuclear submarines would be armed with ballistic missiles. "By their super routine journey under the pole," *Life* opined, "the men of *Nautilus* may have opened an arena for hideous battle." A book coauthored by Commander Anderson was released within months. The *New York Times,* in its review, summarized the transit's fearful implications: "The journey effectively brought to the attention of the world the potential role of nuclear-powered submarines, capable of prowling beneath the polar pack and launching missiles from any of the countless lagoons and channels of open water that divide it."[44]

As yet, the Soviet Union had announced no SSNs of its own. Few doubted their construction, however, to counter the Americans deploying "from their side." As for missiles, the Soviets were pursuing an ICBM program. (In that field, the Eurasian superpower was thought by analysts to be ahead of the West.) And that fall, the first recorded discussion of nuclear-powered submarines for the Royal Canadian Navy took place.

At an IGY reception, meantime, Soviets guests toasted the Americans and their achievement—and sought out whatever information they could as to *Nautilus* and its transpolar success.

Meanwhile, having logged a radar fix on Spitsbergen, *Skate* steamed the ten-degree meridian to the vicinity of the Pole. On 12 August, the boat crossed that extremity, after which a search for open water commenced. Forty miles beyond 90° N, Calvert maneuvered beneath a large polynya, then ordered a vertical ascent. Caution attended: no search-and-rescue plan existed, of course. Surfaced, sun lines taken, word of success was transmitted to naval receiving stations.

("You know you were all right, but we don't," CNO had told him.) "My orders were pretty clear," Calvert added. "The military usefulness of an ocean area [his operational orders read] is dependent on at least periodic access to its surface." Accordingly, *Skate* was navigating the central Arctic to develop and demonstrate techniques for surfacing *within* the canopy.

Continuing to survey bathymetry, *Skate* surfaced then flooded down nine times within the Arctic pack, using the boat's inertia to break through thin ice ("skylights"). As well, Calvert logged rendezvous (third surfacing) with Alpha, a floe-rafted IGY drifting station at 85° N, 136° W—or so Alpha estimated in a reply message to the boat. No observations had been taken for several days, the station radioed. But, fortuitously, "many polynyas in vicinity but best only fifty yards from our main buildings." On 14 August, *Skate* surfaced next to Alpha, with its tiny cluster (twenty-nine personnel) of humanity, "Slowly the periscope came out of the water. We were surrounded by Arctic civilization. Small brown huts dotted the ice. A high radio antenna rose over them. The squat silo shape of a radar dome lay farther astern. Near it stood a tall pole with the American flag."[45]

Calvert put far-northern waters astern. As on the approach, the boat exited via the deep-water Greenland-Spitsbergen Passage. Destination: Bergen, Norway—as ordered.[46] There a reception was hosted, with a band and crowds to greet the Americans. And in Oslo, a ceremony was held at the *Fram* Museum. Among the attendees: Colonel Joseph O. Fletcher, USAF. (See chapter 6.) In the days following, congratulatory messages for *Skate* poured in.

Base Resolute

On Cornwallis Island, Van Gorder and his team were partaking of "wonderful hospitality and help" from Squadron Leader Becker. The base commander and his men were particularly busy just now: the annual resupply ship was swinging to its anchor. Resolute was hosting a *pair* of visitors from the far south.

The mooring mast for *719* had been erected three hundred yards west of the runway.[47] In support, RCAF personnel had graded a narrow taxiway and a circle, its radius such that the ship would swing clear of the strip. Unfortunately, preparations had bared permanently frozen ground. (On-island, permafrost penetrates down more than a thousand feet.) Stripped of its insulating layer, already the taxiway was muddy and uneven, with soft spots. As at Churchill, it

Skate (SSN 578) at Ice Station Alpha, 14 August 1958—first U.S. camp installed on sea ice. Passing *Nautilus* in the Denmark Strait, *Skate* reached the vicinity of 90° N on 12 August. The following March, the boat returned—the first attempt to sail the basin by submarine in winter. *Skate* surfaced at the Pole, the first to do so. "The voyage confirms the use of the Arctic Ocean for both military and commercial purposes." (Dr. Kenneth L. Hunkins)

was necessary to walk *719* to and from its mooring. Conditions here were far more hazardous, however. The muddy taxiway, for one, was barely sixty feet wide.

A "difficult" mooring had concluded without incident. Returning a refueled thus *heavy* aircraft to the runway would bring the expedition close to failure.

Meantime, the navy (assisted by the NADU support team and RCAF personnel) refueled and replenished the airship. Helium was added, to replace that valved. Refueling—from a cache of drummed fuel—proved tedious and was enjoyed by no one.

The run to "Res" had logged just under twenty-four hours aloft—1,244 miles. Average ground speed: fifty-one miles per hour. Fuel for the Churchill-to-Resolute run: forty gallons per hour.

The base here is a no-nonsense sanctuary. Though centrally located, in 1958 its facilities held few necessities; luxuries were absent altogether. A series of barrack blocks provided interconnected living, berthing, kitchen, and messing spaces. Raison d'être: weather reporting and its airstrip—indispensable support for the joint stations at Mould Bay, Alert, Eureka, and at Isachsen. As well, Resolute is an alternate for Thule's air traffic. That year also, a seismological station, cosmic-ray counters, magnetic recorders, and other gear were installed in support of IGY programs. And at water's edge, a new tide gauge stood.

RCAF staff assigned: a detachment of a hundred-plus civilians—added to which were a variety of transients, arriving/departing aircraft and scientists, along with Department of Transport, Mounted Police, and RCN personnel. As well, Becker added: "various dignitaries from all walks of life and countries."

For the Polar Project, base Resolute was ideally located—in mid-archipelago and reasonably close to the Arctic Ocean. The strip at Point Barrow, in contrast, sat a continent away from South Weymouth. Basing at Thule would have meant confronting rugged Ellesmere Island,

The U.S. Navy at Resolute Bay—a half-day layover. The airship will be refuelled and re-provisioned, its envelope topped off with helium. Note the soft ground—disturbed permafrost. Surface conditions here will nearly end the expedition. Returning from T-3, the decision will be taken to overfly the mast and, instead, carry on south to Churchill. (Cdr. A. J. Schou)

whereas the approach from Resolute would be over comparatively flat terrain. Alert was—and remains—a highly classified installation. And "Res" boasted a good communications net, for the transmission of weather data. Also, it had fuel. "It was sort of a natural site to operate from," Greenaway explained. "Resolute Bay was a trans-shipment point so, logistically, it was ideal. Resolute met all the requirements for the airship."[48]

Cornwallis Island is an unobstructed tableland—its inland horizon line unadorned rock and gravel. When the author flew with the Canadian Ice Patrol (in 1989), ice observers referred to the island as "the asteroid."

The soft, flat-lying sedimentary rocks of the central and western archipelago offer superb sites for airfields—but few good harbors. The igneous and metamorphic bedrock of the eastern Arctic, in contrast, offers deep, well-protected anchorages. A rugged, complex terrain grants few large, flat sites for construction.

100 MI FROM
MAGNETIC POLE

[Opposite, top] "Main Street" at Resolute Bay, August 1958. (AD1 Elmer B. Lord)

[Opposite, bottom] Wing Commander Keith R. Greenaway, RCAF, (l.); Cdr. B. Hickman, USN, NADU operations officer; and Lt. Cdr. James Goodman, USN, command pilot of the support Willie Victor at Resolute, on the Northwest Passage. (Cdr. A. J. Schou)

[Left] *719* in the midnight sun, 8–9 August 1958. Basing out of Resolute, U.S. Navy lighter-than-air would log but one sortie across the archipelago, into the Arctic Ocean. (Cdr. A. J. Schou)

Physical landscapes reflect the underlying bedrock and, as well, the processes that—over geologic time—have exhumed and sculpted them. Present-day landforms have directed, in one way or another, the swirl of human migrations, by dictating natural routes of transportation, hence settlements. From barest camp to bustling city, the physical character of a site—access and water, factors of climate, defense, plant and animal resources—these and other variables intertwine with economic, social, and political forces when man elects to settle.

Some habitations are less products of geography than of politics. Resolute is one. In 1947 the task force establishing an advance base met with heavy ice in Barrow Strait en route to Winter Harbour, on Melville Island. Rather than lose a year, and because the site was adequate, Resolute was chosen. The bay is accessible to ships without reinforced hulls (the ice congestion is just to the west) and is centrally located. The bay is shallow in places, however, requiring lightering during sealift resupply. And it is susceptible to ice accumulation. Moreover, the open water to the south produces summer sea fog when the wind is from the west.

Still, Resolute has become the "crossroads of the archipelago."

That long-ago August, light winds and clear skies were forecast for the next thirty-six hours for the western archipelago and the route to T-3. The layover here would be as planned: twelve hours.

Finding a few minutes, Parker scribbled a note. Over loose shingle (what passes here for pavement) he crunched his way to the base post office, near Operations. His words sketch his impressions—and the flight plan: "Made it here to Resolute in fine shape. We're leaving for Ice Island T-3 in a few hours when we refuel and top up with helium. Saw one polar bear eating a seal on an ice floe last night. It is daylight all night long now."[49]

Takeoff for the Arctic Ocean: 0900 hours, local time.

Equipped with his five senses, man explores the Universe around him and calls the adventure Science.

—Edwin Powell Hubble

6 Ice Island

The sky is dull and uninviting. In east-central Alaska, flight conditions below optimum are commonplace. High Arctic operations (above 75° N) were not yet routine. Still, in 1946 the demands attending polar flying were fast becoming a U.S. Air Force specialty.

For the 46th Reconnaissance Squadron Weather, Ladd Air Force Base, at Fairbanks, Alaska (today Fort Wainwright), morning delivers a well-worn routine: an aircrew rise early, don flight gear, mess. A briefing follows. Cold-weather operations call for particular care to aircraft and equipment; here, even routine tasks take longer. Specialists conclude their preflight checks and inspections. Today's mission—to collect weather data over the Arctic Ocean—will be a twelve-to-sixteen-hour penetration into nameless nothingness.

The forecast holds no particular threat, only cloud. A great deal of Arctic flying is logged above low stratus—the surface with its distractions obscured. It matters little. The Arctic Ocean is an unrelieved waste: old polar ice and younger floes in continuous movement, broken by long, narrow leads, hummocks, and snaking pressure ridges—thickened ice. The Pole holds little mystery to these airmen, certainly no romance. It is but a turn point on the charts, the place at which the return leg to base thankfully commences.

For scenery, the north geographic pole is utterly undistinguished.

It is August. USAF flights to the Pole have commenced, to gain weather information. Usual flight track, known as "Ptarmigan," is from Ladd AFB direct to 90° N by way of Point Barrow. This day, a B-29 again has been ordered up. Designed to bomb the Japanese home islands, the Superfortress is superb for long-range air reconnaissance. Impenetrable heretofore, the central polar basin is abruptly accessible. Data collection accelerates. Soon, logging the North Pole will cease to be newsworthy. By 1947, indeed, missions will be flown every few days for weather and for reconnaissance.[1] Hardly routine, but this is just another mission for the Alaskan Air Command. However, this penetration will alter the course of science and research *on* the Arctic Ocean.

The B-29 lifts clear, banks a wide turn, assumes a northerly heading. Distance to the geographic pole: 1,730 miles. The Yukon Basin is crossed, then the alpine peaks of the Brooks Range, which rise up—unseen—then pass astern. The North Slope is crossed. The converted bomber drones out over the polar pack at 180 knots.[2]

About three hundred miles out the navigator "sees" it on his radar. (No visual sighting is possible.) An enormous object is filling the screen. It appears dark against the brilliant returns of the pack—a signal characteristic of low, icebound terrain. Startled yet seasoned, he checks his equipment. The returns are genuine: this is no electronic gremlin, no deceiving "angel." The signal is unmistakable: land where none is known to exist—an island roughly fifteen by eighteen miles. Such had never before been reported in this ocean. Baffled and speculating, the aircrew completes its mission.[3]

In Washington, word of the sighting stirs interest. The object—whatever it is—is designated Target X (later T-1), its existence classified secret. Subsequent flights realize further detections. And with each plot, the target is mapped at different coordinates. At first, these are thought to be errors—understandable, given the rigors of polar air navigation. But a specific rate of movement is finally noticed. The air force is tracking an exceptionally large fragment of ice.

Speculation as to its possible origin and probable future soars.

When at last the mass is sighted visually—from seventy-five miles—it presents an undulating surface distinct from the chaos of the pack. Its pale blue color contrasts as well. Low-level runs above the target confirm an amazingly smooth surface, unlike the rugged confusion of sea ice. Later, pilots are nearly unanimous that an emergency landing could be made on all the large "ice islands" eventually discovered.

Could these peculiar bergs be exploited—as airfields, perhaps, or as communications bases or weather stations? These and related questions are granted intense military scrutiny.

Ice as Platform

Before earth-orbiting satellites, to study the ocean one went to sea. The predecessors of modern "drifting stations" were ice-strengthened ships, deliberately frozen in and allowed to shift with the pack. First to demonstrate the drifting laboratory technique, Fridtjof Nansen and the crew of his ice ship *Fram* had conducted a three-year sequestration (1893–96) of scientific studies in the Arctic Ocean.

Emulating Nansen, Leningrad's Arctic Institute had been first to exploit ice-as-platform. Deploying ski-equipped airplanes, Severnyy Polyus-1 ("North Pole-1") was established in May 1937 twelve miles off the Pole. Led by Ivan Papanin, a party of four had recorded measurements of air, ice, and ocean for nine Zenlike months. Shifted south on the Transpolar Drift Stream, the floe, with its camp—and its record of notes, data and observations—was exported out of the polar basin. Retrieval: by icebreaker, off the southeast coast of Greenland.

Excellence in polar exploration and sciences is a function of geography. Prior to its dissolution, the Soviet Union was earth's largest unbroken area under one flag—its north-facing coastline arcing from Bering Strait to the Baltic: 170° west longitude (opposite Alaska) to 30° east longitude (opposite Norway). Arctic and subarctic territories constituted more than half this colossus.

Impetus: development of a commercial route along the north-facing coast of Eurasia, a zone extending from the Barents Sea east to the Strait. Following the 1941–45 spasm, during which the

Target 3 (T-3). This ice island was radar-detected in July 1950 by the U.S. Air Force, seen visually that August. The Alaskan Air Command occupied T-3 in March 1952, to assess the platform for military-sponsored research. (Dr. Maynard M. Miller)

Soviets ceased nearly all research, polar programs resumed, reinvigorated. Meantime, a trickle of information escaped the Soviet superpower.[4]

Ptarmigan flights kept track of Target X and, to pass the time, looked for other ice masses and undiscovered land. Often T-1 escaped detection; when it was again reported, the mass floated a bit farther east, its shape unchanged.

No new islands had yet been discovered. But T-1 was sighted repeatedly—usually by radar, due to darkness and cloud. The peripatetic berg was following what appeared to be an erratic, clockwise course off the Canadian Archipelago to about 75°, thence westward, then north, across the Pole. Its consistent outline implied great thickness and strength. Shifted from routine flight paths, in 1949 T-1 was "lost" north of Greenland. Average rate of drift: approximately 1.2 miles per day.

The military potential of ice islands, meanwhile, had become a persistent topic. In May 1950, Lieutenant Colonel Joseph O. Fletcher, USAF, CO of the 58th Strategic Weather Reconnaissance Squadron, ordered crews flying the Ptarmigan route to make special radar and visual searches. On 20 July, a large target was sighted and photographed two hundred miles (86°) from the Pole. On the 29th, another, smaller target (T-3) was radar-detected at 75° N.

A reexamination of photographs realized the existence of dozens of ice islands. Most were small, many stranded in interisland channels of the archipelago.[5] An unusual rippled pattern photographed in April 1947 during a joint USAF/RCAF flight was (it was later realized) T-3. The photographer: Squadron Leader Keith R. Greenaway, RCAF.

The U.S. Air Force foresaw dividends from "floating islands." Mobile, stable, and immune to fracturing, these oddments offered natural platforms wandering a maritime blank. Equipped for both survival and research, ice islands presented semipermanent rafts within the polar pack. Immersing himself, Fletcher pushed hard for occupation. In mid-1950 the Alaskan Air Command issued orders to establish an experimental drifting base.

Unknown to the West, the Soviets had already established a second long-haul drifting station, SP-2—one element of their 1950 offshore program. Its existence was not announced, its data withheld.

Impelled by superpower anxieties, the emphasis was shifting from reconnaissance to a new era of protracted, systematic investigation. Transpolar warfare had become possible, given the

B-29 and Soviet Tu-4 long-range bombers. Logistic and other problems attendant to reconnaissance, navigation, detection, landing, supply, survival, and rescue in the North began to garner intensive examination.

[Opposite] The War Hunt Ice Shelf, Ellesmere Island, Canadian High Arctic. These floating shelves are nurseries for ice islands—fragments that break free from the seaward edge to drift with the pack. Note the pattern of ridges and troughs. (Royal Canadian Air Force, courtesy George D. Hobson)

Seeking experience, the U.S. Navy had conducted its own exercises, operating off Greenland and in the Bering Sea. Special ice reconnaissance over the Beaufort Sea was being flown, to support the annual resupply of the Naval Petroleum Reserve No. 4, at Barrow. Funded by ONR, the Arctic Research Laboratory was established—a support facility for contract research. In the eastern Arctic, the joint U.S.-Canadian weather stations required annual resupply. As well, experiments were under way to equip aircraft for pack-ice landings. In April 1950 a C-47 deployed a two-man party off northern Alaska—the first sea-ice landing by U.S. aircraft. Brief touchdowns at selected coordinates are continued by both services, to gather oceanographic, ice, and geophysical data. Equivalent to the Soviets' "jumping" surveys (using aircraft specially equipped as laboratories), there were no borrowings: the Americans knew nothing of the others' technique. "Believe me [Fletcher recalled] had we been able to show our authorities the information [as to Soviet initiatives], it would not have been so difficult to get authorization and support for Arctic Basin investigation."[6]

In 1949 the U.S. Army had organized a Snow, Ice and Permafrost Research Establishment to conduct basic and applied research in snow, ice, and frozen ground. The army also was using the base at Fort Churchill as a cold-weather testing site. A decade later a nuclear-powered research facility *under* the Greenland ice cap (Camp Century) would be operational.

In November 1950 the matter of "floating islands" went public. A paper by Lieutenant Colonel Fletcher and Captain Lawrence S. Koenig, USAF (Fletcher's ice project officer), was presented in Washington. Interest in ice islands soared.[7]

Preparations for an experimental camp were pushed to completion. In February 1951 reconnaissance found a candidate floe about a hundred miles off northern Alaska. Test landings successful, conditions were pronounced "perfect." Over three days, equipment and personnel were deployed.

The full encampment comprised four Jamesway huts equipped for weather observations.[8] The occupation proceeded well, until high winds began shoving the pack. When a lead boomed open on the far side of the runway, no emergency was declared: unless the airstrip or the camp itself fractured, no threat seemed immediate.

After three weeks, however, the experiment came apart. A lead opened close by, then closed with terrific force. Unnerved, the party radioed then fled the bivouac. Two Jamesways were annihilated by moaning ice; in a brief span, the camp was reduced to chaos. The men were evacuated off. Three days later, all debris had vanished.

The experience stalled a second try. Still, the virtue of *thick* ice had been underscored. And the notion of a floating, semipermanent station clung stubbornly. The next ice-rafted outpost would exploit not merely a floe but an *ice island*.

Occupation of T-3

At length, the Air Weather Service decided that a drifting weather station was a military necessity. Dropsondes from aircraft were not providing the accuracy inherent to surface observations. As

well, the frequency and regularity of the airborne observations were wanting. And so the matter of a U.S. drifting station was driven to conclusion: Project Icicle.

Under Colonel Fletcher (designated as project officer), preparations were discussed, organized, coordinated, then executed. Supplies and equipment were shunted from Alaska to a new staging area: Greenland's Thule Air Base. Why? T-3 was now the target of opportunity. T-1 had gone aground. And T-2 floated remote from staging bases; further, it might soon escape—exported into the high North Atlantic. Though small, T-3 floated well within range and was approaching the Pole.

On 14 March 1952 (the sun had reappeared), a special reconnaissance located the "missing" slab. Five days later, the expedition sortied. Steering for the island's last known position, the formation comprised three C-54s escorting a C-47—the smaller ship holding essential gear and those selected to remain. After about eight hours, the leading C-54 began to circle, transmitting a homing signal. Headings were adjusted in the following planes.

As the C-54s orbited, preparations for landing concluded. The C-47 pilots searched for a suitable place to set down as, aft, equipment was reorganized, snowshoes pulled out, cameras

[Opposite] Stresses at failure limit, pack ice fractures—precursors of leads, pressure ridges, and rafting. Floe-ice encampments thus are vulnerable, including loss of runways. (Dr. Kenneth L. Hunkins)

[Left] Nearly invulnerable to ice pressure and breakup, ice islands offer semipermanent platforms for extended occupation. (Dr. Gerry H. Cabaniss)

checked, outerwear donned over flight gear. A low-level inspection disclosed a surface rougher than hoped; as well, a strong wind was whipping up snow. Ski drags verified a deep cover. Following two brief touchdowns and one aborted try, a final touchdown was made—and quickly slowed. The ship taxied under full throttle in billowing snow. When a campsite was selected on one of the ridges, the engines were cut. A *Life* photographer on board described what happened next: "There wasn't any rush to get out. We all sat for a moment in the sudden stillness. Then I crawled out to take a picture. The general [General William D. Old, commanding general of the Alaskan Air Command] followed me out, took one unbelieving look around and trudged off down the landing track. He didn't like what he saw. He came back and told Fletcher, "I don't see how any man can live on this thing. We must take right off if we can."[9]

Expecting this, Fletcher had arguments ready. He and the general went off by themselves, to confer.

As the project's future was debated, eight men tramped onto the nearest ridge to orient themselves and to look around. Walking surveys were made, photographs taken, the landing gear dug out. Beneath the snow (about three feet), the ice appeared solid enough. At length, permission for three to remain was granted; the rest would return to Thule.

The air force flag was planted.

Snow too deep for landings by the heavier planes, General Old ordered the C-54s not to try. Instead, 3000 pounds of equipment—tents, tarpaulins, rations, equipment, clothing, stoves, oil, and gasoline—were airdropped, while 1,200 pounds of supplies were manhandled off the C-47. Gradually, fuel and equipment for at least forty days was collected. The debut shelter, a four-to-six-man double-walled mountain tent, was erected. Meantime, the aircraft was refueled from drums and JATO (jet-assisted takeoff) bottles attached.

[Opposite] The inaugural camp on T-3 (1952). Semipermanent facilities installed, oceanographic, acoustic, geologic, geophysical, meteorological, and biological research would persevere to 1974. Note the transit, for sun shots of position in summer, star shots in boreal dark. (Hazard C. Benedict)

Nearly five hours after touchdown, the three who would stay were bid farewell. As the C-47 wobbled off, gathering speed, again there was tension: the project would degrade to tragedy if the plane could not lift clear. JATO cut in; the aircraft surged forward, then climbed steeply away. The C-54s flew a final pass, waving wings, after which the formation faded south. "We were probably as isolated as anyone can be in this world," chief scientist Dr. Kaare Rodahl, a Norwegian expert on Arctic medicine and nutrition, later remembered. His fellow colonists were Fletcher and Captain Mike Brinegar, USAF.

Organizing themselves and their equipment, the party settled in. Kerosene heaters and primus stoves were coaxed to reluctant life, a meal prepared. "Sitting on ration cases in a circle around the tent pole, warming our hands over the blazing stoves, we chewed some frozen sausages, biscuits and fruit, and drank hot chocolate which we had prepared."[10]

The first days were spent in exploration and in arranging camp. The foundation, they found, consisted of dense, solid ice—a practicable foundation immune from ice pressure. Though punishing in terms of survival, the slab was suitable (Fletcher radioed) for occupation. Indeed, the trio fared well enough on the (slowly) meandering island. Life on ice, the air force concluded, was sustainable. Icicle's first phase a success, a facility for research is inaugurated.[11] Now enjoying loyal support, Fletcher had risked his career—and won.

Hundreds of military and civilian personnel would follow. As a place to do research, T-3 was an immediate attraction. Scientists see the Arctic through a prism of disciplines: geophysicists, geologists, biologists, meteorologists, oceanographers, and other specialists would come. Responsibility for support, safety and resupply rested with the air force. That first April, a party of scientists joined the homesteaders, to investigate the origin and nature of ice islands and the properties of that ocean and its seabed. The all-important weather station was set up. Readings radioed from T-3 were found to improve forecasts for the entire hemisphere.

Hugely fruitful scientifically, T-3 will host a tenacious, near-continuous occupation into the 1970s. Meantime, this early phase persisted to November 1953, when abandonment was recommended: the island had wandered near to Alert, on Ellesmere. Two weather stations in the same general area were redundant. An evacuation concluded by May 1954.

In 1955 a five-man team returned for the season, arriving over T-3 on 25 April. Covered, silent, and reliquary, the derelict camp was exactly as left. Five months' observations conclude with an air evacuation.

A period of relative inactivity ensued, with T-3 unmanned until the surge attending the International Geophysical Year of 1957–58. A systematic international collaboration on a planetary scale, the IGY tendered an enormous leap. The Poles were proving critical to plate tectonics (then just emerging) and, as well, to understanding the atmosphere and climate change—the latter also emergent. "We were all very pleased [according to Dr. Arthur Collin, a Canadian researcher] to be a part of the IGY. . . . The scientific challenge of understanding the geophysics, of understanding the nature of the bottom, of understanding the motion of water masses under that ice-covered ocean, that was a very, very high, very challenging and extraordinarily exciting scientific opportunity which has left a mark on all of us, I think."[12]

In 1956 the U.S. National Committee for the Geophysical Year had requested logistic support for *two* Arctic Ocean camps. For its part, the U.S. Air Force agreed to provide logistical

support. And so, in March 1957 specialists were landed on T-3, to assess conditions. Judged unsuitable, the old camp was abandoned, a new IGY base installed. Exploiting a newly constructed five-thousand-foot runway, commercial trailers were airlifted in by C-130.

As drifting station Bravo took shape, a scientific team assembled at Thule. Consonant with the two-station program, Ice Station Alpha also was deployed onto floe ice as part of the U.S. commitment to the IGY.

On 30 June 1957, the IGY commenced. The *Sputnik* shock registered that October. In the North, operating from the ice, the USSR was mounting an extraordinary campaign. Leningrad would all but run a shuttle over the Arctic Ocean. In 1954 the Soviets had logged about 750,000 miles over the central basin. Using their "jumping laboratories," annual airlift operations landed at selected coordinates, compiling measurements. As well, Severnyy Polyus-4 was deployed that April, Severnyy Polyus-5 in 1955, and in 1956 SP-6—the first station to exploit an ice island. The program was predicated on two well-instrumented drifting stations as well as

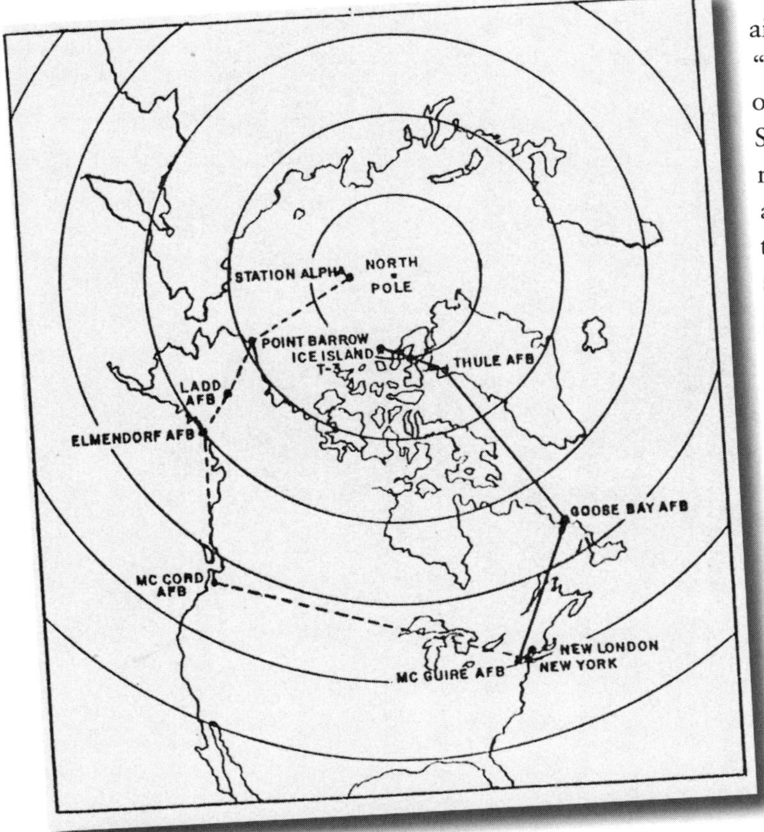

air-mobile detachments (a program known as "Sever," North) recording spot observations over large sectors. For example, the 1957 Sever comprised seventeen aircraft and 270 men. Mission: to close out SP-4, relieve SP-6, and establish SP-7—the latter two dedicated to IGY research. As well, *automatic* weather stations and radio beacons (for tracking drift) were deployed. Sever was in the field from 28 March to 10 June and again that fall for resupply of the SP bases.[13]

On board T-3, research was directed to understanding the characteristics of a largely uncharted basin. Scientific agenda: seismic reflection and refraction investigations (sending sound waves through underlying strata to help decipher basin geology and structure); gravity and magnetic observations; the physical, chemical, and biological properties of pack ice and the water column; coring and dredging of the seabed.

Throughout the IGY, Bravo, on T-3, would compile an invaluable record of environmental observation and data.

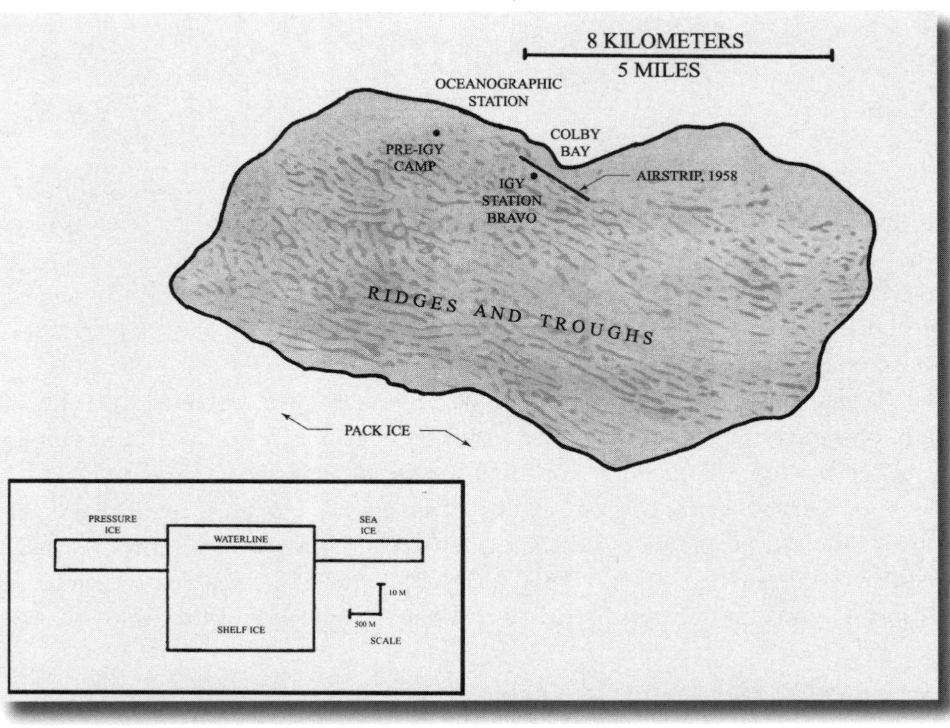

Rendezvous

The 1958 field season had Bravo hosting specialists from the Air Force Cambridge Research Center, in Massachusetts, and contractor and other-agency personnel: from Columbia University (Lamont Geological Observatory), Dartmouth College, the Arctic Institute of North America, the U.S. Geological Survey, Woods Hole Oceanographic Institution, and the Canadian Department of Fisheries. The Underwater Sound Laboratory (USL) also came on board. In August on-island personnel would experience a singular at-sea rendezvous. That spring, though, no one slated for Bravo was aware of the ONR expedition by airship.

About fifteen USAF support personnel, along with six to twelve civilian scientists and field assistants, would deploy to Bravo.[14] Among the latter, a few would encamp for about six weeks, then rotate off before the runway softened; others would pursue their work into early fall, when the surface refroze and the runway reopened.

In Washington and Boston, investigators slated for T-3 began to assemble. After a thorough physical, each man was issued an ID card and orders—then shunted north in Military Air Transport Service C-124s, most from McGuire Air Force Base, New Jersey, a few from Dover, Delaware. At Goose Bay, Labrador, transports refueled, then pushed on for Thule—the largest military installation in the eastern Arctic.

Thule is on northwest coast of Greenland: 76° 33′ N, 68° 50′ W. A weather station, initially, with a gravel strip, it had become a sprawling air base. To ease boredom in twelve-month tours, amenities for personnel were thoroughly modern. Among the off-duty distractions: a gymnasium, library, hobby shop, exchange, theater, clubs. ("The officers' club," a visitor recalls, "was inexpensive and the slot machines were generous.") Outpost duty for five to six thousand officers and men, in 1958 its summer population peaked at approximately ten thousand.

Thule's primary mission: staging, recovering, and supporting aircraft, including forward-based fighters of the Strategic Air Command. As well, Thule resupplied the weather stations at Eureka and Alert—and, as long as it floated within range, T-3.[15]

The Bravo-bound field team was outfitted with cold-weather gear and instructed as to Arctic survival. Last-minute items were squared away. Survival and research equipment (seismographs and geophones, seismic cable and electrical line, surveying instruments, a gravimeter, stakes, a power auger and corers, sample bottles, current meters, water-level recorders, more) was loaded onto a C-54. The first field party reached T-3 on 1 May. Commanding officer of the support detachment this field season: Lieutenant Colonel James J. Giles, USAF.

Three months later, U.S. Navy airship BUNO 126719 was at Resolute for replenishment. Resolute had no fuel truck, so drums were manhandled onto a truck and sledge for shunting to the mast. There the liquid was pumped on board—a time-demanding and onerous evolution. Maximum flight endurance was wanted, so "it took a lot of drums." As well, palletized cylinders had been towed to the site, where their helium transferred on board via manifold.

The refueling and topping-off required almost eight hours. (The American airmen had not messed: "Rations and Quarters were not furnished to you at this station," the orders for the officers read.)

The flight crew embarked. Collins scrambled to the left seat, Hickman right. Van Gorder took the jump seat, Lord between the two pilots. The others—Schou, Koza, Greenaway, Malloy,

[Opposite, top] Exploiting logistical capabilities developed during the Second World War, the International Geophysical Year of 1957–58 held a strong polar component. The U.S. Air Force installed and supported *two* ice-rafted camps in the Arctic Ocean. T-3 and Alpha floated about 400 miles apart, yet they were reached from opposite ends of the continent. Both were staffed by civilian scientists and sustained by air force personnel. (USL *Echo*, 13 June 1958)

[Opposite, bottom] Ice Island T-3. The pre-IGY camp was abandoned in September 1955; Bravo installed in March 1957. Note the idealized cross-sectional profile (insert). (Adapted from Smith, 1960; Jeffries, 1992)

[Top] Circumpolar zones are extreme environments: knifelike cold and wind, lightless winter. Here a *polyarnik* braves boreal dark at Severnyy Polyus-6 (1956–59)—the first Soviet station deployed onto an ice island. Measurements from SP-6 and SP-7 represented the USSR's contribution to the IGY in the Arctic Ocean. (Arktika Muzei)

[Bottom] On the ice, runway construction and maintenance imposed major logistical headaches during the 1950s and '60s when airlift support relied on large aircraft and long, prepared runways. (Dr. Gerry H. Cabaniss)

Parker, Johnson, Eels, and Dunlevy—deployed aft to their takeoff positions. Preflight concluding, Bailey, Gray, Harris, Mulligan, Nusom, and Swenson were ushered up the ladder. (Quite at home, Robertson was already on board.) The passengers were shown where to stow their gear. Mulligan had experience with military aircraft; still, he was surprised by the car's generous space. Instructions dispensed, the newcomers bantered among themselves and assessed unfamiliar surroundings as the airmen readied for departure.

On the handing lines and alongside, Manship and his ground crew waited.

The takeoff had been scheduled for 2100, local time. But an electric motor on the generator cooling fan burned out. An hour's wait was sweated out. Wind velocity: near calm. Light winds and clear skies were forecast for the western archipelago and for the run to Bravo. Before that, however, 760 feet of muddy taxiway interposed between a heavy aircraft and runway gravel. "None of us," Squadron Leader Becker admitted, "had any idea of how complex the task of merely moving the airship from the mast to the runway would be."

The airship was cast off. Unmasting was a routine if precise evolution. But the ship's heaviness and the taxiway's deplorable condition (and width) combined to jeopardize escape. Scant leeway was available over which to maneuver past the deeper traps. *719* had backed away perhaps a ship's length when the starboard gear met a soft spot. As the wheel sank nearly its full diameter, the car assumed a list to starboard. ("You could hear the moans and groans from a hundred spectators," Becker recalled.) Cries of alarm rich in idiom arose as orders were barked. Alongside, men tugged, heaved, and held fast as the flight deck watched, helpless.

The ship was mired, its wheel immovable.

Improvisation is priceless, particularly at remote sites under harsh field conditions. Where the conventional solution is often unworkable, a good idea can squeeze success from seeming failure. After futile tugging, an RCAF corporal found inspiration. Someone hollered, "Get the forklift!" Within minutes, Becker recalled, "the RCAF corporal [name lost to history] came bombing down the taxiway full tilt with the detachment's only forklift." Planks were laid down, the lift shunted beneath. Under Manship's direction, the lift's arms were positioned. Care was essential: the undercarriage could not accept undue strain. Yet the group had to work quickly: a stray gust might shear off the wheel as the ship answered.

Men were disembarked, to lighten ship. "The corporal pulled the up-lever," the base commander continues, "and the undercarriage slowly came out of the gravel and mud." Fill plugged the hole left by the muddied wheel, planks were positioned, the car eased back down. The lift still beneath to help support the ship, a walk to the runway resumed.

Concluding three hours' exertion, *719* reached firm runway gravel. Ground crew holding fast, Collins and Hickman concluded their checks. At about 0130 local time, satisfied that all was ready, Collins signaled Manship, who acknowledged and barked to his men. Lines released, throttles at takeoff power, the aircraft hesitated, then accelerated slowly forward.

Runway gravel dropped away. Time: 0134: Resolute time, 9 August. "The people clapped," Becker would recall, "the forklift operator smiled and the Station Commander wiped some sweat off his brow."[16]

Van Gorder noted a disagreeable departure to his diary: "Stuck in mud after unmasting—used forklift to raise stbd gear out. Ship heavy—take-off hairy."[17]

[Opposite] Minutes west of Resolute, Northwest Passage below: Barrow Strait and floe ice as they would have appeared from the airship. Cornwallis Island spreads away to starboard (north). (Author)

The control car was crowded; nineteen were on board. A blinding sun flamed a gorgeous sky. Aviation Machinist's Mate Elmer Lord, at the flight engineer's station that early morning, would recall "the sun glaring us in the face. I could hardly see the instrument panel."[18] Farther aft, Gray jotted in *his* journal: "Cleared Resolute at 0105 with party aboard blimp about 14000 lbs. negative wt. Clear skies sunny."

The airship climbed away. Naked rock, splotches of green and a small lake slid beneath, then—to starboard—the Inuit village. Nearly ice free, the bay floated a few grounded floes on the curve of its cinnamon shore. A series of gravel terraces (old beach lines) were crossed.

Barrow Strait danced in the peculiar light of an Arctic summer midnight. At five hundred feet, Collins turned to starboard, eased his wheel, and set his heading—due west. He would follow the Northwest Passage to the Bathurst Island group and there alter course to starboard—north. A corner of Griffith Island slid beneath.

It happens.

With no introductory warning, the starboard engine coughs, coughs again, then quits. The ignition is on, so the prop continues to spin. The airship robbed of power, the noise and vibration level change instantly. Airmen know the cadences of their engines. Koza and Schou, topside during the takeoff and climb-out, react instinctively: the pair surge down-ladder, dropping to the deck behind Collins. What the hell is wrong?

The intricacies of ship's propulsion were the province of the flight engineer, or "first mech." He tended to occupy the flight-deck stool when not on his rounds of checks and inspections. Man of the moment: AD1 Lord. He scanned his panel before (without a word from Collins) sprinting aft to the engine compartment. "Second mech" Johnson rushed to the engines as well. The symptoms suggested fuel starvation. At the dead engine, Lord hustled to remove the fuel filter to check for metal, grit, or water in the sumps. Perhaps thirty seconds pass. Both mechanics were thus engaged when, incredibly, the steady throb of the port engine vanished as well—coughing, then a complete loss of power. Both props windmilled on. Inside, an awful silence pervaded the control car. "It was," one crewman recollects, "pretty quiet."

Flight could be had with one engine. But *719* had metamorphosed into a free balloon—a *heavy* free balloon. The aircraft began to settle.

Professional airmen react reflexively. Greenaway was near the radioman's station; he'd been talking with the tower and happened to have the "mike." His instinct is to Mayday; retaining his equanimity, he sends a bearing and distance instead. Should they ditch, Resolute will be able to pinpoint its position.[19] As Collins and Hickman play the controls, assessing the ship's responses to loss of propulsion, the flight deck confers (via intercom) with the mechanics. Standard emergency procedures are initiated. More seconds pass.

Aft and topside, the passengers sense the mechanical insurrection. The navy's guests are not airmen; none are familiar with airships. In a plane, loss of propulsion equals loss of lift—a disastrous forfeiture. Were they going in? One passenger, overcome and close to terror, barges onto the flight deck in an excited state, frantic for reassurance.

For perhaps a minute the mission continued on, but losing altitude. Throughout the descent—an anxious arc toward the blue gray of Barrow Strait, Lord and Johnson work frantically. To the relief of all hands, the starboard engine sputters to life, then resumes its useful work. It now

drums perfectly—a wonderful sound. Descent has been checked: the altimeter has ceased to unwind. Collins can hold altitude on one engine. At this point the ship is no more than fifty feet off the water.

More seconds tick by. The port engine catches as well, tunefully rejoining its seemingly appeased companion. Less than five minutes have passed.

The cockpit instruments betray—nothing. The two Wrights hammer reassuringly. Aft, Lord and Johnson have found nothing conclusive: no water or foreign matter in the strainers and filters. The pilots, huddling forward, talk through the problem. What had happened? Might it reoccur? Should the flight press on? Fuel starvation was the obvious suspect. Still, the officers have no solid answers. (Routine thirty-hour or sixty-hour checks on each engine were performed not long after the casualty.) The decision is taken. At forty-five knots, base Resolute will not be too far astern should loss of locomotion recur. Van Gorder elects to press westward.

His judgment will be vindicated: "They [the engines] never coughed from then to the next seventy-eight hours."

Candidates for rough engine operation: dirt or (more likely) water or carburetor ice: the reaction was typical of icing.[20] Another possible culprit: reduced octane rating, since stored fuel slowly deteriorates. The most probable explanation: condensation from the drummed fuel taken on at Resolute that somehow had evaded the filters. Flow of adrenalin ebbing, the U.S. Navy returns to the mission at hand.

A number of probes had been planned using Resolute as base. The first: an overflight of Alert, the Canadian base on Ellesmere Island. When word of the expedition was released, however, officials responsible for Bravo had requested a rendezvous. And so the operational plan had been changed to include the ice camp riding T-3.

Cape Cockburn is about 105 miles west of Resolute, at the southwest tip of Bathurst Island. From that position, *719* would press northwest, crossing the Queen Elizabeth Islands to the rim of the Arctic Ocean. The heights of Griffith Island slid astern. And in less than an hour, the cliffs and hills of Lowther Island were visible to port. The coast and undulating interior of Bathurst Island passed astern, its distinctive light-colored rock filling the view to starboard. The mission pressed west at five hundred feet. Airspeed: about forty-five knots.

Resolute, for its part, reported that the base would do everything possible to repair soft spots in the taxiway and near the mast. Becker warned, however, he was not optimistic that the surface could be made firm by the time *719* returned. Not long after, radio contact was lost.

Ice conditions in the Northwest Passage—Baffin Bay to the Beaufort Sea—vary from year to year. Along its western reaches, the ice never clears out completely. A mile or two beyond Lowther Island, the east-most ice edge was reached. Westward, little open water was evident.

In the channels and inlets of the Arctic islands, sea-ice persistence and coverage are dictated by local conditions. East of Resolute, the ice is mostly first-year floes. Following spring breakup—and except for bergs—Lancaster Sound and much of Barrow Strait is ice free by mid-August. And so the aircrew had found it. West of Cornwallis Island, the ice is chiefly old ice—thicker, harder. Below, close pack (floes whose edges are largely in contact) veneered much of the channel. Atop the canopy, meltwater glowed in aquamarine—pocking a brilliant plain of white.

At its southwest corner, Bathurst Island forms a low marine plain with a prominent hill. At Cape Cockburn Collins turned. New course: 340°—direct to Mackenzie King Island, about 240 miles to the north-northwest. Their track would pass east of Byam Martin Island—the shortest route across the archipelago.

Resolute is close to the north magnetic pole; there a magnetic compass points straight down. Not long after the turn, the mission passes close to Pole—twenty-five miles. The passengers are informed. They gather in the stern compartment, a bare but ample space with a wraparound view.

Over a realm so vast as to seem unlimited, the navy pushed northwest through Austin Channel; it separates the banded browns of Byam Martin from the Bathurst group. To the west, Melville Island lay brown and vacant. Through the windows to starboard, Bathurst's coastal inlets were gripped in ice. Black smears of deep *liquid* water had vanished. An ocean sheet of consolidated pack (old ice in which the floes are frozen together) capped the surface. "Now cruising over ice pack toward T-3," diarist Van Gorder recorded, "sun shining brightly. 19 on board. We are heading 340 degrees T. by N-1 compass. Mag reads 210 degrees."[21]

Byam Martin Channel was below, and the Bathurst group edged astern one by one—ragged shores corseted in white.

Weather held ideal: light winds, unlimited visibility. A polar high over northwest Greenland was influencing the entire area, cleaning the sky dome of clouds as far south as central Hudson Bay and west to Victoria Island. Though visibility typically is poor in summer, the dome of boreal sky can be brilliant—and free of blemish, a crystalline hyperclarity granting extreme visibility.[22]

Hazen Strait. Excluding the central basin, the Queen Elizabeth Islands host the most severe ice conditions in the Arctic. The black patches are meltwater ponds that puddle the close-packed surface. Ahead lies Mackenzie King Island and, beyond, the Arctic Ocean. (J. Gordon Vaeth)

Approaching Hazen Strait, the crew saw Lougheed Island seemingly etched in place. A glimmering plain spread away the full ring of a flat horizon—here at least eighty miles off. Imbedded in frozen sea, the contrasting browns of western islands of the Queen Elizabeth group lay gripped in white. As if in an ethereal machine, the men hung above an earlier, primordial earth.

The author has seen this sector. Meeting such display, a sense of insignificance is underlined. "It was a totally dead environment of wind and sky," Amundsen and Ellsworth remarked of the Polar Sea from *Norge,* "and gave a peculiar feeling of nothingness." The North is impressive, intimidating. Against such spectacle, the self-important workings of humankind seem altogether fragile. Like the tundra grasses, men are clinging colonizers—technological conceits notwithstanding; here, beyond congenial warm, humans are but clever interlopers.

The navy machine—swallowed in emptiness—floated utterly, spectacularly alone. Seven hours out, Mackenzie King Island was beneath. Six caribou (the first wildlife since Resolute) were sighted inland. The airmen were just south of the 78th parallel—roughly equidistant from the weather station at Mould Bay on Prince Patrick Island and a sister station at Isachsen, on Ellef Ringnes Island—the latter about 140 miles to the northeast of their coordinates.

Minutes later, *719* hung near Brock Island, on the Canadian polar margin. A flat, featureless surface was crossed. The U.S. Navy droned offshore, into the Arctic Ocean.

Ahead: Bravo. That August, T-3 was drifting more or less parallel to the archipelago, 115 or so miles out. Having shifted close to the Pole, the ice-island mass had inscribed a full circuit in the gyre since discovery. On its second orbit now, Bravo floated at about 79° N, 121′ W—approximately 760 miles off the north geographic pole.[23]

Visibility deteriorated as the airship pressed offshore. Low stratus and fog are common in summer—the result of warm air advecting over ice-filled sea. Indeed, August is one of the foggiest months. This day, the layers hung like smoke—cloud tops and fog between three hundred and eight hundred feet. Occasionally, *719* pushed through them. Air temperature: about 35° F.

In the plotting compartment, navigation occupied Greenaway and Malloy. The wing commander was using the jump seat or, as convenient, the stool between the two pilots—as did Robertson, who often came forward. Mostly, though, Greenaway stood beside his counterpart at the navigator's station, helping Malloy interpret images on the radar. Greenaway's experience in sorting out sea ice from land was unrivalled—and, here, indispensable. His navigator-colleague took drift sights and maintained the log; Greenaway took all the heading checks with the astro compass (using the mounts fore or aft) and concentrated on the gyro steering.

Greenaway experienced a flash of insight in these hours. Although broken by leads and open water, the polar pack is a near-continuous sheet. Ice fills every quadrant. Fixing one's position here resembles the technique employed above a conventional sea, that is, celestial navigation. In a nonrigid airship, however, the envelope overhangs the car, foreclosing sightings on the sun for heading checks. Fortunately, the fog and cloud cover were broken sufficiently to permit drift observations—and, Greenaway realized, to make heading checks using the sun's *reflection* on patches of open water or the ice itself. "Over the Arctic Ocean, fortunately, the sun was available at all times, and I used it continuously to maintain the desired heading." Without this assist, the Canadian explained, dead reckoning calculations would have been "tricky."[24] No matter. In command of the requisite arcana ("probably the world's best navigator," Van Gorder remarked), Greenaway found his responsibilities on board—in his phrase—a very simple exercise.

An hour or so offshore, the ONR mission closed on T-3. South Weymouth was two weeks astern.

Ice camps are blots on a pallid blank. Now there was fog. The radio beacon at Bravo broadcast a weak signal. At about 0930, contact was established ten miles out. Encased in gray, the ship homed in after a final alteration of course, using a radio-compass bearing on the T-3 beacon. For some reason the NADU Super Constellation (at that moment on the ramp at Resolute) had not located Bravo during its weather check near T-3. "We had a chuckle over this," Greenaway smiled, recalling the rendezvous, "because we navigated right to the ice island."

Lord, for one, had been wondering if they were going to find the ice camp. The machinist's mate also recalls an edge to his thoughts: if for any reason they had to land, would anyone ever find them in fog far to sea in the Arctic Ocean?[25]

Nine hours out. Time: 1102. Van Gorder, in the jump seat, told Collins to descend until visual contact was made. Through thin, low-hanging murk, the blimp eased onto the beacon. "Then," Lord recalls, "all of a sudden there it was." The descent ceased at two to three hundred—a concession to Bravo's high antennas. "We were very worried," Greenaway recalled, "about crashing into the antenna masts which were not visible until we were right on them." Adding, "We were not able to see the huts until we were almost directly over them." Successive passes over the beacon commence. "At this altitude," Van Gorder would note in his report, "horizontal visibility

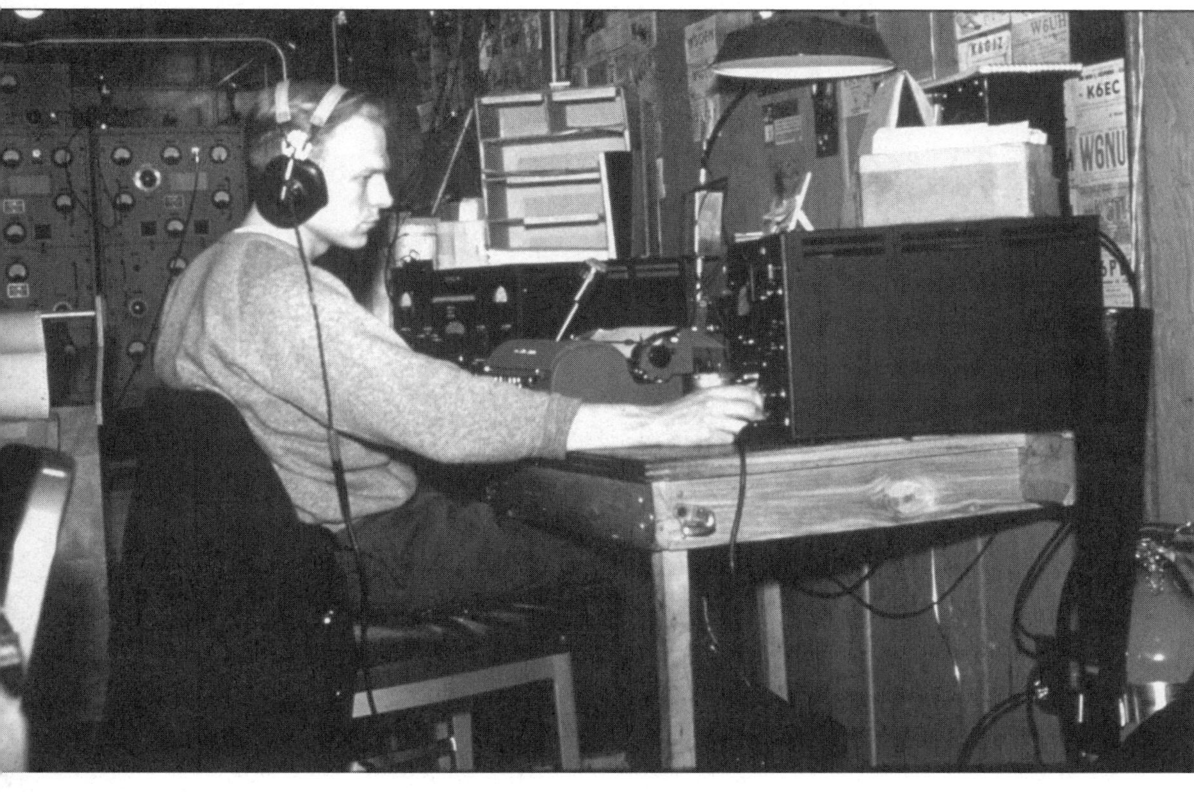

The amateur station at Bravo. AC1 William Detter, USAF, works top-of-the-line Collins Radio equipment in the base's communications center. Part of the Military Affiliate Radio System (MARS), amateur stations provided emergency communications worldwide for remote outposts. (Dr. Arthur E. Collin)

was nil, but vertical visibility permitted observation in a narrow cone beneath the ship through which the personnel and structures on T-3 could be seen."

Cameras were aimed, hopefully. Fascinated by this novel form of transport and polar rendezvous, the guests from ONR kept a watchful eye as *719* ambled low and slow in a near-hover at the IGY encampment.

Excellent voice communication had been established on VHF. But conditions for a landing were problematic: conferring with Colonel Giles, the navy was assessing the advisability of touching down.

The main camp heard the aircraft orbiting. But the fog was dense. And widespread. Arthur "Art" Collin, a Canadian researcher, was the only non-American then at Bravo. For a PhD student, "it was extraordinarily exciting" to be taking oceanographic measurements for the IGY in waters innocent of data.[26]

On the ice were some personnel unaware of the rendezvous. Others heard the loitering blimp, suspended in gray, but caught no glimpse of it.

> Aloft in a Navy blimp over Fletcher Ice Island, Aug. 9 (delayed) (AP)—Bearded scientists waved and danced in the icy streets today when the Navy's Arctic hopping blimp appeared over this floating ice island.[27]
>
> It was their first visual contact with the outside world since the last plane landed here in June. Despite a heavy layer of white fog, pilot Henry Collins of Conshohocken,

Pa., brought the huge silver airship low enough to circle the camp several times and make a mail drop.

Parka clad men poured out of the one story huts as the oil skin packets fluttered down to the gray blue ice.

NADU had intended to land, to unload equipment and mail. This called for ideal conditions. Denied same, the blimp could hover into the wind as deliverables were swung out through the cargo doors and lowered away. A routine if precise operation, this required a minimum one-eighth-mile visibility—that is, of horizontal vision. At the runway, service personnel and researchers had collected, among them Colonel Giles. Via field radio, he conferred with his visitor. A quiet man and excellent leader, the colonel was no hardboiled military type. Still, "there was no question," one investigator recalled, "that there was only one senior officer in the camp."

Was the navy, Giles asked, going to touch down?

That summer, July had had 25 percent clear days; August would record only 9 percent. Nearly a thousand miles beyond the Arctic Circle, despite dead calm, a landing was ruled out.

And no Bravo-bound cargo reached its ice: none was packed for free-fall delivery. Further, any heavy drop would endanger the men below. "A decision was made not to attempt a drop of supplies to T-3," Van Gorder explained in his report to ONR. "Packaging was not adequate for a high, fast delivery, and the low visibility conditions that prevailed introduced an unacceptable risk to the T-3 personnel for either a free drop or a line drop." His navigator agreed. "With such poor visibility," Greenaway said, recalling the rendezvous, "we could easily have dropped the equipment on the huts or the staff."

"Low fog over T-3," Gray scribbled to his notes, "Unable to stop and unable to land anything."

This decision would prove double-edged; the nondelivery held repercussions. Logistically, IGY Bravo rated priority support, and its runway was melted out: *719* represented the sole means of *gentle* melt-season delivery to T-3. (The ice island floated beyond the reach of rotary-wing support.) Those monitoring the mission back in Washington were decidedly unimpressed. At ONR, one staffer admitted to being "disgusted" that the Bravo payload had stayed on board. Nor was Dr. Harris pleased ("obviously upset," an associate remembered.) The Polar Project had conveyed much-needed cargo (and mail) to within two hundred feet of its destination—and withheld transfer.

A drop *was* made. Koza had gone aft; on the second pass, on word from the flight deck, he tossed out two bags through the after cargo doors. One was an oilskin-wrapped bundle of mail. The Bravo residents were informed by radio; "We were watching," one laughed, "for our mail bags to come floating out of the sky." Each plopped down unseen, missing the lakes and runoff plaguing residents. (The melt season had begun on 8 June; by July, about half this island had been water covered—at rendezvous, a quarter.) Mulligan conducted an air drop of his own: an improvised flag "to stake," he said, "a future claim for the AP and the world's only floating news bureau."

Below, a two-man party searched for the errant bags, retrieving one. The second would lie undiscovered until next year's thaw.

Among the letters was one prepared by Dr. Harris to USL colleague Hecht, on T-3. The drop also included a souvenir *poste restante* envelopes—that is, addressed to Bravo personnel but requesting a return to sender. When finally recovered (water damaged), these became outgoing mail. The T-3 cachet was applied and the envelopes dutifully dispatched via Point Barrow. Date of pickup: 2 September 1959. Delivery: via navy icebreaker *Staten Island* (AGB 5).[28]

One item of official business had just been conducted. Norman Gray—at that moment suspended in fog, straining for a downward view—had written an offer of employment to a young researcher. By coincidence, Gray's letter was on board *719*. As yet, addressee Art Collin was unaware that Gray was floating overhead and, as well, ignorant of his offer—which, as it turned out, was accepted.

Bravo was superbly isolated; morale therefore could be brittle—seemingly mundane factors conspiring to dampen the most ardent personality. In the hierarchy of outpost life, the arrival of aircraft ranks supreme—or rather, the mail, supplies, fresh faces, and gossip that accompany aircraft. Each is a balm for stale routine and protracted isolation. This season, Bravo had logged few visitors and none in weeks. In that context, the rendezvous was a genuine disappointment.

[Opposite] Ice Station Bravo, 9 August 1958. Position: 79° N, 121′ W–760 miles off the geographic pole. U.S. Air Force and civilian personnel have collected at the runway. As *719* flies low passes, Lt. Col. James J. Giles, commanding the support detachment (ear to radio, r.), confers with the airship. "We are all looking a little apprehensive," Dr. Collin recalled, "because we don't know if we are going to get any mail!" (Dr. Arthur E. Collin)

[Opposite, top] A meltwater run atop T-3, August 1958. Life-on-ice had deteriorated: all resident-personnel were confronting a soggy at-sea existence.

[Opposite, bottom] Temperatures over pack ice seldom deviate far from freezing. At Bravo in 1958, air temperatures held above freezing almost continuously from June to September. Ablation and melt realized ice pedestals in the camp area. And until freeze-up, the runway was closed. (Dr. Gerry H. Cabaniss)

"We *were* disappointed," Dr. Collin recalled, "because we had looked forward to this magnificent vessel coming over us. We hadn't seen anybody for some months; we were looking forward to seeing some people. As it turned out, we didn't see any new faces."[29] Even a glimpse of the ship had eluded most personnel.

Independent of the rendezvous, morale at Bravo had darkened. Residents had had to adapt to their rounds of work and sequestration—for each a personal trial met according to temperament. Settled into the rules, rhythms, and rituals of outpost existence, some had been on ice since April. Moreover, at-sea conditions had degenerated. At any outpost, weather can exert a depressing effect. That July–August, the melt and ablation had intensified—the thermometer holding just above freezing. Beneath a monotonous gray, day had followed disagreeable day. T-3 had become a sodden, disagreeable world: snow and slush had vanished, and the slab itself was ablating.[30] In the maritime neighborhood, at SP-7, the Soviets recorded the highest temperature in five years. Of these months, a *polyarnik* (polar researcher) will write: "We had to walk up to our knees in melt water. It was very difficult to work under these conditions: our feet froze. Those who had the foresight to take along footwear that was two or three sizes too large felt great: they could also pull fur "boots" over their woollen socks. . . . The water was attacking the tents."[31]

Atop the T-3 slab, water had impounded; as levels rose, ponds coalesced—especially early in the thaw—until most of the snow melted and drainage became better established. Runoff channels advanced slowly upstream, their discharges cascading off the island into the sea. By July, few broad areas stood above water. Movement had become difficult for personnel—and nearly impossible for the largest tracked vehicles.[32] Simple errands metamorphosed into expeditions—heavy slogs across ponds and channel flows—some dramatic. Access to work sites called for stamina, personnel being obliged to half-walk, half-wade. (The long route to Art Collins' "ice hole," for one, cut across every stream draining that sector.) Absorbing solar radiation, carelessly placed items drilled the surface, sinking from view. Moisture penetrated clothing, footwear, and sensitive equipment—particularly electrical gear.

The rate of ablation and melt was astonishing. In the main camp area, smoke and soot from the diesel hut, along with dirt from general traffic and flotsam, had darkened the surface, increasing the absorption of radiant heat.[33] Ironically, the trailers and other buildings shielded the sun. Now Bravo sat atop pedestals. Parachutes had been draped alongside structures, to retard the loss. But as the ice edges rounded off, some trailers became unstable and required extra bracing. And to gain entry, wooden steps had been improvised. "The combination of the steps, parachutes, and buildings standing ten feet or so in the air," a scientist recalled, "made the camp look rather seedy."[34]

Most important, perhaps, the runway had melted out—thereby shutting down Bravo's life-support system. Sole resupply option: paradrops. But for weeks, supply flights had been promised then repeatedly postponed. In consequence, all fresh supplies were exhausted—including mail and luxury items. Inventive with what they had (meals continued excellent), the cooks were exploiting the emergency "C rations." But private caches of beer, candy, and cigarettes were empty: with flights running late, most residents had run out—seemingly. And so hoarding had begun. One clue to forced privation: all ashtrays were buttless. And experiments with tea leaves were under way. Smoking had become clandestine—generosity had ended. "To this day," Collin

laughs, referring to the growing sense of indigence, "I'm not sure that everybody I knew ran out completely." "I can recall," Gerry Cabaniss remarked, "about ten of us standing around in the supply building sharing a single butt." A geophysicist and recent graduate, he and Charles Plummer were field assistants for Dr. David Smith, a Dartmouth College geology professor on T-3 to study its morphology and hydrology. "When things got desperate," Cabaniss adds, "we searched for old butts in the ice, dried them out, and smoked those." As for the unaddicted, Plummer remembers, "It amused us non-smokers to see cigarettes made of tea and anything else being smoked."[35]

It must be said: No one at Bravo had concern for airships. Indeed, when word of the rendezvous got 'round, some personnel were dismissive—a stunt. Still, the collective yearning for resupply nourished open minds. Residents took note—a general sense of pleased surprise. The U.S. Navy would deliver a break in routine—*and* the absolute novelty of support by airship. More to the point, fresh supplies, mail, and new faces would arrive.

Dr. Cabaniss recounts that singular moment in polar (and naval) aeronautics:

> The Day of the Blimp was typical: all the scientific party was in the field; the temperature, about freezing; a fog or low cloud cover obscured the sun, but there were occasional breaks through which a pale blue sky could be seen. We had been informed that the blimp was scheduled, but we didn't believe it—our supply flights had been

[Opposite] Air force support personnel at Bravo, 1958. Parachutes drape the surface, to protect facilities from melt and ablation. Polar bears are afraid of nothing. Dogs were both companions and provided early-warnings of bear. (Dr. Arthur E. Collin)

[Right] Melt-season airlift support to Bravo. Paradrops supplemented basic resupply with fresh fruit and vegetables, steaks, cigarettes, mail, and various other items to sustain morale. (Dr. Kenneth L. Hunkins)

> scheduled for weeks but never came through. Some of us considered ourselves too blasé to be concerned with such obvious touristy types of showmanship; however, all of us would have appreciated such things as cigarettes and mail. . . . Around lunch time we heard the engines of the blimp but couldn't catch a glimpse of it through the clouds for some time. Suddenly the clouds parted slightly and we saw this long, ghostly, silvery airship for a few seconds. It was much longer and more slender than we had expected—as well as more beautiful.[36]

Encased in murk, the airship proved hard to pinpoint, even by sound. On its first pass, engine noise skimmed directly cross-station. Art Collin recalls the moment: "I caught a glimpse of a silver underbelly passing over me, just momentarily. I didn't see the engines, I didn't see any markings, I simply saw that silver belly of the blimp pass over me. It was moving very slowly. Moments later, it disappeared; the fog closed in behind it." A noise wake marked its ambling, low-level passage before it dissolved. Plummer also chanced to be in camp. Joining those grouped at the runway, he scanned the sagging gray. "We heard it circling for some time, but couldn't see it" in the low ceiling, he told me. "Finally, we saw it, largely obscured by the fog."[37]

In the control car, a special satisfaction pervaded. NADU had gained its singular objective; until this hour, Bravo had been but a mark on a chart. Its naval aviators had prevailed. Characteristically reticent, Captain Van Gorder betrayed no emotion to his notes, only a brusque resume: "Arrived at T-3 Floating Ice Island at 1102 [EDST]. Low fog all over ice cap. Very thin though and we circled over camp at 300 ft. Talked to Col. Giles and Navy personnel. Dropped mail and departed at 1132."[38]

Thwarted in its escape from the States, the expedition had met eight days of delay. This is to be regretted. Had polar airspace been entered as scheduled, naval aviation might have floated over the pack as *Nautilus* steamed beneath the canopy. When *719* logged Bravo, however, the boat had already put the basin well astern.[39] On 9 August, as *719* idled over Bravo, *Nautilus* was cutting the North Atlantic at two hundred feet making maximum speed for Portland, England.

[Opposite] Rendezvous. Visibility—the range of horizontal vision—cut by low-level fog, no touchdown is made. (Naval History and Heritage Command)

Anderson was not on board: *Nautilus* had logged a rendezvous of its own. Late on 7 August, off Iceland, the CO had been plucked off by air force helicopter then flown to a Keflavik runway. Anderson was on his way to the White House. There, before assembled media, President Eisenhower announced the transpolar crossing, after which he presented *Nautilus* the first Presidential Unit Citation ever awarded in peacetime. Anderson was awarded the Legion of Merit.

Suspended above Bravo, AP's Mulligan was much moved by the airship's own feat. His copy reciting the arrival evokes the emotions of that long-ago rendezvous—two mere specks in a pallid blank near the top of the planet:

> A ghostly glitter in the golden Arctic sky, a Navy blimp dipped its huge silver bulk below the horizon and lazily circled T-3, a floating chunk of nowhere 700 miles from the North Pole.
>
> Never in history had a nonrigid aircraft ventured this far north. The nearest land was Brock Island, 100 miles to the southeast in the Canadian Archipelago. The nearest airport, Resolute Bay on Cornwallis Island, 520 miles to the southeast.
>
> Averaging 50 miles an hour, as slow as a trailer truck on the new Massachusetts Turnpike near its home base at Weymouth, the blimp had waddled 5,400 miles to prove that lighter-than-air craft still deserve a place in the jet age. . . .
>
> The day was Saturday, Aug. 9, 1958. The time, 9:55 a.m. [15:55 Greenwich Standard]. Lt. Comdr. Henry Collins of Conshohocken, Pa., the baby-faced, sandy-haired command pilot, leaned forward on the yoke to maneuver his block-long ship down through the heavy morning haze that had settled over the island, now a dingy white blotch in the polar pack's eerie mosaic of green and blue sea ice.
>
> "Keep going down until you see the station," said the expedition commander, Capt H. B. Van Gorder of Canandaigua, N.Y. The rest of the 18 crewmen, scientists and observers crowded about the windows and portholes, with cameras and light meters poised.
>
> For the first time since the blimp left Weymouth two weeks before, all nine bunks in the top deck were empty of off-duty snoozers. Even the cribbage players, whom neither polar bears nor walrus could distract, had deserted the wardroom tables, and the cook, Seaman Wendell Dunlevy of Columbus, Ohio, had left a pile of potatoes in a state of semiundress on his galley work bench. Suddenly a low, long hut painted a garish orange [all the trailers, in fact, were unpainted], swam into view. Then another and another, until a whole street of little houses stretched across the ice, like a grotesquely misplaced suburban development. Men could be seen pouring out the huts, waving frantically, happily, as the blimp's back cargo doors swung open and Lt. H. D. Koza of Lyman, Neb., began pushing out mail and supplies.
>
> An off-season visit by Santa Claus could hardly have caused more excitement for the 25 scientists and technicians manning this lonely outpost as part of the International Geophysical Year research program. It had been four months since the last plane touched down on their icy runway, now turned to slush by the summer sun, and two months since their last mail drop. . . .

Seated at the navigation table behind the pilot cabin, Captain Van Gorder scribbled a triumphant sitrep (situation report) to the Office of Naval Research in Washington, sponsors of the expedition. The blimp, he wrote, had "conclusively proved its worth in Arctic research." After numerous false starts and embarrassing detours to Akron and Lakehurst—due mostly to warm air over the Hudson Valley that had caused it to valve helium and lose lifting power—it had carried out its mission. It had supplied a far north base at the height of the summer sun season, when airplanes can't land, and given the geologists and glaciologist aboard a comfortable roomy laboratory plus an unprecedented view.

For naval commands three thousand miles south, a situation report—the mission's thirty-third—was drafted. That naval message: "Arrived floating ice island T3 at 1653Z X Extensive fog up to 300 feet over general area X Breaks allowed visual sighting camp X Radio beacon operating and communications excellent X US Navy unit T3 sends best regards X Departed for Resolute Bay at 1741Z."

Moving off Bravo, course was set for return to Cornwallis Island and the runway at Resolute. Flight time at the IGY ice-island station: forty-eight minutes.

Within weeks—in September—an airdrop to T-3 *did* occur. The camp's impoverished isolation eased. Brief and unsatisfying, the navy's August visit, Plummer recalls, had been "quite anticlimactical." Resumption of paradrops was, in his view, "a much bigger event": under marginal conditions, the low-level release had the chutes barely open before their loads thumped down. A retrieval party scrambled out. Hauled into camp, each crate was unpacked with undisguised eagerness.

"Morale," Plummer adds, "soared after the airdrop." Fresh fruit and vegetables—and ashtray butts—reappeared. At the mess hall, a cornucopian spread was laid out. Collin savored his first grapefruit in weeks. "The meals became spectacular after the first drop," he smiled. "The cooks were in their glory, and outdid themselves."

P R I O R I T Y

Ø9 AUG 58

EEP E257

P Ø9183ØZ
FM SENAV NADVU
TO REEPW/CNO WASH DC
INFO RFEPFZ/CANAIRHED
RFEPNV/CANAIRLIFT
REEBC/COMONE
REEBQC/COMNABONE
REEGK/COMEASTSEAFRON
REEPC/FLEWEACEN
REEFAL/NAS LAKEHURST NJ
REEFAL/AIRSHIP WING ONE NJ
R5EPC/RADIO WASHINGTON
REEBS/NADEVU SOWEYMOUTH
REEPC/ONR WASH DC
GR 52
ET
AIRSHIP ARCTIC FLIGHT X SITREP 33 X ARRIVED FLOATING ICE ISLAND T3
AT 1653Z X EXTENSIVE FOG UP TO 3ØØ FEET OVER GENERAL AREA X BREAKS
ALLOWED VISUAL SIGHTING CAMP X RADIO BEACON OPERATING AND COMMUNICATIONS
EXCELLENT X US NAVY UNIT T3 SENDS BEST REGARDS X DEPARTED FOR RESOLUTE
BAY AT 1741Z

ET

DIST: 33 ACT

SECNAV UNSECNAV ASTSECNAVAIR ØØ Ø9 Ø1 Ø2 Ø3 34 Ø5 5Ø Ø4 55 Ø6 6Ø
92(1ØCC) 6ØTF ØØ7 CR NAVAIDE FLAGPLOT BFR CNO/OOD
DLVY NR192 ALDAPE/RM

PAGE ONE OF ONE

Ø9/183ØZ

As scientists, we need to provide the best information we can. After that, it is a value call.

—William J. Schull

7 Homeward

Course southeast, the airship put Bravo astern. As if redressing the intrusion, the sodden gray reclaims the aerial visitor. Heading: direct for Resolute via Borden Island, the Findlay Group, and the Bathurst Islands.

The navy had elected to oblige the request of IGY officials for support for Bravo. On board *719,* the airmen had assessed their options. Should they press to Alert *before* returning to Resolute or, instead, return direct? The latter would consume less fuel, leaving ample margin for the return run to Churchill. This, indeed, had factored into the decision not to line-drop to Bravo or to land: dumping fuel would have mandated a landing and mooring at Resolute Bay. Fog had settled the issue. A push to Alert and the return leg to Cornwallis Island—about forty hours flying—would not leave fuel sufficient to reach Churchill. That option also involved Resolute. Why? A runway refueling there was not practicable—no equipment.

"The poor conditions at the mooring area at Resolute," Greenaway said later, "were uppermost in the minds of everyone." Unease nagged. Contact with radio Resolute had been lost, so the status of repairs at the mast and taxiway were unknown. When communication was reestablished, the navy would know.

Prudence ruled out Alert—postponed it, anyway. Course had been set for Resolute. The decision to extend the operation or to withdraw to the south would await word on conditions at the mast and on the forecast. "If fuel consumption remains low and weather good," Van Gorder mused, "we may overfly Resolute and go direct to Churchill."[1]

In a joint interview, Van Gorder and Schou were asked about the siren call of Ninety North. Hadn't they been tempted? An iconic coordinate for centuries, 90° north latitude was less than eight hundred miles from Bravo—about sixteen hours' flying. An overflight would have realized priceless publicity. "We wanted to do it. But," the captain continued, "caution tempered me. I kept thinking about that landing at Resolute, and I could almost visualize the airship going off that narrow [taxiway]." "We had," Schou added, "accomplished our mission."[2] Returning to Resolute via the Pole would have added forty hours to the nine flown, putting the expedition close to prudent limits and committing *719* to Resolute. Greenaway concurred: a lunge for the geographic pole from T-3 "would have been taking too great a risk." Anyway, a try was still possible, combined perhaps with a probe to Alert.

Weighing options and the attendant risks, hopeful of further operational hours at these latitudes, judgment had restrained temptation.

Some have deplored the mission commander for not pressing an aggressive deployment. Dr. Miller, for one, lamented lost opportunities. The North Pole, he contended, would have been "scientifically valuable and a dramatic capstone" for NADU, for ONR, for the U.S. Navy.

Armchair hindsight is often fraudulent. In the end, and alone, every on-scene commander must calculate his risks—and decide.

The withdrawal continued.

Fog and low clouds are common in summer—the advection of relatively warm, moist air over melting ice and cold water. *719* plodded shoreward, the sea surface poorly visible—toward Borden Island, the channels of the Arctic islands, the Northwest Passage. Speed: forty knots, altitude about five hundred feet. When glimpses of the pack or an occasional lead were granted, no reference points assisted the navigators.[3]

During this run a bit of research was conducted. In the after compartment, Guy Harris prepared to drop small, Mark 61 practice depth charges—brought along as acoustic-energy sources for geophysicists and their instruments back at Bravo. (Signals generated by small explosions in the Arctic Ocean can be recorded at great distances.)

This was Harris' second Arctic tour that year. In May he had been flown from Point Barrow to Alpha, to assess capabilities and arrange an acoustic program for the field season. Now, near Bravo, he initiated tests in underwater sound. Harris was enjoying himself. Northern research, he enthused, provides "honest-to-God, man-sized adventure."

The charges were readied. "The oceans are the part of the world that we know the least about today," Harris explained. "We actually know less about our oceans than we do about outer space." The North, he added, has great strategic value, because it separates—yet is shared by—the United States and the Soviet Union. "No matter how the military matter is settled, the Arctic still will be of importance economically and politically. We must become familiar with it and learn to live on it because the competition in the world today is centered there."[4]

On signal, Harris tossed out a Mark 61. To do this, he recalled later, "I had to hang from the tail end of the blimp, using a safety belt. After assembling the depth charge, I waited for word from the other end of the blimp that a spot of open water had been located. And at the right moment I dropped the charge."

At intervals, others followed. "We were successful," he said, "in hitting the water with every one of the charges. The blimp proved to be an effective vehicle for this purpose."[5] Further, he suggested that ice charting might prove practicable using airships as "mapping platforms."

At about 1600, a dark line appeared: Borden Island. Sea fog cleared. Old, shore-fast ice presented a brilliant halo, contrasting with the island's browns and tans. Except for a brief late-summer span, the archipelago is indistinguishable from its maritime girdle.[6] And the northwest Queen Elizabeth group is the most remote in the High Arctic.

[Top] Dr. Guy S. Harris, head of the Research Division, Underwater Sound Laboratory and chief scientific observer for the five-man team of specialists on board to evaluate the airship for polar work. (Walter L. Clearwaters)

[Bottom] North of Byam Martin Channel, approaching the Bathhurst group on the return leg from Bravo. Here the canopy is persistent, ice pressures extreme; old polar pack grips the islands from shore to shore. (Hugh A. Mulligan)

The coast ended eight hours over cheerless pack. Landfall brought relief. At any time, sodden sea ice is miserable for emergencies. In 1926, *Norge* had logged two days above the polar pack. "Flat and snow-covered," Ellsworth wrote of reaching Alaska, "it was the most desolate looking coast line imaginable, but it was land and that was enough."

A dozen caribou were sighted. Enclosed by fast ice, the Queen Elizabeth group hosts few mammals. Caribou occur in scattered groups—an adaptation (presumably) to limited food supply. The animals are obliged to forage more than one icebound island and therefore migrate seasonally between them, a resource once providing food, clothing, and tools for the Inuit—but few now hunt them.

The channels of the archipelago become increasingly icebound as one proceeds north and west. At the head of May Inlet (Bathurst Island), a group of musk ox and a bear were sighted. A few thousand musk ox roam the western islands, moving more or less continuously in search of forage. The world's largest concentrations occur on Banks Island, about four hundred miles to the southwest.[7]

All hands enjoyed the sighting. The animals are known for forming ring formations. "I remember circling," Lord told me, "and [we] got them to form a circle back to back." "When the musk oxen heard the engines of the blimp," Harris recalled, "they became alarmed and all fifteen quickly formed a protective circle, heads out." Effective against wolves, the ring formation makes these shy creatures easy to hunt with rifles.

Bathurst Island lies north of Barrow Strait, between Cornwallis and Melville Islands. Here the eroded edges of parallel folds in bedrock realize a striped pattern. A result of slight differences in lithology, hence color, the effect is striking from the air. Drowned by the sea, they appear as long, narrow straits and inlets along the island's west coast, which just now lie beyond the horizon. The surface is weathered and plateaulike, with a few cliffs along a bleak, lifeless shore. "Flying from Resolute [Harris would tell reporters] we saw mosses and lichens, the only growing things. We saw snow only occasionally. Actually, there is never much snow there, since in winter there is no open water to evaporate into the atmosphere. But now, at the height of the growing season, we could see much white ice with pools of light blue, which looked like beautiful lace work. Now and then, there was a break or open water, and we saw many *polynyas*—that's Russian for lakes." (Actually, it means in Russian what in means in English—openings in ice over water.)

These areas of open water, he added, constantly change position and shape. The hushed majesty of this vacant, sprawling realm, the sheer physical magnificence of empty earth, sky, and ice can mark a man. "The North Arctic [Harris enthused] is a region of indescribable beauty. Now, [in the melt season] the sun is shining bright night and day. The low, slanting rays give a yellow-orange characteristic to the light. That, together with the grey-blue sea ice, is something which must be seen to be appreciated."[8]

Its bleak aspect notwithstanding, the Bathurst group is home to a rich concentration of wildlife. Polar vegetation is sensitive to local conditions. One determinant of survival is wind. On the large island, Polar Bear Pass is a comparatively benign natural environment: a well-vegetated tundra, hence an oasis for wildlife. Here, for example, forty-two species of birds are found.[9] In addition, Peary caribou (hunted by Resolute Inuit), musk oxen, and polar bear exploit this habitat, as do Arctic fox, lemming, and ermine. This is a flourishing enclave whose vegetation and animal life form a balanced (if constrained) ecosystem. The southeast coast, moreover, is an important duck and ptarmigan hunting area. And in the adjoining waters: walrus and seal.

Back within range, contact reestablished with Resolute, Greenaway conferred with the meteorological officer. Decision of the hour: to land or to overfly. Conditions at the mast and the forecast will settle the issue.

Seventeen hours after takeoff, at 2120 CST, 9 August, the flight crew again had the Canadian field beneath the control car. Was a firm ground surface available? Was a landing prudent?

Repairs *had* been ordered. But the attempt had further degraded the surface. During construction of a taxiway, the permafrost had been disturbed: insulating gravel removed, soft spots had formed—conditions that had beset departure a day earlier. Deterioration had accelerated—courtesy of twenty-four-hour sun and warm temperatures. The mast site now was very soft despite newly applied fill. And the taxiway was not much better. "When we came back over,"

Greenaway recounted, "you could look at this great circle" around the mast and "you could see these real damp areas"—large wet patches in the tundra.

As the navy loitered, a "detailed discussion" (Becker's phrase) assessed the wisdom of landing. The base commander was not encouraging: to moor again, Becker warned, would reintroduce trouble. "They were airmen and not construction engineers or permafrost experts," Greenaway reminds. "They moved in, leveled it—because we'd left tracks—disturbing that again; only made it worse."[10]

As it happened, high pressure and weak gradients were forecast to hold along the entire flight track to the south. Fuel on board would grant fifty hours flying—with seventeen already logged. The leg to Churchill would consume another twenty-four. Conferring with Collins, mission commander came to his decision: no further gamble on the soggy tundra of Cornwallis Island. The expedition would bypass its quicksand: an attempt to moor might again mire the ship or, worse, shear off its undercarriage. "It was agreed [Becker recounts] by the aircraft commander and the station commander that it would be in the best interest of all concerned if the airship overflew Resolute. . . . We never did appreciate how inadequate the landing carriage of the blimp would be when subjected to four inches of wet muddy gravel with a permafrost base."[11]

In his report, Captain Van Gorder outlined his reasons for discontinuing the operation, for pressing back south: "It was desired to avoid another ground handling evolution under the rather hazardous and trying conditions at Resolute Bay. In addition, all available weather data pointed to the desirability of concluding operations in the area prior to mid August when weather conditions pertinent to air operations deteriorate rapidly. When communications with Resolute were reestablished, the en route and Churchill terminal weather forecasts were obtained. The decision to overfly Resolute was made and the flight was continued to Churchill."[12]

And so the operational hours with which to assess the platform in Arctic airspace were abbreviated. And the opportunity for the Pole vanished.

A position report (the thirty-fifth) summarized a new flight plan: "Arrived Resolute Bay at 100320Z X Overflying for Churchill X ETA 110300Z X fuel remaining 40 hours." To his notes, Van Gorder jotted, "Now 2300—arrived Resolute at 2120—still had 40 hrs fuel aboard and I decided to continue on to Churchill. Est. another 24 hours before arriving there. Saw caribou and herd of muskox."[13]

To *his* journal, Gray recorded a short single line: "Continuing on to Churchill."

> The flight crew, as well as the support personnel [Greenaway later wrote] were greatly relieved at not having to face a second landing at Resolute with the possibility of encountering serious trouble taxiing to and from the mast. [The thawing permafrost and consequent deterioration of the surface was] the real factor that caused us to cancel [further probes. If ground conditions had been better] we would have done several more flights out of there. And of course this may have caused the weather to have been a greater factor later on. Because we were flying in very good weather and, if we had stayed there longer, we might have had poorer weather and therefore this would have been something we could have analyzed. But we didn't. Weather [therefore] was not a factor on this exercise. The weather was good.[14]

These lost hours would prove irretrievable.

The return proved uneventful. For the passengers, the southbound passage—a protracted lunge for homeport—was agreeable enough, if more or less anticlimactic. With a long run before them, this group settled in.

In the spaces forward, the watch dutifully rotated. "It is now 0045 [Greenland Standard Time (GST), 1845 Central Standard Time (CST)]," Van Gorder recorded to his diary. "We are heading south in broad daylight—the sun setting just on the horizon—clear sky. Have been flying about 4 hours now—will be relieved shortly for a few hrs rest." Off-duty personnel climbed topside, to mess, sip coffee, chat, bunk out. Following a shave and breakfast, the captain was back in the pilot's seat by 0830. Airspeed: fifty knots.[15]

The rendezvous with Bravo and the depth charging were between them the scientific climax. Still, the expedition was far from concluded: The flight crew faced a thousand air miles to regain Churchill; South Weymouth lay a further 1,600 miles on.

Although crowded (nineteen occupants in all), control car spaces proved to be ample and shirt-sleeve comfortable. An informal routine evolved: there were working spaces to explore (when invited), living facilities topside, and, if needed, bunks. Beyond the windows, shifting panoramas created innumerable opportunities for distraction.

The North is at once wondrous and intimidating, so extravagant is the scale. Impressions from any penetration are unforgettable. Desolation—raw, moody, imperturbable—scrolled past, each extraordinary image replaced by the next. After eight hours at 250 knots (this author discovered, via Lockheed Electra), the polar terrain may appear more or less unchanged. "No matter how far east or west you go," another writes, "you are still there."

Below, all was vacant and still—a world sunk in timelessness. "The land," airman-author Ernest K. Gann once marveled, "seemed stunned into silence, still waiting for first breath, as if not yet sure of its liberation from glacial ice." Of the subarctic forests, Schou recalled, "You could literally see the reflection of the airship on the lakes . . . and not only see the grey outline but also the colors of the orange panels on the nose and the blue lettering. . . . [T]hey showed up on the water just like a mirror." In some lakes, large fish lay in coves, wholly undisturbed by the airship's passage. Had they wished, the airmen could have trolled the quiet waters.[16]

For the in-flight guests, restrictions were few. No one could mill about forward until takeoff was squared away, a heading taken. It was impermissible to enter any working space until asked to do so. When opportune, however, guests were rotated through to watch the pilots. With its wraparound Plexiglas, the compartment was a prime attraction. "Here of course," one scientist remembers, "the view was superb."

Fundamentally, this was an operational test of the platform. Accordingly, the scientists were along less to conduct tests than to observe, to assess airships for support of polar science. Hopeful of positive opinion, the navy's invitation was calculated public relations.

And so, save for Harris and his "bombs," little in the way of actual work would be conducted. Scientists are naturally curious: each was observing, assessing, noting. By every account, all were fascinated. One or two tended to be interested in the ship itself, others attentive to the pageantry beyond the windows. Each returned delighted with his (brief) association with U.S. Navy lighter-than-air.

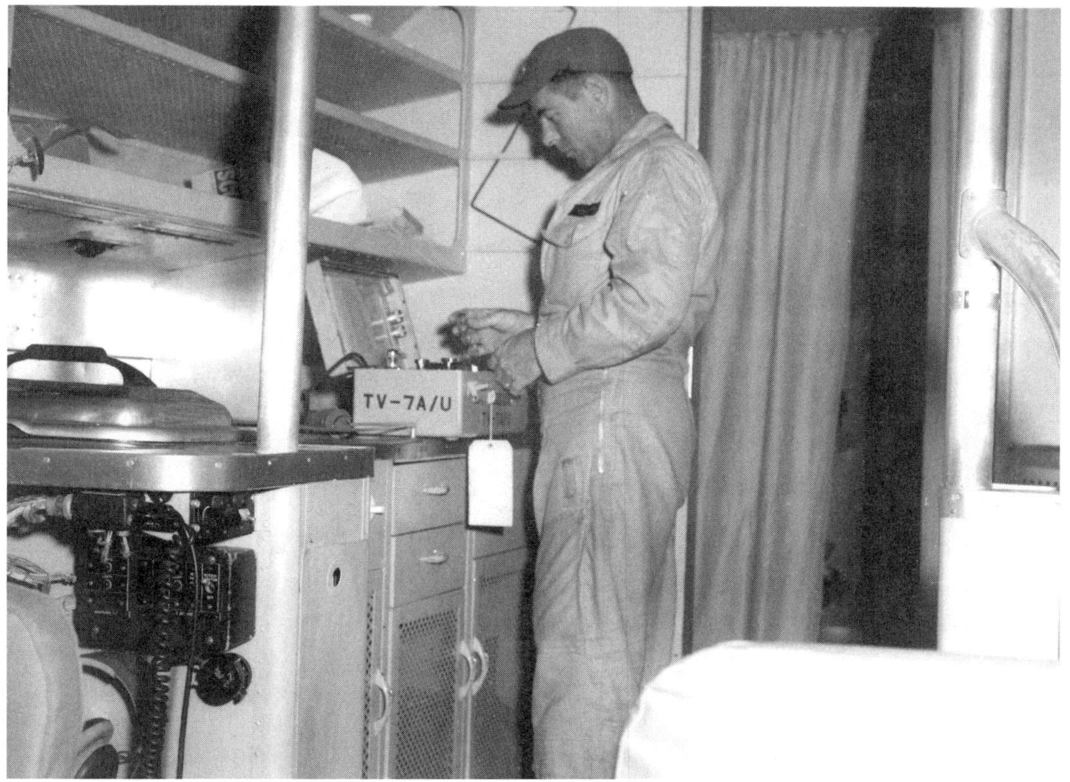

Galley space, portside: Crew chief Fred Parker checking suspect vacuum tubes. The view is forward. Note the shelf and cabinet spaces. The airship's wardroom is aft (left), the lavatory and bunk spaces forward, behind the curtain. (ATC Frederick L. Parker)

Walter Bailey, the tall geographer, did not bother to bunk out. He'd been granted a singular opportunity: to examine firsthand in continuous daylight, at low altitude and a leisurely pace, a stunning geography. The ablation season was nearly done: with snow and ice at minimums, August is ideal for aerial observation. And there was, Bailey recalls, "so much to be seen." The patterns of water and ice, landscape, soil, wildlife, vegetation—greener and darker as the ship returned south—plus a myriad of channels, bays, and inlets scrolled past his aerial perch. A single regret nagged. His professional interests included interpretation of Arctic features from aerial photographs. However, his camera gear had been off-loaded in Ohio, to help lighten ship.[17]

Gray, the forbearing Canadian hydrographer, also was enjoying himself. He had no specific tests to conduct, and he had had no time to plan them.

> I had almost no advanced notice that I was selected to make the trip—consequently I did not have an opportunity to collect any data or consider what observations I should make. It was just that—"an observer." Life aboard was casual—no set routine as far as the passengers were concerned. The blimp traveled at an altitude of 500–600 feet, and the weather was clear and details on the ground clearly visible. It was difficult to judge the size of an object unless one had a known object for comparison—a musk ox or a rabbit. . . . We talked, viewed the landscape, and occasionally flaked out in one of the nine bunks. If one wanted a nap, just look for an empty bunk.[18]

The novelty of a blimp and its loitering traverse charmed the passengers. All preferred the lower deck. "Topside" was unpopular: it intruded into the "bag" and was windowless; to some, it seemed dim and uncomfortable—the bunk compartment especially. Although he recalls the wardroom and galley as pleasant, Mulligan, for one, avoided the bunk spaces, finding them airless and claustrophobic. And if anyone snored, he remembers, it seemed to echo. So, save for meals, he stayed below. There he prepared copy, chatted agreeably with companions, parked by the large windows, dozed.

The excursion (by his account) proved pleasant enough: the ride smoother than a surface ship, less noisy than an airplane.

Commodore "Robbie" Robertson had found the bunks not long enough. (*Labrador*'s skipper was a big man.) "I don't know why it is," the commodore told me, grinning, "but the people who design ships and aircraft, they think the average height is six-foot or six-foot-three. Well, I'm six-foot-seven. It's awfully hard to fit into a six-foot bunk. If you're tired enough, you can. That applies to every ship, I don't care what kind it is."[19]

Although the others had no obligations save to observe/assess, Mulligan had copy to prepare. News gathering has changed little since 1958, though its transmission has enjoyed a revolution. Computers, satellites, and instant communications are a commonplace today; in 1958 wire-service material moved by telephone or teletype. (Satellite service did not reach Arctic Canada until the seventies.) Before that, a heavy dose of inventiveness, perseverance, and luck were called for if a reporter was to get a call relayed to the next station and, finally, on to the Toronto bureau of the Associated Press.

Mulligan had no deadlines. And in light of the platform's decidedly subsonic progress, filing regular reports seemed unnecessary—conveyed along at forty miles an hour, he noted, wryly, he was having a great day. Still, granted time to prepare, Mulligan radioed some of his copy direct. Mindful of military communications, he kept much of his en route reporting brief.

Some of the longer dispatches he handed to the crew chief, Parker, to send by continuous wave. Somewhere near the Distant Early Warning Line, however, the line's nearest main (Hall Beach?) or auxiliary station relayed Mulligan's copy. It offers a day-in-the-life floating above the subarctic sprawl of Canada:

> Up in the glassed-in cockpit, sometimes called the pilot house by sailors who went to sea before they got into the air, Lieutenant Comdr. Henry Collins of Conshohocken, Pa., keeps the blimp's nose level with the horizon by manipulating the control yoke. Next to him in the "idiot seat" copilot Lt. Comdr. A. J. Schou of Morgan, Minn., exchanges flight plans with the escort Constellation some 500 miles away.
>
> In the navigation room behind the cockpit, Wing Comdr. Keith Greenaway of the Royal Canadian Air Force, who wrote a book on polar navigation, checks weather information with radioman William T. Eels of Binghamton, N.Y. Engineer Elmer Lord of Contoocook, N.H., pores a practiced eye over the maze of dials on the instrument panel and occasionally dashes aft to make adjustments in the fuel lines.
>
> In the glassed-in observation station at the aft end of the gondola, geographer Walter Bailey and Capt. Frank Nusom, both of the Office of Naval Research, busy themselves with maps, charts and the moving sea and landscape below.

[Top] AT1 William H. Eels in a private moment in the airship's wardroom, topside. (ATC Frederick L. Parker)

[Bottom] Commodore O. C. S. Robertson, RCN, (l.) and Lt. (jg) J. Malloy, USN, take their in-flight ease in the wardroom. (ATC Frederick L. Parker)

One flight up, however, the stage setting suddenly shifts from aircraft to seacraft. The wardroom with its steaming coffee cups and luscious pin-up pictures is a babble of idle chatter and serious planning, the meeting ground of the on-duty thinkers and the off-duty dreamers. Capt. H. B. Van Gorder of Elmira and Canandaigua, leader of the Arctic trek and commanding officer of the Naval Development Unit at South Weymouth, Mass., discusses progress of the trip with Commodore O. C. S. Robertson of the Royal Canadian Navy, an old Arctic hand who helped set up the DEW Line.

At a table opposite, Comdr. Ben Hickman of Cuyahoga Falls, Ohio, duty pilot, continues to needle Guy Harris of the Navy Underwater Sound Laboratory and me about the whale steak they ate back at Churchill. The whale steak, consumed with scientific ardor if not gastronomic delight, has been a topic of jest ever since. Aromas of a more appetizing dish drift in from the galley where Wendell Cunlevy of Columbus, Ohio, a rigger who likes to cook, presides over a skillet of roast chicken. Meals are first rate aboard a blimp, a far cry from the pemmican and muk-tuk of Peary's day.

Science and tourism blend nicely in the rubber rocket.

The leg to Churchill more or less retraced the outbound track: southeast across Barrow Strait to Prince Leopold Island and Prince Regent Inlet to the Gulf of Boothia (the inlet's "dead end"), thence to Committee Bay. Repulse Bay and Roes Welcome Sound would bring *719* again over the inland sea named for Henry Hudson.

As forecast, the weather continued superb: ideal visibility and ceilings along the entire track. And except for a few hours north of Churchill, the aircraft enjoyed a meteorological bonus: tailwinds.

Enjoying the tour, Mulligan continued to prepare copy for AP's nameless readers back in the midlatitudes. Bemused by the airship, he nonetheless seemed pleased by its peculiar amenities.

The blimp is a block-long bundle of schizophrenic contradictions. It takes off like an airplane, dump's ballast like a submarine, works its rudders like a sailboat, rides the air like a free balloon and tosses and pitches in heavy winds like a destroyer.

But over the Arctic, reputed to be the calmest of oceans, it causes no more heart palpitations than a romp up the escalator in Macy's.

Peary on his dogsled, Amundsen on the deck of his little schooner and Byrd in the cockpit of his tri-motor plane conjure up a vision of the fur-clad explorer courageously thrusting a frozen beard into the howling face of nature. Aloft in a Navy blimp an excellent heating system keeps icicles off the modern explorers' chin growth, and stainless steel sinks and electric razors stand ready to rob him of that time honored facial characteristic. Of the 19 scientists and Navy men who made the 1,700 mile hop over the Arctic Circle from Churchill, Manitoba, to the floating ice island called T-3, not one so much as nursed the stubble of an incipient beard. Clean shaves, binoculars and khaki flight suits were the uniform of the day.

As if to lay to rest all jokes about peddling refrigerators to the eskimos the blimp carried a well stocked freezer into the heart of the frozen north and even had ice cream on the supper menu.

A full day would bring Churchill. The onboard atmosphere—while informal—was still decidedly navy. Little military routine was noted—no saluting. One of the few courtesies Mulligan recalled was reserved for the wardroom: if the captain entered, no one sat down until he did. And the enlisted men held to respectful address: calling each guest "sir" or "Mister." For the correspondent, the officers' khaki shirts were a source of genuine amazement. Each navy man retained a starched and altogether neat appearance, whereas everything *he* had brought was rolled up in a bag—and looked it. "I don't remember anyone acting like they were on a long camping trip," he says, half-joking. "You tried to be as civilized as you could."[20]

The crewman manning the circuit would, now and then, volunteer headline news. Talk of politics: little. Instead, at least one Yankees fan was on board—so the latest ball scores were enjoyed. Canadians are mad for hockey, of course, but August is the off season. Fun was had with the pronunciation of "about:" on board, "a-boot" became the only acceptable usage.

Mulligan recalled cold feet (physical, not metaphorical). The floor of the WV-2 had been chilly; the blimp's, he discovered, was no better. Remedy: several pairs of heavy wool socks, courtesy of the Hudson's Bay store at Churchill.[21]

Also on hand to ease the chill: a personal flask. Outbound, supply exhausted, the burly correspondent had replenished at the Arctic Circle Bar, the sole spa gracing Resolute. Alcohol is banned from military aircraft; in deference to his hosts and to avoid awkward explanations, the navy was kept uninformed. Ah, but when the "heavies" retreated topside, an "informal cocktail hour" commenced. Mulligan discovered that Guy Harris was an extrovert blessed with a fine sense of humor who also enjoyed a nip—or four. What's more, Harris was a superb raconteur with an inexhaustible fund of tales. The two bonded. Enjoying themselves, these devotees were pleased to extend cocktails into the late polar "evening." Robbie Robertson, if it be known, stopped by. A piquant old salt, he found it difficult (as he said) to be convivial with a glass of ginger ale. And he also was handy with a yarn. The commodore delighted in good company and *un petit verre* (a little glass). "Commodore Robertson was a good travelling companion," Greenaway affirmed, "and often enlivened the conversation with his salty jokes and sea-going tales."

Robertson's official position was a bit awkward. A man who liked pushing technology, he delighted in his LTA assignment and appreciated the peculiar virtues of the platform. Still, he was along for a cold-eyed assessment, to evaluate airships for logistical support. The commodore had no ax to grind; indeed, his views had been solicited precisely because he was *not* American. Climbing on board for the first time, Robbie had been granted a "quick and dirty indoctrination." He would log most of his time in the flight-deck area, observing. Courtesy of altitude and slow speed, he could (as he later joked) open the sliding windows and "spit on the polar bears" as the airship ambled past.

Taking a turn at the controls, he found that a blimp is temperamental—reacting to the wheel like a nervous stallion, begrudging of control and correction. Airships tug insistently off course. It was a chore just to keep ship's bow aligned with the horizon. Left uncorrected, the ship wandered across the charts. The slightest wind tugged insistently. A seat-of-the-pants "feel," he realized, was essential if a pilot was to maintain both altitude and heading.

Airships are sensitive—like submarines—to their medium. Emerging from beneath a cloud, the helium is warmed (for example); this lightens ship. Low-altitude craft, they are intimate with the terrain. Above scrub or forest (which absorb heat), airships tend to lose altitude; in open tundra, updrafts pushed them higher. A disagreeable wallow or porpoising can result. Pilots anticipate these effects and correct for them before altitude or heading are disrupted.

The commodore was a saltwater sailor. "I got the goddamn ship porpoising," he recounted, laughing. "I was having a hell of a time. A little hatch opened and a very irate rigger looked down and said: 'Jesus Christ, if you don't keep her steady how am I going to keep the grub on the stove!" "They are," he concluded, "difficult beasts to handle" and not easy to navigate—"they drift like hell."[22]

En route to Massachusetts the aircrew had a relief for each man—excepting the senior navigator. Though assisted ably by Malloy, Greenaway had no opposite number; he alone knew the Arctic islands by air. His maestro's skills were therefore indispensable. And unlike the commodore, the wing commander was a *crew member*. Greenaway would remain on duty, unrelieved, for nearly this entire leg—more than three full days.

"I felt," he explains, "I needed to be available and on the scene at all times because of my own familiarity with the area and the navigation techniques required," both of which were alien to these navy airmen. "I didn't feel it was fair to them to head up to the wardroom bunk and flake out for four or five hours and leave them alone." He would hold to his duties fully to the Ontario–New York line. Malloy proved to be an excellent navigator—skilled with the radar and adapting quickly to the expedition's peculiar demands. "His resistance to fatigue," Greenaway reported, "was excellent as he shared long hours at the navigation station with me without apparent difficulty."[23] Greenaway observes in his book, "High latitude flying presents no undue risks providing the crew take the trouble to prepare themselves as a team. The success of a flight depends even more than usual on crew co-operation. Pilots must appreciate the importance of regular and uninterrupted astro compass checks as well as the necessity of small alterations to maintain the desired heading."[24]

Asked about this, the longest leg, Greenaway downplayed its rigors. "The navigation was at a pace where you could enjoy yourself," he chuckled, remembering. And his duties were less demanding, he insisted, than might appear. "The pressure wasn't the same as if you were flying at high speeds. . . . And again, from my point of view, it was fascinating. So when things are fascinating and you're stimulated, sleep is not necessarily foremost in your mind."

Navigation depended, in part, on mission and platform—and the navigation aids available. For this mission, navigational duties were necessarily divided. Malloy spent most of his time at the navigator's desk, aft of the command pilot's seat. There he plotted the track chart. The wing commander, for his part, took observations using the astro compasses and read the charts. He circulated from the flight deck (where he provided the pilot with alterations of heading) to the navigator's station; he left the former to take astro readings aft—and to mess. "Although I used the jump seat or the moveable stool, much of my time was spent standing beside Malloy at the navigation station monitoring the navigation. In the high latitudes [he added] I assisted him with the radar scope interpretation as I had more experience in sorting out sea ice from land. In addition, I took the heading checks with the astro compass and concentrated on the gyro steering."[25]

One cardinal rule: do not drift off track. "You had to watch that you didn't let the airship get downwind. Like sailing. You can get into difficulties, you lose a lot of time and fuel by having

Face lined with fatigue, Wing Commander Greenaway takes a meal during the southbound run. As senior navigator, he had no opposite number to spell him. And he alone knew the Arctic islands and subarctic Canada by air. The Canadian airman remained on duty, unrelieved, from takeoff at Resolute to the Ontario–New York line—more than three *days*. Note the table-top recesses. (ATC Frederick L. Parker)

to fly upwind. That was the critical thing, make sure that you maintained the correct angle into the wind to maintain the desired track. Because if you didn't, and got downwind very far, it took a long time to get back at forty knots."[26]

In-flight demands notwithstanding, the wing commander's affection for these hours was plain in his recollections. Further, his hosts had prepared themselves thoroughly and well. "In my view," he remembered, "one of the most remarkable characteristics of the crew was its compatible nature. A harmonious condition remained throughout the entire exercise even though the hours were long and the environment unfamiliar."[27]

Robertson echoed these sentiments. "You must remember," the commodore emphasized, "I knew nothing about it as a craft. The thing that impressed me most of all was the efficiency of the crew. Every man seemed to know *exactly* what to do, how to do it, and he could also fill in for any other [crew member]."

Asked for impressions (quite unlike fixed-wing flight time), Greenaway replied characteristically. "It was marvelous—from my point of view. Not having experienced airship flying at all, it was a marvelous way to view the country. And being a sort of amateur geographer, it was fascinating, very fascinating. . . . You had a marvelous opportunity to observe." And more than geography was enjoyed. The airship, he enthused, proved to be "wonderful for observing wildlife—no question about it."

The control car, he noted, was comparatively quiet—except for the engine compartment, which he had to traverse to reach the astro compasses aft. As well, the blimp was comfortable and spacious—all in all, a good working environment. On first inspection, Greenaway had been a bit surprised by its creature comforts. Still, "knowing the [U.S.] navy, I felt you were well looked after."

During the return run, the senior navigator subsisted largely on fruit juices—ready sources of carbohydrate energy. Several "very tasty" steaks rounded out his menu.[28]

By 0800 CST (1400Z, Greenwich Standard Time), *719* hung over Committee Bay and was approaching the mainland. Landfall: Rae Isthmus. Ahead, the settlement at Repulse Bay dotted the chart. About thirty minutes later, the ZPG-2 again met 66° 33′ N—the Arctic Circle. The languid blue gray of Roes Welcome Sound spilled southward. And beyond, as yet out of view, the inland expanse of Hudson Bay.

Badinage aft had subsided. Alone with his thoughts, each passenger now was absorbed—a wordless transaction with the wildness scrolling beneath. Forward, an occasional comment pecked the snore of the engines that falling subarctic afternoon.

Near 2000 the sun touched the west skyline. A bit more than an hour later, Churchill hove into view—forty-four flying hours since takeoff on Cornwallis Island.

According to reports, benign weather was forecast to hold over Ontario for another thirty-six hours. So the navy will not loiter. Rather than moor, the ship will refuel on the runway, then lift off for South Weymouth.

Touchdown was logged at 2120, conditions "good." Ground crew: about three dozen locals seasoned with support-group expertise. (The NADU Willy Victor was on the field, having climbed away from Resolute earlier that day.)

The refueling resembled that at Lakehead: the ship held to the runway, fuel for the final leg was pumped on board, props idling.

Greenaway had disembarked for the Weather Office. The charts were granted a discerning scan; he then received a brief from the on-duty forecast officer. Conditions suitable, he filed a flight plan, climbed back on board. "Things looked good all the way right through, except for some air mass thunderstorms down in the Ottawa area," he recalled. "I spoke with Collins again on this. So the decision was made we should just go straight ahead, which was about another thirty-six hours" of flying.

Two relief crewmen climbed ship's ladder, and some provisions were placed on board.

Here the scientific party disembarked. Gray, Swenson, Harris, Bailey, and Nusom grabbed personal gear, bade farewell, and scrambled off. Only Mulligan and the commodore would attend the run to South Weymouth. Ashore, quarters and transportation out were arranged. Gray, for one, checked into the officers' mess for the night. Next day, he was flown to Ottawa. His sabbatical with the Americans: eighteen days, altogether. A bit less than two (forty-four hours) had been spent with navy LTA.

The refueling concluded in less than forty minutes. In twilight, seventy minutes following touchdown, the expedition again was airborne. Destination: eastern Massachusetts.

A sitrep is transmitted after *719* climbs clear: "Airship Arctic flight X Sitrep 41 X Arrived Churchill 110330Z X Refuelled and departed for NAS South Weymouth at 110440Z X ETA 33 hrs." One line reaches the captain's personal notes: "Off at 2240 for So. Weymouth!!"

The ship pushed southeast, toward the head of the Ottawa River. About ninety minutes out, the mouth of the Nelson River was crossed. York Factory lay a few miles to starboard; to port, the glint of Hudson Bay had paled and gradually darkened until it surrendered to twilight. The sun was touring below the disc-horizon—the aircrew's first "night" in eight days. Pushing inland, the bay eased from view; *719* reentered Canada's dark-green boreal sea. Ahead: the Manitoba–Ontario line.

The Churchill–South Weymouth run: thirty-three hours. Resolute well astern, the adrenalin earned outbound—sighting Hudson Bay, the landing at Resolute and a nearly abortive takeoff, the rendezvous with Bravo—had dissipated. Grinding out the return miles, all hands were eager for homeport and reunions with family—and a shower.

Off watch and on, caffeine fuel punctuated the dragging hours. (The coffee urn was always on.) Rotated off, crew climbed topside: to mess, stretch out, chat, log a bit of reading. In the wardroom, cribbage helped pass time. In-flight routines can regress into a kind of boredom; the hours can lag. The record 1957 transatlantic flight offers an extreme example. Of the uninspiring hours over vacant sea on board ZPG-2 141561, one (civilian) crewman recorded: "It was a request of all hands not on watch to be awakened or informed of the sight of anything other than the shadow of the airship. Viewing Cape Juby [Portugal] from 700 ft. was the subject of discussion for almost 48 hours. Probably the most exciting half hour was during the time that the NADU WV-2 vectored in on the airship during the seventh day. Seeing and talking to them close at hand after seeing nothing but several whales and a shark for three or four days was as enjoyable as going home for Christmas."[29]

At sunrise, 11 August, *719* reentered Ontario airspace. "It is now 0645 [Van Gorder recorded shortly after], and we are hedg home. Weather en route should be good. Our ETA is 0900 tomorrow. A wonderful trip across the forest and lakes of central Canada. Saw several moose and beaver."[30]

The Severn River was crossed an hour after sunrise. A carpet of trees unrolled to the circuit of horizon—the taiga belt encircling the subarctic. The Albany River was reached about midmorning; at noon, the first road in seven days was sighted, near Cochrane, not far from the border with Quebec. "Nearly everyone in town," Greenaway recorded, "was out in the streets." Droning past, the blimp was low enough for the airmen to wave.

That evening, the valley of the Ottawa River shimmered below. The pilots would hold to this winding ribbon as it spilled toward the Canadian capital. Northwest of Ottawa, course was altered to avoid thunderstorms: excellent visibility and good ceilings granted an easy circumnavigation of the cells. Except for threatening thunderheads, ideal weather persisted.

As Ottawa neared, Robertson joked, "We all made crude noises."

West of the capital, course was altered. Ahead, buried within the first night-dark since Akron, lay the St. Lawrence River and the international border.

Professional satisfaction pervaded. Nonetheless, Greenaway remembered, "I sensed there was some degree of frustration in not being able to make more than the one abbreviated flight. Yet, on the other hand, everyone was relieved that things had gone as well as they did considering the difficulties at Resolute."[31]

An Associated Press dispatch was prepared, the expedition's last while under way:

[Opposite] Homeport South Weymouth, about 0800 hours, 12 August 1958. The ship is thirty-two hours out of Churchill and three *days* from liftoff at Resolute Bay. (ATC Frederick L. Parker)

South Weymouth, Mass., Aug. 11 (AP)—A Navy blimp, the ZPG-2, which swooped down Saturday over an American scientific outpost on a floating ice island only 600 miles from the North Pole, was nearing its home base tonight to report on the use of blimps for Arctic research.

The airship radioed at 11 p.m. (EDT) that she was approximately 350 miles from this Naval Air Station and expected to land at 8 a.m.

Her skipper, Lt. Comdr. Don Collins, reported "a very successful voyage."

A Constellation plane, which escorted the craft, came in at 8:30 o'clock tonight.

Ground speed: forty-two knots. In the early hours of 12 August, almost due south of Ottawa, the aircraft reached the New York state line. Canadian airspace astern, Greenaway granted himself a bit of relief and retreated topside, to stretch out.[32] For his part, Van Gorder penned a concluding note to his diary: "Over Utica at 0200 and back in the U.S. Not much running on airship except two engines. Sure will be good to get a shower. New ETA: 0800."[33]

New course: east, to trace the Mohawk Valley to the Hudson.

Passing southwest of Albany, the pilots had the river beneath at about 0400. Another course change: dead south, to follow its shining path. Approximately halfway between Albany and Kingston, near Catskill, course again was altered—this time east, toward the Massachusetts line and, beyond, the haven of South Weymouth.

Shortly before 0800, the airship (now dubbed "Snow Goose," for the migratory bird that returns each year from Arctic breeding grounds) reached the station. The aircrew were thirty-two hours from Churchill, three days from the "hairy" takeoff at Resolute Bay. A final sitrep to CNO was transmitted: "Airship Arctic Flt X Final sitrep X Arr NAS SoWeymouth 121230Z."

A garish dot in view: ship's painted bow. The pilots circled, to accommodate waiting newsmen. At 0826, *719* rolled out to a ground crew for mooring.

The Navy Department had concluded *two* "firsts." Lieutenant Commander Frank Adams, acting CO, had taken *Nautilus* toward Portland, England—slowing so as to make arrival on the 12th. Congratulations were streaming in from CNO, ComSubPac (Commander, Submarine Force, Pacific), and other commands, as did messages on various subjects regarding arrival, celebrations, and related matters, including word of the Presidential Unit Citation. At 0900, 12 August, *Nautilus* surfaced for the final sea miles. About 1300, Commander Anderson was dropped back on board, via helicopter. The boat entered Portland harbor at 1430, securing within hours of U.S. Navy airship 126719. Portside welcome: bands, fireboats, tugs, small boats, crowds, reporters, and ceremony—the citation presented by the U.S. ambassador to England and First Lord of the Admiralty.

The transit had been a technology demonstration, a counter to the Soviet Union's *Sputnik* the previous fall—and U.S. failure on the launchpad. In Washington, President Eisenhower was smiling for reporters and the newsreels. One "race" with the Russians had been won. "We didn't know we were heroes until the President told us," Electrician 1/C James Irwin remarked. The nation exulted: the passage was "America's answer to the *Sputnik*," an admiral was quoted as saying.

Though it was undeniably a Rickover triumph, the admiral had received no invitation to the White House ceremony for Anderson. Asked about this, the admiral was instantly annoyed. "I'm too busy to worry about any snubs," he snapped, then turned away.[34] Once again (according to supporters), Rickover was the persecuted, misunderstood genius. This mask, indeed, was one the admiral had cultivated assiduously since the earliest years of the nuclear navy; by 1958, the role was a cardinal source of the man's influence and power.[35]

The Defense Department released an announcement following the formalities:

> *Nautilus* left Honolulu on July 23rd and after a rapid submerged voyage through the Bering Strait went under ice off Point Barrow, Alaska and proceeded due North to become, at 11:15 p.m. (EDST) on August 3rd, the first ship in history to reach the North Pole. After steaming over 1,800 miles under the polar pack the submarine on August 5th entered the open waters of the Greenland Sea West of Spitsbergen and continued south to the Atlantic to become the first ship to make the Northwest Passage via the polar route. The submarine covered a total distance of about 8,000 miles, of that about 97 percent was undersea.[36]

The submariners had underscored their prowess by transecting the top of the globe—an unqualified sensation. *Nautilus* had pushed from Hawaii to England in twenty-one days, logging

[Opposite] *Nautilus* is welcomed to New York City following her record transatlantic run from Portland, England, 25 August. Only one nuclear boat has since called in New York. (U.S. Naval Institute Photo Archive)

8,146 miles, including nearly two thousand miles beneath the icecap. When the boat emerged and its passage was reported, a torrent of *Nautilus*-related copy was unleashed. *Life* magazine, for one, "desperate for info," came to New London to interview Commander McWethy. Dockside, a clutch of *Time-Life* reporters began interviewing *Nautilus'* crewmen. Other news was swept from the columns, including that of a navy airship fresh from Arctic airspace. The reaction to *Nautilus'* latest triumph—as it would be everywhere—was frenzied. "Jets flew overhead and other planes swooped and circled low. Fireboats sent plumes of spray into the air. Ships and harbor craft made a din of whistles and horns. The Royal Marine Band, in white cork, helmets, played martial airs."[37]

Six days of fanfare ensued in the United Kingdom, after which the boat raced west. Average speed (twenty-one knots) established a new transatlantic record for submarines. In New York City, crew, Rickover (the president's personal representative), and local luminaries were granted a ticker-tape parade.

As news, the transit proved tireless. *Nautilus* and its crew (Anderson told me) were granted an "astounding amount of attention." The weeks following included luncheons, receptions and speeches, interviews, honors, letters, telegrams. Worldwide interest would persist for months.

In South Weymouth too, disembarking, the navy crew faced a clutch of reporters. An impromptu press conference was held in the New England sun.

Questions focused on highlights and on the airship's capabilities near the north geographic pole. His men in line behind, Captain Van Gorder went directly to the point: "At the beginning of the flight I stressed that our mission was to investigate the feasibility of using the airship for Arctic research. I can now report that there is no longer any doubt that the blimp can carry out this assignment as well as, or better than, any other air platform in Arctic research." There was nothing routine about the mission, he continued, adding that neither ship nor crew had ever been in any serious difficulty. He recounted the impromptu fueling at Lakehead, the high winds at Churchill, the cross-wind landing at Resolute, and the platform's miserly fuel consumption. Smiling, "We even had a chance to count the polar bear population in the far north and the moose population in the Canadian forests."

A laugh attends his remark as to the expedition's biggest headache: "The reluctance of the airship to get out of the United States." High temperatures notwithstanding, "Once we were out of Akron, we had beautiful weather all the way."

He was glad to be back, his enthusiasm plain. "Lighter-than-air craft of this size," the captain insisted, "could operate from both large and small bases. Even tied to a mooring tower, the ship can withstand fifty-mile-an-hour winds. It can use narrow runways. It can refuel from fifty-gallon drums brought to it on ships." The machine moored behind him, he opined, had the ability to work in the Arctic in its warm months better than any other. And "it's a lot warmer in the Arctic at this time of year than people think." Continuing, the airship had passed within twenty-five miles of the north magnetic pole, about five hundred miles from the geographic pole. Northernmost penetration: 79° 10′ N. Distance flown: 6,200 statute miles. And throughout, the aircraft had not exceeded an altitude of 2,100 feet above sea level.

This was a tribute to Greenaway. Canadian authorities, the captain continued, had extended all necessary aid in accomplishing the mission.[38]

What about the long return leg? The men had spent their time, Schou responded, "mostly sleeping, and reading a bit. We had no strict watches; just cap-napped when we had the chance. There were a couple of cribbage games on board, though."

Follow-up? "We'll report our results to the Navy Department," Van Gorder concluded, "and it's up to them. However, as far as we're concerned, we're ready to stay home for a while."[39]

Maynard Miller, ONR's project officer, was no less pleased with the results. "Everyone involved in the project," he told me, "felt that it was a success and that it proved what we had set out to do." Not all naval aviators (airship) were inspired, however. When I queried a seasoned LTA airman (retired) if the project was a significant aeronautical achievement or, instead, a more or less standard mission into unusual airspace, the reply was unembellished: "The latter."

[Right] Cdr. Anderson and *Nautilus* back at Groton, Connecticut. The transpolar crossing garnered intense coverage, salving the sting of orbiting Sputniks. Worldwide reaction hijacked competing news, including that of the air expedition to IGY Bravo. (U.S. Naval Institute Photo Archive)

[Opposite] Epic track of *Nautilus:* Pearl Harbor to New York City via 90° N, 22 July–25 August 1958. (U.S. Naval Institute Photo Archive)

During nine days with the project, Captain Van Gorder had added nearly 119 flight hours to his logbook. As it happened, these were to be his last in lighter-than-air.

The concluding leg had consumed just over seventy-eight hours—more than three full days of near-continuous flying. The aircrew—understandably—was drained and tired. Schou, for one, had been at the controls thirty-one hours since Resolute; Koza, his relief, had logged just under sixteen hours in the left seat, slightly less than sixteen as copilot. Both ship and crew had logged fifteen days out of homeport, much of it in alien airspace. Flight time for the mission: just under 173 hours—more than seven days in the air.

Interview concluded, news photographers snapped wives and children greeting husbands and fathers.[40] The airmen then were shunted to private quarters for a hot meal and some rest. Among the attractions that long-ago morning: their first showers in six days.

The local press trumpeted the return; away from the Boston area, however, rather brief copy concluded coverage—fed, in turn, by yet another dispatch from Mulligan and "the budget" of the Associated Press:

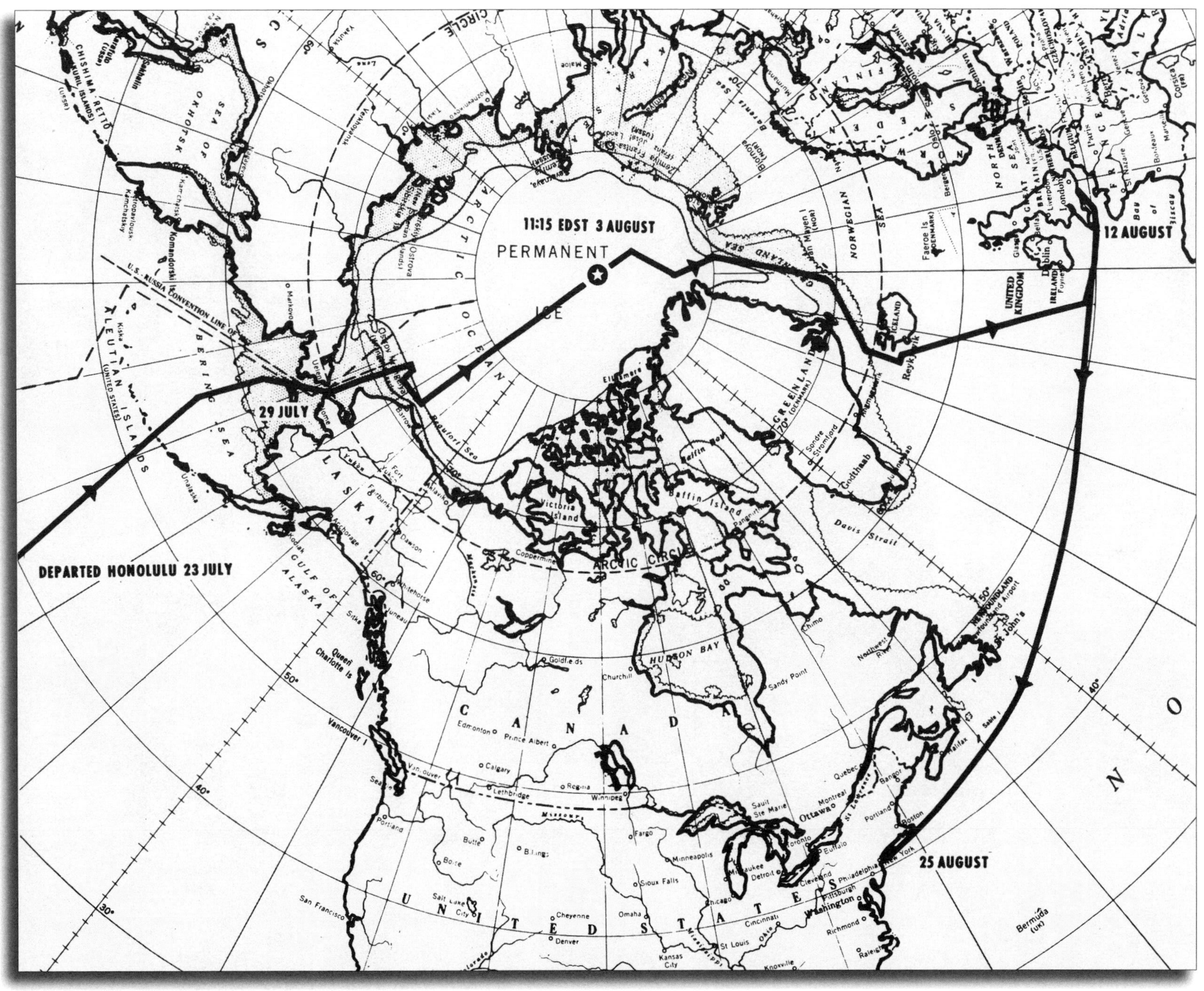

DEPARTED HONOLULU 23 JULY
29 JULY
11:15 EDST 3 AUGUST
12 AUGUST
25 AUGUST
PERMANENT
ICE
ARCTIC OCEAN
ARCTIC CIRCLE
BERING SEA
SEA OF OKHOTSK
GULF OF ALASKA
ALASKA
ALEUTIAN ISLANDS
(UNITED STATES)
U.S.-RUSSIA CONVENTION LINE OF
CHISHIMA-RETTO
(KURIL ISLANDS)
Komandorski Is
CANADA
UNITED STATES
HUDSON BAY
Davis Strait
Baffin Island
Victoria Island
GREENLAND
(DENMARK)
ICELAND
Reykjavik
UNITED KINGDOM
IRELAND
NORWEGIAN SEA
NORTH SEA
NEWFOUNDLAND
St John's
Bermuda
(UK)
Washington
Ottawa

[Top] Disembarked, the fourteen-man aircrew pose for newsmen and photographers. Note the mast watch at a flight-deck window. (ATC Frederick L. Parker)

[Bottom] Capt. Van Gorder is interviewed. Note the clamshell doors of the after compartment. (Capt. H. B. Van Gorder)

[Top left] Pleased with their results and glad to be back, Capt. Van Gorder and command pilot Lt. Cdr. Collins grip-and-grin for photographers and newsmen. (ATC Frederick L. Parker)

[Top right] Lt. Cdr. Schou welcomed by his wife and children. (ATC Frederick L. Parker)

[Bottom] Lt. Koza reunited with his family. (ATC Frederick L. Parker)

South Weymouth, Mass., Aug. 12 (AP)—Capt. H. B. Van Gorder reported enthusiastically today there is no question of the ability of a blimp for supply line work or research in the Arctic.

Just back from a nearly 8,000-mile round trip from South Weymouth Naval Air Station to a point about 500 miles of the North Pole, Capt. Van Gorder told a news conference the airship—christened the Snow Goose by its crew—can work in the Arctic in the comparatively warm summer months better than any other aircraft. Van Gorder is commanding officer of the naval development unit here. . . .

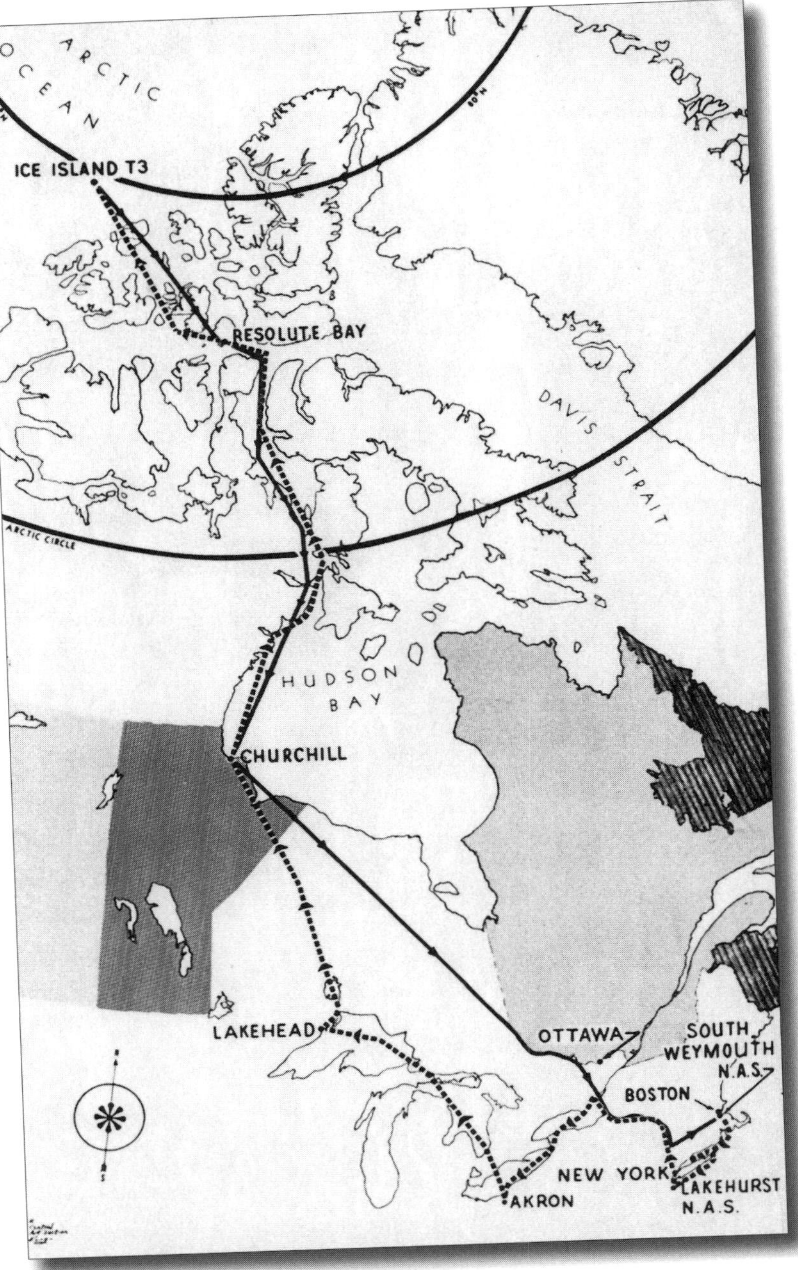

[Left] Track of the ONR Polar Project as flown, July–August 1958. (Brigadier General Keith R. Greenaway, RCAF [Ret.])

[Opposite] Aviators flight log for 9–12 August 1958. (Parker Papers)

Capt. Van Gorder paid tribute individually to the 18 members of the crew and observers who were on board on the most northerly part of the flight from Churchill, Manitoba to T-3, the floating ice island 500 miles from the pole which is a research base. . . .

The airship, crew and observers were given a quick inspection by customs and immigration officials on their arrival and then the families of men stationed here greeted them as they disembarked in the bright warm sunshine. . . .

Capt. Van Gorder, in paying tribute to the crew, particularly praised Wing Commander Keith Greenaway of Ottawa, Royal Canadian Airforce expert on polar navigation. He said Greenaway made an estimate 35 hours before their return that the airship would arrive at South Weymouth at 8:27 a.m. today.

The airship wheels touched the runway at 8:26.

Within the U.S. Navy's high command and elsewhere, the operation into Arctic Canada had been followed closely. A slice of this was concern, lest an accident embarrass the naval service. Still, the flight was well received: department spokesmen expressed pleasure with the airship's performance and with the overall results of the expedition. The ONR project, it was suggested, might open a new area for research into inaccessible areas. Genuinely pleased, CNO ordered up congratulations. Naval messages reached NADU headquarters at South Weymouth, addressed to its commanding officer, and New London, Connecticut, for the CO of the Underwater Sound Laboratory: "Congratulations to the officers, scientists and crew upon successful completion Arctic Airship flight. This is another example of a job well done. Arleigh Burke"

AUGUST 1958

Date	Type of Machine	Number of Machine	Duration of Flight	Character of Flight	Pilot
9-10-11-12	ZPG2	126719	77.5	POLAR ONR	LCDR COLLINS
					CAPT VAN GORDER
					CDR HICKMAN
					LCDR SCHOU
					LT KOZA
					PARKER ATC
					EELS AT1
					LORD AD1
					JOHNSON AD2
					DUNLEVEY AM2
					NAV W/CDR GREENAWAY
					LTJG MALLOY
					COMMODORE RRANVY OCS ROBERTSON
					PASSENGERS
					N.G. GRAY HYDROGRAPHIC
					P.B. SWENSON AINA
					HUGH MULLIGAN A.P
					E.A. NILSON ONR
					GUY S. HARRIS USN UNDER WATER SOUND
					WALTER H BAILEY ONR

T4 TO T6 / +6 TO +4 — COMMENTS

LOCAL TIMES / PASSENGERS / TO LAND: 0100 – 0825. FLT #5 – 2 fatim. (FUEL AND PROVISION STOP AT FT. CHURCHILL ENGINES RUNNING NOT MASTED)

REMARKS: RESOLUTE TO "T 3" TO CHURCHILL, MAN. BY AM. RESOLUTE DIRECT TO MARTIN CHANNEL OVER MACKENZIE KING IS. TO ICE ISLAND T 3 77N 121W ARRIVING T3 AT 091653Z EXTENSIVE FOG UP TO 300 FT OVER GENERAL AREA. BREAKS ALLOWED VISUAL SIGHTING OF CAMP AND MAIL DROPS WERE MADE, DEPARTED FOR RESOLUTE BAY 091741Z, DIRECT VIA BORDEN IS., LOUGHEED ISLAND, BATHHURST IS. TO CORNWALLIS ISLAND AND DIRECT TO CHURCHILL, MAN VIA PRINCE LEOPOLD ISLAND AND SUMMERSET ISLAND THROUGH PRINCE REGENT INLET TO COMMITTEE BAY, REPULSE BAY, ROE'S WELCOME SOUND, WAGNER BAY, MARBLE IS. IN HUDSON BAY TO CHURCHILL, MAN. TOUCH DOWN AT CHURCHILL 110320Z DROPPED OFF GRAY, SWENSON, HARRIS, BAILEY, NILSON, PICKED UP DOLLISON CDR GUINN + PROVISIONS OFF CHURCHILL 1104Z DIRECT TO WEYMOUTH +4 LAND 1208 52

U. S. NAVY AIRSHIP FLIGHT

FLOWN FROM RESOLUTE NWT.

TO FLETCHER'S ICE ISLAND "T 3" AND RETURN TO CHURCHILL, MAN.

DATE OF FLIGHT 9 AUGUST 1958

PLANE NUMBER 126719

PILOT LCDR DONALD COLLINS

NOTES W/CDR KEITH R. GREENAWAY RCAF NAV; CAPT. CO NADU.

Total time to date

16—18616 GPO

The adaptation of men and machines, on a mass scale, to arctic conditions will be a long and tedious process. That some progress is being made is reassuring, but only a concerted effort of science, technology and colonization will produce significant results.

—Department of the Navy,
Naval Arctic Operations Handbook (1949)

8 Epilogue

Unlike *Nautilus,* the Polar Project is a footnote to exploration. Militarily, the exercise was embryonic. In terms of scientific potential in the nascent Space Age, it remains an engaging might-have-been.

A proponent of nuclear power, Admiral Arleigh A. Burke, USN (Ret.), recalled that long-ago era: "They [*Nautilus* and airship 126719] were undertaken at a time when the Arctic was considered the last earth frontier. Both the nuclear-powered submarine and the airship were exotic new, yet-to-be-proven additions to the fleet."

Much here is unsaid. Although nuclear propulsion was untried before *Nautilus* (and was frightfully expensive), the submarine as such was acknowledged naval hardware and had been for decades. Further, the Silent Service enjoyed a broad political base. The airship, in contrast—an unproven, alien thing—had yet to be worked into the overall scheme of operations. Nor was it destined to be. As *Nautilus* ably demonstrated, the nuclear-powered submarine had been cast for stardom. Navy LTA would be slated for termination. Even the hottest performance from NADU, one presumes, would likely have changed nothing.

The landing concluded the expedition's operational phase. A report of findings with recommendations would close out the project. Accordingly, at NADU headquarters, digestion of results and preparation of a preliminary draft commenced.

Media interest evaporated. This, in part, was a function of *Nautilus'* competing story and the resulting media glare.

Late in August, the Associated Press alerted its managing and Sunday editor–subscribers to impending copy as to the "blimp odyssey." A few days later, the copy went on the wire. For Mulligan, it concluded a most unusual assignment.

> The U.S. Navy made history in the Arctic recently both under the sea and in the air. The underwater feat of the atom-powered submarine *Nautilus* was the more dramatic, opening a transpolar route. But six days after that achievement, an ungainly blimp

named "The Snow Goose" poked into the North Pole regions, intent on proving the value of lighter-than-air ships as research and supply vessels in those waters.

According to the "helium heads," as navymen sometimes refer to its blimpsters, the trip was a triumphant success. Just why and how is reported by AP newsfeatures writer Hugh Mulligan in a colorful story upcoming shortly on this circuit for AMs [morning newspapers] of Sunday, Aug. 31.

Mulligan was the only newsman aboard the blimp. The article forms part of a "polar package" on the Aug. 31 budget. The other entry is Roger Greene's profile of *Nautilus* skipper William Robert Anderson, which moved earlier in the week.

At NADU command, meantime, a preliminary draft was prepared. In mid-October, following some rewrite requested from Washington, a final report was submitted to the Chief of Naval Research.

Its import was unequivocal: the feasibility of northern deployment stood verified. "Airships can operate effectively and safely in the Arctic area during the period 1 May through August. Earlier and/or later operating is possible with proper base facilities. [The logistics were surmountable]: prolonged support for LTA operations in the Arctic are generally the same as those required for HTA operations—that is, quarters and messing facilities, fuel supply, aerological and communication facilities, etc. Provisions for ground handling, mooring, and a supply of helium are essential additions."

Two platforms were proposed: the ZPG-2 workhorse and the modernized K type. The former, NADU maintained, could provide long-range photographic and visual reconnaissance as well as air-drop and retrieval capability for supplies and personnel—given ideal weather. Modified for Arctic operations, the smaller K-ship had the range and endurance to reach much of the North. Moreover, the latter could land "at any desired position."

Displacement craft—submarines, airships—are sensitive to their medium. For LTA, a four-month polar window seemed applicable in terms of wind, temperature, and daylight. September twilight fades quickly to boreal dark. Cold air is dense, conferring greater buoyancy. And a twenty-four-hour sun confers more *uniform* buoyancy, unlike the light-to-dark cycles of temperate latitudes. "Airship flight operations with the ZPG and/or [modified K] type airships in support of research in the Arctic Ocean can be conducted on a regular flight schedule basis, from an advanced base during the period 1 May through 15 August. The airship can provide low altitude, slow speed visual and photographic reconnaissance over the Arctic ice pack within a radius of 1,500 miles from base. Delivery and pickup of supplies, equipment, and personnel are feasible . . . at selected positions on the ice pack under average prevailing weather conditions."[1]

Confident of its results, NADU was keen to follow up. Van Gorder requested that the specific research efforts of all federal agencies be assessed and the suitability of the platform to meet requirements resolved. An "early indication" regarding a second penetration—during calendar 1959—was sought.

The report to ONR seemed to conclude the matter. No formal response was forthcoming: its recommendations ignored, evidently, the Polar Project had been dismissed by official Washington. And soon, the entire LTA program would expire. "The operation," in Dr. Miller's metaphor, "was successful, but the patient died."

The hills of New England flamed with October, then faded to winter drab—and still no word. Apparently, NADU had failed to ignite the interest of government agencies with Arctic-related agendas.

Seeking client-users, the NADU commander presented his findings at the Cambridge Research Center, an air force–funded laboratory. The center was sponsoring a conference. Agenda: to devise a logistics plan for the 1959 Arctic field season. It was late November 1958. "If one is to explore the Arctic and look at the terrain [the captain advised in his paper] "there is nothing better than a flight in an airship at an altitude of about 500 feet and with an air speed of about 40 knots; it gives the viewer lots of time. The airship is an ideal platform for observation, photography, and as a vehicle for special instruments."[2]

Fiscal support had evaporated. And so a plea to his conference audience for funding: "The Naval Air Development Unit has a continuing project to conduct operations in the Arctic. However, the Office of Naval Research does not have the money for this program, so if it is desirable to operate airships in the Arctic, somebody must have the requirement and the money to back up the requirement. [Required funding?] "One large [ZPG] and one small airship [K], for a period of three months, would cost about $100,000. This figure includes personnel expenses, fuel, helium, and transportation of masts and helium."

Deployed, say, from T-3, a blimp could multiply the outpost's scientific returns. "Instead of using the light aircraft at T-3, as was proposed earlier in the session, why not use a smaller airship, not based at Resolute Bay or some other base near the Arctic Ocean, but right on T-3? The airship could then take people and a small amount of equipment out onto the pack for minute observations."[3]

Airplanes (it must be said) could not begin to deliver comparable support by way of lift and endurance, but they could provide support quickly, and in more units at less cost in terms of infrastructure and manpower. At Barrow, the Arctic Research Laboratory (ARL) had had no air capability until 1952, after which it had leased aircraft. When ski-equipped Cessna 180s were secured, its new birds were thrown to seaward. By 1963, ARL's fixed-wing aircraft were logging a quarter of a million miles—and 60,000 miles more by chartered machines. Its Cessna pair, indeed, carried out a gravity survey that year from Point Barrow fully to the Pole, with landings on T-3 and its drift camp ARLIS II (ARL Ice Station II)—the first single-engine aircraft to reach 90° N.[4]

Northern research is possessed by weather; weather surrounds polar fieldwork. What limitations, the captain was asked, are imposed by winds? Is icing a problem? Logistical and support requirements? Logistical support for northern deployment was about the same as that required for planes, he told his audience—augmented by ground-handling equipment, extra personnel, masts, and helium—the latter dependent on mission. About 100,000 cubic feet would supply a summer's operations—three trailers transportable by C-124. To moor and unmoor, a ZPG-2 would require thirty ground handlers, including crew and maintenance personnel, two blimps from forty to fifty. Personnel needed on T-3? A K-ship would need about fifteen or twenty for landings and takeoffs (roughly doubling Bravo personnel) plus an assist from the scientists.[5]

No second probe was ordered. Airships hadn't galvanized potential users—or so it would seem.[6] Why is not clear even today. Explanations can be inferred, however. One factor was the

Cessna 180 deployed by the Arctic Research Laboratory, spring 1960. The navy pioneered use of light aircraft for support of research both ashore (Alaska) and on the ice. These aircraft operated in company, so that no man's life depended on one engine. (Dr. Gerry H. Cabaniss)

availability (and flexibility) of fixed-wing support, as noted in one preceding paragraph. Another: the status of NADU within the naval organization. "My experience," Greenaway speculated, reflecting on the question, "is that no R&D element in any military service has the clout of an operational element." NADU, in other words, was dismissable. It never fanned any enthusiasm, certainly, from relevant bureaucracies. Decades later, Van Gorder told me, "Simply, there was no response to my recommendation." It's a rueful comment.

Years into the political wilderness, lighter-than-air was already operating on borrowed time. However improbably, a new role for naval airships might, just might, have bred a reprieve. In that context, a quiet effort may have been mounted to scuttle any recommendation as to a follow-on operation.

Dénouement

In the U.S. Navy, no command was primarily concerned with airships. Development, administration, and operation remained in the hands of the naval air organization; there it was a stepchild to heavier-than-air. From the earliest years, the navy had failed to recognize the airship as a special

Naval Air Station Lakehurst, New Jersey. Force reductions by the chief of naval operations and successive elimination of bases would—by 1959—confine all LTA to Lakehurst. The program continued by virtue of ad hoc measures and much improvisation. In 1961 all fleet airship commands had been disestablished. (U.S. Navy)

type, a vehicle requiring attention by officers qualified in and familiar with its peculiar problems. Other naval types—carriers, submarines, airplanes, even missiles—were accorded this special handling. In brief, LTA had not been integrated into the "mix"—nor was it destined to be. In June 1957 it was announced without explanation that two antisubmarine squadrons would be decommissioned. This action halved the number of ASW units. Cutbacks by CNO continued—the successive elimination of operational fleet LTA units. Extinction would be total: training, R&D, test and development, fleet units. By 1960 twelve squadrons had been eliminated, reducing operating strength from forty-three ships to ten. As well, successive elimination of bases from normal operations had confined all LTA activities to Lakehurst. "Practically speaking, this has shrunk the Navy to a token participation in LTA activities. The 'art' may be kept alive but it will be a precarious existence with no real foundation upon which a substantial wartime capability could be built. The numbers of airships remaining in each category is so small that operations which, with adequate numbers and reasonable access to bases would be routine, become 'all-out' events without necessary reserves and alternates for flexibility."[7]

An early casualty: BUNO 126719. Less than two months following its assignment to Airship Squadron 2 (ZP-2) at NAS Glynco, Georgia, *719* was ferried to Lakehurst for deflation and storage. It was September 1959. The squadron was being decommissioned. Time on the airframe: less than 1,400 hours.

During 1959–60, four ZPG-3W ships were delivered to Navy Lakehurst. The ZPG-3W was the blimp's ultimate defense configuration. Primary mission: airborne early warning. The "3W" was the culmination of a quarter-century's experience: "all that had been learned by the Navy and Goodyear on the past programs came together in this ship [a seasoned LTA officer was to recall]. All of the troublesome things were eliminated and all of the best in improvements were incorporated. . . . The ZPG-3W was more powerful, faster, longer-ranged, quieter, more habitable, very dependable, had trouble-free systems and longer range radar."[8]

With an envelope volume of 1,500,000 cubic feet, the ZPG-3W was the largest and—at eighty-two knots top speed—the fastest nonrigid ever flown. The platform was too late. The ballistic missile was the prime strategic threat, obsolescing AEW. At sea, the nuclear submarine had evolved into a first-order strategic system. The modern, fast, deep-diving SSN seemed beyond the reach of the ASW airship—and, as it happened, just about everything else.

On 26 June 1961, the termination order reached the air station's teleprinter. CNO was decommissioning all fleet airships, disestablishing the lighter-than-air commands. Excluded were two ZPG-2s—to be kept flying for two R&D projects, one classified. Before year's end, all fleet squadron aircraft were in war-reserve storage. And the R&D flying was hurried to a premature end.

A final flight by the last operational ship—BUNO 141559—was made on 31 August 1962. When *559* touched down that afternoon, an era of naval aviation concluded at Lakehurst.

There would be no resurrection. In December 1962 all airships in war-reserve storage were ordered stricken. The salvage work and disinvestment was concluded in 1964.

At Goodyear, engineers and technicians were reassigned; the firm's airship infrastructure withered. As Commander Widdicombe phrased it, "After twenty-five years GAC [Goodyear Aircraft Corporation] was left only with a lot of information in the files and an LTA tradition." The technology has been kept alive by modest commercial operations and a few adherents.

Considered solely as a research-and-development project, the ONR mission to T-3 is among the most fascinating in the history of LTA aeronautics. It is certainly unique. The airship men failed to prove their platform to the navy's satisfaction, but they cannot be judged harshly. As Commander Fleet Airship Wing 1 pleaded their case:

> It is a matter of record, but little-known and largely unrecognized, that the airship has played an important role in the R&D phase of many of our operational ASW equipments. These include, among others: airborne radar, MAD, aircraft sonar (both dipping and towed), exhaust trail detector (sniffer), JEZEBEL [sonobuoy], and infrared detector. The same characteristics which made the blimp so attractive a vehicle for prosecution of these projects should insure its continued usefulness in future R&D work. However, R&D projects aimed towards improvement of the vehicle itself have had a low priority and little support that virtually no changes have been made in airship design within the past 10 years.[9]

In the postwar era of naval aviation, it is doubtful if as much was achieved by so very few against so many formidable obstacles.

Potential Applications

How the tug of gravity is overcome is an engineering trade-off. As long as air weighs eighty pounds per thousand cubic feet and helium eleven pounds, the principle of lighter-than-air transport will remain fundamentally sound. Technology-rich options are available to engineering design teams: strength/weight advances in alloys, plastics and fabrics; satellite-based forecasting and weather radar; INS and GPS navigation and autopilot systems; vectored thrust; and avionics suites tailored to mission requirements.

Since the demise, countless proposals, workshops, conferences, hearings, articles, and programs have reevaluated LTA for various military and civil applications. Concepts have ranged from the fanciful and merely impractical to rigorous engineering analysis. Various study vehicles have "flown" paper trails, yet all have adhered stubbornly to the drawing board.

The obvious question arises: Why? The simple reason is economics. There were usually cheaper existing solutions (and constituencies) to a particular need or requirement.

The 1980s witnessed the largest-ever military buildup in peacetime. From 1983 through 1985, the U.S. Navy lavished $57.5 billion on ASW alone.[10] In this context, the Pentagon could afford a few tens of millions for reassessing—one might say rediscovering—the airship. The navy and, as well, the U.S. Coast Guard, Air Force, customs, and various antidrug and police agencies held interest.[11] *Naval* rationale: high-speed, low-flying cruise missiles. A stay-with-the-fleet, early-warning sentinel was wanted. "The airship," according to one announcement, "does not replace any existing system; it is unique in its capability to provide continuous airborne surveillance to battle groups." No conceivable airplane could deploy the huge arrays required for optimum warning.[12] Detection (hence engagement) capabilities increase with altitude: air defense lifts the radar and communications horizon for surface units.[13] Operational performance: fifty hours at forty knots, with good on-station "loiter." At-sea refueling would allow the platform to remain with fleet units. Payload: an array of large-aperture radar systems to detect, track, and identify stealth and low-radar-cross-section targets.[14]

The "battle surveillance airship" was brought to the brink of revival. And there it stalled: a casualty to budgetary squeeze and competing factions wary of its impact on related projects. Engineering was less daunting than doubt. Politically fraught, stripped of a sponsor, the blimp as fighting machine proved vulnerable.

The end of the Cold War led to neglect of antisubmarine warfare. Today, a new generation of quiet submarines holds major implications for naval forces and control of the sea lanes. Pentagon interest in ASW revived in 2003—a response to the growing threat of quiet conventional and nuclear boats, especially in the littorals.

The threat environment of terrorism rekindled interest. LTA platforms have been proposed for homeland security and, for the navy, support of warfare in littoral areas. A hyperlong-endurance vehicle could provide sensor-loaded surveillance over Afghanistan.

The circumpolar North is a sprawl of forest (taiga), muskeg, permafrost tundra, and northward-facing margin in which are scattered a miscellany of camps, outposts, bases, communities, weather stations, and projects. Its spaces lie beyond the ground transportation net. Sheer scale and the absence of a road-rail infrastructure impede access for investigation, development, resupply. And the latter is crucial. Accordingly, people as well as light, valuable, and urgent freight move almost invariably by air. Heavy or outsized cargo—notably fuel—is reserved for seaborne delivery, exploiting the short season of breakup.

Airships are superb for visual and sensor search—a prime mission during the Second World War. The control car hangs *below* the bag, granting a full-horizon view for low-level surveillance. Civil applications endure—geophysical, geological, oceanographic and climate-change survey, maritime law enforcement (illegal immigration, narcotics, antipiracy, pollution, fishing rights, harbor protection), wildlife census, whale watching, ecotourism.[15] The North is huge geographically, complex geologically. As with planes and helicopters, airship-deployed magnetic, gravity, and other remote sensors could pinpoint promising locations, then deploy field parties for "ground truth."[16]

Interest persists in heavy-lift support in remote places—such as dam construction, transmission towers, pipelines, resource extraction—moving something heavy in, lifting large quantities. Conveying mining equipment fully assembled instead of taking it apart for transport brings savings in labor and time.[17] Systems of year-round transportation through permafrost are frightfully difficult to engineer, then maintain. In northern Canada, *winter* roads are used primarily to supply the aboriginal communities with goods, food, fuel, and other essentials. Warming implies that government will be unable to sustain this winter-based linkage. "Basically, we [Manitoba Department of Transportation & Government] have no alternate. Yes, we can have airplanes and you can fly stuff in, but cost and capacity . . . limit how much you can get into the community. Yes, you can fly the fuel in at a very expensive rate . . . about ten times the normal cost. Yes, you can bring in foodstuff, but a lot of other things are eliminated by the high transportation cost."[18]

Geographically, Arctic Eurasia and Canada dominate the North. From St. Petersburg to the Bering Sea, the curve of Russia is largely devoid of heavy-duty roads. As in the United States and Canada, Russian officials suffer periodic outbursts of "helium fever."[19] Still, no airship has penetrated the subarctic since 1958. And no military airship has flown in nearly fifty years.

The North is a world apart. Bases are scattered, alternates few, the weather capricious. Dr. Hugo Eckener—*Graf Zeppelin* his instrument—had helped demonstrate the feasibility of transoceanic air transport. He deemed the Arctic a natural operating environment for airships. Among his reasons: its cold, dense air and the lighter winds of late spring and summer. "Most of the bad weather reported in the Arctic," he remarked in 1947, "is that observed from the surface, not from the air. It seems to me," he continued, "that the large cargo-carrying dirigible can bring supplies to isolated spots in the Arctic regions more cheaply and with greater ease than any other way."

One nagging concern: icing. The outer cover of *Graf Zeppelin* had inhibited buildups—unlike metal surfaces. "As with airplanes," the explorer Vilhjalmur Stefansson wrote, "dirigibles have found in the Arctic that they can usually control the formation of ice by rising and dropping to levels of different temperatures." Still, General Greenaway considered deicing for the ZPG-2 "very primitive." The ship had been vulnerable to icing. In this regard, the expedition had been blind lucky: air temperatures had held above freezing. NADU's all-weather evaluations had suggested that snow and ice accumulated mainly during moor-outs, rather than in flight. Airborne, the ZPG-2 carried thousand- and two-thousand-pound buildups with ease.

"The operation," Greenaway wrote, "demonstrated that a ZPG-2 airship can provide low altitude, slow speed, visual and photographic reconnaissance over a wide radius in the Arctic, and that it is also an excellent platform for scientific investigations."[20] Still, the airship was not a workaday vehicle. Deemed "rather fragile," it needed more R&D for it to offer a reliable, cost-effective mode of polar transport. Among the liabilities: the need for masts, helium, and ground-support personnel. "Mooring and ground handling facilities superior to those available at Resolute," he continues, "are required at forward bases to ensure safe operating conditions." For NADU, relatively good weather had been an operational necessity, especially low winds.

Demonstrably, a slow-speed aircraft was deployable. And yet: "We were very fortunate with the weather," General Greenaway reminded. "I doubt whether the Navy crew members fully appreciated this fact because it was a totally new environment for them. It is not uncommon to have freezing rain throughout that area at that time of year." In retrospect, perhaps, less congenial weather might have provided a better test upon which to judge. The Canadian does not dismiss the airship; its value lies, probably, in specific tasks, such as heavy lifting into roadless areas—with which the northlands abound.[21]

Commodore Robertson had endorsed LTA—with reservations. The blimp, he said, was a "bloody good" platform. He conceded, however, that airships were not continuously deployable in the North. Moreover, "it would take an enormous amount of logistic support to keep one up there." Robertson had had to conclude that fixed-wing aviation was more efficient and better adapted to high-latitude operations.

Official view aside, the commodore recalled loping low and slow over Arctic Canada with warmth.[22]

Fellow passenger Dr. Norman Gray summarized his experience. "I can only judge the suitability of a blimp from a hydrographic standpoint [he wrote]. The blimp traveled at an elevation of five hundred to one thousand feet with a speed of about sixty knots. In my opinion this would make it extremely vulnerable to adverse winds. For reconnaissance it might be useful when used under favorable conditions, but a fixed-wing aircraft would provide better and faster coverage."[23]

No military airship has deployed since 1962. The art has been kept alive by modest commercial operations, countless studies and reassessments—and by visionaries. Heavier-than-air is expensive in terms of energy, hence cost—the price of lift. The military, for its part, has a huge demand for on-station sensor platforms as well as lift capability—moving assets throughout the world. According to the study manager for the *Advanced Mobility Concepts Study* (Office of Force Transformation in the Office of the Secretary of Defense): "The results all agree that there is nothing that can beat surface ships for pure mass and volume, but an airship's potential ability to move a large mass far inland offers tremendous additional capability. Airships could fill the gap between the contributions of surface shipping and cargo airplanes."[24]

A clear and sustaining market for LTA technologies has proven elusive. Investor esteem is low: airships, apparently, offer little more than vehicles for advertising, passenger tours, and broadcasting—an adjunct to the Olympics and public spectacles. Praised in its day as a great feat of the age, who recalls *Norge*—the first aircraft to reach the North Pole?

[Opposite] *Skate* and *Seadragon* (SSN-584) at 90° N following rendezvous under the ice, 2 August 1962. As Dr. Lyon predicted, the all-season capability of nuclear submarines opened up a "new engineering domain" for strategic warfare and for science—true under-ice navigation. (U.S. Naval Institute Photo Archive)

History matters. Airships are subject to a great deal of prejudice. Fanciful claims exacerbate the record. Three generations have matured since the last rigid airship was dismantled; the naval nonrigid too is forgotten. Skeptics dismiss any application—whether far-northern or midlatitude—as impractical. This mind-set and competing, overlapping systems have deterred risk capital and vexed reinvention.

SSN/SSBN Polar Operations

Nautilus and crew had garnered instant, worldwide acclaim. An irrepressible flow of press, radio, and television commentary would persist for months. *Life, National Geographic,* and *Saturday Evening Post,* among others, added to the colloquium, as did professional publications that analyzed the implications. The Arctic Ocean had become, abruptly, strategic seaspace.

Anderson's *Nautilus 90 North* zoomed onto the best-seller list. Translated, the story would sell briskly in nearly two dozen countries.

Canadian editorial reaction was one of unease. "Canadians must be struck by the fact that the voyages of the *Nautilus* and the *Skate* were made in waters which border, for the most part, Canadian territory," one newspaper noted, arching an editorial eyebrow. "They demonstrate that, with atomic submarines, these waters can present either an area of great defensive strength or of great defensive weakness."[25]

The following March, *Skate* again steamed north: this time to demonstrate winter-patrol capability. The first submarine to brave boreal winter, *Skate* surfaced at the Pole—the first to do so.[26] "The art of routine surfacing through sea ice was devised on board *Skate* in the winter of 1959, by intuitive engineering, rudimentary knowledge of ice mechanics, and trial. A routine surfacing was defined as a stationary, vertical ascent at a specified rate of rise in feet per minute that was calculated to exert a vertical impact force on the sail . . . within the submarine's design strength."[27]

After breaking through into near-dark, overcast, and a bitter wind, a simple memorial service was held in the glow of flares for Sir Hubert Wilkins, next to the hull. To a volley of shots and according to Wilkins' expressed wish, his ashes were committed to the raging snows.

In February–March 1960, *Sargo* (SSN 583) transited the Bering–Chukchi shelf under heavy ridged ice, lingered under the canopy investigating newly developed under-ice sonars. *Sargo* surfaced through thick ice into boreal dark, including at 90° N. Eight scientists were on board, headed by Dr. Waldo K. Lyon. In May 1960 *Triton* (SSN 586), Captain Edward L. Beach, commanding officer, completed a submerged circumnavigation of the world ocean. In August 1962 *Skate* returned north, proceeding in company with *Seadragon* (SSN 584) to 90° N, where both surfaced in the same polynya. Two years before, with superb seamanship, *Seadragon* had negotiated (east to west) the inland waterway between Canadian islands—the first transit of the Northwest Passage. A very tall Canadian was on board. Quite in character, Commodore O. C. S. Robertson, RCN, enjoyed the cruise.[28]

The risks were high. "I realized," Admiral Calvert remarked, "it [under-ice cruises] was the most dangerous thing I had been involved with since World War Two [eight wartime patrols]."[29] If submarines learned to operate there, the strategic returns were immense. "We were aware,"

Frank Adams, the boat's "exec" remarked, "of the strategic implications, the scientific importance . . . of the [*Nautilus*] trip."

Soviet and British submarines have cruised the Arctic. For its part, Ottawa has accepted chronic bystander status. *Official* threat to Canadian sovereignty: the Soviet undersea fleet. Still, Washington's refusal to ask permission—unreported submarine movements, the reinforced supertanker *Manhattan* (1969), the icebreaker *Polar Star* (1985)—have abraded public opinion.[30]

SSNs for the Royal Canadian Navy have been argued since *Nautilus*. As late as 1987, a white paper maintained that an SSN program was essential if the RCN was to acquire under-ice capability. "Not surprisingly, the Canadian SSN programme was also intended to strengthen Canadian Arctic sovereignty in the face of US submarine operations in the region. After all, it is the US not the Soviet Union which denies that the waters of the Northwest Passage are internal to Canada."[31]

Canada borders on three oceans. "We are unquestionably a maritime nation," a rear admiral argued, "with an enormous stake in the seas both as a mercantile and a coastal state."[32] Following months of debate, the Brian Mulroney government canceled plans (1989) to acquire ten to twelve SSNs.[33] The procurement, General Greenaway remarked, had represented a needed asset. "As a sovereign nation, we've got one ocean and a third of our coast area which is ice covered. So, if you're going to have any capability of surveillance as a sovereign state or under alliance, you need the [nuclear submarine] capability. So, fundamentally, to pull our weight, we need[ed] it."

Nautilus rewrote the tenets of warfare, her crew disciples of nuclear power throughout the fleet.[34] In 1958 nuclear-powered ballistic missile submarines (nicknamed "boomers") were under construction. In November 1960, USS *George Washington* (SSBN 598) cast off for the Norwegian–Barents Sea area with sixteen missiles—the first Polaris deterrent patrol.[35] In 1963 construction began on the *Sturgeon*-class nuclear attack submarine—each boat capable of year-round Arctic operation. Armed with Trident II missiles, *Ohio*-class SSBNs currently ply the world ocean. Patroling "boomers" represent the most invulnerable weapons system yet devised—the ultimate in stealth technology, a seaborne deterrence in the nuclear age.[36]

The nuclear submarine (as Dr. Lyon had foreseen) is the quintessential polar platform. When *Nautilus* put the basin astern and came home, a bathymetric record (more than 11,000 soundings) and other measurements returned with her. Unnumbered tracks now crisscross the Arctic Ocean. "It is a fact of the cold war," Adams reminded me in 1989, "that we're *both* operatin' up there." Priceless data sets—water temperature, optical transparency, electrical conductivity, gravity, bathymetry, sea-ice thickness—have been compiled for military and civilian science.

The platform confers a quantum jump in accessibility: prior to *Nautilus,* no submarine had logged more than fifty miles under ice.

Cold War sub-watching subordinated science to military mission. *Every* Arctic cruise collected ice thicknesses and other information relevant to operations. Yet few civilian researchers were on board, to exploit the platform for civilian science.

Lloyd Keigwin is associated with Woods Hole, a civilian oceanographic institution. G. Leonard Johnson is with ONR. "Civilian oceanographers and some forward-thinking naval officers [they wrote] have pushed for nuclear submarines as platforms for basic research since the early sixties. However, these individuals have never achieved a critical mass and their efforts have not persisted. Most importantly, until the recent demise of the former Soviet Union, the Navy's nuclear submarine fleet was secure in its military mission. Now [1992] it is appropriate to explore new missions."[37]

As Commander McWethy had forecast, "The prime peacetime task of the nuclear-powered submarine in the Arctic is survey work."

A *Sturgeon*-class boat was assigned to civilian research.[38] Nuclear submarines are superb vehicles for working the maritime North. "You felt [Anderson told me] you owned the oceans. The way to explore the Arctic," he said, "is in shirtsleeves with a cup of coffee. And that was the condition in *Nautilus* in most parts of the ship."

In January 1993 the Navy Department announced that one of its fast-attack boats held orders for the Arctic—and that the U.S. oceanographic community was invited. Cruise: unclas-

Soviet nuclear icebreaker *Arktika* at the geographic pole, August 1977—the first surface vessel to bull its way fully to 90° north latitude. (Arctic and Antarctic Research Institute)

sified. Data: full access. That August, the SCICEX-93 (SCience ICE EXpedition-93) stood out to sea. The USS *Pargo* examined hydrography and circulation in the central basin. The boat itself was tested as an oceanographic platform, as was the nascent partnership between civilian researchers and the submarine command.[39] "It [*Pargo*] demonstrated the capability to make a wide variety of measurements and to collect samples both from the surface and submerged. It provided an acoustically quiet, stable and fast-moving vehicle for underway geophysical observations both above and below the submarine. Most encouraging for the scientists was the competence and enthusiastic support of the officers and crew of the *Pargo* for the scientific mission."[40]

A second cruise occurred in 1995, and a five-year program was established: about a month per year. Oceanographers envisioned a research SSN *dedicated* to science. In the course of seven deployments, the total body of unclassified data on the Arctic Ocean more than doubled. But the navy began to retire its *Sturgeon* class. The last SCICEX was in 2000. Reason: budgetary support, including insufficient funds from the science community. A unique opportunity was lost. "Remember," Norman Polmar reminds, "when the Cold War ended the Navy had about 95 SSNs in service; they are now [2002] down to just under 50. Obviously, the older boats would go first, and the current SSN force is too heavily committed for SCICEX operations."[41]

The Arctic Ocean is "the private sea of the submariner who is free to move in any direction and at any speed under the ice covering the sea." So wrote Waldo Lyon in 1963. Two decades thereafter, he said: "Many areas within the Arctic Ocean remain uncharted, for which data will be collected by submarine, or by drift-ice station, taking years to accomplish. It's a big place," he reminds.

USS *Nautilus* would log more than 500,000 miles, shattering records for submerged distance and speed. The first SSN deployed with the Sixth Fleet; in 1960 the boat operated with the Atlantic Fleet and in NATO exercises. During the Cuban missile crisis, *Nautilus* deployed as part of the naval quarantine of that "imprisoned island."

On 26 May 1979, after nearly a quarter-century, a last signal provoked a final flurry of headlines. *Nautilus'* nuclear reactor was shut down for the final time. "The *Nautilus* belonged to Rickover, even more than to the nation that had paid for her, more than to the Navy that operated her, more than to the shipyard that built her. And the submarine was the world's most revolutionary undersea craft to go to sea since the end of the previous century. The *Nautilus* was the world's first 'true submersible.'"[42]

Decommissioned in March 1980 and designated a National Historic Landmark, the boat stands at ease—centerpiece exhibit at the USS *Nautilus* Memorial and Submarine Force Library and Museum. Final berth is close to the U.S. Naval Submarine Base, New London, where the boat's keel first met the sea.

Ice Island T-3

The 1958 rendezvous with Bravo was followed by a decade of continued research in the basin exploiting T-3 and floe-ice platforms. As U.S. Air Force interest in the Arctic declined, that of the navy burgeoned. In 1962 custody of T-3 was transferred to the navy and ARL, at Barrow. Resupply—fuel, freight, personnel—continued almost entirely by airlift. By drift's end (1974), the ice island had floated programs in geology, glaciology, gravity, seismology, geomagnetism, tectonics, marine biology, oceanography, upper-air phenomena, meteorology, climatology, and underwater acoustics.

The potential for accident haunts every outpost. Attending T-3's protracted at-sea occupation: fire, runway incidents, a tragic explosion, a medical emergency that proved fatal. A marauding bear nearly took a camp commander. *Skate* and *Sargo* made rendezvous, resupply icebreakers bulled to its position. In 1970 a T-3 researcher was murdered. "Overriding the excitement of scientific discovery, however, is the tense awareness of the region's strategic position in a world divided by Communism."[43]

[Top] *Archerfish* (SSN 678) during Submarine Ice Exercise I-79 (March–May 1979). Intended to advance sonar system technology, the SCICEX program included, typically, an ice-breaker, aircraft, or drifting station. The vision of a SSN *dedicated* to Arctic research was not to be realized. (Cdr. Charles M. Wood)

[Bottom] Decommissioned in March 1980, *Nautilus* here is under tow in the Panama Canal (1985), en route to final berth at Groton, Connecticut. (U.S. Navy)

[Top] T-3, summer 1960. Resupply of the ice-island base—fuel, freight, personnel—was almost entirely by airlift. The occupation carried on—with interruption—for more than two decades. Here an arriving icebreaker dots the horizon. (Dr. Gerry H. Cabaniss)

Occupation ended in 1974. The last confirmed position for T-3 was recorded in August 1983: 83° N, 4′ W—on approach to Fram Strait. Images of the remnant showed a C-47 wing still visible. The peripatetic berg was exported out into the high North Atlantic. Decades after calving, its ice was reconciled to the sea.

The West is hardly alone on or beneath the Arctic Ocean. Russia has fielded more than three dozen Severnyy Polyus drifting stations. Five have exploited ice islands. Beneath the canopy, submarines from several nations penetrate the deepwater basin.

The Ward Hunt Ice Shelf again calved, in 1982. Recognizing the opportunity, Polar Shelf established a runway and camp on a large fragment—a multimillion-dollar outpost for researchers and support staff. "Hobson's Choice" was exploited to broaden Canadian expertise, for joint programs with other nations, and for bolstering Ottawa's claim to offshore sovereignty. Pushed into the archipelago, hence useless scientifically, its ice was abandoned in 1992.

Frustrated by its inability to track foreign submarines and lacking SSNs of its own, Canadian armed forces had hung a hydrophone off the ice island, to monitor for acoustic evidence.[44]

Climate Change

Earth is made habitable by certain atmospheric gases. Carbon dioxide concentration in the atmosphere has increased since 1958, when systematic measurements began—the so-called Keeling Curve. Global warming and ensuing effects on climate patterns have been on the table for

[Top] Instrument hut at ARLIS 5 (1970)—a "quiet camp" for acoustics work. Note the tape recorder. Submerged, information is transferred acoustically; for the submariner, sound is his "eyes" and a tool of detection. Knowledge of the acoustic behaviour of sea ice, ambient noise, propagation, and related disciplines has advanced using ice-based research. (Beaumont M. Buck)

[Bottom] An Ilyushin Il-14 at Severnyy Polyus-9, 1960—a floe-based station. The Soviet Union sustained a *continuous* offshore presence from 1954 to 1991. To date, Russia has deployed five drifting stations onto ice islands, the United States two, Canada one. (Boris Vdovienko courtesy R. E. G. Davies)

[Opposite] The Arctic cryosphere is changing. International teams are monitoring sea-ice thickness and extent, mountain glaciers, ice caps and the Greenland Ice Sheet, ice cover on lakes and rivers, extent and duration of snow cover, thawing permafrost, and changes in Arctic ecosystems. A nearly ice-free summer is now considered likely for the Arctic Ocean by mid-century. (Author)

decades. Today, most scientists are predicting a considerable—and accelerating—change, due to alterations in global heat exchange. Few would argue that the science is settled: science is about probability, not certainty. Still, decades of peer-reviewed work have realized consensus: human-generated warming of the industrial era. Unabated, rising risks are posed. "It appears mankind may have messed up the earth's climate so severely that the effects are irreversible," Dr. Maynard Miller remarked. "Certainly the increase in atmospheric carbon dioxide is, in the short term, irreversible."

A warming is predicted for the Arctic. A global temperature database points to an average 0.1° C warming of Earth's land areas per decade since 1900.[45] Climate is dynamic and complex: trends can be difficult to tease from the data. Still, the six best climate models show loss of summer sea ice in twenty-five or thirty years.[46]

Mountain glaciers are retreating around the world, sea-ice and snow areas in the Northern Hemisphere have receded, earlier springs are recorded. Off the North American and Eurasian polar margins, the shipping season will be extended; ashore, at remote settlements, permafrost degradation (sagging infrastructure) will dictate more reliance on air transportation—or abandonment. In September 2009 two German vessels were the first commercial ships to navigate the Northeast Passage—inaugurating, perhaps, the passage as a reliable route. Climate change is causing the Arctic Ocean to transition to a seasonally free sea: "the most profound environmental state change on Earth. Risks of political, economic and cultural instability are inherent."[47] Russia literally has planted its flag on the bottom at the Pole. Absent statesmanship, the high seas surrounding 90° N will become contentious.

> Sovereignty is going to be getting more attention, because the climate models show, especially over the long run, that there is going to be less sea ice . . . , such that it [the maritime Arctic] will be navigable all year round. This has important climate implications and is one of the reasons why the changes in the north are so critical. No ice, no snow, and you change the complete way in which heat moves around within the climate system in the north. The north is the thermostat for the globe, and therefore, if we fiddle around with that thermostat, everything is going to change.[48]

The twentieth century began with a race to the north geographic pole. It ended with major programs designed to understand the Arctic Ocean and to predict global climate change. In a warming world, teams are monitoring sea ice, high-latitude and mountain glaciers, permafrost, and circumpolar biota. Paralleling a global tendency, glaciers and sea-ice cover have exhibited negative mass balances. Currently, high-latitude research in atmospheric, biological, ecological, geological, and oceanographic sciences commands international focus.

All nations have a stake in the Arctic. Currently, national-security data are being applied to environmental problems. As well, proponents of climate change legislation warn that global warming poses a threat to national security—a threat multiplier that could lead to conflict over sector claims and resources. "Climate-induced crises like drought, starvation, disease and mass migration," they argue, "could unleash regional conflicts and draw in America's armed forces, either to help keep the peace or to defend allies or supply routes. . . . This is increasingly accepted wisdom among the national security establishment."[49]

At high latitudes, changes in snow and sea ice, glaciers, ice sheets, and permafrost are precursors to trends elsewhere. Ice-core studies (for example) are but one element of a multidiscipline, multinational program of climate-change research.[50] "It's not new that the environment is on the international agenda," a researcher observed. "What's new is that it's at the top of the international agenda." Observing the earth system in unprecedented detail, modern-day monitoring exploits remote sensing from space and from buoys, submarines (occasionally), aircraft (regularly). From the ice, drifting stations surveil the Arctic basin and its canopy.

It is an irony that, a half-century ago, LTA had intrigued Dr. Maynard Miller for reconnaissance and support of ice-rafted research. Reflecting on the data-buoy program of later years, "The airship [an expert opines] with its great range and capability to hover/land could have been used most effectively in implanting a large field of data buoys throughout the Arctic Ocean. The large number of ground support personnel—probably the most significant drawback of the airship—would have been required for only the short time needed for the buoy installations. Then the ship could have withdrawn and the buoys left to send back data for a year (or more)."[51]

Modern transportation is relentlessly transforming. Arctic Canada has changed irretrievably since a U.S. Navy airship retreated south.

Resolute is a communications and administrative center still. A staging area, the base logs "movements" of commercial, research, charter, and military aircraft. (Few private pilots reach its runways.)[52] The outpost is manned year-round, with summer's inrush swelling the local roster.

Not long after *719* cast off, control of Fort Churchill was relinquished by the Canadian armed forces; the site was leveled in the seventies. Billing itself as the "Polar Bear Capital of the World," Churchill is a destination for tourists.[53]

Alert is highly classified, the most northerly habitation in North America.[54]

Residents, settlers and scientists, businessmen and contractors, tourists and adventurers shuttle in and out of the North. There is no place that cannot be reached by some type of aircraft. "Voyages that once took months, created hardships and cost human lives can now be made in less than a day," Ottawa notes with satisfaction. "These days," according to one researcher, "people fresh out of university who want some information from the Arctic are just magically transported out there." Airlines crisscross Arctic Canada, offering scheduled service to out-of-the-way communities and to virtually all settlements. And charters are available to go almost anywhere.

To explore Arctic coasts or to trek the tundra, outfitters are available. Resolute has several—a hub for fishing and photographic excursions, bear and sea-ice expeditions. One can hike, sledge, kayak, ski, or snowmobile across frozen sea or wilderness—or overfly the North Pole.[55]

Still, Canada's Arctic islands are not easy—an empty, difficult physical environment. "Even the most pampered outing," a magazine warned, "involves such rigors as cold weather, rustic accommodations, limited menus and primitive transport."

The Protagonists

The military and civilian personnel who converged on the Arctic Ocean in the IGY summer of 1958 have retired.

The U.S. Navy flight crew did not fly again together. The Polar Project, as it happened, brought Captain Van Gorder's final LTA hours. Six months following the T-3 rendezvous, the NADU commanding officer received orders to relieve the chief of staff, Commander Naval Forces, Northern Europe, NATO. "The Commander was a British Vice-Admiral," he recalls, "and since I had had previous success in working with [the] British, the Van Gorders were on their way to Norway in a hurry." Continuing, "It ended abruptly my attempts for an Arctic mission follow-up." While in Norway he met by chance the chief apostle of ice-island exploitation: Lieutenant Colonel Joseph Fletcher, USAF.

Two years later, he was ordered to Washington as program director in the Bureau of Naval Weapons. Following retirement from naval service in June 1962, Van Gorder was appointed dean and director of the Advanced Management Program at Harvard Business School. In September 1974 he again retired—this time to west-central Florida.

Commander Aage Schou retired in 1969. Total flight time: more than 4,800 HTA hours and a further eight hundred in LTA. He also called Florida home, riding out his retirement not far from his former commanding officer. The two airmen met frequently.

In 1979 Commander Henry Collins, the expedition's command pilot, died in eastern Pennsylvania.

Lieutenant Harold Koza retired from the naval service in 1960, worked for the Army in aviation armaments, retired again in 1977. He qualified in reciprocating and jet aircraft, as well as night fighters and special (nuclear) weapons. Until his death in 1994, he resided in Alabama.

Fred Parker, crew chief, retired after twenty-two years of active duty, including twelve in lighter-than-air. Until 1994 he resided in California. Elmer Lord, an aviation machinist mate, was transferred to the Fleet Reserve in 1959, following twenty years of naval service. He resided in New Hampshire.

Dr. Maynard Miller, Project Officer for the probe, is a captain in the U.S. Naval Reserve. The recipient of numerous awards, he remains a tireless scientist, administrator, teacher. Dr. Miller has lectured and published widely. He currently is director of the Glaciological and Arctic Sciences Institute for the University of Idaho. In 1994 he was reelected to the Idaho House of Representatives.

After thirty-one years in uniform, Keith Greenaway retired from the Canadian Forces in 1971. His log records at least a dozen overflights of 90° N and thousands of hours above the Arctic Circle. Admired internationally, the brigadier general is a member of Canada's Aviation Hall of Fame. He remained active until recent years as an advisor and consultant to his government. This fine man and superb officer died in 2009.

Commodore O. C. S. "Robbie" Robertson, RCN, lived with his sailor memories on the shore of Lake Ontario not far from Toronto. Ever handy with a yarn, and until his death in 1994, HMCS *Labrador,* the ship he had commanded, steamed "full ahead" (in memory) with great affection. Hospitable, he kept (as he promised) "a bloody good bar."

Squadron Leader William Becker, RCAF (Ret.), resided in his nation's capital. Delighted to recall Resolute's "strangest aircraft," he was unequivocal in his impression of it. "The visit of the U.S. Navy airship to Resolute Bay," he told me, "was memorable in every way. The skill and courage of the crew cannot be underestimated."

Dr. Guy Harris was associated with the Navy's Underwater Sound Laboratory for a quarter-century. An indefatigable researcher, Harris died in 1966—"one of my big losses," Dr. Lyon recalled. A USL building has been dedicated to Harris' memory.

Norman Gray, the patient Dominion Hydrographer, headed the Canadian delegations to the International Hydrographic Conference at Monaco in 1957, 1962, and in 1965. Retired in 1967, he tended a farm near Ottawa.

Walter Bailey, the ONR geographer whose camera had been off-loaded in Akron, lived quietly in southwest Missouri.

Of the other observer-scientists on board *719,* sea-ice specialist Paul Swenson could not be located for this work. Captain Frank Nusom, USN, is deceased.

Of the submariners who converged on the Pole that IGY summer, all are retired. Commander William Anderson was detached from *Nautilus* in 1959. Promoted to captain, he did not seek flag rank: after duty as an aide to the secretary of the navy, Anderson resigned from the navy to enter politics. Representing his home state of Tennessee, Anderson served four terms in the U.S. House of Representatives. A successful businessman, he resided near Washington, D.C., until his death in 2007.

Promoted to captain, Lieutenant Commander Frank Adams held command of the attack submarine *Swordfish* (SSN 579) for nearly three years, then logged three patrols as CO of *Ben-*

jamin Franklin (SSBN 640) before retirement in 1969 for a career in industry. Lieutenant Commander Paul Early commanded USS *Sargo* and USS *John Adams* (SSBN 620), among other assignments. Retired, he lived not far from New York City. Advancing in rank, Lieutenant Shepherd "Shep" Jenks was a member of the commissioning crew of the first Polaris boat, USS *George Washington,* and was on board for its inaugural patrol. He went on to command the USS *Skipjack* (SSN 585) and USS *Abraham Lincoln* (SSBN 602) before retiring in 1971. Lieutenant Kenneth Carr served as commanding officer of USS *Flasher* (SSN 613) and USS *John Adams* (SSBN 620). Following duty as deputy and chief of staff to the commander in chief, U.S. Atlantic Fleet, he retired from the navy in 1985, a vice admiral. Becoming commissioner of the U.S. Nuclear Regulatory Commission, he retired again in 1991.

Until his death, Dr. Waldo Lyon was busily engaged. A titan of the under-ice submarine, he logged twenty-three polar cruises, totaling more than two *years* at sea. A fixture at the Arctic Submarine Laboratory (a former part of the U.S. Navy Electronics Lab), his last years were absorbed with declining funding. ("I am still in full battle to keep the Lab. in existence," he wrote in May 1995, "and making Navy Command understand we have never solved submarine warfare requirements in ice-covered seas.") His fellow conspirator, Captain Robert McWethy, USN, resides on the opposite coast, not far from the U.S. Naval Academy.

Lieutenant Colonel Joseph O. Fletcher—champion of the T-3 occupation—retired from the U.S. Air Force for a second career. In 1989 he received the Distinguished Presidential Rank Award, the nation's highest civil-service honor. A scientist-administrator, Dr. Fletcher was director of the Environmental Research Laboratories of the National Oceanic and Atmospheric Administration, an important player in the study of global climate change.

Late in September 1958, the T-3 runway refroze—and staff rotated off for the fleshpots of Thule and points south.

Among the alumni of that summer, all continued professionally. A field assistant in 1958, geophysicist Donald Plouff worked for the U.S. Geological Survey in California. His bibliography includes more than a hundred publications. Dr. Charles Plummer, another T-3 field assistant, received his PhD in 1969 and went on to conduct field work in Antarctica. He has been cited for outstanding service, and one of that continent's glaciers has been named for him. Gerry Cabaniss found himself back on T-3 before the end of 1958; eventually, he would log 531 days on the ice—four tours. A geological consultant, Cabaniss resided in New Mexico. In 1961, under the auspices of the Arctic Research Laboratory and sponsored by ONR, Dr. David Smith conducted further on-ice research on board ARLIS II—another ice island. Following positions in both academia and consulting, he founded his own consulting firm in California.

Arthur Collin completed his PhD soon after quitting Fletcher's Ice Island. He has enjoyed a distinguished scientific career, devoting thirty-four years to public service and succeeding Norman Gray as Dominion Hydrographer. Vice president of a private firm, Dr. Collin resides in Ottawa. He still uses, he reports, Tabasco sauce on his eggs—a habit acquired while on board T-3.

Special Correspondent Hugh Mulligan was the sixth reporter in Associated Press history to hold that designation. His innumerable bylines include the junkets of presidents, space shots, and the world's trouble spots, including Vietnam. Mulligan commuted from his Connecticut home to New York City—that is, when he wasn't touring with Bob Hope or traveling with the pope.

Appendix 1
Mission Background and Statistics: Polar Project, U.S. Navy Airship BUNO 126719

WHEN A U.S. NAVY AIRSHIP crossed the Arctic Circle on 6 August 1958, two "firsts" were logged: the first nonrigid airship (or blimp) to reach the line, and the only military airship yet to do so.

No lighter-than-air (LTA) craft had penetrated Arctic airspace in more than a quarter-century, not since *Graf Zeppelin* had explored and photographed the islands north of European Russia in July 1931. Northernmost penetration: 81° 50′ N. Further, no airship had penetrated the North American Arctic since *Norge,* in May 1926. Indeed, *719* was but the fifth airship—and the sixth LTA machine—to reach far-northern latitudes.

The air expedition was an unclassified evaluation sponsored by the Office of Naval Research (ONR). The 1950s were a time of keen research and military interest, propelled by Cold War tensions, in the circumpolar North. The multinational enterprise known as the International Geophysical Year of 1957–58 intensified these campaigns throughout the planet. Objective of ONR's Polar Project (as the mission was called): to evaluate the suitability of U.S. Navy LTA in support of Arctic science.

On 27 July 1958 the airship cast off from Naval Air Station (NAS) South Weymouth, Massachusetts, on what was to be a twelve-day mission. An interior route via Hudson Bay had been recommended in Ottawa and, upon consideration, chosen—to avoid the unpredictable weather and bold coastlines of the Canadian Maritimes, where conditions for a slow, low-altitude aircraft were uncongenial. High air temperatures realized several delays before Canadian airspace could be penetrated; *719* crossed the international border on 2 August. In Canada, the navy landed first at Fort Churchill, on Hudson Bay in northern Manitoba, where a mooring mast along with fuel and helium had been prepositioned, thence the Royal Canadian Air Force (RCAF) base at Resolute Bay, on the Northwest Passage in the Canadian Archipelago—just shy of 75° N.

On 9 August, *719* unmoored at Resolute for the Arctic Ocean and rendezvous at the IGY drifting station installed on Ice Island T-3—an iceberg of freshwater shelf ice adrift with the polar pack. IGY Bravo was a collection of trailers and buildings manned by a scientific party supported by U.S. Air Force personnel. Nine hours after casting off, *719* was orbiting the main encampment area. At that moment, the ice island floated at 79° N, 121° W—approximately sixty miles to seaward of the Canadian polar margin and 760 miles from the north geographic pole.

Due to poor visibility, the decision was taken not to land. Two bags of mail were dropped to the ice; however, the scientific equipment slated for Bravo remained on board. Three days following this singular Arctic rendezvous, BUNO 126719 concluded 78.3 hours of near-continuous flying when the aircraft touched down at NAS South Weymouth on 12 August.

The expedition logged 6,200 miles over sixteen days. Flight time: nearly 173 hours—more than seven days in the air. Northernmost penetration: 79° 10′ N. At no time throughout the mission did the ship exceed an altitude of 2,100 feet above sea level.

The evaluation demonstrated—to naval LTA airmen, anyway—that nonrigid airships (blimps) had a capability for low-altitude visual and photographic reconnaissance from an advanced Arctic base over a wide radius. The Second World War (it should be recalled) had established the strategic importance of the circumpolar North—an exposed flank in the superpower contest. As one consequence, the U.S. armed services' demand for information on that region proved insatiable. The logistics inherent to deploying, then resupplying, field parties scattered throughout a vacant, vast geography were formidable—and remain so today. In addition to long endurance and substantial lift, however, airships can hover into the wind. Accordingly, they can augment fixed-wing support to seaward (such as to ice-rafted camps) as well as ashore—providing useful reconnaissance and resupply during the boreal warm, when sea ice is too sodden for exploitation by heavier-than-air (HTA) craft.

In light of mission results, an operational season from about 1 May to 15 August was recommended by the Naval Air Development Unit (NADU)—the research-and-development (R&D) command assigned to execute the assessment for ONR. No follow-up mission was ordered, however. And in June 1961, the chief of naval operations (CNO) announced that the fleet airship program was slated for termination.

The Polar Project remains today—as it was in 1958—unique in the hundred-year history of U.S. naval aviation.

Appendix 2
Flight Crew, Scientists, and Passengers: Polar Project, U.S. Navy Airship 126719

FOUR PILOTS (ONE ENLISTED) flew the mission into Arctic Canada, assisted by two navigators—a RCAF wing commander serving as senior navigator. The enlisted crew consisted of two flight mechanics, two riggers, two electronic technicians, one radioman, and one electrician. In Akron, Ohio, the flight crew was reduced temporarily by one pilot and four technicians in order to ease static heaviness due to high air temperatures. Six men boarded the airship at Lakehead Airport, Ontario (now Thunder Bay), among them Captain Harold B. Van Gorder, USN, expedition leader; Commodore O. C. S. Robertson, RCN, an observer for his government; and ADC Herman England, USN. As well, two men were "valved" during the refueling, joining temporarily the supporting WV-2. Five civilian scientists plus an Associated Press feature writer met the expedition at Fort Churchill, northern Manitoba, on Hudson Bay; however, this group continued north to the RCAF base at Resolute Bay, Cornwallis Island, on board the "Willie Victor." Commander B. Hickman, USN, operations officer of the Naval Air Development Unit (NADU), NAS South Weymouth, also joined *719* at base Resolute.

U.S. Navy Flight Crew

Captain Harold B. Van Gorder, USN	officer in charge
Lieutenant Commander Henry D. M. Collins, USN	command pilot
Commander Aage J. Schou, USN	pilot
Lieutenant Harold A. Koza, USN	pilot
AC1 George Kalnin, USN	pilot
Lieutenant (junior grade) James Malloy, USNR	navigator
Wing Commander Keith R. Greenaway, RCAF	senior navigator
AD1 Elmer B. Lord, USN	first mechanic
AD2 Floyd W. Johnson, USN	second mechanic
ATC Frederick L. Parker, USN	crew chief
AT1 William H. Eels, USN	electronics technician
AT1 Francis M. Hughes, USN	electronics technician

AE3 Rudolph J. Cabral, USN	aviation electrician
AM1 James P. Quinn, USN	first rigger
AMC William H. Dunlevy, USN	second rigger
Commander B. Hickman, USN	NADU operations officer

Observers and Civilian Scientist-Observers

The scientist/observers assigned to the NADU mission for ONR joined the expedition for its High Arctic hours only—climbing on board at Resolute Bay. This group accompanied the single probe across the Arctic islands thence offshore, for rendezvous with IGY Bravo—an ice-island rafted camp in the Arctic Ocean. The scientists disembarked when, upon the return, the ship overflew melting permafrost at the Resolute mast site and, instead, refueled well to the south, at Fort Churchill. The Canadian observer and AP correspondent accompanied *719* the entire southbound run back to homeport: U.S. Naval Air Station South Weymouth, Massachusetts.

Captain Frank A. Nusom, USN	Office of Naval Research
Commodore O. C. S. Robertson, RCN	Canadian Joint Staff, Canadian Embassy, Washington, D.C.
Dr. Guy S. Harris, acoustics expert	Navy Underwater Sound Lab
Mr. Walter H. Bailey, geographer	Office of Naval Research
Mr. Paul B. Swenson, sea-ice expert	Arctic Institute of North America
Dr. Norman G. Gray, hydrographer	Dominion Hydrographer (Canada)

Media Representative

Mr. Hugh A. Mulligan, feature writer, Associated Press.

Ground Support Team

The support team was conveyed to and from the advance bases supporting the flight on board a U.S. Navy WV-2 (BUNO 131388). Helium, mooring masts, fuel, and about thirty men were required at both the Fort Churchill and Resolute mast sites, to assist in ground handling. The support team was flown ahead of the airship, to allow time to organize and train novice ground crews. (Two mooring masts had been shunted up and erected a few weeks earlier, in June.) Ground handlers were lent by the U.S. Air Force at Lakehead Airport (a refueling stop), by the U.S. Army First Test Center at Fort Churchill, and, at Resolute, by Royal Canadian Air Force personnel. The WV-2 support team consisted of an aerologist, two airship pilots, a ground handling officer (GHO), and a half-dozen ground handling and maintenance personnel, among them ADC Herman England, USN.

In charge of ground crew and material support in Arctic Canada: Lieutenant Commander Cecil Manship, USN. Lieutenant Commander James Goodman, USN, commanded the WV-2 throughout the exercise.

Appendix 3
Performance Summary and History of BUNO 126719, U.S. Navy Model ZPG-2 ("Snow Goose")

THE NONRIGID AIRSHIP (or blimp) ordered into the Canadian Arctic in August 1958 was of standard configuration. The ZPN-1 prototype for the "N" series had been delivered to Naval Air Station Lakehurst, New Jersey, in June 1952. Improvements and a host of innovations were incorporated into the production model—designated ZPG-2 by the U.S. Navy. Between October 1953 and December 1956, twelve were procured from the contractor, Goodyear Aircraft Corporation. Intended for antisubmarine patrols of long duration in collaboration with surface vessels, the ZPG-2 was specifically designed for one-engine, two-propeller operation when cruising at air speeds below forty knots. Extended missions impose physical and psychological demands upon aircrews; in-flight habitability was deemed vital. A two-deck control car—eighty-three feet in length—was the design solution. Crewmen messed and berthed "topside," a refreshing remove from the lower deck, with its operating and antisubmarine warfare (ASW) equipment. For extended missions, a fourteen-man flight crew was on board.

Length: 342.7 feet
Height: 96.8 feet
Envelope diameter: 75.4 feet
Envelope volume: 1,011,000 cubic feet of helium
Area of envelope: 7,019 square yards
Gross static lift (97 percent inflation, standard conditions): 58,636 pounds
Nominal dynamic lift: 6,000 pounds
Gross lift: 64,636 pounds
Airship weight, empty: 46,300 pounds
Normal gross weight (static-lift condition): 58,636 pounds
Maximum gross weight (6,000 pounds "heavy"): 64,636 pounds.

The ZPG-2 was powered by a pair of R-1300-2A engines, a seven-cylinder, single-row engine rated at 700 BHP (brake horsepower) at 2,400 rpm. During normal operation each unit delivered power through a transmission system via long driveshafts to 16-foot, 7-inch Curtiss Electric reversible-pitch propellers. A unique arrangement of clutches made it possible to drive each propeller by its engine or to drive both propellers with either engine. The ship could maintain airspeed of forty to forty-three knots for seventy-five hours with a fourteen-man crew, provisions, and equipment, and with about four thousand pounds of useful lift available for cargo. The still-air range was three thousand nautical miles under these flight conditions.

When selected for far-northern operations, ZPG-2 Bureau Number (BUNO) 126719 (the fourth production unit) was at Lakehurst, undergoing major overhaul. For its singular mission—to evaluate airships in support of Arctic science—the aircraft was assigned to the Naval Air Development Unit (NADU), NAS South Weymouth, Massachusetts, an R&D command for the Office of Naval Research. During July–August 1958, the necessary modifications were effected, after which ground checks and test flights were logged. Alterations related principally to navigation in high latitudes, near the magnetic pole. The platform itself received minor modifications. The specific changes:

1. The sonar and sonobuoy equipment were removed as weight-saving measures.
2. An N-1 compass—essential to navigating in the High Arctic—was installed.
3. An APN-77 navigator, providing drift angle and ground speed, was installed.
4. The G2 compass installation was modified to incorporate free gyro operation, thus permitting use of the autopilot in geographic areas of little or no accurate magnetic-compass operation. (As it happened, the ship would pass within twenty-five miles of the north magnetic pole in Viscount Melville Sound, southwest of Bathurst Island.)
5. The ship's nose was painted a bright orange pattern to enhance visibility over polar terrain.

The platform held eight crew stations for antisubmarine duties: command pilot, pilot, copilot, navigator, antisubmarine warfare (now undersea warfare) plot officer, radio operator, radar operator, and electronic countermeasures (ECM) operator. For the Arctic expedition, the ASW and ECM positions were unoccupied.

Significant Chronology, ZPG-2 BUNO 126719

Construction begun: Summer 1953
First flight: 13 January 1954
Accepted by U.S. Navy: 24 January 1954 (26.1 hours on airframe)
Delivered to NADU command, NAS South Weymouth: 26 January 1954
First major overhaul: June–July 1956, NAS Lakehurst
Transferred to Airship Squadron 3 (ZP-3): 5 September 1957
Second major overhaul: May 1958
Reassigned to NADU: 27 June 1958 (922.0 hours on airframe)
Departure for Arctic Canada via Fort Churchill, Manitoba: 27 July 1958
Return to NAS South Weymouth: 12 August 1958
Assigned to Airship Squadron 2 (ZP-2), NAS Glynco, Georgia: 1 August 1959
Last flight: 27 September 1959 (1356.8 hours on airframe)
In storage: October 1959 to September 1961 (NAS Lakehurst)
Placed into war reserve storage: September 1961 (NAS Lakehurst)
Stricken and salvaged: June–December 1963.

Appendix 4
Fact Sheet on USS *Nautilus* (SSN 571)

CONSTRUCTION OF A NUCLEAR-POWERED submarine was recommended to Congress by the late Admiral Forrest P. Sherman, Chief of Naval Operations, on 25 April 1950. In a statement to the Committee on Armed Services of the House of Representatives at that time, Admiral Sherman said:

> "You are aware that for some time the programs of the Navy and the Atomic Energy commission have included development of a nuclear power drive for submarines. It now appears that during fiscal 1952 we shall need to commence the design of a ship concurrently with the design and construction of power plants. The advanced nature of this project is significant."

The Joint Resolution (H.J.Res.277) approved 1 July 1951 made funds available for the SSN, as well as for the other vessels in the 1952 fiscal shipbuilding program.

The contract for the first SSN was awarded to the Electric Boat Co., Groton, Conn. (now the Electric Boat Division, General Dynamics Corporation), on 21 Aug. 1951. Basic designs were prepared by the Bureau of Ships.

On 13 December 1951 it was announced that the SSN would be named the NAUTILUS. This is a name famous in submersible history. Robert Fulton's experimental undersea craft in 1801, the imaginary ship in Jules Verne's "Twenty Thousand Leagues Under the Sea," and several U.S. Navy submarines, have all been named NAUTILUS.

During World War I the Navy submarine NAUTILUS, the H-2, became a highly successful type, and was imitated by England, Russia, Italy, and Chile. She had a speed of 14.1 knots surfaced, and 10.6 knots submerged. She was built by the Union Iron works for the Electric Boat Company.

During World War II the U.S. Navy had another NAUTILUS, the SS 168. She made 14 war patrols during the war, sinking 89,625 tons of Japanese shipping, and was the first U.S. Navy submarine to sink a Japanese carrier. Three of her torpedoes sank the carrier SORYU at Midway, after the enemy ship had been attacked by torpedo bombers and left dead in the water. She displaced 3,000 tons, and was one of the three largest submarines ever built by the U.S. Navy.

The propulsion plant of the new NAUTILUS is being designed by the Argonne National Laboratory of the Atomic Energy Commission together with Westinghouse Electric Corporation. Research, design, and production work in the development of an atomic power plant to propel the ship are being carried on at the Atomic Energy Commission's Bettis Field site near Pittsburgh, and at the DuPage County, Illinois site near Chicago, Illinois. Actual erection of the land prototype nuclear reactor and associated steam propulsion system is being carried on by Westinghouse at the Atomic Energy Commission's National Reactor Testing Station near Arco, Idaho. It will be the power plant of an actual submarine in a portion of a submarine hull, and will be identical, as far as is possible, with the reactor, propulsion equipment, and submarine hull section that will go to sea. It is being built on land so that tests can be made under more favorable conditions.

Construction of another land-based prototype of an atomic power plant for submarines was authorized by the Atomic Energy Commission on 21 February 1952. Design and construction of this nuclear reactor is under the supervision of the Knolls Atomic Power Laboratory, operated by the General Electric Company for the Atomic Energy Commission. This prototype will be used for final development work leading to construction of an intermediate neutron energy reactor for propulsion of a submarine.

Because the NAUTILUS will be capable of prolonged submerged operation, special provisions for conditioning and revitalizing the atmosphere inside the submarine are being incorporated in its design. This is being done in order that the endurance of the crew will also be greatly extended.

In the shipbuilding program presented to Congress for fiscal year 1953, a second nuclear powered submarine was included for the intermediate neutron energy reactor. This was reported out of committee on 2 April 1952 by House Report No. 1681, to accompany H. R. 6140.

The costs of the two vessels, as appearing in the House Reports, are an estimated $29,000,000 for the NAUTILUS, and $32,700,000 for the second SSN. These are only the Navy's construction costs, however, and do not include the Atomic Energy Commission's construction costs.

The cost of the NAUTILUS and of the second nuclear submarine is considered to be comparable to costs of other submarines being built today for the Navy. For example, the average Bureau of Ships cost for the TANG class submarine is $16.5 million for each vessel. Considerable research and development work is connected with construction of nuclear submarines and this is responsible for their higher cost.

Appendix 5
Memorandum: Commanding Officer USS *Nautilus* to All Hands, 21 June 1958

Memorandum:
Commanding Officer USS Nautilus
To All Hands On Board,
21 June 1958.
Subject: Security of information regarding Operation Sunshine.
Ref: (A) CNO TOP SECRET Msg [Message] 182131Z of June 1958

1. The Chief of Naval Operations in reference (a) has directed in the national interest of the United States that all information regarding Operation Sunshine be retained in the category of *TOP SECRET sensitive* information.
2. I cannot impress upon you too strongly the grave responsibility which rests on each of you individually to carry out this order. Not only is it necessary for each of you to "forget" entirely everything that has happened or been divulged to you regarding this operation, but you must also actively participate in maintaining a plausible cover story for what we have [been] or will be doing. I cannot imagine a situation requiring greater discretion, common sense, alertness and loyalty.
3. Remember that the strength of the chain depends on the weakest link. Neither rank or rate, nor the lack of it, nor time on board, nor years of service, nor any other factor, change the degree to which you are personally responsible.
4. You may come in contact with those who conjecture that NAUTILUS has done this or that or plans to do this or that. Do not let conjectures on the part of others cause you to lower your guard.
5. *Specific instructions.*
    a. *From this moment forward* do not discuss *any facet* of Operation SUNSHINE with *any person on board or ashore* by either verbal or written means. In privacy it is permissible to consult with the Commanding Officer or Executive Officer on factors relating to the subject.

b. Immediately search through your personal things—letters, papers, notes, etc.,— and seal them in an envelope or package to be marked with your name, labeled TOP SECRET Control Officer—Lt White. Department and division officers and leading petty officers do the equivalent within their own organizations with regard to logs, charts, records, etc.
c. Put away in a secure stowage all portable equipments, indicative of Arctic operations—special portable navigation gear, depth senser [*sic*], temperature and salinity recorders, etc.
d. Prior arrival Pearl [Harbor] stow securely all cold weather clothing.
e. Because beards are somewhat indicative of cold weather operations shave them off prior arrival Pearl.
f. Gunnery Officer be prepared to repaint numbers topside on appropriate calm day enroute Pearl.
g. Hold back any reports that might tend to furnish some correlation with operation SUNSHINE.
h. All hands on board execute disclosure agreement form provided by Top Secret Control Officer.

6. The following will be used as a basis for all written and verbal discussions concerning or implying NAUTILUS' operations:

Early in 1958 the Chief of Naval Operations, based on the extreme success of NAUTILUS' 1957 West Coast deployment, decided to send NAUTILUS back to the Pacific for continued orientation of Pacific Fleet personnel in the significant aspects of nuclear propulsion and nuclear submarine operations.

At this time NAUTILUS was scheduled to make a late summer cruise to the Arctic in company with [USS] SKATE [(SSN 578)] and [USS] HALFBEAK [(SS 352)]. Because little time would elapse between the Pacific cruise and the Arctic cruise, it was necessary and logical to install all gear needed for the Arctic cruise prior departure New London. Installation of Arctic equipment, including the inertial navigator, filled two other requirements: (1) it provided time for thoroughly testing equipments, particularly the navigator, (2) it carried out CNO's policy to equip all nuclear submarines for Arctic operations on a permanent basis.

In the spring of 1958 the Fleet Ballistic Missile [FBM] submarine group in Washington made an urgent request for an endurance cruise to be conducted by an SSN during Fiscal 1958. It was decided to assign this cruise to NAUTILUS incident to the transit from Seattle to Panama.

Requirements for this cruise were two distinct categories: (1) atmosphere control studies, (2) special highly classified studies relating to the problems of operating FBM submarines.

Because of the long sealed boat runs of [USS] SEAWOLF [(SSN 575)] and SKATE the atmosphere control study took on a slightly different aspect and became secondary to category (2) above, details of which are, again, highly classified.

Due to this fact, a long continuous sealed-boat run became of secondary importance and CNO, in order to fulfill a long standing high priority request by CinCPacFlt [Commander in Chief, Pacific Fleet] and ComSubPac [Commander, Submarine Forces Pacific] split the endurance cruise into two phases with a period at Pearl for indoctrination of other PacFlt personnel in between the two phases.

The new schedule will undoubtedly change the timing of, or even cancel, the scheduled summer cruise to the Arctic. This is the result of the extremely high priority placed on the FBM submarine studies. Perhaps the cruise will be made in the Fall. At this point the future schedule of NAUTILUS must be considered indefinite, however, C.O. [Commanding Officer] NAUTILUS believes NAUTILUS will return to New London via the [Panama] Canal, arriving New London by mid-September.

NAUTILUS departed Seattle on 9 June and sailed south along the track shown you by the Navigator. It was a routine cruise—material problems were few and atmosphere control was the best experienced to date.

Elaborate plans were made for the first equator crossing by a nuclear powered ship. However, on 20 June, still considerably North of the equator, the ship received the change in OpOrd [operation order] diverting us to Pearl. Failure to cross the equator at this time and the prospective delay in getting home are naturally disappointing, however the visit to Hawaii will add another interesting chapter to the most travelled submarine in history.

/s/ W. R. ANDERSON

Appendix 6
Mission Statistics: 1958 Transpolar Voyage, USS *Nautilus* (SSN 571)

USS *NAUTILUS* (SSN 571) was the world's first nuclear-powered submarine. Granted a revolutionary capability—that is, freed from surface oxygen—she was the first vessel to reach the north geographic pole, in the central Arctic Ocean. (Muscling multiyear ice, the Soviet Union's nuclear icebreaker *Arktika* was the first *surface* vessel to gain 90° N latitude, in August 1977.) Operation Sunshine—a Pacific-to-Atlantic transpolar crossing of the basin via the Pole consumed nineteen days and logged 8,146 miles. Ninety-three percent of *Nautilus*' underway time was logged submerged. The run to Bering Strait from Pearl Harbor—2,901 miles—was made at an average speed of nearly twenty knots, a then record for a long submerged cruise. Average speed for the entire mission: over seventeen knots.

Chronology, Phase II, Operation Sunshine (all times EDST)

Departed U.S. Submarine Base, Pearl Harbor	0200	23 July
Entered Bering Strait	0100	29 July
Slipped under Arctic pack off Point Barrow, Alaska	0837	1 August
Reached 90° north latitude	1115	3 August
Emerged from under polar pack, northeast of Greenland	0954	5 August
Arrived rendezvous, off Iceland	1100	7 August
Commanding Officer transferred to helicopter, at sea	2315	7 August
Commanding Officer arrived Washington, D.C.	1045	8 August
Arrived Portland, England	0830	12 August
Departed Portland, England	0700	18 August
Arrived New York City	0800	25 August

When *Nautilus* logged 90° N latitude, more men—116—were assembled at that long-sought extremity than at any time in the history of exploration.

Among its many "firsts," *Nautilus* was the first combatant ship equipped with an inertial navigation system (INS). Her automatic control gear held the 319-foot-long hull exactly on course—piercing the geographic pole precisely. Still, four compasses of various types also were mounted. *Nautilus* was equipped with separate acoustic and sonar systems to monitor the sea-ice canopy overhead as well as three for measuring distance to the seabed. Her continuous record of ice thicknesses and water depth (more than 11,000 individual soundings) represented the first-ever contour map for the polar basin. Water depth at the Pole: 13,410 feet. Before the 1958 transit, the central Arctic Ocean had been essentially uncharted, with a mere scattering of soundings available—and those largely from short-term drifting stations deployed on the shifting pack.

A closed-circuit, upward-beamed television system was mounted, allowing officers and crew to view the pack's underside as it passed overhead.

During Operation Sunshine, *Nautilus* steamed ninety-six hours beneath ice, logging 1,830 miles from Point Barrow, Alaska, into then open sea just beyond the pack-ice margin, exiting into the northeast Atlantic on the East Greenland Current, between Greenland and Spitsbergen. Throughout the epic sortie, the submarine and its systems performed superbly—not so much as a lightbulb failed.

On her 1957 attempt, *Nautilus* had pressed to within 180 miles of 90° N but was obliged to reverse course (carefully) and retreat: a fuse had blown, compromising navigation. For the Phase 1 attempt in June 1958, the navy rushed the season: in the Chukchi Sea (continental shelf), shoal water and deep-draft ice keels blocked passage to abyssal water. Before *Nautilus,* no ship had steamed north of 83° 21′ under its own power—a record set by a Soviet icebreaker in 1955. (Intentionally beset, Fridtjof Nansen's ice ship *Fram* drifted for months within the polar pack, reaching 85° 57′ N.)

En route to Portland, England, and a rave-up welcome, the boat logged her 60,000th submerged mile. Like her fictional namesake, *Nautilus* had steamed Jules Verne's famous "20,000 leagues under the sea."

Notes

Preface

1. Dr. Gerry H. Cabaniss, letter to author, 20 December 1989. An undergraduate in 1958, Cabaniss was a geologist field assistant assigned to T-3 that IGY summer.
2. Ibid.
3. The CO had disembarked—plucked by helicopter—at a rendezvous point off Iceland. Flown to an Icelandic runway, he was on his way immediately to Washington. At sea, the boat submerged and took departure for Europe.

Chapter 1. The North American Arctic

1. "As many Canadians see it, the mention of Canada to a foreigner, particularly an American, instantly conjures up images of hockey players, Royal Canadian Mounted Policemen, lumberjacks, igloos, and, of course, canoes and moose. The list goes on." Calvin Trillin, "Funny Food," *New Yorker,* 23 November 2009, 70.
2. The 60th parallel has figured large. In 1870 the Hudson's Bay Company territories of Rupert's Land and the Northwest Territory were transferred to the new dominion. The parallel became the southern boundary of the Northwest Territories when the provinces of Alberta and Saskatchewan were created in 1905.
3. Flight Lieutenant Keith R. Greenaway, RCAF, *Arctic Air Navigation* (Ottawa: Defence Research Board, 1951), 86, 124. Richard E. Byrd had noted this threat to aviators. "No idea of the extremely irregular character of Ellesmere Island," he wrote of a 1925 expedition, "can be gathered from the maps and charts. In fact many of the mountains we saw were uncharted." When *Navigation* was released, Greenaway became an authority on the subject. Loaned to the Americans in 1958, the Canadian airman would navigate a U.S. Navy airship to the Arctic Ocean and return.
4. The Greenland ice cap is dwarfed by that of Antarctica, which covers 4.8 million square miles. This is the largest desert on earth and contains 70 percent of its freshwater. In places, this colossal weight has depressed the bedrock more than 8,200 feet below sea level. As in Greenland, the ice is domed and flows to the margins. Icebergs are one result.
5. Ernest K. Gann, *Fate Is the Hunter* (London: Hodder and Stoughton, 1961), 175.
6. Average annual temperatures are lower than in any other part of Canada, ranging from 21° Fahrenheit (-6° Celsius) at Baffin Island to -4° F (-20° C) on northern Ellesmere. A record low temperature of -65° F (-54° C) was recorded at Isachsen, on Ellef Ringnes Island, in March 1956. The record high for the islands—84.2° F (29° C)—was measured at Cambridge Bay, on Victoria Island, in July 1930.
7. By way of comparison, New York City, which lies at about 41° north latitude, receives forty-two inches annually.

8. One consequence of extended cold and brief thaw is the formation of perennially frozen ground. The result is a rock-hard mixture of soil, rock, and ice. In summer, thin spongy soil or deep bogs result. Half of Canada's land surface is so afflicted. Indeed, one-fifth of the land area of the world is underlain by permanently frozen ground. The phenomenon is a chronic construction headache: when its surface is disturbed, the soils lose their ability to support a load and then settle as the ice melts.
9. In the distant past, though, the islands were occupied. Some campsites are little more than rearrangements of rock slabs—over which were erected whalebone supports, covered in turn with hides. These seem absurdly primitive; one is left to marvel how their builders' prehistoric occupants could possibly have survived there.
10. See Peter C. Newman, "Canada's Fur-Trading Empire," *National Geographic* 172, no. 2 (August 1987), 192–228, for a history of the enterprise. Rather recent financial losses notwithstanding, "The Bay" remains a major economic force in real estate and is Canada's biggest department-store chain.
11. A. P. Low, "Report on the Dominion Government Expedition to Hudson Bay and the Arctic Islands on Board D.G.S. *Neptune,* 1903–1904"—the first comprehensive report on the islands acquired in 1880. The cruise produced a wealth of geologic, topographic, zoological, and biological data, as well as frank descriptions of the native peoples. The penetration was much more than a scientific expedition; it was the first specifically dispatched to assert Canada's authority in the Arctic islands.
12. "The Week in Review," *New York Times,* 11 September 1988, sec. 2, 3. The occasion of this remark: the signing of one of a series of agreements with Ottawa giving native Canadians in Arctic Canada title to a vast sweep of new territory. On 1 April 1999, Nunavut became a homeland larger than any province.
13. John Honderich, *Arctic Imperative: Is Canada Losing the North?* (Toronto: University of Toronto Press, 1987), 3–4. See also Kenneth C. Eyre, "Forty Years of Military Activity in the Canadian North, 1947–87," *Arctic* 40, no. 4 (December 1987), 293.
14. Brig. Gen. Keith R. Greenaway, RCAF (Ret.), interview by author, 24–25 October 1988.
15. Oil was discovered at Norman Wells in 1920. In 1932 a refinery was in operation; by 1939 output was 20,000 barrels per year. Driven by wartime demands, production soared to 1.2 million barrels in 1944.
16. When in 1940 German forces occupied Denmark, the way was opened for their possible occupation of the Danish possession as well. In view of the threat, Greenland authorities adopted a resolution expressing the hope that, in view of the extraordinary political and military situation, the U.S. government would remain mindful of Greenland's exposed position. The Danish ambassador, acting as a free agent, signed an agreement concerning the defense of the island with Secretary of State Cordell Hull in April 1941.
17. Eyre, "Forty Years of Military Activity in the Canadian North, 1947–87," 294. The Cold War delivered continuing change. The Arctic's abrupt strategic significance intensified Ottawa's awareness of its responsibilities toward Canadian ownership and control. "Large wartime defence projects in the north such as the air staging routes, the Canol pipeline, and the Alaska Highway had been carried out almost exclusively by the armed services of the United States, and American citizens outnumbered Canadians in many parts of the north. There was no threat to Canadian de jure sovereignty, but Canadian de facto sovereignty was much less secure. Canadian government activities in the north therefore began to be given a much higher priority, and northern development was recognized as something that should be encouraged rather than as an expense that could be put off indefinitely." Graham Rowley, "Bringing the Outside Inside: Towards Development of the Passage," in *Politics of the Northwest Passage* (Kingston and Montreal: McGill–Queen's University Press, 1987), 39–40.
18. Canada, *House of Commons Debates,* 10 September 1985, 6463.
19. Neither the United States nor Canada looked on the North as a place to be protected due of some intrinsic value. Rather, it was seen as a direction, an exposed flank; Eyre, "Forty Years of Military Activity in the Canadian North, 1947–87," 294. Most Canadians did not consider the Cold War threat to be as great as the Americans did.
20. The value of Arctic observations was not lost on Berlin. In addition to weather reconnaissance penetrations for its forecasters, ground stations were established briefly in Spitsbergen, Franz Joseph Land, and in eastern Greenland. By spring 1944, all had been evacuated. See for example, "German Meteorological Activities in the Arctic, 1940–45," *Polar Record* 6, no. 42 (July 1951), 185–226.

21. Moira Dunbar and Wing Commander Keith R. Greenaway, RCAF, *Arctic Canada from the Air* (Ottawa: Defence Research Board, 1956), 500. This became an instant, indispensable reference. The knowledge gained in the ensuing decades notwithstanding, it remains an authoritative work.
22. One of the icebreakers, *Edisto,* reached 82° 33′ N, the farthest penetration to that date by a ship under power. On the return, a new route was investigated. Steaming south from the passage, the two ships passed through Prince Regent Inlet and the Gulf of Boothia, through Fury and Hecla Strait into Foxe Basin, thence to the Labrador Sea. They were the first ships to reach the Atlantic from Lancaster Sound via this route. But permission had not been requested ahead of time, so Ottawa protested. This was not to be the last time U.S. vessels were criticized for insensitivity to Canadian territorial sovereignty.
23. *Calgary Herald,* 13 August 1958; *Vancouver Sun,* 15 August 1958, sec. 3, 5.
24. *Toronto Star,* editorial, 15 August 1958, sec. 6, 1.
25. Early-warning programs were conceived at a time when, it was thought, Soviet bombers would remain the primary strategic threat. Soviet missile capability developed sooner than anticipated, so the line declined in relative importance. By about 1960 the major element in each superpower's arsenal was the ICBM. Technological advances permitted the closing of intermediate stations; eventually, the line was allowed to lapse into obsolescence. In response to the advent of the air-launched cruise missile, however, continental air defenses were modernized. In 1985 Prime Minister Brian Mulroney and President Ronald Reagan signed a $1.5 billion agreement to construct the North Warning System. Designed to replace the aging DEW Line, plans for the NWS included eleven manned and thirty-seven unmanned radar stations. The NWS went operational in 1988.
26. Robertson outlined the rationale for Labrador: "Expanded arctic research is mandatory if North America is to extend her military frontier to the Soviet Arctic littoral. While much thought has been given to our eastern and western frontiers, a vacuum exists in the Arctic Ocean due to our lack of basic knowledge of this region. Intensive and effective research being pursued by the Soviets, without fanfare, is filling this vacuum, and unless we meet this challenge, we will invite a scientific Pearl Harbor. . . . The concept that the Arctic is a barrier to an aggressor is no longer acceptable—the Arctic is a highway to those who have the wit to use it"; T. A. Irvine, *The Ice Was All Between* (New York: Longmans, Green, 1959), xxii. When asked about the maiden trip, Irvine offered a startling fact: "That was," he says, "the first year the [Canadian] Navy ever looked at ice" in the High Arctic. Letter to author, 17 January 1993.
27. Ibid., 16–17. In 1954–56 Irvine served under Robertson on board *Labrador.*
28. A government booklet explains: "There is no doubt that the government's intentions were honorable. The government succeeded in stabilizing the feast-and-famine cycles. The incidence of tuberculosis was reduced. Mortality rates dropped. But most of the changes that affected the Inuit were made without consulting them."
29. The first sighting of Resolute Bay was recalled: "Our [1953] arrival at our promised land was a shock. It was desolate. We could see no living thing. There was only grey gravel and snow as far as the eye could see. What was to become of us?" Some of the transplants still see themselves as exiled people. At Grise Fiord, unaccustomed to the walrus and seal diet and missing their former home, some accepted a government offer to move them back to Quebec. A compensation claim posted by the community was resisted by Ottawa, however. *Toronto Star,* 4 July 1991; *New York Times,* 11 September 1988.
30. Michael Foster and Carol Marino, *The Polar Shelf: The Saga of Canada's Arctic Scientists* (Toronto: NC, 1986), 11. Washington had asked for northern gravitational data—vital to its nascent space program. "They [the Americans] came to us and asked if we would supply the data on gravity in the Arctic," a Canadian geophysicist recalls, "or if not, they would go up there and get it themselves. We decided it would be better if we supplied the data." George D. Hobson, interview by author, 25 April 1993.
31. Ibid.
32. Joseph T. Jockel, "The US Navy, Maritime Command, and the Arctic," *Canadian Defence Quarterly* 19, no. 3 (December 1989), 26.
33. Reconnaissance of Possible Soviet Activities in the Canadian Arctic 1, DRB paper, "Russian Activities on the Canadian Side of the Pole," undated (submitted August 1954), quoted in Gordon W. Smith, *Ice Islands in Arctic Waters* (Ottawa: Department of Indian Affairs and Northern Development, 15 May 1980), 67.
34. Canada, *House of Commons Debates,* 14 August 1958, 3512.

Chapter 2. Platforms

1. Charles P. Burgess, *Airship Design* (New York: Ronald., 1927), 3–4.
2. The DC-7C was the first truly transoceanic airplane. The De Havilland Comet inaugurated passenger jet service, in May 1952. The Boeing 707 was the first successful jet airliner.
3. *Los Angeles* was the fourth aircraft to cross the Atlantic. First to transit was the navy's *NC-4,* in May 1919. John Alcock and Arthur Brown succeeded on 14–15 June in a twin-engine converted Vickers bomber. That July, the British R-34 made the first east-to-west crossing—and the first round-trip. The airmen flew in relative comfort, in marked contrast to the open cockpits of their HTA colleagues. In all, ninety-one persons flew the Atlantic before Lindbergh, sixty-five of whom did so by airship.
4. Contrary to misconception, the fire did not conclude the zeppelin's first crossing. *Hindenburg* logged ten round-trips for the 1936 North Atlantic season. The airship took fire while completing her first arrival of the 1937 season.
5. When the author contacted Goodyear, the firm responded, "As for rigid airships, Goodyear has no plans in this field. Here again, cost is the big bug-a-boo. It is estimated that it would cost between twenty-five and fifty million dollars to duplicate an airship like the *Akron* or *Macon* today. Secondly, because of the unfortunate disasters which many famous rigid airships met back in the 1920s and 1930s, there seems to be a public distrust of such types of aircraft. Additionally, mankind seems to have become orientated to the jet age. Travelers want to get there quickly. Jets take them where they want to go, quickly and comfortably." Letter to author, 11 July 1966.
6. R. E. G. Davies, "MEGAJET: The Next Airliner Generation," Transportation Research Board Annual Meeting, 9–13 January 2000, Washington, D.C., courtesy Mr. Davies.
7. Curators have not hesitated to exploit the accident as entertainment. At the National Air and Space Museum, footage of the fire was shown continuously in the now-disestablished Balloon and Airship Gallery. One cannot imagine tragic footage of, say, a DC-3 or 747 being granted similar attention in a gallery nearby.
8. T. L. Blakemore and W. W. Pagon, *Pressure Airships* (New York: Ronald, 1927), v.
9. In March 1987 its aerospace subsidiary was sold by Goodyear to the Loral Corporation. The deal allowed management to retain control of the core of their operation—tire manufacturing. Airships have always been a highly visible but generally unprofitable sideline.
10. Ongoing research may yet confirm a "kill." See Richard G. Van Treuren, "The World War Two K-Type Airship: Reassessing Effectiveness," *Naval History* 12, no. 3 (May–June 1998), 41–44.
11. For 1948, the total "Aviation Navy" budget amounted to about $749 million. Thus, the four million dollars earmarked for LTA was less than 1 percent of the naval aviation total. Development funds for the prototype represented about 2 percent of the Navy's R&D funds for all naval aircraft.
12. Why did Douglas bother? It had been approached by the BuAer's LTA Design Section; following a bit of arm-twisting, Douglas decided—reluctantly—to compete. The intent: to put price pressure on the sole supplier; see Ed Heinemann, *Combat Aircraft Designer* (Annapolis, Md.: Naval Institute Press, 1980), 236–37. There was no shopping for airships. "We had a market, of course, that was ours alone," a Goodyear negotiator was to remark. "Nobody else made them."
13. Long missions were routine from the earliest years. Great War blimps had an endurance of about twenty-four hours. The rigid airship offered a remarkable performance: even "local" flights were from six to eight hours' duration. *Macon* (ZRS-5) could range nearly six thousand nautical miles for strategic search; its longest flight, in July 1934, had the ship aloft almost eighty-three hours—more than three days.
14. "In service use, it was found that there was little or no advantage in fuel consumption or in airspeed to driving both propellers with one engine versus simply shutting down one engine and flying the ship single-engine. The clutch was simply extra weight and complexity. . . . Additionally, the gear boxes and shifting proved to be very noisy. This was bad for habitability. The gear boxes were also trouble-makers." Lt. Cdr. R. W. Widdicombe, USN (Ret.), "Operational Experience with Large Navy Patrol Airships, 1940–1961," Memorandum-Report, 1 November 1985, courtesy Lieutenant Commander Widdicombe.
15. *Aviation Week,* 26 February 1951, 188.
16. Widdicombe, "Operational Experience with Large Navy Patrol Airships, 1940–1961."
17. Wilkins was airship conscious. He not only planned to gain the Pole but, as well, proposed to bore upward, surface, and rendezvous with *Graf Zeppelin.* In exchange for reporting rights from the airship,

newspaperman William Randolph Hearst had guaranteed $150,000 if the two machines exchanged mail and passengers at the pole, $100,000 if they only rendezvoused there, and $30,000 if they met somewhere in the Arctic. See J. Gordon Vaeth, *Graf Zeppelin* (New York: Harper and Brothers, 1958), 112.

18. "But Stefansson pointed out that while we might superficially prospect most of the Arctic by airplane," Wilkins would write, "we would not be able to do real exploration from the air. He suggested that instead of airplanes one should use submarines and travel slowly under the ice, coming to the surface in the open leads and carrying along sufficient equipment to investigate in a leisurely way many things of interest in many branches of science." Hubert Wilkins, *Under the North Pole: The Wilkins-Ellsworth Submarine Expedition* (New York: Brewer, Warren & Putnam, 1931).
19. Cdr. Robert D. McWethy, USN, had served for eleven years with submarines; in 1948 he was teaching navigation at the General Line School in Monterey, California. "We had a segment on polar navigation," he remembers, "and there was nothing in the books on the subject." Having heard that the air force was working on navigational techniques in the Arctic, he secured a flight, to observe. "My first clue that the Arctic Ocean might be a place for submarines came in 1948 when I flew over the Pole with the Air Force on their 103rd weather mission out of Ladd AFB [Air Force Base]. . . . I believe it was in August, and I was amazed at the amount of open water in the ice pack." Letter to author, 21 March 1994.
20. Stewart B. Nelson, *Sabotage in the Arctic: Fate of the Submarine Nautilus,* self-published, www. Xlibris .com, 151.
21. Ibid., 164.
22. Ibid., 170.
23. Commander James Calvert, USN, *Surface at the Pole* (New York: McGraw-Hill, 1960), 143.
24. Noting that Wilkins had failed because of inadequate preparation, the release claimed that the Soviets were "equipped to solve the problem of under-ice polar exploration. . . . The use of submarines in polar exploration, together with planes and ice-breakers, will speed the final conquest of the Arctic." "Soviet Maps Trip Undersea to Pole," *New York Times,* 28 December 1937.
25. Capt. Edward L. Beach, USN (Ret.), interview by author, 12 October 1993.
26. In the shipbuilding program presented to Congress for fiscal year 1953, the second SSN *(Seawolf)* was included for the long-lead nuclear reactor and associated steam-propulsion system for submarines.
27. Norman Polmar and Thomas B. Allen, *Rickover: Controversy and Genius* (New York, Simon and Schuster, 1982), 297; Beach interview. At Electric Boat shipyard, overall supervision of design and construction was vested in various branches of BuShips. Yet "Rickover maintained complete and absolute control and direction of the submarine's reactor and propulsion machinery, and all personnel selection and training related to the nuclear portions of the ship . . . because of his special relations with Electric Boat, and because only he could discuss propulsion, shielding requirements, and many other matters that affected aspects of the submarine, he became involved in the design and construction procedures for virtually all of *Nautilus*"; Polmar and Allen, *Rickover,* 154.
28. Vice Adm. Eugene P. Wilkinson, USN (Ret.), interview by Public Broadcasting System, "Submarine," PBS (WNET), 1993.
29. The ship's military significance, Truman said simply, was "tremendous." *Nautilus*' reactor, the president noted, would have as revolutionary an effect on the navies of the world as had the first ocean steamship. "But the peaceful significance of the *Nautilus* is even more breath-taking. When this ship has been built and operated, controllable atomic power will have been demonstrated on a substantial scale. I wish I could convey to everyone," he said, "what a tremendous and wonderful thing has been accomplished. It is amazing what our scientists and engineers have done. Think what was involved in creating the engine that will go into this submarine."
30. Navy news release, *Nautilus* files, U.S. Naval Institute, Annapolis, Md. "The Soviets realize that conquest of the world is not dependent upon land and air power alone. As a result they are feverishly constructing a navy—and why? Because the Soviet Union realizes that only by their gaining supremacy of the seas can they realize their ambition of world conquest. . . . America's Naval supremacy must be maintained to combat this growing Communist menace to the freedom of the world"; ibid.
31. Warfare was the objective. Hence the emphasis on applied sciences: oceanography, cryology, sea-ice studies, field work in target detection/recognition, weapon requirements, approach doctrine. Methods

of access to the surface had to be devised, hull changes incorporated, sound transmission and reverberation studies conducted.

32. *Nautilus* would exercise with every kind of surface and air ASW weapons system, including blimps. "I don't know why they didn't try the blimps," Early remarked; "perhaps because we operated in the open ocean distant from their bases. Everywhere we went P2V aircraft would try to track us, to no avail." Rear Adm. Paul J. Early, USN (Ret.), letter to author, 5 September 1992.
33. A remark by Beach is emblematic of the advances *Nautilus* embodied. "We used to say," he recounts, "that if we had one nuclear-powered submarine like the *Nautilus,* or like the *Triton,* in the war, we could have won the whole war by ourselves. All we would have needed was enough torpedoes." Beach interview.
34. In 1937 Sir Hubert was in charge of the Alaskan-Canadian search section that was looking for the lost Soviet aircraft commanded by Sigimund Levanevsky, which had vanished on a flight from Moscow to Fairbanks. Wilkins remained committed to his notion, "always thinking," according to an author, "about submarine operations in the Arctic. In fact he has felt that the search he was now undertaking could have been better made from a submarine, bobbing up and down through the ice and forming the mobile base for a number of search parties. . . . However, there was no suitably equipped vessel available at the time, so air search was the only practicable alternative." John Grierson, *Challenge to the Poles* (London: G. T. Foulis, 1964), 474–75.
35. "German U-Boats in the Arctic, Part III," *Office of Naval Intelligence Review* (August 1951), 329–30.
36. Rear Adm. J. A. Furer, Coordinator of Research and Development, memorandum, to Senior U.S. Naval Officer, Italy, 29 June 1944, box 101, RG 298, National Archives.
37. All available material on handling a ship in ice had been studied. The best source, according to Cdr. J. B. Icenhower, USN, *Sennet*'s CO, was a translation of the Russian *Instructions for Handling a Ship in Ice.* "The very first requisite of the embryonic ice pilot," Icenhower wrote, "is to develop a very healthy respect for the tremendous power of the ice. Never allow the peaceful appearance of an ice field to lull you into a sense of false security. On the other hand, don't fear the ice. A great deal of progress into ice can be made by a submarine capably handled." Waldo K. Lyon, *The Polar Submarine and Navigation of the Arctic Ocean,* Research Report 88 (n.p.: U.S. Navy Electronics Laboratory, 21 May 1959; reissue of final report), 84.
38. Early letter.
39. Dr. Waldo K. Lyon, interview by author, 13 October 1996.
40. Waldo K. Lyon, "Submarine Exploration of the North Pole Region: History, Problems, Positioning and Piloting," *Pole Nord 1983, Editions du CNRS* (1987), 315.
41. To transit from Point Barrow to Spitsbergen (summer only), a diesel-electric boat would have had to steam about thirty-three days.
42. U.S. and Canadian icebreakers surveyed the Beaufort Sea and channels of the Arctic Islands during 1950–54 to construct bathymetric/oceanographic charts.
43. USS *Redfish* Confidential Letter Serial 042, "Report of *Redfish* Participation in Beaufort Sea Expedition," 7 October 1952; USS *Burton Island* Confidential Letter Serial 071, "Beaufort Sea Expedition, 12 August to 4 October 1952, Report of," 1952. ASW aircraft and surface ships had virtually no ASW capability in ice-covered seas.
44. Capt. Robert D. McWethy, USN (Ret.), letter to author, 25 October 1993. "Nuclear power is not a requirement for basic under-ice submarine operations, but nuclear power does provide mobility and freedom from delays caused by finding a place to surface and stopping to charge the batteries of a diesel-electric powered submarine." "Significance of the Nautilus Polar Cruise," U.S. Naval Institute *Proceedings* 84, no. 5 (May 1958), 34.
45. Lyon field journal, 30 October 1956, 46.
46. Advised of the proposed Arctic cruise via the Pacific, "Rickover, in his usual emotional display objected, but was difficult to see just what he objected [to] because of so many parenthetical displays against Op Nav. He appeared to object to extra mileage required by sending boat to Pacific Fleet and then across." Lyon field journal, 14 February 1958, 71.
47. Lyon field journal, 2 September 1957, 55. Experimental operations using diesel boats were confined to the shallow, flat-bottomed Chukchi Sea. "Only a few soundings by Nansen's drift of the Fram (1893–96) and the Soviet ice station (Papanin, 1938) were known." Waldo K. Lyon, "The Navigation of Arctic Polar Submarines," *Journal of Navigation* 17, no. 2 (May 1984), 160.

48. By way of comparison, *Los Angeles* had an overall volume of 2,599,110 cu. ft.; *Akron* and *Macon,* 6,850,000 cu. ft.; and *Hindenburg* 7,062,150 cu. ft. *Hindenburg* and the sister ship *LZ-130* were the largest machines ever to navigate the air.
49. Louis Mancini, letter to author, 30 November 1990.

Chapter 3. Preparations

1. "Navy Blimps Perform," editorial, *Aviation Week,* 25 March 1957, 21.
2. The Polaris missile was developed in this period, as was the platform that deployed it: the nuclear-powered submarine. The implications for strategic warfare in polar seas were profound.
3. The Second World War had mobilized science for the national defense, locking academia and the military in enduring embrace. It had been a technological chess match between the opposing sides. Examples: radar, magnetic detection of U-boats, the atomic bomb. Scientists and engineers in their government-funded laboratories were as responsible for victory as the soldiers, seamen, and airmen.
4. Faith in extravagant technological fixes had come to dominate national security. In 1952 the Lincoln Laboratory had been asked to consider ways to guard North America against bomber attack. (Among those consulted: Wing Commander Keith R. Greenaway, RCAF.) The solution: lines of radar stations across northern Alaska and Canada. Today, the laboratory is active in such abstruse fields as machine intelligence, satellite communications, radar system engineering, and laser-beam control. Principal client: the Department of Defense.
5. Included in this group was Richard E. Deal, aviation structural mechanic (3rd class). A boatswain's mate 2nd class in 1933, Deal was one of but three survivors from the foundering of USS *Akron* (ZRS-4) on the night of 3–4 April. This loss proved to be the beginning of the end for the rigid airship in the United States.
6. The plane's radar was the product of a three-year Lincoln program. Taking possession, NADU delivered the ship from the West Coast. Tower operators are known for their careful etiquette. When the WV-2E glided in at Tucson, a thirty-seven-foot rotodome atop its fuselage (the first ever mounted), a comment was irresistible. "My god, here comes a flying saucer," the controller remarked. Capt. H. B. Van Gorder, USN (Ret.), telephone interview, 28 September 1989.
7. Interview by author, audiocassette, Beachwood, N.J., 20 April 1998.
8. The flight's command pilot, Cdr. M. H. Eppes, USN, received the Distinguished Flying Cross and, later, the 1955 Harmon International Trophy for Aeronauts, presented by Vice President Richard M. Nixon. Each member of the crew was awarded the Air Medal, including the Goodyear representative on board, the first civilian ever to receive it.
9. The experimental *Voyager,* which in December 1986 made the first nonstop flight around the world, eclipsed the distance mark set by *Snowbird* (more than 25,000 miles) but not the duration of nine days.
10. CO, NADU, Memorandum, to Chief, ONR, "Special Report on Extended Flight of ZPG-2, BUNO 141561," 25 September 1957, Mills Papers. The final report on the all-weather evaluation would prove a useful reference for officers planning the Polar Project.
11. Dr. Maynard M. Miller, "An Experiment in Arctic Airship Exploration," provisional manuscript (1992), 5, courtesy Dr. Miller.
12. Ibid., 3.
13. Capt. Harold B. Van Gorder, USN (Ret.), interview by author, 4–5 December 1989.
14. According to the Associated Press feature writer who would accompany *719* northward, "Demise of the blimp program was very much in the wind then but not in the news much except in military circles or newspapers near airbases." Hugh A. Mulligan, note to author, 23 June 1985.
15. The U.S. Air Force had initiated high-latitude operations after the war. The rationale: the strategic importance of the region and the air force's role in defending it. An intensive program of research thus was under way. Tactical problems inherent to operations, weather reconnaissance, studies of rescue and survival, communications headaches attendant to polar flying, the scientific and military potential of floating ice islands—all held interest. The tracking, occupation, and scientific exploitation of Ice Island T-3 were in large part funded by the air force.
16. The notion for the IGY was born in 1950. An orbiting satellite was a major goal, for the Americans and Soviets both. The first public announcement of U.S. plans to launch "small, earth-circling satellites" as part of its participation was made in July 1955.

17. “Details of LTA Study and Polar Feasibility Operation” (as submitted by letter to Chief of Naval Research by VNRRC3-1, May 1958), Van Gorder Papers.
18. Cdr. Max V. Ricketts, USN (Ret.), letter to author, 27 July 1990.
19. Greenaway, *Arctic Air Navigation,* 2.
20. This is the area about which the earth’s magnetic field is focused in the northern hemisphere; it is located hundreds of miles from the geographic pole. All magnetic compasses point there rather than to true north. Depending on one’s position, allowances for the displacement must be made. The closer one gets, the less reliable a magnetic compass becomes. Further, the magnetic pole wanders. In 1958 it was located in Barrow Strait, west of Resolute; today, the magnetic pole lies near Lougheed Island, in the Findlay Group. When the author overflew the site in August 1989, the cockpit’s magnetic compass “walked” in wild circles.
21. *Canadian Aviation* (September 1953), 44.
22. It should be recalled that the shortest route for U.S. bombers and missiles to targets in the Soviet Union was across maritime boreal wastes. Keith Greenaway’s contributions to the Strategic Air Command cannot be overestimated. It was his work on grid techniques and gyro steering that led to an improvement in SAC’s polar navigation, hence in bombing accuracy.
23. Cdr. Cecil Manship, USN (Ret.), letter to author, 15 January 1990.
24. Squadron Leader William P. Becker, RCAF (Ret.), letter to author, undated (1993).
25. The U.S. Navy could have obtained the necessary assistance from the air force. But the airship would be operating over Canada and, further, the wing commander was both familiar with the mission and had helped sort out the route. From a diplomatic point of view, then, his presence represented a decided asset. In short, the Canadian airman was the logical choice.
26. Quarters and messing for eight officers, six enlisted men, and one civilian, plus 4,600 gallons of aviation fuel were requested. In the Arctic, supplies are a chronic preoccupation. Accordingly, it was vital that the Canadians be alerted as to visitor requirements, to avoid depletion of essential local supplies. Thus, the NADU aircraft conveyed as many supplies as possible for the upcoming operation.
27. Coral Harbour is a civilian airfield on Southampton Island, in Hudson Bay. It was fortunate that the engines were not shut down, because no auxiliary power unit was on hand to restart them. If a shutdown had been made and the batteries failed, the NADU WV-2 would have been stranded. Following a meal (“food like you never saw,” Van Gorder recalled), the airmen lifted off, the midnight sun pouring in the windows as the Willie Victor pushed north for Resolute. Van Gorder interview.
28. Capt. Paul B. Ryan, USN, U.S. Naval Attaché and Naval Attaché for Air, confidential letter, to Group Captain E. M. Mitchell, RCAF, Director of Air Services, RCAF Headquarters, 30 June 1958, Record Group [hereafter RG] 24, accession 1983–1984/216, box 3579, file S9610103-1, pt. 5, National Archives of Canada.
29. Confidential letter, Capt. Paul B. Ryan, USN, Naval Attaché and Naval Attaché for Air to Air Marshall Hugh Campbell, RCAF, Chief of Air Staff, Department of National Defence, 3 July 1958, ibid.
30. Confidential letter, Campbell to Ryan, 8 July 1958, ibid.
31. President Eisenhower had directed the Department of Defense to develop the necessary vehicles and provide logistic support. Management of these aspects of the program had been assigned to the ONR and, in turn, to the Naval Research Laboratory.
32. “Reporters from around the world converged on Cape Canaveral and cranked up suspense during a two-day delay due to weather and holds. Shortly before noon on December 6, 1957, the countdown finally reached zero. Two seconds after ignition the Vanguard rose four feet off the pad—and suddenly exuded thunder and flame. . . . [The rocket] settled back to earth and was consumed, but the nose cone fell clear, and the little ball of satellite came comfortably to rest nearby, chirping innocently.” Walter A. McDougall, *The Heavens and the Earth: A Political History of the Space Age* (New York: Basic Books, 1985), 154. The first U.S. satellite followed *Sputnik 1* three months later, in January 1958.
33. Memorandum, ONR to Office of Information, 14 July 1958, Van Gorder Papers.
34. This was solved by Op 311, which ordered the charts. Lt. Shepherd M. Jenks, USN, made a special trip to Washington and brought them to the boat, “where for the next two months he resorted to all types of locked door antics in order to lay out a track and study the problems involved with navigating in high latitudes under the ice pack.” CO, *Nautilus,* to CNO, “Operation Sunshine I; report of,” 28 June 1958, A-3, courtesy Dr. Lyon.

35. Early letter; Cdr. William R. Anderson, USN, with Clay Blair Jr., *Nautilus 90 North* (Cleveland: World, 1959), 111.
36. On 6 March: "Working on writeup of plan for modified SS for under ice experiments; meeting with McWethy 1300, then to Pentagon, and stayed overnite with McWethy writing program." Lyon field journal, March 1957, 47; Capt. Robert D. McWethy, USN (Ret.), letter to author, 21 March 1994.
37. Lyon field journal, 21 August 1957, 50.
38. "According to our operational plan," Anderson would write, "she [*Trigger*] would remain outside the pack during our penetrations, to assist gathering data on underwater transmissions and, frankly, to furnish moral support"; Anderson and Blair, *Nautilus 90 North,* 79. Unsaid is that *Nautilus* had objected to its inclusion. Capability was so disparate that much time had been expended just to effect rendezvous. "Cannot see any merit in her assignment," Lyon complained to his notes, "even for any so called safety measures[.] This is old fashion thinking, based on diesel boats alone where one can go same place and same manner as other of pair"; Lyon field journal, 10 September 1957, 5, 8.
39. Prior to the 1957 cruise, no ship had ever been north of 83° 21′ under its own power—a record set by a Soviet icebreaker in 1955. In 1895, under Nansen, the ice ship *Fram* had drifted with the polar pack to 85° 57′.
40. Senior Scientist's report to CO, *Nautilus* (field journal, 61–64, 57). In Lyon's view, these constituted the "most essential field work." "The USSR [he continues] has been very active the past ten years in the Arctic basin gathering bathymetric data by aircraft landings on the ice and by drifting stations. The U.S. Navy should gather these data in a shorter time and in the much more precise and meaningful form of continuous contours by submarine, the submarine surfacing at the end of each survey leg to fix position by electronic aid" (62).
41. Lyon field journal, 19 June 1958, 88–89.
42. Ibid. [italics added]. CNO had no cash kitty—that is, Admiral Burke couldn't get Lyon funds for the charter without divulging its purpose. "So I paid for the plane; got my money back [laughing]." Interview by author, 13 October 1996.
43. *Nautilus'* probes were independent of the IGY. As the *Times* noted, "The voyage was a demonstration, rather than a scientific expedition." Admiral Early underscores this: "It [*Nautilus'* 1958 try] was the continuation of the exploratory work in the Arctic that had begun in 1957. And this was a continuation of experimental under-ice work by diesel boats and Dr. Lyon that began in 1946. *Nautilus* had far more endurance and thus was a better platform for Dr. Lyon's work." Early letter.
44. Since the crew knew the physicist and associated him with the Arctic, Lyon had been smuggled on board in stream, at Seattle, then kept hidden until castoff. "They locked him in a cabin below where he remained for 12 hours," *Life* reported, "sustained only by occasional sandwiches which his conspirators slipped through to him. Then the sub slipped out of Puget Sound, her destination was announced to the crew, and Lyon was released."
45. CO, *Nautilus,* to CNO, "Operation Sunshine I; Report of," 28 June 1958, 2.
46. Ibid., B-11.
47. Ibid., 2–3.
48. Lyon field journal, 19 June 1958, 90. "Only hope we get chance to try again; if this chance is denied then a serious set back to arctic submarine program is likely to result—surely my own career as well as Andy's [Anderson] will feel the impact of this decision and turn back"; ibid., 18 June 1958, 86.
49. "I was very nervous about the thing leaking out and creating such a turmoil that the White House or Pentagon would cancel the trip." Lyon field journal, 87, 89; Capt. William R. Anderson, USN (Ret.), interview by author (notes), 24 August 1990.
50. Early letter.
51. Today, the Associated Press and United Press International receive special consideration as part of the media's "automatic pool." Both are guaranteed a seat on *Air Force One,* whereas the daily newspapers and the networks must rotate their places. Hugh A. Mulligan, interview by author, 17 August 1989.
52. On the 14th, via memo to the Department's Office of Information, ONR had provided a "Public Information Plan" for the flight. Among its points, the document outlined the expedition's fundamental mission. "The primary purpose of this trip," ONR advised, "is to test the feasibility of using blimps as a basic vehicle/platform for scientific research in the Arctic. While several scientists will be on this trip, and will conduct observations and experiments as practicable, the testing of blimp operations north of the Arctic Circle will remain the foremost consideration in this flight."

53. U.S. Department of Defense, Office of Public Information, news release, "Navy Blimp to Make Northernmost Flight," 17 July 1958, Naval Historical Center, Washington Navy Yard, Washington, D.C.
54. Anderson interview.
55. Since 1939 there had been virtually no ice information on Soviet Arctic waters, including the approach now crucial to *Nautilus:* the Russian sector of the Bering Strait area and western Chukchi Sea.

Chapter 4. False Starts

1. Greenaway, *Arctic Air Navigation,* 65, 67.
2. *Boston Traveler* (editorial), 29 July 1958.
3. Among these were a manometer panel, a superheat indicator (superheat is the temperature differential between the helium and atmosphere), a ballonet fullness indicator, a ballast quantity indicator and dump switches, a free-air temperature indicator, various controls for the air-pressure system, and rope-release switches.
4. Normally, the aircraft commander (AC) observed the flight crew. The first pilot made the takeoffs and landings and directed all in-flight assignments. The copilot was an assistant to the first pilot. Should the AC participate in flight duties, the first pilot was relieved temporarily, usually for rest and chow. Any changes in the flight plan were made or approved by the AC. The flight crew was divided into watches; the AC, however, set his own hours and assumed overall responsibility for the crew.
5. Hugh A. Mulligan, dispatch, 27 July 1958, AP files, courtesy Mr. Mulligan. All dispatches following are from this source.
6. Cdr. Aage J. Schou, USN (Ret.), with Capt. Harold B. Van Gorder, USN (Ret.), joint interview by author, 4–5 December 1989.
7. Adjustment of trim (nose up or nose down) was accomplished using three internal ballonets. One in the center-bottom of the "bag" was exploited principally to help maintain internal pressure. The forward and aft ballonets were analogous to trim tanks on a submarine: more air forward made the nose heavy, by displacing helium from that location. More air aft caused the tail to drop.
8. Many everyday items maintain their shape through the use of internal air pressure. Normal operating pressure in the ZPG-2 was a bit more than two inches of water—a fraction of that required in, say, an automobile tire or a regulation football.
9. The 707 had emerged from the factory in 1954. Pan American bought the first and inaugurated transatlantic service in October 1958. In all, Boeing was to build 857 707s. Goodyear, by comparison, would sell a mere dozen ZPG-2 aircraft.
10. "Minnesotan Co-piloting 1st Navy Blimp to Arctic," *Minneapolis Star,* 28 July 1958.
11. Sitreps were dispatched to the CNO and to commands and locations appropriate to the exercise. Among these were Fort Churchill; Headquarters, Canadian Air Force; Commander, Eastern Sea Frontier; Fleet Airship Wing 1, NAS Lakehurst; Radio Washington; ONR; Fleet Weather Central, in Suitland, Maryland; and NADU. Copies also were distributed to both the secretary of the navy and the under secretary, to the assistant secretary of the navy for air, and to their naval aides.
12. *New York Herald Tribune,* 31 July 1958.
13. In 1610 the Dutch explorer sailed in *Discovery* through the strait and into the bay that now bears his name. This was the first European expedition to winter in the Canadian Arctic. But the spring brought mutiny: Hudson and eight of his men were set adrift, to perish in a small boat. The mutineers sailed *Discovery* home.
14. Wing Commander Keith R. Greenaway, RCAF, "To the Top of the World by Airship," *Canadian Aviation Historical Society Journal* (Fall 1980), 84. See also his "U.S. Navy Airship Flight to Ice Island T-3," *Arctic Circular* XII, no. 2 (September 1959), 22.
15. Greenaway, letter to author, 10 March 1990.
16. CO, NADU, to Chief Naval Research, "Interim Report no. 1 on RTED Project no. NDSW-ONR 46120: Conduct airship flight operations in support of research in the area of the Arctic Ocean," 14 October 1958, Van Gorder Papers.
17. Gray had arrived on 25 July. Instructed with "almost no advance notice" to be in Churchill at 0900 on the 28th, he had flown in early (no weekend flights were available). Gray found himself with ample time to sample the sights. The scientist walked around the nearby town and, among other diversions, visited the grain elevator, a whale processing plant, Fort Prince of Wales (via canoe), an Inuit mu-

seum, and the local hydrographic research lab. Daily calls to Operations brought news only of the airship's tribulations. For example, his journal entry for Tuesday, 29 July (the scheduled date for arrival), records: "Called Operations about 1000 hrs. report that blimp at Lakehurst N.J. ????" Norman G. Gray, letter (with enclosure) to author, 8 November 1989.

18. The Chukchi Sea has been charted by oil-company geophysicists and by the U.S. Navy. The Amoco Corporation, for one, acquired extensive acreage in federal lease sales in the Chukchi and Beaufort Seas off the North Slope.
19. Second World War submariners had tasted of Aleutian weather. The log of *S-23* for 13 February 1943 records these lines: "Heavy sea over bridge. All hands on bridge bruised and battered. Officer of the Deck suffered broken nose. Solid stream of water down hatch for 65 seconds. Put high pressure pump on control room bridges; dry after two hours. . . . Barometer 29.60; thirty knot wind." Clay Blair Jr., *Silent Victory* (New York: J. B. Lippincott, 1975), 267–68.
20. Lyon field journal, 28 July 1958, 94.
21. "No untoward psychological or psychiatric problems became manifest," the skipper was to report. "Quite the opposite, the entire crew were endowed with a particular zeal and pride to see the successful fulfillment of this historic cruise." CO, *Nautilus,* to CNO, "Operation Sunshine I; report of," Q-1, courtesy Dr. Lyon. A captain of the SP section of the Bureau of Ordnance was riding *Nautilus,* to observe under-ice operations and possible effect on crews of Polaris boats.
22. In the interests of "selling" nuclear power, the crew became accustomed to a constant flow of visitors, necessitating some "hot-bunking." It was perhaps a year or so before *Nautilus* was able to log being under way with no visitors. Vice Adm. Kenneth M. Carr, USN (Ret.), letter to author, 7 June 1989. Then-Lieutenant Carr had joined *Nautilus* in 1953. Except for a twelve-month hiatus in 1956–57 for nuclear power training, he was part of her complement until late 1960. "Current nuclear submarines," he opined, "have not yet reached the habitability that *Nautilus* achieved."
23. "Welcome Aboard USS *Nautilus,*" public information handout files, U.S. Naval Institute.
24. One NASA spacecraft designer with time in submarines has remarked that a submarine is a very high-tech ship—very compact and full of machinery, like a spacecraft.
25. "Beneath North Pole on a Well-Planned Adventure," *Life* 45, no. 9 (1 September 1958), 57–72. All quotes from ship's enlisted complement are from this source.
26. Anderson and Blair, *Nautilus 90 North,* 198.
27. Like Anderson with Dr. Lyon for the June penetration, Lieutenant Jenks had accompanied the first two ice reconnaissance flights. On 18 July he returned to *Nautilus* at Pearl Harbor.
28. Lyon interview.
29. Its seafloor is complex: distinct basins and intervening ridges. Continental shelves—the drowned land between the coast and oceanic depths—end abruptly in steep slopes. Vast abyssal plains, seamounts, mountain ranges, and trenches have since been mapped. Except for scattered soundings and some geophysical investigations, in 1958 little was known of this topography.
30. Dr. Waldo K. Lyon, "The Navigation of Arctic Polar Submarines," *Journal of Navigation* 37, no. 2 (May 1984), 165.
31. Early, letter to author, 5 September 1992.
32. Lyon field journal, 2 August 1958, 95.
33. Anderson interview.
34. Oil-soaked insulation had ignited, generating acrid smoke, making it difficult for crewmen to see and breathe. "That night," Anderson recorded, "as I lay tossing in my bunk, I shuddered to think what might have happened to us if that small fire had occurred beneath the ice, in a place where we could not break our way to the surface. The answer was all too obvious: *Nautilus* would have been lost"; Anderson and Blair, *Nautilus 90 North,* 127. "We learned in that fire," the boat's former chief engineer remarked, "that a safe breathing system is necessary for every member of the crew especially if we could not surface, as under the ice. Such a system was designed by Lieutenant Don Fears, the Auxiliary Division Officer, from sample parts he obtained in San Francisco. It was installed while we were in Mare Island Naval Shipyard and since has proven effective. All submarines now are fitted with them"; Early letter.
35. "A simple mistake at that latitude where longitudinal lines begin to converge, could throw us into the dreaded game of longitude roulette. Conceivably, we could be led into the wrong ocean or, even worse,

up against an ice-locked coastline. The ship's navigator's were subjected to a barrage of friendly jokes about liberty in Alaska and, inevitably, Murmansk." Anderson and Blair, *Nautilus 90 North,* 95.

36. Although unbroken ice may extend for ten or more miles, even in the coldest weather fracturing occurs. Information regarding comparatively thin ice and polynyas—relatively large areas of persistent open water—are of obvious importance to submarines.
37. Anderson and Blair, *Nautilus 90 North,* 223.
38. Early, letter to author, 5 September 1992.
39. Lt. William G. Lalor Jr., USN, "Submarine through the North Pole," *National Geographic* CXV, no. 1 (January 1959), 17.
40. The argument of who, in fact, was the first man to stand at the geographic pole is long-standing. Beaumont M. Buck is a seasoned Arctic hand. "I for one don't believe it was *Nautilus.* It was the first man atop the ice to carry with him a GPS [Global Positioning System] receiving system, whoever that was. Maybe no one yet?" Undated letter (1994).
41. The earth's oldest known formations, indeed, lie amid the tundra wastes of northwest Canada, near Great Slave Lake. Dating back 3.96 billion years, these remnants are nearly as old as Earth itself. Rocks from western Greenland are nearly as old.
42. Commodore O. C. S. Robertson, RCN (Ret.), interview by author, 26 October 1988.
43. *Daily Times-Journal,* 5 August 1958.

Chapter 5. Northward

1. Van Gorder interview.
2. Postcard, 4 August 1958, courtesy Frederick L. Parker.
3. In Canada, sovereignty is a persistent theme. With Confederation, vast areas of western Canada were made available. So as to consolidate sovereignty from sea to sea, an "almost frantic" occupation of the prairie spaces became deliberate national policy.
4. Predictability of acoustic properties and ambient noise is crucial to the design of sonar equipment. The two features that most influence underwater sound in northern waters are ice cover and the depth/temperature profile. The navy was devoting resources to the basin's acoustical mysteries. Most of the observational data taken at T-3, for example, reached the open literature. Notable exception: acoustic research.
5. Easygoing and engaging, the commodore added a comic note. When asked for his reaction when ordered to join the project, he chuckled, "Well, it took two big rums to settle my nerves when they asked me if I'd go." As for navigating near the magnetic pole: "Once you get up above eighty-seven [degrees], every direction according to the compasses, including the gyro, is south. Well, what happens is you just go around in circles. You could spend the rest of your life doing this [until] either you run out of beer, or run out of food, or run out of fuel." Robertson interview.
6. Flight Diary entry (portion), 7 August 1958, courtesy Captain Van Gorder.
7. The landscape here is replete with signposts. "I think the most fascinating thing I can remember about the flight," Fred Parker recalled, "was the stories that Greenaway could tell about the Arctic region. He had names for just about every little lake or hole in the ice we passed over and told us stories about Eskimos we saw out by themselves that would travel like that for months across the ice, then meet with their families after the hunt at some predetermined point." Letter to author, 7 October 1989.
8. Much of the tundra appears treeless. In many places, however, it is covered with "a thick matting of short, ancient willows and birches. You realize suddenly that you are wandering around on *top* of a forest." Barry Lopez, *Arctic Dreams: Imagination and Desire in a Northern Landscape* (New York: Charles Scribner's Sons, 1986), 29.
9. Hugh A. Mulligan, dispatch to AP, 10 August 1958 (delayed), courtesy Mr. Mulligan.
10. In May 2008 the U.S. Fish and Wildlife Service listed polar bears in Alaska as an endangered species—a symbol of climate change.
11. Map reading becomes difficult north of the tree line. The surface looks like the map only when there is little or no snow. For most of the year, it is covered and, except for areas of bold topography, obscures lakes, rivers, coastlines. "This is a situation for which many airmen are unprepared when they first venture into the barrens, and a little forewarning can be helpful." Dunbar and Greenaway, *Arctic Canada from the Air,* 9.

12. Keith R. Greenaway, in *Moving Beyond the Roads: Airships to the Arctic Symposium II (Proceedings),* University of Manitoba Transport Institute, 21–23 October 2003, 45–46. According to a book of Arctic stories, the children's reaction was fright: a huge whale was about to swallow them up.
13. The Arctic Circle has no practical meaning. It is simply the line north of which one can see the midnight sun.
14. In 1948 a U.S. embassy airplane was reported overdue on a flight from Churchill to The Pas, Manitoba. The ensuing air search was unusually extensive. In the end, three dozen aircraft were involved, including the blimp XM-1 basing at Winnipeg. This was the first such use of a nonrigid. On 25–26 September, XM-1 had pushed to about 54° N when, abruptly, the search concluded. *Arctic Circular* 1, no. 8 (December 1948), 92–94. Cdr. Charles Mills, USN (Ret.), copilot, recalled the subarctic wilderness as "absolutely serene."
15. The bodies were found in 1930 on White Island. The expedition's records also were recovered: well-preserved diaries, logbooks, a journal, photographic plates. After an erratic, 517-mile flight, the balloon had been forced down due to lack of ballast about 288 miles from the point of ascension. Calculating their position, the party then decided to sledge south and east. Alternately sledging and drifting, the men came ashore after eighty-five days. Four days later, expedition records ended.
16. Walter Wellman, *The Aerial Age: A Thousand Miles by Airship over the Atlantic Ocean* (New York: A. R. Keller, 1911), 15, 185.
17. "We looked ahead," Byrd was to write, "at the sea ice gleaming in the rays of the midnight sun a fascinating scene whose lure had drawn famous men into its clutches, never to return. . . . We were now getting into areas never before viewed by mortal eye." Upon return to Kings Bay, in Spitsbergen, he was met by (among others) Amundsen and Ellsworth, "two good sports"; Rear Adm. Richard E. Byrd, USN (Ret.), *Skyward* (New York: Blue Ribbon Books, 1928), 187, 195, 201. Doubts concerning Byrd's claim have persisted; *Norge,* most now acknowledge, was the first aircraft to gain 90° N.
18. Roald Amundsen and Lincoln Ellsworth, *First Crossing of the Polar Sea* (New York: George H. Doran, 1927), 207.
19. Following his court-martial, Nobile went abroad; in 1937 he was serving as consultant for the Soviet Union's dirigible construction trust. The notion of exploring the Arctic with airships burned still. "Since dog expeditions [round the Pole] are rather risky and not even the strongest icebreaker can penetrate so far," he remarked, "the airship is certainly the given means by which that region can be surveyed fairly comfortably. It can carry a larger scientific staff and equipment than planes. Also it allows the observer to descend lower toward the ground. After some more experiments I should think that even the dropping and picking up of landing parties should present no unsurmountable difficulty." H. P. Smolka, *40,000 against the Arctic* (New York: William Morrow, 1937), 97.
20. See William Barr, "The Soviet Contribution to the *Italia* Search and Rescue," *Polar Record* 18, no. 117 (1977), 561–74. See also Maurice Parijanine, *The Krassin,* trans. Lawrence Brown (New York: Macaulay, 1929), for an account of the icebreaker's rescue of the main group of survivors.
21. Samoilovich had invited Nobile to participate in an expedition by the icebreaker *Malygin.* When *Graf Zeppelin* rendezvoused with *Malygin* in the Franz Josef group, the zeppelin made a water landing. Nobile shook hands with his fellow airman from *Norge,* Lincoln Ellsworth.
22. Atmospheric purity in the circumpolar Arctic was documented. One cubic centimeter of air taken over Leningrad contained 52,000 dust particles, whereas over Severnaya Zemlya the same volume contained but two to three hundred.
23. See Gordon Vaeth, *Graf Zeppelin: The Adventures of an Aerial Globetrotter* (New York: Harper and Brothers, 1958), chap. 9, and, for a personal account, Ernst Krenkel, *RAEM Is My Call-Sign,* trans. R. Hammond (Moscow: Progress, 1978), 121–41. Krenkel, a radioman, was among the passengers. "As I explored the inside of the envelope," he said, "the dirigible flew further and further north. We passed over Archangel and the White Sea before coming to the Barents Sea. Floating ice appeared and on one of the ice-floes we spotted a polar bear, to the delight of the entire expedition. This, naturally, aroused great interest among those who had never seen one before. The noise produced by the almost 3,000 horsepower harnessed in the dirigible disturbed the lord of the Arctic and he hurriedly jumped into the water and swam to another ice-floe, supposing that it would be quieter there." In 1937 the radioman would gain international acclaim as a member of the first expedition to establish a floe camp mere miles off the Pole.

24. Vilhjalmur Stefansson, *Arctic Manual* (New York: Macmillan, 1944), 499; Cdr. Charles A. Mills, USN (Ret.), interview by author, 20 April 1998.
25. Greenaway, letter to author, 3 April 1991; "U.S. Navy Airship Flight to Ice Island T-3," 24.
26. How many Canadians were on the archipelago in 1958? An estimate: about three hundred officials, perhaps a hundred in business and other nonofficial occupations, plus two thousand or so Inuit. DEW line sites added about 250 more, with about four hundred at Frobisher Bay on Baffin Island—a major administrative center for the eastern Arctic. Grand total: approximately three thousand.
27. Becker letter.
28. "During the nineteen-fifties there were no flight operations or traffic controllers, as such, at Resolute. A radio operator monitored all aviation frequencies and provided information to the aircrew as requested (i.e., wind speed and direction, barometric pressure for setting the altimeter, and other information), and passed messages to the appropriate ground staff." Greenaway, letter to author, 3 September 1990.
29. Thomas B. Kilpatrick, letter to author, undated (1989).
30. Becker letter.
31. At the White House, the orbiting Soviet sphere had inspired the idea of a "super-routine" crossing of the Arctic, a feat (presumably) surpassing that of simply gaining the Pole. "But," *Life* noted, "if the transpolar trip was to be a propaganda success, she had to do it neatly, safely, quickly."
32. Alfred S. McLaren, "Analysis of the Under-Ice Topography in the Arctic Basin as Recorded by the USS *Nautilus* during August 1958," *Arctic* 41, no. 2 (June 1988), 122. Under-ice topography has been recorded by more than fifty U.S. and British submarines.
33. Capt. Frank M. Adams, USN (Ret.), audio prepared for author, (mailed) 22 September 1989.
34. Early letter.
35. Capt. Shepherd M. Jenks, USN (Ret.), audio prepared for author, September 1989.
36. *Spectator* (Hamilton, Ont.), editorial, 11 August 1958.
37. Mr. Alvin Hamilton, *House of Commons Debates,* 14 August 1958, 3540.
38. Anderson was reported in the *Times* (London) as having said, "There appears to be no upper limit to the size you may build submarines and I think cargo submarines carrying priority cargo such as oil are definitely coming along in the future." Quoted in Canada, *House of Commons Debates* (14 August 1958), 3511. See also Cdr. William R. Anderson, USN, "The Arctic as a Sea Route of the Future," *National Geographic* CXV, no. 1 (January 1959), 21–24.
39. Much would be made of a commercial seaway in which neither ice nor weather are barriers. A polar route would shorten by about four thousand miles the sea distance from Tokyo to London. The commercial potential of this "new northwest passage" using nuclear-powered submarine-tankers and cargo-carrying submarines was touted. The shipment of oil and iron ore from its northlands to world markets (for example) garnered scrutiny in Ottawa. Climate change has resurrected the matter of Arctic routes for shipping. See, for example, *New York Times,* 11 September 2009.
40. Beginning in 1949, "Rickover became the most vocal and most visible symbol of the navy's drive for nuclear propulsion. His efforts, his control, and his single-mindedness overshadowed in purpose those of all other individuals, regardless of their contributions or advocacy." Norman Polmar and Allen, *Rickover,* 178.
41. When Anderson and Lyon met with Rickover concerning the cruise planned for June, the admiral, "in his usual emotional display, objected, but it was difficult to see to just what he objected because of so many parenthetical displays against Op Nav. He appeared to object to extra mileage required by sending boat to Pacific Fleet and then across." Lyon field journal, 14 February 1958, 71.
42. Vice Adm. James Calvert, USN (Ret.), (telephone) interview by author, 8 December 1993. Nine civilian scientists accompanied the cruise, including two oceanographers from the Navy Electronics Laboratory, a gravity specialist, an ice forecaster, an oceanographer from the Hydrographic Office, and an electronic scientist from the Underwater Sound Laboratory (USL). The latter's function: to make underwater acoustic observations.
43. "U.S. Can Blow Up World from Below Admiral Declares," *Toronto Star,* 11 August 1958; "Soviet Blasts *Nautilus'* Use as War Threat," *Toronto Star,* 12 August 1958.
44. "Shadow beneath the Ice," *New York Times Book Review,* 4 January 1959.
45. Calvert, *Surface at the Pole,* 107–8.
46. In November 1931 Wilkins' *Nautilus* was towed four miles from Bergen and scuttled. Images from submersible dives in 2005 show the boat to be in reasonably good condition.

47. "Building the mooring mast," Becker recalls, "was quite a challenge to our limited engineering staff. The major problem was quite simple to understand but most difficult to solve. Cornwallis Island, in the dead of summer, melts down to a depth of some four inches. The next 1,250 feet is permafrost"; Becker letter. An innovation was used for the support wires. NADU's advance crew had found the permafrost impossible to penetrate. Pondering the matter en route back to South Weymouth, Van Gorder chanced to mention his problem to a U.S. Army colonel at Fort Churchill. The solution: shaped explosive charges, procured from the army. Captain Van Gorder interview.
48. Greenaway interview.
49. Postcard, 8 August 1958, courtesy Frederick L. Parker.

Chapter 6. Ice Island

1. In addition to weather data, these flights conducted radar surveillance. As well, research projects were conducted—for example, air sampling for nuclear fallout and measuring the earth's magnetic field. And aircrews were keeping eyes open for any undiscovered landmasses.
2. Stripped of armament and turrets, the B-29 was fitted with additional fuel tanks. In the nose, the meteorologist made his observations, with coordinates for each set of readings provided by the navigator.
3. Interpretation of radar pictures was greatly influenced by highly variable snow and ice conditions. The shifting of old pack ice crumbles new ice, forming pressure ridges and patches of uneven, broken ice. These showed up clearly on the radar scope but were easily mistaken for coastlines or islands.
4. At the Arctic and Antarctic Research Institute, I asked Dr. Ilya P. Romanov about data exchange. "We are very grateful for American scientists and specialists," he said, "because all of the data they obtained during their expeditions they have published. They [the data] are not confidential." Soviet researchers "badly need" Western results, to compare with their own. Was the reverse true? Wasn't Soviet data a state secret? "It is always impossible to get [our] data," was the reply. Interview by author, 19 May 1992.
5. Extensive shelves float attached to the north coast of Ellesmere Island, in the Canadian High Arctic. Subsequent work concluded that these freshwater features are, in fact, an ice-island nursery.
6. J. O. Fletcher, "Origin and Early Utilization of Aircraft Supported Drifting Stations," in *Arctic Drifting Stations: A Report on Activities Supported by the Office of Naval Research,* proceedings of the symposium, Warrenton, Virginia, 12–15 April 1966 under the auspices of the Arctic Institute of North America and the Office of Naval Research, November 1968, 5.
7. "I remember my interest and excitement when Col. Joseph O. Fletcher, then in command of the Air Weather Squadron at Fairbanks, Alaska, read his descriptive paper. Afterward, several of us sat up late into the night conjecturing about the origin, composition, and probable future of these paradoxical floating 'lands.' We were especially curious as to where they had come from." Maynard M. Miller, "Floating Islands," *Natural History* LXV, no. 5 (1956), 235.
8. A prefabricated structure similar to a Quonset hut, the Jamesway was designed expressly for Arctic use.
9. "North Pole 103 Miles: Temperature 60 Below," *Life* XXXII, no. 13 (31 March 1952), 13–17.
10. Kaare Rodahl, *North: The Nature and Drama of the Polar World* (New York: Harper and Brothers, 1953), 189.
11. In 1990 the author sojourned at an ice-island camp established by Canada. Accommodations were wood cabins: plain yet ample. Relative to conditions faced by early explorers and later military personnel, it was a pampered existence. The experience served to underscore the skill, resolve, and sheer grit of Fletcher and his team, confronting hostile, empty ice. Rather than retreat to a heated cabin or kitchen space, they had two tents connected by a snow-lined passage.
12. Dr. Arthur Collin, interview by author, 25 April 1993.
13. *Polar Record* 9, no. 61 (January 1959), 337.
14. Charles C. "Carlos" Plummer, an undergraduate geology student, was one of two field assistants for Dr. David Smith, deployed onto T-3 to study the island's morphology and hydrology. "I had never heard of ice islands, much less T-3, but it sounded interesting and adventurous. I was something of a romantic then and glorified in doing the unknown or seldom done and going to exotic places. The pay was exceptionally good ($450 month), but I probably would have gone for nothing"; letter to author, 10 February 1990. Donald Plouff, a geophysicist now with the U.S. Geological Survey, remarked: "I quickly volunteered to participate in the arctic work [on T-3] as a chance to do a variety of geophysical work in a unique area." It was, he continued, "a great opportunity to gather data and, hopefully, new ideas from a strange region of the Earth"; letter to author, 22 June 1989.

15. "Military personnel for support [of T-3] plus air resupply were requested by us from Headquarters USAF and were provided alternately by the Northeast Air Command (NEAC) and the Alaskan Air Command (AAC), depending on the position of T-3 relative to Greenland's Thule AB [Air Base] and Point Barrow, Alaska. The T-3 scientific program was conducted under the supervision of a T-3 Chief Scientist whom our Laboratory designated, while the military provided logistics and was responsible for safety of all personnel." Col. Louis DeGoes, USAF (Ret.), letter to author, 21 February 1989. Following extended duty with the Cambridge Research Center, DeGoes retired from the air force. During 1967–81, he served as executive secretary of the Polar Research Board, National Academy of Sciences.
16. Becker letter.
17. Van Gorder, diary entry (portion), 9 August 1958.
18. Elmer B. Lord, letter to author, undated (1989).
19. The airfield commander remembered this incident. "Although the takeoff was a jubilant affair," Becker recounts, "the happiness was not to last. Radio communications between Resolute tower and the airship indicated that an engine was running rough. Shortly thereafter, the tower was advised that the engine had stopped." Becker letter.
20. Carburetor ice can occur in clear, humid air with temperatures well above freezing—conditions different from those conducive to external icing.
21. Van Gorder diary, 9 August 1958.
22. One of the men at SP-2 (1950–51) was to write of April's extreme visibility: "Surprisingly transparent air provided marvelous visibility, and even distant hummocks could be studied in the finest detail. It seemed that the horizon had moved out to infinity." G. N. Yakovlev, *Ice Routes of the Arctic,* originally *Ledovyye puti Arktiki* (Moscow: Mysl, 1975; repr. under the authority of the Director General Intelligence and Security, National Defence Headquarters, Ottawa, DGIS Translation Library no. 1653, 4 October 1977), 27.
23. Data on long-term motion had come from the tracking of beset ships and manned drifting stations. In the Canada Basin, the gyre pushes ice toward the high North Atlantic or into another orbit. Hostage to this circulation, T-3 would circle three times during its known history before export, in 1983.
24. "The only practical way to keep course in high latitudes where compass variation is great," Wilkins had observed, "is by piloting, that is using dead reckoning governed by observation of surface conditions, wind drift, direction of snow banks, pressure ridges, lanes of open water, or other objects. A combination of that method with frequent sextant observations will necessarily fully occupy the time of a navigator flying in high latitudes"; quoted in John Grierson, *Heroes of the Polar Skies* (New York: Meredith, 1967), 167. As gyroscopes became more precise (less drift), the frequency of heading checks declined to about every half hour or so. These and related manual techniques developed for high-latitude navigation set the stage for the devices now used and are fundamental to today's inertial, computer-assisted systems.
25. Lord letter.
26. I asked Collin if IGY Arctic programs had emphasized military requirements. The scientific challenge had, he said, predominated. "In my view a very large proportion of the professional interest that I encountered was genuinely scientific. The understanding of the Arctic Ocean was very, very elementary at that time. There were no charts of the bottom, for example; there was no bathymetry in the Arctic Ocean at that time. We had a general idea of the western basin and the eastern basin. We had a general idea of the Lomonosov Ridge; but nothing more than that. So the geologic, the geophysical interest was extremely high. . . . At the same time we were fully aware of the issue of submarines under the ice: of the potential balance of power that could take place with submarine fleets operating [in the Arctic]. We had our assumptions of the capabilities of submarines under the ice, but of course we were all learning at the same time. . . . I think it was obvious to all of us that any additional information in the polar basin, for example, was information which contributed to an understanding of submarine operations: sonar ranging for example, densities for example, temperatures for example, bathymetry for example—all that information, classified and unclassified, all contributed to a better understanding of submarine operations in the polar basin." Collin interview.
27. The dancing-in-the-street image is dismissed. Don Plouff, for one, labels this "nonsense." "We were not 'dancing in the streets'; we may have waved," Carlos Plummer remarked. Also, "No scientists were in the camp," Gerry Cabaniss recalls, "and it's doubtful many of the military support personnel would have danced."

28. Hal Vogel, *Ice Cap News,* April–June 1996, 48–56.
29. Collin interview.
30. Under these conditions, the question of safety arises. "We were all aware," Collin observes, "that we were, at times, extremely isolated. And with weather conditions being as variable as they can be—in mid-summer in the Arctic Ocean there is a chance that cracks and leads will form, where you can get very low fog, and visibility and flying conditions become impossible—you can find yourself in a serious predicament if you have serious illness or a serious injury. So we took many steps to make sure that that didn't happen." Collin interview.
31. Yakovlev, *Ice Routes of the Arctic,* 65.
32. David D. Smith, "Development of Surface Morphology on Fletcher's Ice Island T-3," Air Force Cambridge Research Center, Scientific Report no. 4, 15 February 1960, 13. The 1958 ablation season was unusually warm and long; it commenced at T-3 on 8 June and ended on 2 September. Fifteen days during this period had an average daily temperature below freezing—an ablation season of about seventy-two days. At Alpha, melting was so intense that many of the buildings had to be moved.
33. Even minute amounts of particulate matter affect albedo—the ratio of light reflected to that received. Sediments entrained within sea ice greatly influence the Arctic's heat budget.
34. Cabaniss letter.
35. Ibid.; Collin interview; Dr. Carlos C. Plummer, letter to author, 10 February 1990.
36. Cabaniss letter.
37. Collin interview; Plummer letter.
38. Van Gorder diary, 9 August 1958.
39. The IGY, one can speculate, was a cover for the NADU mission: to contact and (or) to track *Nautilus.* The coincidence of the 27 July departure of *719,* four days after *Nautilus* left Pearl astern, is striking. And each concluded its respective operation on 12 August. There is mention, moreover, of potential military applications in the Pentagon's announcement regarding the expedition (see page 72). This line of conjecture is readily demolished. Eisenhower's express orders were clear: the boat's objective was to remain top secret. Coordination with NADU, of necessity, would have enlarged the need-to-know population. Only eleven senior commanders were informed of the mission and plans; Lieutenant Commander Early was told that twelve naval officers not on *Nautilus* knew. The two missions, Dr. Miller insists, were "separate and not coordinated operations." "As far as I'm concerned," Adams told me, "coordination would not have been a good idea; [it] did not fit in to our plans or our objectives." Finally: "You could count on both hands," Anderson remarked, "the number of people both in the navy and in the White House who knew anything of the voyage." Thus, he could "guarantee" that Van Gorder knew nothing of the boat's operational orders. Dr. Maynard M. Miller, letter to author, 28 January 1990; Capt. Frank M. Adams, USN (Ret.), audiocassette prepared for author, (mailed) 22 September 1989; Anderson interview.

Chapter 7. Homeward

1. Van Gorder diary, 9 August 1958.
2. Schou and Gorder joint interview, 4–5 December 1959.
3. "Depending entirely on Dead Reckoning," Greenaway reminds, "tends to increase the intensity of devotion to navigation duties. The islands provided a quick reference and ready check on one's bearing—as the sun didn't set at this time of year one could become disoriented quite quickly when flying long hours and using Greenwich Time." Letter to author, 3 April 1991.
4. *Sun* (Springfield, Ohio), 4 June 1962; unidentified New London area paper (clipping).
5. At least one airman recalled Harris' team as "excited" when *Skate* acknowledged their acoustic signal. On 9 August, however, *Skate* was nearing Spitsbergen en route to the basin—and received word that *Nautilus* had crossed the Pole seven days earlier.
6. In 1947 "Borden Island" was found to be *two* islands. In August 1989 the author passed slightly to their east. At four thousand feet, the sea-ice canopy arched away to the Pole, brilliant and forbidding in the crystal light of morning. Despite flawless visibility, from that vantage land could not be distinguished from the enclosing sea ice.
7. See *New York Times,* Science Times section, 14 December 2009.

8. Unidentified, undated clipping (1958).
9. At least seventy-five species of birds migrate to Arctic shores each summer to breed. Some journey from as far away as South America and Antarctica to join the ptarmigan, owls, ravens, gulls, and others that stay year-round. Several migratory-bird sanctuaries have been established in the archipelago; there, all activities are strictly regulated, and research is conducted.
10. Greenaway interview.
11. Becker letter.
12. CO, NADU, "Interim Report no. 1."
13. Van Gorder diary, 9 August 1958.
14. Greenaway, "U.S. Navy Airship Flight to Ice Island T-3," 25, and interview.
15. Van Gorder diary, 10 August 1958. Some confusion prevailed as to what time it actually was on board. Greenaway explains: "We used Greenwich Standard Time (GST) for navigation as all data in the Air Almanac referred to GST. At the time, Britain was on double daylight time but this was never used and the letter Z following the time indicated GST. South Weymouth was on EDST and the Central Time Zone in which Resolute Bay was located, used Daylight Time. Resolute used Standard Time. Some of the crew, and others, left their watches on EDST, while others changed to local time. This confusion of time references and the fact that it was daylight all the time only added to the problem." Letter to author, 22 September 1990.
16. Schou and Gorder joint interview.
17. Walter H. Bailey, (telephone) interview by author, 8 April 1989.
18. Norman G. Gray, letter to author, 25 July 1990.
19. Robertson interview.
20. Mulligan interview.
21. The purchase resulted in an amusing sidebar. When his expenses were submitted, one of the head accountants ("a shiny-pants bookkeeper") insisted on a receipt for the socks. Having none and piqued by the request, he stuffed the (unwashed) footwear in an envelope with an accompanying note. "I'm sure," Mulligan smiled, "they're not in the AP files anyplace now"; ibid.
22. Robertson interview.
23. Greenaway letters, 24–25 October 1988, 22 November 1989.
24. Greenaway, *Arctic Air Navigation,* 128.
25. Greenaway elaborates: "Throughout the exercise my main concern was to ensure that we were maintaining the correct heading. All of the flight north of Churchill required steering by directional gyroscope because of the proximity of the Magnetic Pole. This required taking three observations an hour on a celestial body to correct for gyro precession. This type of navigation was foreign to my naval companions who were only familiar with steering by the magnetic compass." Letter to author, 10 March 1990.
26. Greenaway letter, 24–25 October 1988.
27. Greenaway letter, 22 November 1989.
28. Greenaway letter, 24–25 October 1988.
29. Report (copy), Ed Moore, Field Service, South Weymouth to Jack Peace, Section Head Field Service [Goodyear], "Extended Flight, ZPG-2 BuNo 141561," 18 March 1957, courtesy Mr. Moore.
30. Van Gorder diary, 11 August 1958.
31. Greenaway, letter to author, 3 April 1991.
32. Why had he remained on duty to the U.S. border? "South of Churchill," Greenaway explained, "I was familiar with the topography as I had flown over it many times. But at the low altitude we were flying it was difficult to pinpoint our position if one were not acquainted with the region. Thus I felt I needed to be available at all times." Ibid.
33. Van Gorder diary, 12 August 1958.
34. "U.S. Can Blow Up World from Below Admiral Declares," unidentified clipping.
35. "I was present one time," Capt. Edward Beach recalled, "when the Chief of Naval Operations—a man I highly admired, said he was just relaxing, he said, 'You think I run the Navy, don't you. Well I've got news for you: I work for Rickover just like all of you bastards.' That's what he actually said. What he meant, of course, was that when Rickover wanted something, he knew how to force the Navy to produce what he wanted"—the CNO included. Beach interview.
36. U.S. Defense Dept., Department of Defense, Office of Public Information, news release, 8 August 1958, courtesy Naval Historical Center, Washington, D.C.

37. *New York Times,* 13 August 1958. In the adjacent column, including an image of Anderson rejoining his ship off Portland, the paper had a short piece on the return of *719* to South Weymouth from Canada—its final piece concerning the expedition.
38. Naval Attaché Paul Ryan acknowledged Canadian support in a letter to the Chief of Air Staff, Ottawa. "On behalf of the U.S. Navy," the captain wrote Air Marshall Campbell, "may I express our profound thanks for the excellent cooperation and competent assistance rendered the U.S. Navy airship by the Royal Canadian Air Force on its recent flight to the Arctic. As you know, the airship returned to its base at South Weymouth, Massachusetts, on 12 August having established the fact that the airship is a suitable vehicle for Arctic research. . . . I am informed that the participation in the flight of Wing Commander Keith Greenaway, RCAF, was most helpful to the success of the mission." Confidential letter, 18 August 1958, RG 24, Acc. 83-84/216, box 3579, file S961-103-2, pt. 5, National Archives of Canada.
39. "Navy Blimp Returns to South Weymouth after Polar Journey," *Quincy Patriot Ledger* (Mass.), 12 August 1958. A sampling of local headlines includes, "Navy's Blimp Home after Polar Trip"; "Blimp Home from Arctic: Captain Praises Its Ability"; "Joyful End for Arctic Blimp Trip"; and "Weymouth Blimp Returns Safely." For its part, the *New York Times* concluded its coverage on the 13th, with a one-column "Navy Blimp Finishes Trip over the Arctic."
40. "While hugging my three children and kissing my wife," Koza relates, "my fore-and-aft hat fell off the back of my head. Placing hand behind me, [I] caught hat and placed it back on my head still kissing wife. That sequence made the national evening news." Letter-review to author, 13 September 1990.

Chapter 8. Epilogue

1. CO, NADU, "Interim Report no. 1." For much of the boreal year, deployment of a slow-speed aircraft was impracticable. During May–August, however, the average prevailing wind over the Arctic Ocean area is one of light winds or calm. Still, a ceiling is typical, ground fog frequent. The Polar Project, Van Gorder emphasized, was to investigate the feasibility of operations during the polar summer. Operating in winter "was never considered feasible. HTA had successfully provided the supply requirements during that period." Letter to author, 2 May 1991.
2. Capt. Harold B. Van Gorder, USN, "Use of Lighter-than-air Craft in the Arctic," in J. H. Hartshorn, ed., *Proceedings of the First Annual Arctic Planning Session, November 1958,* GRD Research Notes no. 15 (Bedford, Mass.: Air Force Cambridge Research Center, April 1959).
3. During and also after the IGY, scientists repeatedly emphasized the need for stationing light aircraft at U.S. drifting stations. Deeming them impractical initially, the Naval Arctic Research Laboratory initiated lightplane operations, often keeping Cessna 180s deployed on the ice for several days to a week.
4. *Polar Record* 12, no. 77 (May 1964), 181. The laboratory's 180s operated in company, so that no man's life depended on one engine.
5. Van Gorder, "Use of Lighter-than-air Craft in the Arctic." Ground handling is a critical element; most losses and damage occur on the ground.
6. Dr. Kenneth L. Hunkins was in the audience. The meeting, he recalls, stands out in his memory more for a paper on the C-130 as a support platform and the presence of Col. Bernt Balchen, USAF (Ret.)—a legendary officer-airman. As for airships, "while a good idea, [blimps] were not going to replace fixed-wing aircraft by any means." Interview by author, 30 March 1995.
7. Capt. M. H. Eppes, confidential memorandum to CNO, 11 September 1959, [Lt. Cdr. James] Punderson, [USN (Ret.)] Papers. Eppes was the most senior officer with recent fleet experience in LTA.
8. Richard W. Widdicombe, memorandum to Capt. Norman L. Beal, USNR, CND Office of Naval Warfare, 1 November 1985, courtesy Lt. Cdr. Widdicombe, USN (Ret.).
9. Eppes memorandum.
10. See Richard Halloran, "A Silent Battle Surfaces," *New York Times Magazine,* 7 December 1986, for an overview of U.S. and Soviet submarine programs and strategies during the Reagan-era buildup.
11. A 1984 study envisaged airships as logistics support vehicles for a new North Warning System for detecting cruise missiles. The NWS has since replaced the DEW line of radars for North America with completely new sites.
12. "Because airships can accommodate a wide variety of sensor avionics, including large-array antennas, they are well-suited for missions requiring detection and tracking of sea-skimming cruise missiles and

tactical ballistic missiles. Airships can be equipped with direct, relay, and beyond-line-of-sight communications gear configured to function as a switchboard converter terminal for real-time cross-band/link operations." Richard G. DeSipio, "Airships Are State-of-the-Art," U.S. Naval Institute *Proceedings* 119/8/1075 (August 1993), 91–92.

13. During the Falkland Islands war, an inexpensive missile sank a high-technology warship having no early-warning air cover. And in 1987 an Exocet hit the USS *Stark*. In response, battle groups adopted a number of strategies: surveillance airplanes, the Aegis cruiser, the Phalanx machine gun.
14. In the arcane world of computerized war gaming, the early-warning airship converted skeptics. In simulations, the platform typically was assigned a subordinate role, say, as a communications relay. As the game progressed, it was discovered that, thanks to the hypothetical ship, one side could talk to forces it could not reach before. Intrigued, gamers edged the airship toward center stage, where its radar helped one side to see very well. Often, further, the airship helped save the forces that received its services. See DeSipio, "Airships Are State-of-the-Art," 91–92, for a dated assessment.
15. The need for long-range, over-water, low-altitude research aircraft persists. The oceans and continental shelf constitute the airship's natural habitat, where it can deploy sensors and portable gear to remote sites, thus offering an airborne-survey substitute for costly ship-based surveillance.
16. Helicopters have a niche that cannot be duplicated. They are, however, expensive-to-operate, high-maintenance platforms.
17. Development and operational costs for labor, power, and transportation place northern mines at a distinct disadvantage. Mines have finite lives; new deposits must be found. Having to push through a road may mean leaving known or suspected resources undeveloped.
18. Don Kuryk, Manager Technical Services, "Seasonal Transportation to Remote Communities—What If?" in *Moving Beyond the Roads,* 42–43. For Ottawa, climate-change opening of the Northwest Passage holds implications for sovereignty, resources, and environmental protection.
19. During the 1980s, Canada expended R&D funds to study heavy-lift cargo airships for specialty hauling (logs, ore) and for military purposes. "This [airship] revival is of interest to Canada," an observer wrote in 1987, "particularly for northern operations, since our Arctic has special conditions—moderate winds, poor logistics and ocean ice—and the airship has special attributes—flexibility, endurance, payload and hover capability—which seem to uniquely qualify it for this environment and for many diverse tasks, civil and military, which must be performed to provide Canada with a northern presence." C. L. R. Unwin, "The Airship Revival and Canadian Operators," *Canadian Defence Quarterly* (Spring 1987), 44. Proposals notwithstanding, little resulted.
20. Greenaway, "To the Top of the World by Airship," 92. See also Greenaway, "U.S. Navy Airship Flight to Ice Island T-3."
21. Greenaway interview.
22. Robertson interview.
23. Gray, letter to author (with enclosure), 25 July 1990.
24. Lt. Col. Michael Woodgerd, USA, "Mobilus: A Challenge for a New Century," in *Moving Beyond the Roads,* 116.
25. "Atomic Submarines for Canada?" *(Montreal) Gazette,* editorial, 14 August 1958.
26. Not long after its Arctic cruise, Sir Hubert Wilkins visited *Skate*. Lunching with her skipper, the old explorer had suddenly remarked: "Now that you have everything you need to do the job you must go in the wintertime. You haven't really opened the Arctic Ocean for scientific investigation," he went on, "or military or commercial use, for that matter—if you merely demonstrate what you can do in the summertime." Sir Hubert died two months later. Not long after, asking Stefansson's views on a winter cruise, Calvert was similarly encouraged. "You'll find it a lot different from what you saw last August," he was told. Calvert, *Surface at the Pole,* 144.
27. Waldo K. Lyon, "Submarine Combat in the Ice," U.S. Naval Institute *Proceedings* 118 (February 1992), 37.
28. See Cdr. J. P. Steele, *Seadragon: Northwest under the Ice* (New York: E. P. Dutton, 1962); Calvert, "Skate's Breakthrough at the Pole," *Life* 46, no. 18 (4 May 1959), 29.
29. Calvert interview.
30. "The Polar Sea's voyage appeared certain to be one of the major issues facing Prime Minister Brian Mulroney when Parliament resumes. . . . Opposition Leader John Turner . . . described it as 'an affront

to Canada.'" He added that Mulroney's failure to intervene personally with Washington "blatantly encouraged" the United States to ignore Canada's views. *Maclean's,* August 1985, 16.

31. Jockel, "The US Navy, Maritime Command, and the Arctic," 26. A forthright summary of Canadian opinion, it includes American reaction to the SSN proposal.
32. Rear-Admiral (CF, Ret.) F. W. Crickard, "An Anti-Submarine Warfare Capability in the Arctic a National Requirement," *Canadian Defence Quarterly* (April 1987), 24.
33. "What is the Minister proposing? He is proposing we spend up to $10 billion to protect our sovereignty against our closest ally. That is how it appears from this side of the House. . . . There are better ways to protect our sovereignty. We should put fixed sensors off our three coasts. . . . Icebreakers can provide a much more visible physical presence than nuclear submarines." Canada, *House of Commons Debates,* 5 June 1987, 6783. According to a Canadian admiral, "It's also possible that [U.S. submarines] can get to the Arctic without going through Canadian waters. But if they don't, there isn't a damn thing we can do about it, so why embarrass ourselves by objecting?" *Sunday Star,* 11 August 1991.
34. Rear Adm. Carl J. Seiberlich, USN (Ret.), conversation with author, 15 April 1998. *Nautilus* was not merely an improved submarine but a new weapon. Rickover labeled the boat the most revolutionary undersea craft since 1900; see Polmar and Allen, *Rickover,* chap. 8.
35. In August 1966 the USS *Will Rogers* (SSBN 659) was launched—the forty-first and last Polaris submarine. Because of its experience with submarine electronics, the Underwater Sound Laboratory played an important part in development of electronics equipment in support of the Polaris Weapons System.
36. The Silent Service has eclipsed *Nautilus* as a working/living environment. "Current nuclear boats are far more habitable than *Nautilus,*" Capt. Frank Adams, USN (Ret.), remarks. Touring a Trident boat, he made the inevitable comparisons. "I could have taken the USS *Swordfish*—a small nuclear attack submarine [which he commanded for thirty-two months]—and dropped it down into the missile compartment of the Trident submarine. Very comfortable, very roomy, very well laid out for living and maintenance" on eight-week-plus patrols. Remarks prepared for author, (mailed) 22 September 1989.
37. Lloyd D. Keigwin and G. Leonard Johnson, "Using a Nuclear Submarine for Arctic Research," *Eos* 73, no. 19 (12 May 1992), 209, 220–21. "Despite the fundamental importance of polar regions to the habitability of planet Earth," the authors note, "most oceanographers have used only the most inefficient methods of exploring the ocean beneath the ice: drifting on floating ice camps and bashing through the ice with ice breakers. Neither of these methods is an effective way to explore a feature as large and as physiographically varied as the Arctic basin."
38. Ibid.; A. S. McLaren, "Save the *Sturgeon*s to Study Global Change?" U.S. Naval Institute *Proceedings* 116 (September 1990). Today, even the CIA—via its intelligence assets—is sharing environmental data. See *New York Times,* 5 January 2010.
39. Various U.S. Navy assets serve civilian science. In 1991, for instance, the Navy Department began granting access to its underwater Sound Surveillance System (SOSUS), a classified network of seafloor hydrophones. "This is the first time that we can actually eavesdrop on eruptions on the deep-sea floor," a NOAA geologist exulted. The system also enables scientists to study the wide array of noises made by whales. "This technology is going to revolutionize the way people look at and listen to whales," a marine mammalogist predicted. See (for example) *Science News,* 28 August 1993.
40. Marcus Langseth et al., "SCICEX-93: Arctic Cruise of the U.S. Navy Nuclear Powered Submarine USS *Pargo,*" *Marine Technology Science Journal* 27, no. 4 (Winter 93–94), 4–12.
41. "The Science Exercise Program: History, Achievements, and Future of SCICEX," *Arctic Research of the United States* (Fall/Winter 2000), 2–7; Norman Polmar, e-mail to author, 17 August 2002.
42. Polmar and Allen, *Rickover,* 179.
43. *National Geographic,* 128, no. 5 (November 1965), 692.
44. U.S. Navy silence concerning the extent of its operations in Canadian territorial waters is a virtual tradition, hence a long-standing irritant in Ottawa defense circles. "The USN parcels out exceedingly sparing information to its Allies concerning US [submarine] movements," one author observed, "preferring instead to simply guarantee, having heard from them where their submarines are to be, that American boats will not be in the way." Jockel, "The US Navy, Maritime Command, and the Arctic," 27.
45. *Science* 327, no. 5968 (19 February 2010), 934.
46. *Science* 323, no. 5922 (27 March 2010), 1655.
47. *Science* 462/26 (November 2009), 413.

48. Kuryk, "Seasonal Transportation to Remote Communities—What If?" 46. See, for example, "Arctic Shortcut, Long a Dream, Beckons Shippers as Ice Thaws," *New York Times,* 11 September 2009. "Someday the Entire Arctic Sea May Be One Giant Northwest Passage," *Wall Street Journal,* 11 March 2010.
49. *New York Times,* editorial, 18 August 2009.
50. An ice core taken at Vostok, in East Antarctica, extended the record of atmospheric carbon dioxide concentration back 160,000 years. The ice core retrieved by the Greenland Ice Sheet Project proffers a 200,000-year history of climate change. And long-term reconstructions of past conditions have been prepared using tree rings, pollen deposits, lake sediments, shoreline and dune traces, even the appearance or disappearance of civilizations.
51. Beaumont M. "Beau" Buck, undated letter-review (1994). Buck was Special Projects Officer, Undersea Branch, ONR/Polar Research Lab. He logged months on Arctic ice, including T-3.
52. Typically, January and February are slow at Resolute. Activity revives in March, with late August the busiest season after which it drops precipitously. Commercial flights include four scheduled Boeing 727s each week and service (mostly by De Havilland DHC-6 Twin Otter) to communities and outposts within the archipelago.
53. See "Mixed Blessing: The Polar Bears Are in Churchill Again," *Wall Street Journal,* 14 November 1989.
54. Military personnel attend the Alert base year-round, listening to radio signals and keeping in touch with Canadian aircraft and ships. The facility has a restricted landing strip, a radio-antennae farm, weather station, staff quarters, an operations center. Amenities to banish boredom include a bowling alley, skating rink, and bars. Canadians cannot visit or photograph the outpost: "We don't allow media to go there, never have and never will," a spokesman said. "It is a classified station and there would be no advantage to us to have the buildings and antennae arrays photographed." A resourceful newspaper obtained an image nonetheless, purchasing one taken in 1987 via Soviet satellite. This was the first Soviet satellite photograph of Canada ever released. *Sunday (Toronto) Star,* 30 July 1989.
55. In December 1990, a startling tourist package was announced. The Northeast Passage—the polar route across the top of Eurasia from the Bering Strait to Norway—was opened to foreigners. Though plied by icebreakers escorting ice-strengthened cargo vessels and tankers, no passenger expeditions had made the transit. Cost for the twenty-one-day passage via Soviet icebreaker: from $25,000 to $32,000 per person, depending on choice of cabin.

Selected Bibliography

Primary Unpublished Sources

Research has relied, in significant part, on the men who helped plan and who took part in the events of this book. Interviews were indispensable. No less important was an in-depth correspondence plus, in several instances, self-recorded replies to author queries. Private papers, archival records and Department of the Navy reports were essential. Published primary and selected secondary sources also were useful, to corroborate supporting information and to help round out the narrative.

The following individuals—grouped by platform—were interviewed by the author or contributed through correspondence, or both—the bedrock, the foundation, of the work. As well, six among those listed reviewed selected portions of the draft manuscript.

Navy Airship BUNO 126719 (asterisks indicate audio-recorded interviews and submissions)

Mr. Walter H. Bailey
Squadron Leader William P. Becker, RCAF (Ret.)
Mr. Walter L. Clearwaters (regarding Dr. Guy S. Harris)
Dr. Norman G. Gray
Brigadier General Keith R. Greenaway, RCAF (Ret.)*
Mrs. Jeanne Harris (regarding Dr. Harris)
Mr. Thomas B. Kilpatrick (airship *719* at Resolute)
Lieutenant Harold D. Koza, USN (Ret.)
AD1 Elmer B. Lord, USN (Ret.)
Mr. Louis D. Mancini (fabricating the ZPG-2)
Lieutenant Commander Cecil Manship, USN (Ret.)
Captain [and Dr.] Maynard M. Miller, USNR (Ret.)
Mr. Hugh A. Mulligan, feature writer, Associated Press*
ATC Frederick L. Parker, USN (Ret.)
Commander Max V. Ricketts, USN (Ret.)
Commodore O. C. S. Robertson, RCN (Ret.)*
Lieutenant Commander Aage J. Schou, USN (Ret.)*
Captain Harold B. Van Gorder, USN (Ret.)*
Commander Richard W. Widdicombe, USN (Ret.) (flying the ZPG-2)*

USS *Nautilus* (SSN 571)

Captain Frank M. Adams, USN (Ret.)*
Captain William R. Anderson, USN (Ret.)

Captain Edward L. Beach, USN (Ret.) (naval aide to President Dwight D. Eisenhower)*
Mr. Richard J. Boyle (history of under-ice submarines)
Rear Admiral Arleigh A. Burke, USN (Ret.) (former CNO)
Vice Admiral James Calvert, USN (Ret.) (former CO, USS *Skate*)
Vice Admiral Kenneth M. Carr, USN (Ret.)
Rear Admiral Paul J. Early, USN (Ret.)
Dr. Waldo K. Lyon, Arctic Submarine Laboratory (formerly Naval Electronics Laboratory)*
Captain Shepherd M. Jenks, USN (Ret.)*
Captain Robert D. McWethy, USN (Ret.)

Ice Island T-3 (IGY Drift Station Bravo)

Dr. Gerry H. Cabaniss
Dr. Arthur E. Collin*
Colonel Louis DeGoes, USAF (Ret.)
Mr. Donald Plouff
Dr. Charles C. Plummer
Dr. David D. Smith

Published Sources

Books

Amundsen, Roald, and Lincoln Ellsworth. *First Crossing of the Polar Sea*. New York: George H. Doran, 1927.

Anderson, Commander William R., with Clay Blair Jr. *Nautilus 90 North*. Cleveland: World, 1959.

Blair, Clay, Jr. *Silent Victory*. New York: J. B. Lippincott, 1975.

Blanchet, Guy. *Search in the North*. Toronto: Macmillan, 1960.

Byrd, Rear Admiral Richard E., USN. *Skyward*. New York: Blue Ribbon Books, 1928.

Calvert, Commander James, USN. *Surface at the Pole*. New York: McGraw-Hill, 1960.

Dunbar, Moira, and Wing Commander Keith R. Greenaway, RCAF. *Arctic Canada from the Air*. Ottawa: Defence Research Board, 1956.

Foster, Michael, and Carol Marino. *The Polar Shelf: The Saga of Canada's Arctic Scientists*. Toronto: NC, 1986.

Greenaway, Brigadier General Keith R., RCAF (Ret.), and Colonel Morris D. Gates, RCAF (Ret.). *Polar Air Navigation: A Record*. Ottawa: Self-Published, 2009.

Greenaway, Flight Lieutenant Keith R., RCAF. *Arctic Air Navigation*. Ottawa: Defence Research Board, 1951.

Grierson, John. *Challenge to the Poles*. London: G. T. Foulis, 1964.

Hattersley-Smith, G. *North of Latitude Eighty*. Ottawa: Defence Research Board, 1974.

Honderich, John. *Arctic Imperative: Is Canada Losing the North?* Toronto: University of Toronto Press, 1987.

Krenkel, Ernst. *RAEM Is My Call-Sign*. Translated by R. Hammond. Moscow: Progress, 1978.

Leary, William M. *Under Ice: Waldo Lyon and the Development of the Arctic Submarine*. College Station: Texas A&M University Press, 1999.

Lopez, Barry. *Arctic Dreams: Imagination and Desire in a Northern Landscape*. New York: Charles Scribner's Sons, 1986.

McDougall, Walter A. *The Heavens and the Earth: A Political History of the Space Age*. New York: Basic Books, 1985.

Nelson, Stuart B. *Sabotage in the Arctic: Fate of the Submarine Nautilus*. Self-Published, 2007, www.Xlibris.com.

Nobile, Umberto. *My Polar Flights*. Translated by Frances Fleetwood. New York: G. P. Putnam's Sons, 1961.

Osherenko, Gail, and Oran R. Young. *The Age of the Arctic: Hot Conflicts and Cold Realities*. Cambridge: Cambridge University Press, 1989.

Polmar, Norman, and Thomas B. Allen. *Rickover: Controversy and Genius*. New York: Simon and Schuster, 1982.

Rodahl, Kaare. *North: The Nature and Drama of the Polar World.* New York: Harper and Brothers, 1953.
Rodgers, Eugene. *Beyond the Barrier: The Story of Byrd's First Expedition to Antarctica.* Annapolis, Md.: Naval Institute Press, 1990.
Vaeth, J. Gordon. *Graf Zeppelin: The Adventures of an Aerial Globetrotter.* New York: Harper and Brothers, 1958.
Wellman, Walter. *Airship Voyages over the Polar Sea.* New York: A. R. Keller, 1911.
Wilkins, Hubert. *Under the North Pole: The Wilkins-Ellsworth Submarine Expedition.* New York: Warren and Putnam, 1931.

Technical Papers, Professional Periodicals, Archives

Althoff, William F. "Potential Arctic Missions." In *Moving Beyond the Roads: Airships to the Arctic Symposium II (Proceedings),* University of Manitoba Transport Institute, 21–23 October 2003.
Banks, N. D. "Forty Years of Canadian Sovereignty Assertion in the Arctic, 1947–87." *Arctic* 40, no. 4 (December 1987): 285–91.
Barnard, Rick. "Iraqi Conflict Brings Increased Interest in Military Airships." *Sea Power* 46, no. 7 (July 2003): 1.
Canada, Record Group 24, accession 83-84/216, box 3579, file S961-103-1, pt. 5, National Archives of Canada, Ottawa.
Commanding Officer, Naval Air Development Unit. Interim Report no. 1 to Chief of Naval Research on RTED Project no. NDSW-ONR 46120. "Conduct Airship Flight Operations in Support of Research in the Area of the Arctic Ocean." 14 October 1958.
Crickard, F. W., Rear-Admiral (CF, Ret.). "An Antisubmarine Warfare Capability in the Arctic: A National Requirement." *Canadian Defence Quarterly* 16, no. 4 (April 1987), 31–38.
Delmas, Robert J. "Environmental Information from Ice Cores." *Reviews of Geophysics* 30, no. 1 (February 1992): 1–21.
Denton, G. H., R. F. Anderson, J. R. Toggweiler, R. L. Edwards, J. M. Schaefer, A. E. Putnam. "The Last Glacial Termination, *Science* 328, no. 5886 (25 June 2010): 1652–56.
Eyre, Kenneth C. "Forty Years of Military Activity in the Canadian North, 1947–87." *Arctic* 40, no. 4 (December 1987): 292–99.
Fletcher, Joseph O. "Origin and Early Utilization of Aircraft-Supported Drifting Stations." In *Arctic Drifting Stations: A Report on Activities Supported by the Office of Naval Research*, Proceedings of the Symposium, Warrenton, Virginia, 12–15 April 1966, under the auspices of the Arctic Institute of North America and the Office of Naval Research, November 1968.
"German U-Boats in the Arctic (Part III)." *Office of Naval Intelligence Review* (August 1951): 326–31.
Haydon, Commander Peter T. "The Strategic Importance of the Arctic: Understanding the Military Issues." *Canadian Defence Quarterly* (Spring 1988): 27–34.
Hazell, Steven. "Where the Caribou and the Cruise Missiles Play." *Canadian Defence Quarterly* (May/June 1991): 34–35.
Jeffries, Martin O. "Arctic Ice Shelves and Ice Islands: Origin, Growth and Disintegration, Physical Characteristics, Structural-Stratigraphic Variability, and Dynamics." *Reviews of Geophysics* 30, no. 3 (August 1992): 245–67.
Jockel, Joseph T. "The US Navy, Maritime Command, and the Arctic." *Canadian Defence Quarterly* (December 1989): 23–33.
Keigwin, Lloyd D., and G. Leonard Johnson. "Using a Nuclear Submarine for Arctic Research." *Eos* 73, no.19 (12 May 1992): 209, 220–21.
Koenig, L. S., K. R. Greenaway, Moira Dunbar, and G. F. Hattersley-Smith. "Arctic Ice Islands." *Arctic* 5, no. 2 (July 1952): 67–103.
Kuryk, Don. "Seasonal Transportation to Remote Communities: What If?" In *Airships to the Arctic Symposium II: Moving Beyond the Roads (Proceedings),* University of Manitoba Transport Institute, 21–23 October 2003.
Langseth, Marcus, Theodore Delaca, George Newton, Bernard Coakley, Roger Colony, Peter McRoy, James Morison, Jeff Gossett, Walter Tucker, and William Smethie. "SCICEX-93: Arctic Cruise of the U.S. Navy Nuclear Powered Submarine USS *Pargo.*" *Marine Technology Science Journal* 27, no. 4 (Winter 1993–94): 4–12.

Lyon, Waldo K. "The Navigation of Arctic Polar Submarines." *Journal of Navigation* 37, no. 2 (May 1984): 155–79.

———. "Ocean and Sea-Ice Research in the Arctic Ocean Via Submarine." *Transactions of the New York Academy of Sciences,* ser. II 23, no. 8 (June 1961): 662–74.

———. *The Polar Submarine and Navigation of the Arctic Ocean.* Research Report no. 88. N.p.: U.S. Navy Electronics Laboratory; reissue of final report, 21 May 1959.

———. "The Submarine and the Arctic Ocean." *Polar Record* 11, no. 75 (1963): 699–705.

———. "Submarine Combat in the Ice." U.S. Naval Institute *Proceedings* 118 (February 1992): 33–40.

———." Submarine Exploration of the North Pole Region: History, Problems, Positioning and Piloting." *Pole Nord 1983, Editions du CNRS* (1987): 313–28.

Mayer, Norman J. "LTA: Recent Developments." *Astronautics and Aeronautics* 15, no. 1 (January 1977): 58–64.

McWethy, Commander Robert D., USN. "Significance of the NAUTILUS Polar Cruise." U.S. Naval Institute *Proceedings* 84 (May 1958): 32–35.

Nassichuk, W. W. "Forty Years of Northern Non-Renewable Natural Resource Development." *Arctic* 40, no. 4 (December 1987): 274–84.

McLaren, Alfred S. "Analysis of the Under-Ice Topography in the Arctic Basin as Recorded by the USS NAUTILUS during August 1958." *Arctic* 41, no. 2 (June 1988): 117–26.

———. "The Development of Cargo Submarines for Polar Use." *Polar Record* 21, no. 133 (1983): 369–81.

———. "Under the Ice in Submarines." U.S. Naval Institute *Proceedings* 107 (July 1981): 105–9.

Nelson, Stewart B. "Airships in the Arctic." *Arctic* 40, no. 3 (September 1993): 278–83.

Polar Record. Volumes 6 through 12, July 1951 to May 1964.

Polmar, Norman. "Submarines in the Ice." U.S. Naval Institute *Proceedings* 89 (August 1991): 105–6.

Smith, David D. "Sequential Development of Surface Morphology on Fletcher's Ice Island, T-3." Bedford, Mass., Geophysics Research Directorate, U.S. Air Force Cambridge Research Center, Scientific Report no. 4 (1960), 896–913.

U.S. Department of the Air Force. *Ice Islands of the Arctic: Alaskan Air Command's Arctic Experience*. Alaskan Air Command Historical Monograph, 1979.

U.S. Department of the Navy, Office of the Chief of Naval Operations. "Details of LTA Study and Polar Feasibility Operation, Outline of Proposed Technical Research Study by Naval Research Company 3-1." Enclosure A of VNRRC3-1, letter to Chief of Naval Research regarding study "The Use of Non-Rigid Airships in Support of Geophysical Research and Related Studies in the Region of the North Polar Sea." May 1958.

———. *Flight Handbook: Navy Model ZPG-2 Airship*, 1 February 1954.

———. *Naval Arctic Manual,* ATP-17 (A), January 1970.

———. *Naval Arctic Operations Handbook: Part 1. General Information.* Part 2, *Operational Notes,* 1949.

———. Office of Naval Research. *Arctic Sciences Program Summary FY89.*

———. Office of Naval Research. Memorandum to Office of Information, "Public Information Plan for Blimp Flight to Arctic Circle," 14 July 1958.

U.S. Naval Attaché (Ottawa) to Chief of Air Staff, 3 July 1958, Record Group 24, accession 1983–1984/216, box 3579, file S961-103-1, pt. 5, National Archives of Canada.

Van Gorder, Captain H. B. "Use of Lighter-than-Air Craft in the Arctic." In *Proceedings of the First Annual Arctic Planning Session, November 1958.* Edited by J. H. Hartshorn. Bedford, Mass., U.S. Air Force Cambridge Research Center, Geophysics Research Note 15, 1959.

Walsh, Don. "Being There: The Case for the Oceanographic Submarine." U.S. Naval Institute *Proceedings* 126 (December 2000): 87.

Other Periodicals

Addinell, H. "Air Transport: Russia and Her Airships." *Flight,* 1 December 1932, 1153–54.

Anderson, Commander William R., USN. "The Arctic as a Sea Route of the Future." *National Geographic* CXV, no. 1 (January 1959): 21–24.

Barr, William. "The Soviet Contribution to the *Italia* Search and Rescue, 1928." *Polar Record* 18, no. 117 (1977): 561–74.

Bellow, Joe Steven. "Nautilus: Under Way on Nuclear Power." *All Hands,* October 1979, 26–31.

Cadwalader, John. "Arctic Drift Stations." U.S. Naval Institute *Proceedings* 89 (April 1963): 67–75.

Dryden, Hugh L. "The International Geophysical Year." *National Geographic* CIX, no. 2 (February 1956): 285–98.

Fahey, John A. "The Russians Are Coming!" *Buoyant Flight: The Bulletin of the Lighter-than-Air Society* 29, no. 1 (November–December 1981): 2.

Fletcher, Joseph O. "Three Months on an Arctic Ice Island." *National Geographic* CIII, no. 4 (April 1953): 489–504.

Gibson, Alice G. "Development Struggle behind Canada's 'Twilight Computer'." *Canadian Aviation* (March 1955).

Greenaway, Wing Commander Keith R. "New Navigational Methods for Northern Flying." *Canadian Aviation* (September 1953).

———. "To the Top of the World by Airship." *Canadian Aviation Historical Society Journal* (Fall 1980): 83–86, 92.

———. "U.S. Navy Airship Flight to Ice Island T-3." *Arctic Circular* XII, no. 2 (September 1959): 19–26.

Halloran, Richard. "A Silent Battle Surfaces." *New York Times Magazine,* 7 December 1986.

Hunt, William R. "The Rise and Fall of Umberto Nobile." *Musk-Ox,* no. 17 (1975): 3–13.

La Fay, Howard. "DEW Line, Sentry of the Far North." *National Geographic* CXIV, no. 1 (July 1958): 128–46.

Lalor, Lieutenant William G., Jr., USN. "Submarine through the North Pole." *National Geographic* CXV, no. 1 (January 1959): 1–20.

Miller, Maynard M. "Floating Islands." *Natural History* LXV, no. 5 (1956).

Nelson, Stewart B., PhD. "Rediscovering World's 1st Arctic Sub: NAUTILUS of 1931." *Polar Times* 3, no. 10 (January 2007): 35.

Newman, Peter C. "Canada's Fur-Trading Empire." *National Geographic* 172, no. 2 (August 1987): 192–228.

O'Neil, Paul. "Beneath North Pole on a Well-Planned Adventure." *Life,* 1 September 1958, 57–72.

Payne, Lee. "Airships 1962–1988 in Hindsight." *Buoyant Flight: The Bulletin of the Lighter-than-Air Society* 36, no. 2 (January–February 1989): 6–7.

Silk, George. "North Pole 103 Miles: Temperature 60 Below." *Life,* 31 March 1952, 13–17.

Thomas, Lowell, Jr. "Scientists Ride Ice Islands on Arctic Odysseys." *National Geographic* 128, no. 5 (November 1965): 670–93.

Vaeth, J. Gordon. "Airborne Arctic Weather Ships." Wingfoot Lighter-than-Air Society *Bulletin* 13, no. 2 (December 1965): 2–6.

Walker, Hepburn, Jr. "The Surveillance Airship Contract Award: The Dawn of a New Era?" *Buoyant Flight: The Bulletin of the Lighter-than-Air Society* 34, no. 5 (July–August 1987): 2, 4.

Wellman, Walter. "The Polar Airship." Washington, D.C.: Judd and Detweiler n.d. Reprint from *National Geographic*, April 1906.

Wiltsie, Gordon. "Holiday on Ice: Sledging and Camping in the Canadian Arctic." *Travel & Leisure,* October 1988, 138–43, 190–92.

Further Sources

Airship ZPG-2 BUNO 126719, Aircraft Flight Log; Custody Record; Overhaul Record, box 219, boxes 220–21, C. E. Rosendahl Collection, History of Aviation Collection, University of Texas at Dallas.

"A Polar Epic under the Ice." *Life,* 18 August 1958, 20–21.

Associated Press. Dispatches filed by Hugh A. Mulligan, feature writer, July–August 1958, files of the Associated Press, courtesy Mr. Mulligan.

Canada, *House of Commons Debates,* 14 August 1958, 3510–13, 3540–41.

Gray, Dr. Norman G. Personal journal, 24 July–12 August 1958, courtesy Dr. Gray.

Koza, Lieutenant Harold D., USN (Ret.). Aviators Flight Log Book, July–August 1958, courtesy Lieutenant Koza.

Lord, Elmer B. Scrapbook, courtesy AD1 Lord.
Lyon, Dr. Waldo K. Field journal for 1956–58, pages 46–105, courtesy Dr. Lyon.
"Operation Attaché." *Arctic Circular* 1, no. 8 (December 1948).
"Operation SUNSHINE I; report of, CO, *Nautilus* to CNO, 28 June 1958 and *Nautilus* transpolar Voyage; final report of." CO *Nautilus* to CNO, 25 August 1958, courtesy Dr. Lyon.
Parker, ATC Frederick L., USN (Ret.). Aviators Flight Log Book, July–August 1958, courtesy ATC Parker.
———. Scrapbook, Parker Papers.
Richards, William. "Mixed Blessing: The Polar Bears Are in Churchill Again." *Wall Street Journal,* 14 November 1989.
Schou, Lieutenant Commander Aage J., USN (Ret.). Aviators Flight Log Book, courtesy Lieutenant Commander Schou.
U.S. Department of Defense, Office of Public Information. News release, "Nautilus," Washington, D.C., 8 August 1958.
———. News release, "Navy Blimp to Make Northernmost Flight," Washington, D.C., 17 July 1958.
Weymouth Warrior 1, no. 2 (April 1958).
Van Gorder, Captain Harold B., USN (Ret.). Aviators Flight Log Book, courtesy Captain Van Gorder.
———. Personal diary, 7–12 August 1958, Van Gorder Papers.

Newspapers

Akron Beacon Journal
Boston Globe
Boston Traveler
Calgary Herald (Alberta)
Daily Times-Journal (Fort William, Ont.)
Democrat Chronicle (Rochester, N.Y.)
Elizabeth Daily Journal (N.J.)
Kingston Whig-Standard (Ont.)
Minneapolis Star
(Montreal) Gazette
New York Herald Tribune
New York Times
Port Arthur (Ont.) News Chronicle
Quincy Patriot Ledger (Mass.)
Spectator (Hamilton, Ont.)
Star-Ledger (N.J.)
Telegram (Toronto)
Toronto Star
Vancouver Sun
Wall Street Journal

Index

Page numbers in *italics* indicate illustrations. Page numbers followed by an "n" indicate endnotes.

About the Author

WILLIAM F. ALTHOFF, an environmental geologist by profession, has published extensively in technical and in history-related journals. During 1999–2000, he was Ramsey Fellow in Naval Aviation History at the National Air and Space Museum, Smithsonian Institution. This is his fifth book of naval history.

THE NAVAL INSTITUTE PRESS is the book-publishing arm of the U.S. Naval Institute, a private, nonprofit, membership society for sea service professionals and others who share an interest in naval and maritime affairs. Established in 1873 at the U.S. Naval Academy in Annapolis, Maryland, where its offices remain today, the Naval Institute has members worldwide.

Members of the Naval Institute support the education programs of the society and receive the influential monthly magazine *Proceedings* or the colorful bimonthly magazine *Naval History* and discounts on fine nautical prints and on ship and aircraft photos. They also have access to the transcripts of the Institute's Oral History Program and get discounted admission to any of the Institute-sponsored seminars offered around the country.

The Naval Institute's book-publishing program, begun in 1898 with basic guides to naval practices, has broadened its scope to include books of more general interest. Now the Naval Institute Press publishes about seventy titles each year, ranging from how-to books on boating and navigation to battle histories, biographies, ship and aircraft guides, and novels. Institute members receive significant discounts on the more than eight hundred Press books in print.

Full-time students are eligible for special half-price membership rates. Life memberships are also available.

For a free catalog describing Naval Institute Press books currently available, and for further information about joining the U.S. Naval Institute, please write to:

Member Services
U.S. Naval Institute
291 Wood Road
Annapolis, MD 21402-5034
Telephone: (800) 233-8764
Fax: (410) 571-1703
Web address: *www.usni.org*